ENCYCLOPEDIA OF AMERICAN INDIAN REMOVAL

ENCYCLOPEDIA OF AMERICAN INDIAN REMOVAL

Volume 1   A–Z

Daniel F. Littlefield, Jr.
and James W. Parins, Editors

AN IMPRINT OF ABC-CLIO, LLC
Santa Barbara, California • Denver, Colorado • Oxford, England

Library of Congress Cataloging-in-Publication Data

Encyclopedia of American Indian removal / Daniel F. Littlefield Jr.
and James W. Parins, Editors.
      p. cm.
   Includes bibliographical references and index.
   ISBN 978-0-313-36041-1 (set hardcopy : alk. paper) — ISBN 978-0-313-36042-8
(set ebook) — ISBN 978-0-313-36043-5 (v. 1 hardcopy : alk. paper) — ISBN 978-0-313-
36044-2 (v. 1 ebook) — ISBN 978-0-313-36045-9 (v. 2 hardcopy : alk. paper) — ISBN
978-0-313-36046-6 (v. 2 ebook)
   1. Indian Removal, 1813–1903—Encyclopedias. 2. Indian Removal, 1813–1903—Sources. I.
Littlefield, Daniel F. II. Parins, James W. III. Title.
   E98.R4E63   2011
   970.004'97003—dc22   2010037598

ISBN: 978-0-313-36041-1
EISBN: 978-0-313-36042-8

15   14   13   12   11   1   2   3   4   5

This book is also available on the World Wide Web as an eBook.
Visit www.abc-clio.com for details.

Greenwood
An Imprint of ABC-CLIO, LLC

ABC-CLIO, LLC
130 Cremona Drive, P.O. Box 1911
Santa Barbara, California 93116-1911

This book is printed on acid-free paper (∞)

Manufactured in the United States of America

CONTENTS

Preface   ix

Introduction   xiii

Indian Removal Timeline   xvii

Volume 1, A–Z
Abraham (c. 1790–1870s)   1
African-Descended People and Removal   3
Alabama and Indian Removal   6
Apalachicola Removal   11
Arkansas and Indian Removal   13
Armstrong, William (d. 1847)   16
Black Hawk (1767–1838)   20
Black Hawk War (1832)   21
Boudinot, Elias (c. 1804–1839)   24
Brotherton Removal   26
Butrick, Daniel S. (1789–1847)   27
Caddo Removal   29
Caldwell, Billy (Sauganash) (1780–1841)   30
Carroll, William (1788–1844)   31
Cass, Lewis (1782–1866)   33
Cavallo, John (c. 1812–1882)   34
Cherokee Nation v. Georgia (1831)   36
Cherokee Removal   37
Chickasaw Removal   44
Choctaw Removal   46
Clark, William (1770–1838)   50
Coacoochee (d. 1857)   51
Coe Hadjo (dates unknown)   53
Coffee, John (1772–1833)   55

Colbert, Levi (c. 1764–1834)   56

Deas, Edward (1812–1849)   59

Delaware Removal   60

Eastern Cherokees   64

Eaton, John Henry (1790–1856)   66

Ellsworth, Henry L. (1791–1858)   68

Eneah Emathla (Neamathla) (c. 1750s–1830s)   69

Eneah Micco (Neamicco) (c. 1780–1836)   72

Florida and Indian Removal   75

Folsom, David (1791–1847)   79

Food   81

Gardiner, James B. (1789–1837)   83

Georgia and Indian Removal   84

Halleck Tustenuggee (dates unknown)   92

Heckaton (d. 1842)   94

Henry (McHenry), Jim (c. 1815–1883)   95

Ho-Chunk Removal   97

Hulbutta Micco (dates unknown)   99

Hulbutta Tustenuggee (c. 1795–?)   100

Indian Removal Act (1830)   102

Indian Territory   106

Indiana and Indian Removal   107

Ishtehotopa (c. 1800–c. 1850)   109

Jackson, Andrew (1767–1845)   111

Jesup, Thomas S. (1788–1860)   114

Jones, Evan (1788–1872)   115

Kansas Territory and Indian Removal   117

Kennekuk (dates unknown)   119

Keokuk (c. 1780–1848)   120

Kickapoo Removal   122

Land Speculation and Indian Removal   124

LeFlore, Greenwood (1800–1865)   127

Little Rock Office of Removal and Subsistence   130

McCoy, Isaac (1784–1846)   132

Mecina (dates unknown)   133

Medicine and Disease   134

Menominee Removal   135

Metoxin, John (1770–1858)   137

Miami Removal   137

Miccosukee Seminole Nation   140

Miconopy (c. 1800–1849)   141

Mississippi and Indian Removal   142

Mississippi Band of Choctaw Indians   144

Muscogee (Creek) Removal   146

Mushulatubbee (d. 1838)   149

Northwest Ordinance (1787)   151

Nullification and Removal   153

Ogden Land Company   156
Oneidas   159
Opothleyohola (c. 1798–1863)   160
Oshkosh (1795–1858)   162
Ottawa Removal   163
Panoahah (dates unknown)   168
Parker, Ely S. (1828–1895)   169
Parker, Nicholson (c. 1820–1892)   171
Peoria-Kaskaskia-Piankeshaw-Wea Removal   172
Pierce, Maris Bryant (1811–1874)   173
Poarch Band of Creek Indians   174
Potawatomi Removal   175
Quapaw Removal   181
Quinney, John W. (1797–1855)   182
Richardville, Jean Baptiste (1761–1841)   184
Ridge, John (c. 1803–1839)   185
Ridge, Major (1771–1839)   189
Ross, John (1790–1866)   191
Saginaw Chippewa Removal   195
Sanford, John W. A. (1798–1870)   197
Sarasin (d. c. 1832)   200
Sauk and Mesquakie (Fox) Removal   201
Schermerhorn, John F. (1786–1851)   204
Schoolcraft, Henry Rowe (1793–1864)   205
Scott, Winfield (1786–1866)   206
Second Seminole War (1835–1842)   208
Seminole Removal   210
Seminole Tribe of Florida   216
Seneca Removal   217
Shawnee Removal from Ohio   219
Sprague, John T. (1810–1878)   222
State Militias and Removal   223
Stockbridge-Munsee Removal   227
Strong, Nathaniel Thayer (1810–1872)   229
Tennessee and Indian Removal   231
Third Seminole War (1855–1858)   234
Tishomingo (c. 1740–c. 1839)   236
Tonawanda Senecas   238
Trail of Tears   240
Treaty of Buffalo Creek (1838)   241
Treaty of Dancing Rabbit Creek (1830)   243
Treaty of New Echota (1835)   245
Treaty of Pontotoc (1832)   246
Treaty of Washington (1832)   250
Tuckabatche Hadjo (dates unknown)   251
Tustenuggee Emathla (c. 1793–?)   253
Van Buren, Martin (1782–1862)   256

Whig Party 259
Wirt, William (1772–1834) 261
Women during Removal 262
Women's Roles and Removal 267
Worcester, Samuel A. (1798–1859) 269
Worcester v. Georgia (1832) 271
Wyandot Removal 273

Annotated Bibliography 277

Index 291

About the Editors and Contributors 305

PREFACE

The two-volume *Encyclopedia of American Indian Removal* is a continuation of research that the Sequoyah National Research Center staff have conducted or supported for the better part of a decade. We were motivated by the attention to the Trail of Tears generated by the increased efforts by the National Park Service to document and interpret the Trail of Tears National Historic Trail through nine southern states. Because nearly every member of all of the large tribes that were removed from the Southeast traveled through Arkansas on their way west, Arkansas is a pivotal state on the historic routes. However, because the legislation creating the National Historic Trail focuses only on Cherokee removal, we were concerned that removal in general and especially the removal of the other four tribes might become obscured. Thus, in 2006 we began to collect research resources related to all of the removed tribes of the Southeast and, peripherally, those that were removed elsewhere.

Interest in Indian removal has waxed and waned during the past century. Near the turn of the 20th century, writers like Annie H. Abel and James Mooney viewed Indian removal through a romantic lens. The centennial of the Indian Removal Act of 1830 and subsequent removals caused writers like Grant Foreman to take a new interest in removal. With the Indian awareness movement of the 1960s and 1970s, removal became popular again among scholars, who not only examined removal stories but also began a debate on removal policy and the role of Andrew Jackson. Throughout the 20th century, Foreman's was the only major attempt (1932) at a history of removal. Unfortunately, John Ehle's popularized history that appeared in 1988, and Gloria Jahoda's highly romanticized work, written in 1975 but not published until 1995, reinforced many of the common misperceptions about removal held by the public. In 1993, Theda Perdue and Michael D. Green produced a useful brief history and edition of primary documents on Cherokee removal. During the late 20th century, only Arthur DeRosier produced a book-length history of one tribe's removal, the Choctaws'. Research done in recent years related to the National Park Service project represents the latest waxing of interest in Indian removal during the past century. That interest has resulted in Vicki Rozema's 2003 edition of primary documents relating to Cherokee removal, a brief general study of Cherokee removal by Amy Sturgis, and a book-length study of Chickasaw removal by Amanda Paige and other Sequoyah National Research Center staff. Unfortunately, the public has not yet seen other major results of the recent research that has been done.

We consider this encyclopedia to be a major offering to the public. We have been guided in this by a challenge raised by Cherokee scholar Lathel Duffield in 2002. Duffield's study of the historiography of Cherokee removal examines a number of public misperceptions about Cherokee removal and the ways in which historians and other writers have perpetuated misinformation that was published near the turn of the 20th century. He calls for a new start, urging scholars to go back to the original documents and reexamine them to present a more historically accurate story of Cherokee removal. Although Duffield's concern is Cherokee removal, his advice is sound for researchers of all tribes.

While removal looms large in individual tribal histories, the stories of many tribes' experiences have been obscured or lost for most Americans, who, unfortunately, tend to relate removal primarily to the Cherokees. We do not attempt to fill in all the missing pieces of the stories or to correct all public misperceptions. Nor do we attempt to cover all removals in all periods of American history. We have chosen, instead, to focus on the removal period that followed the Indian Removal Act of 1830 because it had a more devastating effect on more tribal people than any other piece of congressional legislation except, perhaps, the General Allotment Act of 1887. In doing so, we consulted what we consider the best available information, realizing, of course, the limitations of some of that information.

As in most encyclopedias, the 125 entries in Volume 1 of the *Encyclopedia of American Indian Removal* are arranged alphabetically. Each entry contains an essay and a list of further readings. The essays focus on events, issues, and people related to removal. Highlighted cross-references in the essays will direct readers to related entries. Volume 2 consists of primary documents, some of which are referred to in the essays of Volume 1, while others are offered to add depth to the reader's knowledge of Indian removal. In addition to the essays and documents, we have included a timeline of removal and an annotated bibliography that will lead readers to major resources for the study of removal. An introduction puts the topic of Indian removal into context, and a detailed subject index provides additional access to the information in the essays.

Primary Documents in Volume 2

The collection of documents reprinted in Volume 2 is the largest modern edition of original sources related to Indian removal. During the past 15 years, several small volumes of original documents related to Cherokee removal became available. This volume's wider scope includes other tribes.

The volume is organized into three sections: "Policy," "Responses to Policy," and "Removals." Within each section, documents are arranged in chronological order. Included in the "Policy" section are laws, debates, speeches, and other documents related to the shaping of Indian removal policy. In the "Responses to Policy" section are documents containing the responses by both Indians and non-Indians to the passage of the Indian Removal Act of 1830, its application to the tribes east of the Mississippi, and its impact on tribes west of the river. The last section contains documents related to specific removals of tribes or remnants of tribes.

In selecting documents to include here, we were guided by a belief that the original documents in the second volume of the *Encyclopedia of American Indian Removal* should not simply support, but also add to, the essays in the first volume. Thus, we chose to reprint as few as possible of those documents that are readily available from other sources. Some, such as the Indian Removal Act, however, are too central to an encyclopedia of removal to be omitted. On the other hand, we have chosen not to reprint removal treaties because of their large number and because they are readily available online at sites such as http://digital.library.okstate.edu/Kappler/. We have avoided excerpting too severely to avoid imposing editorial bias and to preserve contexts for the passages. Each document is preceded by a headnote that creates a context for the writing.

Finally, we have lightly edited the documents, including emendations where necessary and corrections to gross misspellings that might lead to misunderstanding.

Daniel F. Littlefield, Jr.
James W. Parins

INTRODUCTION

Although American leaders had discussed Indian removal since the early days of the nation, removal as federal Indian policy emerged from political debate during the first two and a half decades of the 19th century. The Georgia Compact of 1802 was the first major step, with the United States promising to extinguish Indian land titles within the state. Political pressure from Georgia and elsewhere pushed for immediate action. President Thomas Jefferson proposed in 1803 that Indians be encouraged to move voluntarily from their lands east of the Mississippi to the newly acquired Louisiana Purchase west of the river. In the decade and a half that followed, some Indians did so, but the majority of tribes remained.

By the mid-1820s, Indian removal had become an issue of open national debate. As the American population and economy expanded in the early 19th century, Americans began to think of Indians as "cumberers" of the earth. President James Monroe asked Congress for legislation to fulfill Jefferson's plan, believing, like Jefferson, that the Indians could survive only if they removed to the West, where they could have time to become "civilized" before American expansion caught up with them. Monroe's plan, which was accepted by his successor, John Quincy Adams, turned on voluntary removal. However, a more aggressive approach to Indian removal was pursued by Presidents Andrew Jackson and Martin Van Buren. Jackson's message to Congress in December 1829 made clear the direction his policy would take: instead of a policy based on persuasion, as proposed by former administrations, his policy would be based on forced removal under the threat of tribal destruction.

When Jackson asked Congress for the authority to negotiate removal with the tribes, he initiated an emotional debate in both the public and political arenas. Pro-removal forces won, although they were not unified in motive. Leftover egalitarianism of 18th-century Enlightenment thinking led some to believe that removal was humane, yet the debate was also sprinkled liberally with vicious racism and bigotry. However, it was greed that drove most pro-removal proponents—Americans coveted Indian lands, whether it was for the gold or transportation routes or the fruit and cotton lands of the Cherokees, the cotton lands of the Creeks and Choctaws, the cotton lands and livestock range of the Chickasaws, rich farmlands in the Midwest, or the land speculation of the **Ogden Land Company** in New York. Jackson was also driven by his belief that the American nation would be less vulnerable to attack by foreign powers if the southern states were populated by white Americans, especially the lower Mississippi Valley. Jackson got his wish. The **Indian Removal Act**, which barely passed Congress on May 28, 1830, became one of the most destructive laws in Indian history, ranking alongside the General Allotment Act of 1887 and Public Law 587 of 1954 in its assault on Indian societies and their resources.

The Indian Removal Act set in motion a series of events that historians have styled the "removal period," which usually refers to the 1830s and early 1840s. During this period, execution of the provisions of the Indian Removal Act was widespread. Besides the larger tribes in the Southeast, the Removal Act applied to the Apalachicolas of Florida, who had separated from the Creeks and Seminoles. It also applied to numerous tribes elsewhere, such as the Sauks, Foxes, Kaskaskias, and Peorias of Illinois; the Potawatomis, Miamis, and other tribes of Indiana; the Senecas, Wyandots, and Shawnees of Ohio; the Chippewas of Michigan, as they were then called; and the New York Indians. During the decade 1830 through 1839, the United States ratified eighty-seven treaties and agreements with tribes. Nearly half of them provided for removal, and nearly all of the remainder dealt with liquidation of residual tribal land claims in the wake of removal. Although most removals took place in the 1830s and early 1840s, they occurred as late as 1859. Removal treaties were not confined to those tribes residing east of the Mississippi but included tribes already in the West, such as the Caddos of Louisiana, who also were removed in an attempt to make room for removing tribes or to consolidate tribes in Indian Territory west of Arkansas and Missouri.

Uprooting the vast majority of tribal population east of the Mississippi River had disastrous consequences for the Indians. Cultural discontinuity resulted from the replacement of familiar environments with foreign surroundings. Populations declined because of deaths resulting from armed resistance, unsanitary conditions of forced encampment, rigors of travel, and encounters with epidemic diseases such as influenza, cholera, and smallpox. Individuals were impoverished by limitations on the transportation of private property. For the Sauks and Foxes, there was the brief but costly **Black Hawk War**, and for the Seminoles, there was lingering warfare from 1835 until 1858. Recovery was slow after removal because tribes had to build new economies in new surroundings. For the Americans, on the other hand, displacement of the tribes meant new lands were open to economic development. In the Southeast, the large land masses suddenly available for purchase resulted in large-scale speculation, which, in turn, contributed to a growing banking crisis that finally culminated in the Panic of 1837.

Although the term *removal period* defines only the short period of 1815–1860, removal as federal policy continued for more than a century and a half. In the so-called reservation period of the post–Civil War era, large numbers of tribes were moved from their lands in the Plains, Midwest, and elsewhere to reservations in what is now Oklahoma. Most Americans tend to relegate removal to the 19th century, but it also occurred in the 20th century, even within the memory of many living Americans. For example, eviction of Cherokee families from lands to build Camp Gruber during World War II, of the Dakotas from lands of the Cheyenne River and Standing Rock Reservations inundated by Oahe Lake in the 1960s, and of the Senecas from lands now covered by the Allegheny Reservoir behind Kinzua Dam in the 1960s was no less psychologically traumatic and heartrending for 20th-century Indian people than removal was for tribal people who were forced west in mass migrations in the 19th century. In all cases and in all times, the objective was the same: to rid particular landscapes of Indians to make way for American economic development—in other words, greed. Small wonder that the Yavapai Nation annually celebrates its defeat of the Orme Dam project in Arizona in the early 1980s, preventing the destruction of much of its Fort McDowell Reservation.

Failure to recognize later removals has resulted, in part, because the so-called removal period following the Indian Removal Act has overshadowed all others in the popular mind. Unfortunately, Americans have a highly stereotyped and romanticized concept of removal during that period, based for the most part on the experiences of the five large tribes of the Southeast, commonly called the Five Civilized Tribes. The concept had its roots in the early 20th century, when Indians were thought to be vanishing from the American scene and writers, artists, and founders of the Boy Scouts of America and Woodcraft Indians romanticized, even idealized, Indians. During the second decade of the century, the term **"Trail of Tears"** was fashioned and emerged as a metaphor for the removal experience. Made popular primarily by Cherokee women college students in the 1910s and 1920s, the term had found its place in serious history by the 1930s. By the late 20th century, the Cherokees claimed the term as theirs even though it was also used by other tribes, especially the Choctaws. The Cherokee claim was reinforced by the congressional act in 1987 that created the Trail of Tears National Historic Trail, which was planned to commemorate only the Cherokee removal. Thus, in the popular mind, the Cherokee story epitomizes Indian removal, and most who hear the term Trail of Tears think first of Cherokees.

There are a large number of historical inaccuracies in the mental images conjured up by most people when they hear the term. The removal period occurred before photography came into its own. Sketch artists and writers apparently had little interest in providing visual or word pictures of events on the trail, and only the Potawatomis are known to have been sketched on their journey. The style of news reporting of the day avoided details. The result is only an occasional eyewitness account. Rendering of events was therefore left to the fertile imaginations of 20th-century artists. A typical rendering depicts a group of forlorn people, some sick and some dying, often trudging through deep snow in a trackless wilderness under the watchful eyes of mounted soldiers. The Indians usually belong to the southeastern tribes, most often Cherokees. In truth, those who went overland followed well-established roads, did not encounter deep snow, and only on two or three occasions were accompanied by a small group of soldiers. Most of the southeastern Indians did not walk but used practically every available method of travel of the day: horseback, wagons, ox carts, buggies, steamboats, keelboats, flatboats, canal boats, railroads, and sailing ships.

Stereotyping has popularized the trauma of removal for some tribes and obscured that of others whose experience was no less devastating. American scholars have abetted this process. For example, in the *Handbook of North American Indians* (Volume 4), the section on Indian removal liberally treats the tribes of the Southeast while giving only two paragraphs to all the other tribes to which the Indian Removal Act applied. And on its Web page "Indian Treaties and the Removal Act of 1830," the U.S. Department of State mentions no tribes except the five tribes of the Southeast and mentions only the Cherokees in reference to the Trail of Tears.

A fair and balanced study of removal following the act of 1830 quickly undermines stereotyped interpretations. Terms of removal varied widely, depending on the land the tribes occupied, the natural resources the land contained, the abilities of the tribes to resist, the negotiating skills of the tribes, their destination, and the general health of the people. Conditions of travel varied according to the landscapes through which the people moved and the seasons of the year. In addition, there were always those Americans, both government officials and private citizens, who viewed removals as opportunities to make money and therefore influenced the logistics of removal.

A work like the *Encyclopedia of American Indian Removal* cannot tell every story of removal. It is not inclusive but representative. However, such a study of the removal period of American history can provide a greater understanding of Indian removal by emphasizing such matters as the number of tribes to whom the Indian Removal Act applied, the wide variety of cultures and historical circumstances that precipitated their removals, and the differing conditions of their journeys to the West. Hopefully, it will counter some of the misinformed perceptions of removal that abound in the public mind.

INDIAN REMOVAL TIMELINE

1802   Georgia Compact, in which the United States promises to extinguish Indian titles to lands inside Georgia.

Louisiana Purchase agreement is made.

President Thomas Jefferson proposes voluntary removal of tribes.

Ohio becomes a state.

1810   Ogden Land Company acquires preemptive rights to Indian lands in New York.

1812   Louisiana becomes a state.

1813   Red Stick War begins.

1814   Treaty of Fort Jackson concludes the Red Stick War.

1816   First Seminole War begins.

Indiana becomes a state.

1817   Alabama becomes a state.

Andrew Jackson's forces invade Florida.

Treaty with Cherokees provides for land cession and voluntary removal to the West.

1818   Delaware Treaty of St. Mary's cedes all Delaware land claims in Indiana.

Miami Treaty of St. Mary's provides for their removal from Indiana.

Quapaws cede large area of land in Arkansas.

1819   Illinois becomes a state.

Mississippi becomes a state.

Treaty with Cherokees provides for land cession and voluntary removal to the West.

Main body of Kickapoos remove west of the Mississippi.

1820   Treaty of Doak's Stand, first Choctaw removal treaty, exchanges part of Choctaw land in Mississippi for land west of Arkansas.

Delawares remove from Indiana.

1821   Missouri becomes a state.

Treaty of Indian Springs cedes Creek lands between the Ocmulgee and Flint Rivers in Georgia.

Creeks pass a law forbidding the sale or cession of Creek land.

1823   Treaty of Moultrie Creek provides for removal of Florida Indians to central Florida.

1824   Quapaws cede their remaining lands in Arkansas.

1825   Treaty of Indian Springs cedes most of remaining Creek lands in Georgia.

William McIntosh executed for engineering the Treaty of Indian Springs in violation of Creek law.

1827   Alabama enacts legislation to extend laws over Indian lands.

Treaty of Fort Mitchell cedes remaining Creek lands in Georgia.

Cherokees write a constitution.

Ho-Chunk (Winnebago) "uprising" against lead miners.

1828   *Cherokee Phoenix* is established with Elias Boudinot as editor.

Georgia passes a law attaching Cherokee lands to Georgia counties.

Andrew Jackson is elected president.

Commission is organized to arrange Ottawa and Miami removal.

Western Cherokees remove from Arkansas to Indian Territory.

1829   Alabama enacts additional legislation to extend laws over Indian lands.

Additional acts by Georgia nullify Cherokee law and deny right of Cherokees to testify against whites.

John H. Eaton becomes secretary of war and urges Congress to establish an organized Indian Territory in the West.

1830   Indian Removal Act passes Congress.

Treaty of Dancing Rabbit Creek with the Choctaws provides for their removal.

Georgia law outlaws Cherokee government and confiscates gold fields.

Georgia passes law requiring license and loyalty oath for whites to remain in Cherokee lands.

Mississippi extends laws over Indians within its borders.

Chickasaw Treaty of Franklin is first treaty negotiated under the Indian Removal Act, but becomes null and void.

1831 Georgia law requires license and loyalty oath for whites living in Cherokee country.

Georgia Guard is authorized by Georgia law.

Lewis Cass becomes secretary of war.

Little Rock Office of Removal and Subsistence is established.

Choctaw removal begins.

Cherokee Nation v. Georgia says Cherokee Nation is not a foreign nation under the Constitution.

Samuel A. Worcester and other missionaries are arrested.

Treaty of Lewistown with Senecas/Shawnees of Lewistown provides for their removal from Ohio.

Treaty of Wapakoneta with Shawnees of Hog Creek and Wapakoneta cedes land and provides for their removal from Ohio.

Treaty of Detroit with Ottawas of Blanchard's Fork and Oquanoxa's Village cedes lands and provides for their removal from Ohio.

Treaty with Menominees adjusts relations with New York Indians.

Treaty of cession and removal is made with the Senecas of Sandusky.

1832 *Worcester v. Georgia* declares Georgia's extension of laws to Cherokees unconstitutional.

Treaty of Payne's Landing provides for Seminole removal.

Georgia enacts legislation to outlaw Cherokee government.

Treaty of Pontotoc provides for Chickasaw removal.

Black Hawk War occurs.

Andrew Jackson reelected as president.

Georgia begins confiscating Cherokee property.

Treaty of Washington provides for allotment of Creek lands in Alabama.

Cholera epidemic breaks out in the West.

Stokes Commission is established to prepare Indian Territory tribes for forced removal of others.

Treaty of Fort Armstrong with Winnebagos cedes lands in southwestern Wisconsin and northern Illinois.

Missouri Kickapoos remove.

Alabama extends its laws over Creek country.

Treaty of McCutchensville with Wyandots of Ohio cedes lands.

Indian Vaccination Act is passed.

Treaty of Fort Armstrong with Sauks and Foxes cedes their lands east of the Mississippi and provides for their removal.

Treaty with the Apalachicolas relinquishes their reservations in Florida and fixes the date for their removal.

Treaty of Camp Tippecanoe with the Potawatomis of the Prairie and Kaukakee cedes Indiana lands.

Treaty of Tippecanoe River with Potawatomis cedes land.

Treaty of Castor Hill with Shawnees and Delawares cedes lands in Missouri.

Second Treaty at Tippecanoe River with Potawatomis cedes lands in Indiana and Michigan.

Treaty of Castor Hill with Kaskaskias and Peorias cedes lands in Illinois and Missouri.

Treaty with Menominees cedes lands for Stockbridges, Munsees, Brothertons, and New York Indians.

Treaty of Castor Hill cedes lands of Piankeshaws and Weas in Illinois and Missouri.

1833   Treaty with Quapaws provides for their removal to Indian Territory.

Illinois Kickapoos remove.

Sale of Choctaw allotments begins.

Treaty of Fort Gibson with the Western Cherokees defines limits of Cherokee lands in the West.

Treaty of Fort Gibson with the Creeks defines limits of Creek lands in the West and lays the groundwork for Seminole settlement with the Creeks.

Treaty of Maumee with the Ottawas of Ohio cedes land and provides for their removal.

Treaty of Fort Gibson with a Seminole delegation is used by the United States as a removal agreement by the entire tribe.

Treaty with Apalachicolas cedes lands and provides for removal.

Treaty of Chicago with United Chippewas, Ottawas, and Potawatomis cedes lands and provides for removal.

Supplementary Treaty of Chicago is made with United Chippewas, Ottawas, and Potawatomis residing in the Territory of Michigan south of Grand River.

1834   Apalachicola removal begins.

Treaty requires Caddos to remove beyond the limits of the United States.

Indian Intercourse Acts designates territories beyond Louisiana, Arkansas, and Missouri "Indian country."

Sale of Creek lands begins.

Chickasaws sign an agreement at Washington that supplements the Treaty of Pontotoc.

Creek voluntary removal begins.

Treaty at the Forks of the Wabash with Miamis cedes land in Indiana.

Second treaty at the Forks of the Wabash with Miamis cedes land in Indiana.

Treaty of Tippecanoe River with Potawatomis cedes land in Indiana.

Second Treaty of Tippecanoe River with Potawatomis cedes land in Indiana.

Treaty of Potawattimie Mills with the Potawatomis cedes land in Indiana.

Treaty of Logansport with Potawatomis cedes land in Indiana.

1835   Treaty of Caddo Agency with the Caddos provides for their removal outside the limits of the United States.

Treaty of New Echota provides for Cherokee removal.

1836   Arkansas becomes a state.

Martin Van Buren is elected president.

Lower Creeks engage in a war that results in forced Creek removal.

Seminole removal begins.

Forced Creek removal begins.

Texas becomes a republic.

Menominees sign the Treaty of the Cedars, establishing their Wisconsin reservation.

Treaty of Washington with Michigan Ottawas and Chippewas cedes land and provides for removal.

Ottawas and Chippewas of Mashigo, Grand River, Michilimackinac, Sault Ste Marie, L'Arbre Croche, and Grand Traverse sign cession and removal treaties.

Treaty of Washington with the Swan Creek and Black River bands of Chippewas cedes land and establishes reservation.

Treaty at Tippecanoe River with Potawatomis cedes land.

Treaty of Turkey Creek Prairie with Potawatomis cedes land and provides for removal.

Treaty of Chippewanaung with the Potawatomis cedes land and provides for their removal from Indiana.

A second Treaty of Chippewanaung with the Potawatomis cedes land and provides for their removal from Indiana.

A third Treaty of Chippewanaung with the Potawatomis cedes land and provides for their removal from Indiana.

Treaty of Dubuque County, Wisconsin, with the Sauks and Foxes cedes land and provides for removal.

A second Treaty of Dubuque County, Wisconsin, with the Sauks and Foxes cedes land.

1837   Choctaw-Chickasaw agreement at Doaksville provides for Chickasaw removal.

Chickasaw removal begins.

General John Wool arrives in Cherokee Nation to prevent rebellion against the Treaty of New Echota.

National banking crisis known as the Panic of 1837 begins.

Treaty of Detroit with Saginaw Chippewas cedes land and provides for removal.

Stockbridge-Munsee Constitution is drafted.

Wreck of the *Monmouth* kills 311 Creeks.

Michigan becomes a state.

Treaty of Washington with Potawatomis of Indiana cedes land.

Treaty of St. Peters with Chippewas cedes land.

Treaty of Washington with Sauks and Foxes cedes land and provides for removal.

Treaty of Washington with Sauks and Foxes of Missouri cedes land.

Treaty with Winnebagos cedes land and provides for removal.

1838   Cherokee forced removal begins.

Fort Coffee is abandoned in Indian Territory.

Potawatomis are forced to remove from Indiana on their Trail of Death.

General Winfield Scott arrives in Cherokee Nation to enforce Cherokee removal.

Treaty of Buffalo Creek with New York tribes cedes land and provides land for them in the West.

Treaty with Saginaw Chippewas cedes land.

Treaty of Washington with the First Christian and Orchard Parties of Oneidas cedes land and establishes reservations.

Treaty of the Forks of the Wabash with Miamis cedes land and provides for removal.

1839   Major Ridge, John Ridge, and Elias Boudinot, Cherokees, are assassinated.

Treaty of Stockbridge cedes land and provides for removal of Stockbridges and Munsees in Wisconsin.

Brothertons are made U.S. citizens.

Kickapoos in Kansas remove to Indian Territory.

1840   Treaty of Forks of the Wabash with Miamis cedes land and provides for their removal from Indiana.

1842   Colonel Ethan A. Hitchcock reports on fraud in Indian rationing in the West.

U.S. officials declare Second Seminole War ended.

Treaty of Sandusky is signed.

Treaty of Buffalo Creek provides for Seneca removal.

Treaty of LaPointe with Chippewas of the Mississippi and Lake Superior cedes land.

1843   Wyandots remove from Ohio.

Treaty of Sauk and Fox Agency with Sauks and Foxes of Iowa cedes land and provides for removal.

1845   Florida becomes a state.

1846   Miamis remove from Indiana.

Iowa becomes a state.

1848   Wisconsin becomes a state.

1851   Potawatomis remove from Wisconsin.

1854   Kansas-Nebraska Act organizes Kansas Territory.

1855   Third Seminole War begins.

1857   Tonawanda Senecas buy land from Ogden Land Company.

1858   Billy Bowlegs, the last major Seminole leader, removes from Florida.

1859   Seminole removal ends.

A

Abraham (c. 1790–1870s)

By the time Abraham appeared on the national scene in 1826, he was a confidant of **Miconopy**, head chief of the Seminoles, and a translator—soft-spoken, gentle mannered, and dressed in Seminole fashion. He was a former slave at Pensacola, but presumably about the time of the First Seminole War he made his way to Billy Bowlegs' (*see* **Hulbutta Micco**) town, where he developed a relationship with Miconopy, a relationship that made him a key figure in **Seminole removal**.

African-descended people among the Seminoles, like Abraham, were welcomed because of their usefulness. Not slaves in the sense of American chattel slavery, they instead lived in a social arrangement by which the "slave" paid tribute to the "owner." Many lived in separate villages and owned their own property. They were armed and went to war with the Seminoles. Others, like Abraham, served as interpreters and go-betweens with the whites. By 1826, he was one of the principal men of the tribal town of Pilaklikaha. That year Abraham accompanied Miconopy and a delegation of Seminoles to Washington regarding the Treaty of Moultrie Creek, and as a reward for his services, Miconopy allegedly made him a free man.

Following the Treaty of Payne's Landing in 1832, Abraham was part of the delegation sent to Indian Territory to look over the land, as the treaty required. As the Seminoles understood it, the delegates were supposed to report their findings back to the Seminoles. However, their visit to Fort Gibson coincided with the visit of the Stokes Commission, there to survey conditions in the Indian Territory, and Commissioners Montfort Stokes, Henry **Ellsworth**, and John **Schermerhorn** persuaded the Seminole delegates to sign an agreement on March 28, 1833, stating that they liked the land. Abraham signed as interpreter. Although the Seminoles did not recognize the delegation's authority to sign a removal agreement, the United States interpreted the agreement as a removal treaty and applied it to all of the Florida Indians.

Abraham was a Black Seminole, one of many escaped black slaves absorbed into the Seminole Nation. (Library of Congress)

While remaining friendly with the whites, Abraham was active on the Seminole side in the early stages of the **Second Seminole War**. Before the outbreak of hostilities, he accompanied Yaha Hadjo and others who sought to encourage the slaves in the sugar plantations along the St. Johns River to revolt when the Seminoles gave them a signal. With a number of warriors under his command, he was a leader in the war for a year following the annihilation of Maj. Francis Dade's command on December 28, 1835. He was at the battles on the Withlacoochee and helped negotiate a truce with Gen. Edmund P. Gaines in March 1836.

In early 1837, Abraham went to Gen. Thomas S. **Jesup** under a flag of truce, and Jesup convinced him to use his influence with the Seminoles to bring in others for negotiations. He was successful in persuading Jumper, **Hulbutta Tustenuggee** (Alligator), and others to meet with Jesup for talks, which led to an agreement. The Seminoles promised to assemble at Tampa Bay by April 10. Miconopy was to be held as a hostage to guarantee their actions. A large number of Seminoles and blacks went to Tampa Bay, as agreed, to await removal, but the arrival of slave claimants caused them to scatter. A group of Seminoles under Osceola, **Coacoochee**, and John **Cavallo** freed the hostages. Abraham, among others, however, remained with the army, and Gen. Jesup promised him and his family their freedom if he remained loyal to the United States.

Abraham continued to use his status among the Seminoles to try to get them to remove. He sent word to, or met with, **Coe Hadjo**, Miconopy, Alligator, and John Cavallo. He was successful only with Coe Hadjo, with whom Abraham had a close relationship. He reminded Coe Hadjo of the time that they sat together near Fort Gibson and talked about the richness of the land in the West and how they believed that the Seminoles could survive there. Whether it was his appeal that worked is unclear, but Coe Hadjo assembled his people and prepared them for removal.

Abraham left for the West in February 1839 with Coe Hadjo and his band. The group included 13 free blacks and 48 slaves, who made up 30 percent of the party, and a large number of women and children. Traveling aboard the steamboat *Buckeye,* the party of 204 was stranded for a short time at Little Rock in early April because of low water on the Arkansas River. The party finally arrived at Fort Gibson on April 13, having lost only one person, who fell overboard.

In the West, Abraham remained near Fort Gibson for some time, acting as an interpreter for the army and the Creek Agency in the early 1840s, but he lost his job as interpreter in 1843. His influence with the Seminoles declined, and there were apparently threats on his life for his past relations with the army. However, he remained loyal to Miconopy.

Abraham removed to the Seminole lands in the western Creek Nation after the Seminole treaty with the Creeks in 1845. In 1852, Abraham was part of the delegation that returned to Florida to try to persuade remaining Indians to remove. They met with **Hulbutta Micco** (Billy Bowlegs), whom they took on a tour of Washington and New York in an attempt to convince him of the power of the whites. In his later years, Abraham became a live-stock raiser and apparently lived into the 1870s.

FURTHER READING: Mahon, James K. *History of the Second Seminole War, 1835–1842.* Gainesville: University Press of Florida, 1967; Porter, Kenneth W. *The Black Seminoles: History of a Freedom-Seeking People.* Revised and edited by Alcione M. Amos and Thomas P. Senter. Gainesville: University Press of Florida, 1996; Porter, Kenneth W. "The Negro Abraham." In *The Negro on the American Frontier.* New York: Arno Press and the New York Times, 1971, pp. 296–338.

AMANDA L. PAIGE

African-Descended People and Removal

When the **Indian Removal Act** became law, a significant part of the southeastern Indian societies consisted of African-descended people, both slave and free. Their presence became an underlying element in the pro-removal argument of southerners and in some ways served to expedite Indian removal once it had begun.

The institution of slavery helped create in the southern states a need for the land that Indian removal would provide. Because extensive cotton farming, made possible by slave labor, quickly depleted the soil, new lands had to be opened. Areas available for new cotton land had greatly shrunk by the end of the second decade of the 19th century. The lands occupied by the tribes looked inviting to the states, whose population was rapidly increasing. In addition, a growing fear of slave revolts, such as those planned or led by Denmark Vesey in 1832 and Nat Turner in 1831, beset white planters. They looked at Indian nations and their populations of slaves and free blacks as potential havens for runaways or stolen slaves and were openly concerned about communities of blacks, such as those among the Florida Indians, who were armed.

In carrying out removal, the United States established policies that ensured that slave ownership by Indians did not become an obstacle to removal. Nearly every African-descended person of whatever status living with the tribes at the time of removal, except those stolen by slave traders or white intruders, was sent to the West with the Indians. Slaves, like free blacks, received the same rations and other forms of subsistence on the removal trails as the Indians did and were employed in the removal as wagon drivers, skilled workers, boat crewmen, and interpreters. Those Indians who removed themselves received per capita commutation money. Slave owners received as much for each slave as they did for themselves, their children, and other family members. Thus, Indians were encouraged to take their slaves to the West with them. Evidence indicates that slaves from white-owned plantations took advantage of the presence of African-descended people among the Indians and escaped by joining parties of Indians that were departing for the West. Advertisements for runaway slaves indicate that some were captured after they had crossed the Mississippi, while others apparently made good their escape.

Slaves helped ease the hardships of removal for some Indian owners. For example, Cherokees who owned large numbers of slaves were not required to go to concentration camps in preparation for departure for the **Cherokee removal** to the West. They were allowed to stay in their houses, tend their crops and livestock, sell their property, and join the removal parties at the time they set out from the staging points or after they had taken up the march, some joining as much as three weeks after the departure. Most Cherokees, however, were rousted from their homes by the state militias or federal troops without the opportunity to dispose of their property or gather their personal belongings. They then endured the terrible heat of the summer of 1838 in cramped and unhealthy conditions. Thus, slaves helped create a privileged class of Cherokees who escaped the unsanitary and disease-ridden camps, which were the source—rather than the trail itself—of many stories about the horrible conditions of removal.

Historians have at times conveniently, but erroneously, equated the slave-holding class with the Treaty Party of the Cherokee Nation. In 1835, the year of the **Treaty of New Echota**, Chief John **Ross** held more slaves than any of those usually identified as leaders of the Treaty Party except John **Ridge**, and Ross's brother Lewis owned more than the Treaty Party leaders combined. In fact, Cherokee government officials in charge of removal—including Second Chief George Lowrey, Cherokee leaders of removal contingents, and others—owned about 20 percent of the slaves held by the entire Cherokee population.

U.S. officials used African-descended people to expedite removal once it had begun. For example, when claims for runaway or stolen slaves threatened to delay **Muscogee [Creek] removal** and **Seminole removal**, the United States chose to allow the slaves and free blacks to go to the West with the tribes, arguing that the claims could be settled there. Military leaders in Florida in the early years of the **Second Seminole War** were at times stymied in negotiations when American slave claimants appeared on the scene. The Creek warriors who went to Florida to help the U.S. Army fight the Seminoles were promised they could keep all booty, including slaves. When slave claims to some of the captives were begun by whites, the War Department fought legal attempts to have the slaves held at Tampa Bay, New Orleans, or Little Rock rather than risk discontent among either the Seminoles or the Creeks.

African-descended people—whether members of the tribes, slaves, or free blacks—played active roles in the Florida Indians' armed resistance to removal. The U.S. Army used men such as **Abraham**, Cudjo, and Tony Barnett as interpreters, scouts, and go-betweens in its warfare and negotiations with the Indians. Others worked for the Indians in the same ways as well as serving as warriors in the field. Before switching sides to the U.S. Army, Abraham was in command of warriors at the annihilation of Maj. Francis Dades's command and at the Battles on the Withlacoochee. John **Cavallo** remained much longer in the field at the head of a number of warriors. Gen. Thomas S. **Jesup**, commander of American forces, became convinced that he was fighting a "negro," not an Indian, war and instituted a policy of bribing the blacks to surrender, promising them freedom once they reached the West. Hundreds took advantage of Jesup's offer, thus depriving the Seminoles of arms, skilled workers, crops, livestock, interpreters, and other kinds of support. Jesup's promise became a matter of serious contention between the Seminoles and Creeks in the West.

Some removal treaties accommodated the institution of slavery. The Seminole Treaty of Payne's Landing in 1832, for example, provided for relief for the Seminoles against claims by Americans for runaway slaves in Seminole territory. The United States promised $7,000 to investigate and liquidate any claims determined to be valid. The Chickasaw Treaty of Pontotoc that same year added additional acres to standard allotments according to the number of slaves in the household.

The government accommodated slavery among all the tribes from the Southeast in other ways. For example, its printed forms for removal rosters provided columns for listing the number of slaves in each household, and the army maintained separate rosters in many instances for "negro-Indians," slaves, and African-descended people.

The removal of the southern tribes created a slave trade in the West where none had existed. The numbers of African-descended people who removed with the Choctaws, Muscogees (Creeks), Florida Indians, Chickasaws, and Cherokees to the West is uncertain. More than 500 each removed with the Choctaws and the Muscogees, the Chickasaws held about 1,500 near the end of removal, nearly 500 removed with the Seminoles, and more than 1,500 removed with the Cherokees to lands west of Arkansas. Until removal, Arkansas did not have a slave trade. However, slave claims followed the Creeks and Seminoles to the West, calling attention to the large population of African-descended people in the Indian Territory, who became the focus of a trade that sprang up at Fort Smith on the western border and lasted until the outbreak of the Civil War. The Cherokees and Choctaws, whose societies were more legalistic than the others, were plagued by fewer claims, one major exception being the Beams family claim in the Choctaw Nation, which persisted into the 1850s. They were, however, raided by slave stealers from Arkansas, and the Choctaws and Chickasaws were raided by the same kind of low-life Texans. Historians have examined African-descended people among the Seminoles, Creeks, and Cherokees, but a thorough study of their role in removal has not been done.

FURTHER READING: "Black-Indian History Information." At http://anpa.ualr.edu/ other_resources/black_indian_history/black_indian_info.htm; Littlefield, Daniel F.,

Jr. *Africans and Creeks.* Westport, CT: Greenwood Press, 1979; Littlefield, Daniel F., Jr. *Africans and Seminoles.* Westport, CT: Greenwood Press, 1977; Porter, Kenneth W. *The Black Seminoles: History of a Freedom-Seeking People.* Gainesville: University Press of Florida, 1996.

DANIEL F. LITTLEFIELD, JR.

Alabama and Indian Removal

When Alabama became a state in 1819, four tribes had lands within its boundaries: Choctaw, Creek, Chickasaw, and Cherokee. By that time, the southern states strongly supported President Thomas Jefferson's proposal to use the Louisiana Purchase as a place to relocate tribes from the South and elsewhere. During the next decade, especially during the Monroe administration, the federal government made great headway in formulating a removal policy and achieved some success in persuading members of some tribes to remove voluntarily. It was only after the election of Andrew **Jackson** in 1828 that removal became official Indian policy. As president, Jackson pressed for passage of what became the **Indian Removal Act** and supported the efforts of the states to force the Indians out.

Alabama officials and other citizens, like those in Georgia and Mississippi, were heartened by Jackson's election. Between the election in 1828 and his inauguration in early 1829, all three states passed legislation asserting that state civil and criminal laws applied to the Indians, assuming that the Indians would rather remove than submit. In addition to piecemeal legislation between 1827 and 1829, Alabama lawmakers passed a broader extension bill in 1832 that brought the Indians further under Alabama law. The new bill was designed to usurp the Creek and Cherokee governments and prohibit the Indians from passing laws that violated the Alabama constitution or state laws. Alabama also asserted its legal jurisdiction over the Choctaws and Chickasaws, which effectively undermined the efficacy of their governments and the authority of their headmen inside the boundaries of the state.

The Choctaws were first to remove from Alabama. They held only a relatively small tract of land in extreme west-central Alabama, having ceded their other lands within the state in 1803, 1805, and 1816. The strongest movement for Choctaw removal came from Mississippi, not Alabama. However, the states worked in concert for a common good. The extension of state law, though not applied immediately, was unsettling to the Choctaws. Passage of the Indian Removal Act in May 1830 was followed by an influx of American intruders into Choctaw land. These events and the political machinations of a few prominent Choctaws led to the **Treaty of Dancing Rabbit Creek** in the following September, providing for **Choctaw removal**. It ceded all Choctaw land in exchange for land between the Arkansas and Red Rivers west of Arkansas Territory.

The treaty also allotted Choctaw land to heads of households to provide a home for the Choctaws until they removed. Immediately, land speculation began as land dealers used extended credit and other techniques to obtain purchase agreements for allotments at the time of removal. A number of speculators were based in Alabama, and much of the land went into their hands. However, the speculators fell to wrangling among themselves, causing long delays in clearing titles and thus defeating one of Jackson's prime goals: to put Indian land into the hands of American farmers as soon as possible.

The Choctaws began removing soon after the Treaty of Dancing Rabbit Creek was signed. The people marched overland primarily to Natchez and Vicksburg, where they boarded steamboats to take them to points west or traveled through the Chickasaw Nation to Memphis. By late 1833, most of the Choctaws had left for the West. Among those who remained were the ancestors of the **Mississippi Band of Choctaw Indians** of today.

Muscogee (Creek) removal was the primary focus of Alabamians because of the large land mass occupied by the Creeks and the quality of the land for cotton culture. Whites had been pressing upon their borders and intruding in their lands for years. The condition of the Creeks at the time the Indian Removal Act was passed was the most desperate of any of the tribes in the Southeast. Although they were removed a few years later, they were the only tribe in the Southeast to remove without having signed a removal treaty.

Early voluntary removals had followed the Treaty of Indian Springs. In 1825, the Coweta chief, William McIntosh, signed the treaty, which ceded all Creek land in Georgia and a large portion of Creek land in Alabama in exchange for an equal amount of land west of Arkansas Territory. McIntosh was executed by order of the Creek National Council, and approximately 700 members of the McIntosh party and their slaves emigrated to the West in 1827. This commenced the Creek voluntary removal period. While the group prepared for their journey west, delegations of Creeks worked tirelessly to overturn the treaty. Although they were successful in nullifying the Treaty of Indian Springs and signing a revised version in 1826, the Creeks were ultimately unable to recoup their Georgia lands. As a result, approximately 7,000 Lower Creeks living in Georgia were forced from the state into Alabama on January 1, 1827.

Loss of their Georgia lands created incredible hardships for the Creeks forced into Alabama. Many appear to have been unable to find suitable land and began a decade-long period of decline. In the years following the treaty, many Lower Creeks were reduced to receiving government-provided rations at Fort Mitchell and eating roots, the bark of trees, or the carcasses of dead, diseased animals. Some Lower Creek towns or villages, formerly located in Georgia, dissolved and were never reconstituted within Alabama.

For the Lower Creeks who were unable to establish their lifeways within Alabama, voluntary removal west offered a way to avoid the hardships. Creek leaders countered U.S. encouragement of voluntary removal by attempting to force all Creeks to remain within the Creek Nation. The National Council passed laws prohibiting Creeks from enrolling, or advising other to enroll, for emigration, and death threats were issued to those caught trying to leave the Nation. However, small emigrating parties consisting primarily of friends and followers of McIntosh left Alabama in 1827 and 1828, and in 1829 a large party of almost 1,400 departed for the West.

Despite the large number of Creeks that voluntarily emigrated, Andrew Jackson was unhappy with the progress of removal. In 1830, he stopped all government-sponsored emigrations until the entire Creek Nation agreed to remove. Whereas this decision had little effect on the Creeks opposed to emigration, it had broad implications for those who had enrolled to move west. Many had not planted crops that year in anticipation of receiving government rations. To make matters worse, Creek headmen ordered the slaughter of the emigrants' livestock as punishment for leaving the Creek Nation. With no crops and livestock, many Creeks lived on the edge of starvation. Their problems were compounded by the influx of white squatters who illegally settled in the Creek Nation. Many whites simply cleared a plot of Creek land, while the most brazen forcibly evicted the Creeks from their houses. Other whites traded alcohol to the Creeks or established grog shops on Creek land. Many Creeks contracted diseases, such as smallpox, and died as a result. When the Creeks complained to Washington, Jackson told them that the only solution was emigration.

The Creeks' decision to negotiate the 1832 Treaty of Washington was, in part, a desperate attempt to save their Nation from being overrun by white squatters. Creek heads of family received a 320-acre reserve of land while 90 headmen received a tract of 640 acres. Whites continued to be a problem after 1832, however, because land speculators based primarily in Alabama and Georgia cheated many of the Creeks out of their reserves by various means of fraud. With the promise of the treaty unfulfilled, removal of the entire Creek population appeared to be inevitable. Amidst the land fraud controversy, two more voluntary emigrating parties numbering about 500 left Alabama in 1834 and 1835. Others wished to emigrate but wanted to settle their land fraud cases before leaving.

By 1834 and 1835, the Creeks were divided over removal. Most favored remaining on their ancestral homeland. Among the latter was a band of Lower Creeks who lashed out against white encroachment in the spring of 1836. In response to the Second Creek War, as it was called, Andrew Jackson decided to forcibly remove the remaining Creeks. The Creeks who participated in the war were shackled and marched to Montgomery, where they were placed on steamboats for their journey west. Civilian agents overseen by military officers then removed the remaining "friendly" Creeks by organizing them into five detachments from camps at Wetumpka and Tallassee and two camps near Talladega. A sixth detachment, composed of family members of Creeks fighting the Seminoles, remained in Alabama until the Florida campaign was over. These Creeks were persecuted by local whites as they waited in three emigration camps and were subsequently removed to Mobile Point and later Pass Christian, Mississippi, before continuing west to Fort Gibson in 1837.

Small detachments of Creeks, consisting of individuals or families, continued emigrating from Alabama to the Indian Territory during the 1840s and 1850s. Other Creeks remained with authorization under the first article of the 1814 Treaty of Fort Jackson. Their descendants constitute the **Poarch Band of Creek Indians** currently residing near Atmore, Alabama.

The Chickasaws were the third tribe to remove from Alabama. Their Alabama landholdings when the Indian Removal Act became law consisted of not quite 500,000 acres along the Mississippi border in the northwestern part of the state. They had ceded their other lands in Alabama in 1805 and 1816. In the Treaty of Pontotoc in 1832, adjusted by Articles of Agreement in 1834 in Washington, the Chickasaws ceded their remaining lands in Alabama and Mississippi in exchange for lands in the West.

Like the Choctaws and Creeks, the Chickasaws were beset by a number of problems. Extension of Mississippi and Alabama civil and criminal laws over their lands, followed quickly by passage of the Indian Removal Act, demoralized the people. Intruders moved onto their land, their society was disrupted, they became indebted to local merchants, and they were preyed upon in the state court systems. Also like the Choctaws, they received land allotments to ensure them a place of residence until they removed and the allotments could be sold. Their lands were laid off into counties in 1835, the land was surveyed, and sales began in 1836. The lion's share of Chickasaw land became the property of land speculators, including some of the same Alabamans who had engaged in speculation in the Choctaw Nation. Many, however, lost in their ventures because of the Panic of 1837 in the banking system. Unlike the Choctaws, most Chickasaws received the market value for their allotments.

Unlike other removals, **Chickasaw removal** was contingent upon the Chickasaws finding land that suited them in the West. It was not until early 1837 that they reached an agreement with the Choctaws to occupy the western district of the Choctaw Nation. Removal began in the summer of 1837 and continued under a federal superintendent until 1839. However, the Chickasaw Nation paid commutation expenses for any Chickasaws who wished to remove thereafter. Chickasaws continued to remove as late as 1850. They were the only southeastern tribe who left no remnant east of the Mississippi.

Cherokee removal was the last major Indian removal from Alabama. Land cessions in 1806, 1817, and 1819 had shrunk the Cherokee land base so that by the removal period their Alabama lands consisted of an area in the northeastern corner of the state between the Tennessee River and the Creek Nation. This land was highly desirable to Alabamans because of the extensive orchards maintained by the Cherokees and because of its strategic location in regard to transportation. The Cherokees blocked access to an important segment of the Tennessee River and maintained and controlled an efficient system of toll roads and ferries along important routes from northern Georgia, eastern Tennessee, and the Carolinas. In 1835, some 1,424 Cherokees, 299 slaves, and 32 whites married to Cherokees resided in the Alabama lands.

By that time, Cherokee removal from Alabama had been going on for years. A large number had voluntarily removed following the treaties of 1817 and 1819 and had become part of the Western Cherokee Nation in Arkansas. Gunter's Landing had been the point of departure for captured Creeks who had sought refuge among the Cherokees and for groups of

Cherokees who chose to voluntarily remove. Still, the Cherokees for the most part resisted removal. Many who had taken reservations under the treaties of 1817 and 1819 were beset by whites intent on stealing their property, forcing them to move south of the Tennessee, only to face the same problems a few years later. Following Alabama's further extension of its laws over the Indians in 1832, many of the ferry owners and turnpike regulators had their business enterprises confiscated and turned over to whites. After 1832, large numbers of whites, particularly from Tennessee, Georgia, and the Carolinas, flocked to the region, squatting on Cherokee lands and stealing their crops, slaves, livestock, and other property.

As the deadline for removal set by the 1835 **Treaty of New Echota** approached, the Cherokees made little preparation. Andrew Jackson directed the army to remove the Cherokees by force. Beginning in May 1838, Gen. Winfield **Scott** ordered squads of state militia to round up Cherokees and place them in holding camps until his regular troops arrived. The Cherokees were forcibly rousted from their homes by the Alabama militia and, later, U.S. troops, marched to a camp at Fort Payne, abandoning their homes and other property. The Cherokees' lack of preparation made life harder in the camps, where they suffered from exposure to the sweltering heat, unsanitary conditions, and disease during the summer of 1838 while they were awaiting removal.

The government had begun to remove some Cherokees immediately after the deadline. In late spring, the first four removal groups traveled by wagon, water, and railway across northern Alabama and departed on steamboats from Waterloo. However, low water and disease made the journey west difficult and deadly. As a result, the Cherokee Nation obtained permission to suspend removal until the fall and to conduct the removal itself. Only one of the remaining thirteen major Cherokee removal parties organized in Alabama. With John Benge at its head, the group of slightly more than 1,100 Cherokees left Fort Payne on November 1 and exited the state north of Huntsville on its way overland to **Indian Territory**. A month later, a party that included Chief John **Ross** and his family traveled down the Tennessee River on flatboats, went through the Muscle Shoals Canal, and reached Tuscumbia, where Ross purchased a steamboat that took them to Indian Territory. His departure officially ended Cherokee removal.

FURTHER READING: Foreman, Grant. *Indian Removal: The Emigration of the Five Civilized Tribes of Indians*. Norman: University of Oklahoma Press, 1989; Gibson, Arrell M. *The Chickasaws*. Norman: University of Oklahoma Press, 1971; Haveman, Christopher D. "The Removal of the Creek Indians from the Southeast, 1825–1838." PhD diss., Auburn University, 2009; Hill, Sarah H. "Cherokee Indian Removal," Encyclopedia of Alabama. At www.encyclopediaofalabama.org/face/Article.jsp?id=h-1433; O'Brien, Greg. "Chickasaws in Alabama," Encyclopedia of Alabama. At www.encyclopediaofalabama.org/face/Article.jsp?id=h-1487; O'Brien, Greg. "Choctaws in Alabama," Encyclopedia of Alabama. At www.encyclopediaofalabama.org/face/Article.jsp?id=h-1186.

CHRISTOPHER D. HAVEMAN AND DANIEL F. LITTLEFIELD, JR.

Apalachicola Removal

By 1830 when the **Indian Removal Act** became law, the Apalachicolas were much reduced from the status they had once held. A Hichiti-speaking "people on the other side," in the early 18th century they had consisted of four towns on the lower Chattahoochee in present-day Georgia. Later in the century, some joined the Lower Creeks on the west side of the Chattahoochee, across from present-day Columbus, Georgia, settling in what was known as Big Town. There, in a 1757 peace agreement between them and the Muscogees, they founded what became known as the Creek Confederacy. Between then and the end of the century, this significant tribe declined, and by the time removal began they numbered about 400, living on the Apalachicola River in Florida.

The United States treated with the Apalachicolas separately from the other Florida tribes in the talks that led to the Treaty of Moultrie Creek in 1823. While the other tribes agreed to move to reserved land in central Florida, an additional article in the treaty provided for small reserves for the bands of **Eneah Emathla**, John Blount, Tuski Hajo, Mulatto King, Emathlachee, and Econchatimico on the Apalachicola and Chattahoochee Rivers. Eneah Emathla, a Lower Creek who had been named principal negotiator for the Florida tribes at Fort Moultrie, soon thereafter took his band back to the Lower Creeks. Those who remained were successful farmers and livestock growers who accumulated slaves and other property.

When the **Seminole removal** treaty was signed at Payne's Landing in 1832, the Apalachicolas were excluded, and Andrew **Jackson** sent James Gadsden to negotiate separately with them. In a relinquishment signed on June 18, 1833, leaders Blount and Davy gave up their lands, and the others were given options to remain and continue receiving annuities until Blount removed, at which time support would be withdrawn; to sell their lands and remove to Arkansas at their own expense; or to cede their lands to the United States, join the Creeks and Seminoles in the West, and give up the separate agreement made with them in 1823, in return for $3,000 and the "privileges" guaranteed under the Treaty of Moultrie Creek.

Blount's band was the government's first priority. Blount and Davy led a delegation, including members of the other Apalachicola bands, to the West and visited Red Moccasin, Blount's uncle, who had lived on the Trinity River in Texas for a number of years. They agreed that Blount's band could settle with his uncle's. Back in Florida, Blount hesitated and tried to obtain permission to remain. But Blount could count on no assistance from federal authorities to protect his people. Instead, they threatened to drive him away if he did not remove. They also held back the money due him, saying that he would have to collect it in the West. A delay in departure occurred because eight boys, including one of Blount's sons, were in school at the Choctaw Academy in Kentucky and did not arrive in Florida until December 1833. By 1834, his people's situation had become desperate: some had died of cholera; some had defected to the Creeks and Seminoles; whites had raided them, committing violence and stealing property; intruders had entered their lands; and slave hunters had made claims on their slaves and invaded Blount's land, chasing the slaves with dogs. Finally, in 1834, Blount's band, along with those of Davy and Yellow Hair, left by steamer to New Orleans, traveled up the Mississippi to northern Louisiana, disembarked, and traveled overland to the Trinity River in Texas, where Blount died not long afterward.

The Apalachicolas' troubles followed them to the West. At New Orleans, William Beattie filed suit for $6,500 he claimed the Apalachicolas owed him. The Indians settled out of court for $2,000 and two slaves worth $500 each. Beattie, a Vermonter and an opportunist, was believed to have committed forgery, submitted a fraudulent claim, and swindled the Apalachicolas. Beattie became an underling for John W. A. **Sanford**, whose Sanford Emigrating Company received the contract for **Muscogee (Creek) removal** and led Creek removal parties to the West.

When the **Second Seminole War** began, the Apalachicolas who remained in Florida tried to be neutral. Seminoles and whites raided them, stealing their slaves and other property. They could not plant crops and suffered from lack of food. In the spring and summer of 1836, when Lower Creeks under Eneah Emathla revolted against Creek removal, refugee Creeks fled to the Apalachicola lands. By late spring 1838, the Apalachicolas were desperate and agreed to remove in the fall.

Maj. Daniel Boyd conducted the Apalachicola removal. On October 29, about 250 Apalachicolas and 34 Dog Island Creeks left Pensacola aboard the steamer *Rodney* and the schooners *Vespar* and *Octavia*, bound for New Orleans. From there, the *Rodney* took the entire group up the Mississippi and Arkansas Rivers as far as Little Rock, where they were stopped by low water. Many were sick at they time they left Florida, and by the time they reached Little Rock, six had died. On November 23, they boarded the light draft *North St. Louis*, which went only a few miles up the river before it also grounded. The Apalachicolas disembarked and traveled by wagon over the military road the remaining distance to Fort Gibson. They settled among the Creeks not far from present-day Okmulgee, Oklahoma, and became Tulwa Thlocco (Big Town), one of the forty-four tribal towns constituting the Creek Nation.

FURTHER READING: Covington, James W. "Federal Relations with the Apalachicola Indians, 1823–1838." *Florida Historical Quarterly* 42 (October 1963): 125–141; McReynolds, Edwin C. *The Seminoles*. Norman: University of Oklahoma Press, 1957; "Seminole & Apalachicola Indian Records & Miscellaneous." At http://freepages .genealogy.rootsweb.ancestry.com/~textlance/seminoles/; "Treaty with the Apalachicola Band, 1832." At http://digital.library.okstate.edu/kappler/Vol2/treaties/ app0352.htm.

DANIEL F. LITTLEFIELD, JR.

Arkansas and Indian Removal

Thomas Jefferson considered the Louisiana Purchase an opportunity to set his plan for Indian removal in motion. Believing that the Indians could not survive in close proximity to white Americans, Jefferson thought that their removal to a more distant territory would give them time to become more "civilized" and, therefore, more agreeable neighbors for Americans. By 1808, and for two decades thereafter, the Arkansas River watershed and, later, Arkansas Territory, seemed the most likely location for settlement of the tribes. However, as the territory rapidly became populated, it became clear that Arkansas would be a pass-through territory or state for removing tribes, whose final destination lay beyond its western borders. Nevertheless, Arkansas was a pivotal state that profited greatly from the removal process.

Although Cherokees had migrated and settled in Arkansas as early as 1794, it was not until 1817 that the United States took the first official step to remove Indians to the territory. That year, a treaty with the Cherokees established a reserve on the Arkansas River in west-central Arkansas for those who agreed to voluntarily remove. The Cherokees signed an additional treaty in 1819, the year Arkansas became a territory. In 1820, the Treaty of Doak's Stand provided for voluntary removal of Choctaws beyond the western border of Arkansas. By the late 1820s, however, it was clear that the territory would not provide for the proper settlement of the tribes, and in 1828, the Arkansas Cherokees agreed by treaty to remove beyond the territory's western border.

When removal began, a system of roads crossed Arkansas from east to west to the **Indian Territory**. In the southern part of the state, a road went west from Point Chico on the Mississippi River to Ecore Fabre, presently Camden, and then to Washington and from there to the Choctaw Nation. In central Arkansas, a road left the Mississippi opposite Memphis and went west, crossed the St. Francis River and Crowley's Ridge north of present-day Forrest City, and continued west across the L'Anguille River, which was bridged, to the 64th mile west of Memphis. There it turned southwest to Mouth of Cache, now Clarendon, where there was a ferry across the White River. From there the road passed westerly across the Grand Prairie to Brownsville, then west to present-day Jacksonville, where it joined the old Southwest Trail, turned south, crossed Bayou Meto, which had been bridged, and followed the old trail to present-day North Little Rock. This road was joined in the Grand Prairie by a road that led north from Arkansas Post. At Little Rock, the Memphis road connected with the Military Road, which had been completed in 1827 to Fort Smith. On this road at Dardanelle, many parties crossed the Arkansas River and took a road west to Fort Coffee or the Choctaw Agency. From Little Rock, the old Southwest Trail went southwest to Washington, where it joined the road from Point Chico. In northern Arkansas, a post road left the Southwest Trail in northeastern Arkansas and went by Batesville on the north side of the White River to present-day Gassville, where it crossed the river and went to Fayetteville and the Cherokee Nation.

In northwestern Arkansas, the Missouri Road entered Arkansas near Pea Ridge and went to Fayetteville.

The quality and condition of the roads varied. The military roads were unquestionably the best, but they were far from adequate. Particularly problematic throughout the removal period was the segment of the Military Road between Memphis and the St. Francis River. In 1834, appropriations were made for surveying and reconstructing the road, which was rerouted in some places, but the road from the St. Francis River to Little Rock was considered unfinished as late as 1836 and 1837. Despite efforts at improvement, however, the four-mile stretch directly west of Memphis, usually referred to simply as the "Mississippi Swamp," was flooded much of the time and was either impassable or almost so in most seasons. The swamp, perhaps more than any other single factor, caused removal parties or their conductors to choose water transportation at Memphis rather than land.

Travel by steamboat was much more convenient than travel by land when the water conditions were favorable. In the spring months, the Arkansas River was navigable from its mouth nearly to Fort Gibson. The White River was navigable from its mouth to Batesville, and the Ouachita was navigable as far north as Ecore Fabre. At other times of the year, travel by steamboat was problematic. Many removal parties had to unload and make on-the-spot arrangements for overland travel, for which the people were often not prepared.

In the wake of the **Indian Removal Act**, all members of the Choctaws, Creeks, Florida Indians, Chickasaws, and Cherokees who removed to the West crossed the territory (later, the state) using its roads and waterways. **Choctaw removal** began in the winter of 1830–1831, with some Choctaws traveling across southern Arkansas and others traveling by steamboat up the Arkansas to Indian Territory or stopping at Arkansas Post, where they began an overland trek. Later groups took these routes as well, while others went up the White River to Rock Roe and traveled overland from there. Still others traveled overland from Memphis to the West by way of Little Rock and from there along the Military Road to Indian Territory. The other tribes made use of some of these same routes and others.

During **Muscogee (Creek) removal**, which began in 1828, the Creeks traveled the White and Arkansas waterways or followed the overland routes from Memphis or Rock Roe. The Florida tribes made nearly all of their journeys by steamboat from New Orleans to Indian Territory during **Seminole removal**, 1837–1850. The Chickasaws also traveled by water using the White or the Arkansas or followed the overland route from Memphis during **Chickasaw removal**. Some groups of Chickasaws and Choctaws diverged from the common route and traveled from Little Rock southwest to the Red River along the Southwest Trail. Of the 17 large Cherokee contingents in the mass **Cherokee removal** of 1838–1839, five traveled the Arkansas River, one took the Memphis–Little Rock route, and one traveled across the northern part of Arkansas from the northeast to the northwest. The remaining overland contingents crossed the northwestern corner of the state.

In addition to poor traveling conditions, the removing tribes encountered health problems in Arkansas. The summer months were considered the fever season, when people were plagued by heat, mosquitoes, and biting green flies. The Creeks encountered a flu epidemic while passing through the state, and the Choctaws experienced a great deal of sickness that ended in death for many who had become infected with cholera at Memphis. Upon their arrival in Indian Territory, many members of all the tribes who had not been vaccinated died of smallpox, allegedly brought by a small removing party that arrived by steamboat.

In addition to generating internal improvements, the movement of such large masses of people and animals through various parts of the state was an economic boon to Arkansas. The government supplied rations for both people and animals, depending in large measure on local production of corn, fodder, salt, and livestock, primarily cattle and swine. The production of rations delayed Arkansas's entry into the cotton economy, which, in turn, saved the state from the economic woes that resulted from the collapse of the cotton market and from the banking panics in 1837 and 1839. The government paid for goods and services in silver dollars, infusing hundreds of thousands of dollars into the Arkansas economy during a decade when the common currency was paper money, worth considerably less than specie. As long as the land offices at Batesville and Little Rock would take paper money, those with specie converted it into paper money, which generated as much as 35 percent more at face value, allowing them to buy more acres. Many acquired thousands of acres. Establishment of the Arkansas State Bank and its spinoff the Real Estate Bank in 1836, the state's first two banks, was accomplished by the War Department's investment of Chickasaw funds generated by the sale of their lands in Mississippi. Finally, Indian removal gave rise to a major light draft steamboat business at Little Rock. Uncertain water levels above Little Rock could be plied more months of the year by "lighters" that had a draft of about one and a half feet. A large number of such craft were docked at Little Rock during the removal season.

The end of the economic growth related to removal in the 1830s resulted in a rise of anti-Indian sentiment in Arkansas. As long as the money flowed, few Arkansans were critical of the government's policy of removing large numbers of Indians to the state's western border. However, popular sentiment turned against the Indians, and there arose a cry for the establishment of a line of forts along the border to protect the people from "hostile" Indians. When the tribes proved not to be "hostile," the prospects of large numbers of troops and the money that might be made from supplying them faded. In response, Arkansans developed a seething resentment against the five tribes that lasted until the allotment period at the end of the 19th century. Removal was a significant event for Arkansans. While removal went on, many Arkansans enriched themselves, and on the basis of their wealth, a number founded what would be known later in Arkansas history as the "first families" of the state.

FURTHER READING: Bolton, S. Charles. "Jeffersonian Indian Removal and the Emergence of Arkansas Territory." *Arkansas Historical Quarterly* 62 (Autumn 2003): 353–371; Paige, Amanda L., et al. *Chickasaw Removal.* Ada, OK: Chickasaw Nation Press, 2010; Paige, Amanda L., et al. "The North Little Rock Site on the Trail of Tears National Historic Trail: Historical Contexts Report." At http://anpa.ualr .edu/trail_of_tears/indian_removal_project/site_reports/site_reports.html.

DANIEL F. LITTLEFIELD, JR.

Armstrong, William (d. 1847)

William Armstrong served as superintendent of Indian affairs for the western district at the Choctaw Agency in **Indian Territory** from 1835 until his death in 1847. As such, he oversaw the arrival and settlement of thousands of Choctaws, Creeks, Seminoles, Chickasaws, and Cherokees, and was charged with ensuring that subsistence and other postremoval treaty commitments were carried out. In addition to the five tribes, he oversaw affairs for the Osages, Senecas, Shawnees, and Quapaws. Probably no better example exists of the lasting influence of Andrew **Jackson** in the day-to-day business of Indian removal than Armstrong's public career, which extended well beyond Jackson's administration.

A major responsibility was the purchase and distribution of one year's subsistence rations, which were guaranteed the Indians upon their removal to the West. The amount of money involved was apparently too tempting to Armstrong and others to resist. In collusion with Capt. R. D. C. Collins, the disbursing agent for Indian removal west of the Mississippi, he approved contracts that gave a virtual monopoly to the firm of Glasgow & Harrison with offices in St. Louis and Little Rock to supply subsistence rations. It was during Armstrong's administration that the government bought, using Chickasaw money, a million rations for **Chickasaw removal** without ensuring a proper means of storing them, allowing the goods to spoil at a great loss to the Chickasaws. Armstrong and Collins gave most of the spoiling rations to Glasgow & Harrison and other companies, who were supposed to sell the rations on the open market and replace them later as the tribes needed them. Instead, they issued many of the spoiled rations to newly arrived removal parties. The Cherokees protested, and as time went on, rumors and accusations of spoiled rations, short rations, illegal trading in rations through ration tickets, and other kinds of fraud reached the War Department.

Although the department was reluctant to investigate allegations of fraud, in 1841 the secretary appointed Joshua Pilcher, Indian agent at St. Louis, to investigate. Pilcher, too, not only was reluctant to pursue the investigation but also worked to exonerate Collins. By the time he arrived in Indian Territory, the companies and their main accuser, Austin J. Raines, had left the Territory. Raines had been bought off by Glasgow & Harrison, and so Pilcher gave up his investigation.

That summer, however, Secretary John Bell assigned Maj. Ethan Allen Hitchcock to the task. Evidence convinced Hitchcock that Armstrong was deeply involved in fraud with Collins and Glasgow & Harrison. When questioned, Armstrong claimed no knowledge of wrongdoing and no authority to do anything about it if he had known. Armstrong also denied any role in making contracts and laid responsibility on Collins, who had died in 1841. As for short rations, he said, the military officials stationed in the Indian Territory oversaw the rations to Creeks, Seminoles, and Cherokees at Fort Gibson, and they were not obligated to report to him. Chickasaw affairs were overseen by G. P. Kingsbury, who, by 1842, was also deceased. Armstrong denied knowledge that tickets were issued to the Chickasaws as substitutes for rations. He disavowed any knowledge of how the original Chickasaw rations had been obtained or who had done it. Armstrong also dismissed accusations made by Austin J. Raines, the main accuser, because Raines, too, had died. He refused comment on Collins's role in the contracts because he, too, was dead. Finally, he denied any knowledge of Glasgow & Harrison. In short, Armstrong flatly denied any blame for anything. That Armstrong was openly lying about some of these matters was unquestionable, and he was hiding behind the recent deaths of Raines, Kingsbury, and Collins. Hitchcock knew Armstrong was lying, and he believed him corrupt. Armstrong had come to the Southwest $20,000 in debt in 1835, and by 1842 he had paid his debts and was allegedly worth $40,000 even though his salary was only $1,500 a year.

When Hitchcock reached Washington with his report in April 1842, he created an explosive political atmosphere, unaware, perhaps, of the political influences that sustained Armstrong. Hitchcock assumed that his report would be controversial because it accused public officials. At first he was treated courteously by Secretary John Spencer, Indian Commissioner T. Hartley Crawford, and Winfield **Scott**, general of the army. But when he condemned Glasgow & Harrison and labeled Armstrong a corrupt official who should be removed, he quickly became convinced that a coverup of Armstrong and others was afoot in the executive branch. He heard innuendos that former Secretary John Bell's life would be in danger if his report accused Armstrong because Bell had ordered the investigation. Clerks in the War Department talked openly about the influence and power of the Armstrong family in Tennessee. Spencer, who stayed at the same boarding house as Hitchcock, began to avoid him. Commissioner Crawford began to make excuses for Armstrong. All of these innuendos, intimations, and social avoidances were aimed at convincing Hitchcock to withhold his report.

Hitchcock had also underestimated the close ties of the Armstrong family to Andrew Jackson, who still wielded considerable power in the removal process because of his earlier appointments. Jackson's regard for the Armstrong family came primarily through his love of Robert, William's brother, who had served under him in several military campaigns. In 1843, Jackson named his grandson after Robert, to whom he willed his sword and case of pistols. His feeling for Robert Armstrong spilled over onto his brothers Francis and William. It had been vociferous support for Jackson that had gained Francis his position as Choctaw Agent West and superintendent of Indian affairs for the West. When Francis died in 1835, William took his place. Jackson's devotion to the Armstrong family remained strong well after Hitchcock's investigation and report. Apparently as a result of his closeness to power, Armstrong had enriched himself on a meager salary in a short time.

Hitchcock's report, filed on April 28, 1842, was an indictment of the removal subsistence rations process and, potentially, government officials and contractors. His open criticism of Armstrong forced the executive branch of government to draw constitutional lines to protect political friends. In the wake of its investigation of the transportation of Chickasaws to the West, the House wanted to investigate fraud in Cherokee subsistence. On May 18, 1842, the Whig-dominated House asked Spencer for any reports relating to fraud among the Cherokees—presumably the Hitchcock report—that the executive branch wished to keep from the public. Spencer refused, saying that Hitchcock's report was *ex parte* and to publish it would be unjust to those implicated. It had become a question of principle, and he vowed that the House would not get the report "without his heart's blood."

Afraid Hitchcock would testify before the House, the War Department wanted him "out of the way." Mrs. Spencer urged her husband to appoint him as inspector general of the army as a means to mollify him. Crawford tried to bring him into his office, and Gen. Scott severely challenged Hitchcock's integrity and declared that he would send Hitchcock to his regiment in Florida as soon as the War Department released him from his special assignment. However, Spencer suddenly repaired their relationship, likely because the secretary had received a ruling from the Treasury Department that criminal charges of fraud could be avoided.

Following the House request for Hitchcock's report, Spencer had sent it to the solicitor of the treasury with strict orders to keep it confidential and with questions he wanted the solicitor to answer. Were there grounds for criminal prosecution, and specifically what was his opinion of Armstrong's conduct regarding the contracts? There had been fraud, the solicitor found, Armstrong could have acted better, and the Indians had been wronged, but the loss was not great in comparison with the large amount of money involved. A little thievery, then, could be condoned if it meant hiding the role of government officials involved in it. Although the Whigs held the White House, too, it was evident that the personal relationship between the one man who could clarify the matter, William Armstrong, and former President Andrew Jackson was too strong to overcome.

Hitchcock left Washington in late August 1842 with his report the center of a constitutional debate between two branches of government. The House had renewed its request for Hitchcock's findings. It was ignored by President John Tyler. It may have been executive privilege, but his explanation to the House later suggested that the implication of War Department officials might have been embarrassing. In January 1843, Congress renewed the request. Tyler, in response, argued that the request was a challenge to executive authority but, fearing that continued silence might be construed as giving credibility to the charges, he decided to comply. He argued, however, the futility of investigating fraud because so many of those involved in providing removal subsistence were dead or no longer in the Southwest, the cost would be prohibitive, and prosecution would be ineffectual. Nevertheless, the House Committee on Indian Affairs reported in February 1843, including in their lengthy report the results of Hitchcock's investigation.

Tyler served during a time of instability in the War Department that opened the door to fraud in the removal economy. Five men served as secretary of war and an additional one as acting secretary during his administration, 1841 to 1845, a result, in part, of a growing conflict between the Congress and the executive branch regarding Indian affairs. In 1840, the House Committee on Indian Affairs had produced a scathing indictment of the War Department's handling of Cherokee affairs after the killing of Major **Ridge**, John **Ridge**, and Elias **Boudinot** in the wake of **Cherokee removal**. When the report failed to emerge from committee, member John Bell of Tennessee leaked it to the *National Intelligencer.* Also, allegations of fraud and conspiracy had clouded Indian affairs during the last half of the administration of Democratic President Martin **Van Buren**, 1837 to 1841. When **Whig** William H. Harrison took office in 1841, Bell became his secretary of war. Harrison died shortly after taking office, and Bell and the rest of Harrison's cabinet soon resigned because of succeeding President John Tyler's refusal to sign Whig bills, probably because he was a Democrat at heart, having bolted the party to be elected as a Whig.

During his short tenure as secretary, Bell appointed Hitchcock to investigate the ration system for removed tribes. By that time, new allegations of fraud had surfaced regarding what was known as the Chickasaw incompetent and orphan funds, generated from the sale of Chickasaw allotments at the time of removal. This time, however, the alleged culprits were not Jacksonian appointees but Whig merchants and their political allies. Their depletion of the Chickasaw national fund was overseen by William Armstrong, who steadily defended the merchants' honesty and opposed any attempts to remove merchants from the Indian Territory or to place limits on their activities.

Far from the seat of authority, political appointees such as Armstrong, with less than stellar characters, were left to their own devices. In an era of banking instability, the hard cash paid by the government for goods and services related to Indian removal was more of a temptation than such men could withstand.

FURTHER READING: Foreman, Carolyn T. "The Armstrongs of Indian Territory." *Chronicles of Oklahoma* 30, no. 3 (1952): 292–308; Foreman, Grant. *A Traveler in Indian Territory.* Cedar Rapids, IA: Torch Press, 1930; Paige, Amanda L., et al. *Chickasaw Removal.* Ada, OK: Chickasaw Press; 2010.

DANIEL F. LITTLEFIELD, JR.

B

Black Hawk (1767–1838)

Makataimeshekiakiak, or Black Hawk, was a leading Sauk warrior whose actions in the spring and summer of 1832 helped spark the conflict known as the **Black Hawk War**. He was born in the Sauk village of Saukenuk on the Rock River in Illinois near where it joins the Mississippi. This site was the center of Sauk and Mesquakie resistance to white encroachment. Black Hawk had gained renown and respect within the Sauk Nation as a warrior and as an opponent of the Treaty of 1804 that ceded all Sauk lands located east of the Mississippi River. In the spring of 1832, he led a party of more than 800 men, women, and children from Iowa to resume their residence at Saukenuk, a traditional village site. There they were joined by others until Black Hawk's band numbered around 2,000. The return to the village was precipitated in large measure by pressure from the women of the tribe, who sought to plant their crops in the same fields as they had for generations. This move incited fear within the non-Indian population of Illinois and set in motion events that led to the movement of federal troops to the area from St. Louis under Gen. Henry Atkinson and the raising of the Illinois militia, which set out at once to engage the Indians.

As the white troops advanced menacingly toward Saukenuk, Black Hawk saw that he was outnumbered and led his people north to the Four Lakes area of Wisconsin. With the militia in pursuit, the band continued along the Wisconsin River, losing many warriors along the way to desertion, especially those from other tribes who had joined them. Many of the women and children, however, remained with the band. Near the mouth of the Bad Axe River, the militia and the Indians fought a pitched battle in which the whites were victorious and which resulted in Black Hawk's capture. He was taken to St. Louis and with some of his lieutenants was confined in Jefferson Barracks.

In the spring of 1833, Black Hawk, his son, and some of his lieutenants, including the Winnebago Prophet and Neapope, were taken to Washington,

D.C., to meet President Andrew **Jackson**. At the meeting, Jackson ordered the Indian party confined at Fort Monroe, Virginia, but Atkinson and William **Clark** suggested to Secretary of War Lewis **Cass** that they be taken first through the major cities of the East, then to Iowa to join their people. The captive Indians were led through the streets of Baltimore, Philadelphia, and New York City, where they appeared in theaters. While the intent of this journey was to impress Black Hawk with American might and the futility of opposing the whites, crowds of Americans flocked to see the Indians and even cheered as they were paraded down the streets. Nonetheless, Atkinson, Clark, and Cass's message was heard by Black Hawk. Once he returned to Iowa, he did not again raise arms against the United States.

Black Hawk was a chief of the Thunder Clan of the Sauk Indians. (Smithsonian American Art Museum, Washington, DC / Art Resource, NY)

FURTHER READING: Jackson, Donald, ed. *Black Hawk: An Autobiography.* Urbana-Champaign: University of Illinois Press, 1987; Nichols, Roger L. *Black Hawk and the Warrior's Path.* Arlington Heights, IL: Harlan Davidson, 1992; Trask, Kerry A. *Black Hawk: The Battle for the Heart of America.* New York: Henry Holt and Company, 2006.

JOHN P. BOWES

Black Hawk War (1832)

The first shots in the conflict known as the Black Hawk War were fired on May 14, 1832, and the last were fired less than three months later on August 2. Although the origins of these hostilities were complex, the war bears the name of the Sauk warrior **Black Hawk** because many believed his actions provided the primary spark. The violence may have been short-lived, but it had substantial repercussions. Not only did the Black Hawk War finalize the removal of the **Sauk and Mesquakie (Fox)** Indians from northern Illinois, but it also contributed to the relocation of thousands of other American Indians from the western Great Lakes region.

The causes of the Black Hawk War can be attributed to four main factors. The first of these was the 1804 treaty that officially ceded all Sauk lands located east of the Mississippi River to the United States. The Sauk Indians asserted that the five men who signed that treaty did not have the authority to surrender the lands in question. But the U.S. government refused to invalidate the agreement. Although the terms were not enforced right away, as of 1804 the American government laid claim to all Sauk lands east of the Mississippi River.

The second cause of the Black Hawk War cannot be tied to one specific event. Instead, it encompassed the subsequent expansion of American settlement into Sauk territory in the 1810s and 1820s. Illinois became a state in 1818, and in the years that followed thousands of American citizens moved into the region and began to build homes closer to the land still claimed by the Sauk Indians and their Mesquakie and Ho-Chunk (Winnebago) neighbors. American veterans of the War of 1812 received land grants in the region as payment for their wartime service, and in the 1820s, miners began to pursue more vigorously the lead deposits in northern Illinois and southern Wisconsin. The growing numbers of Americans in the area created conflict with the Native peoples and also led federal officials to push for enforcement of the terms of the 1804 treaty.

Sauk connection to the land stands as the third cause of the Black Hawk War. Enforcement of the 1804 treaty resolutions and the growing calls for Indian removal met resistance among the Sauks because many believed not only that the 1804 agreement was fraudulent, but also that they could not and should not leave the village of Saukenuk and their traditional homelands. Saukenuk, the Sauk village located on the Rock River in northern Illinois, had been the center of Sauk homelands for decades. Black Hawk, a well-respected war leader, and his many Sauk and Mesquakie followers believed that this village and its environs should not be surrendered simply because the United States and its citizens supported an invalid treaty. Therefore, from the late 1820s to the outbreak of war in 1832, Black Hawk and those who shared his beliefs refused to abandon Saukenuk.

The final and arguably most important cause of the outbreak of violence was particular episodes of misunderstanding caused by the heightened tensions among Native peoples and American citizens in northern Illinois and southern Wisconsin. In the spring of 1832, Black Hawk led nearly 1,000 men, women, and children across the Mississippi River with the intention of returning to Saukenuk. Although they were prepared to defend themselves, they did not intend to initiate conflict. Many of the women even carried seed to plant corn and other crops in the fields around Saukenuk. Similar actions in previous years, however, had led Illinois state officials to issue calls for removal and U.S. military officers to intervene. But in April 1832, Illinois governor John Reynolds demanded more immediate action. He viewed the Indian migration as an act of war, called out the state militia, and ordered the pursuit of Black Hawk's band. The first violent encounter occurred less than a month later when overeager and anxious militiamen fired upon members of Black Hawk's band who had been sent to observe possible truce negotiations.

The skirmish that followed the Illinois militiamen's actions became known as the Battle of Stillman's Run. It ended with the death of 11 militiamen and an unknown number of Indians. More important than those numbers, however, was the fact that the skirmish had ended any hope for a peaceful resolution to the situation.

From May to the first days of August, the territory of northern Illinois and southern Wisconsin was engulfed by the events that constituted the Black

Hawk War. The term "war" does not necessarily fit the circumstances of the conflict, however. Although Black Hawk and his followers conducted raids on American settlements, forts, and military forces, the bulk of the action involved attempts by the Sauk and Mesquakie Indians to evade the U.S. Army and cross the Mississippi River into the western territories. They had never been a war party and were not prepared for war. Yet for over two months they faced a military force intent on bringing them to battle.

For most of June and July, the Sauks and Mesquakies evaded their pursuers by staying in the swamps and marshes in the Four Lakes region near present-day Madison, Wisconsin. This location made it extremely difficult for federal soldiers under the command of Brigadier Gen. Henry Atkinson to find and capture the members of Black Hawk's band. The successful evasive maneuvers came with a price, however, because the Four Lakes region did not provide a bountiful food source and the Indians soon began to starve. The growing distress of the Sauks and Mesquakies led them to leave the swamps in mid-July, at which point Atkinson's scouts discovered their trail. The concluding episodes of this conflict occurred over the next two weeks.

Black Hawk's band left a trail of pots, blankets, and other material goods in their wake as they attempted to beat their pursuers to the Mississippi River. The warriors of the band fought several rearguard actions in an attempt to give the women, children, and elderly more time. But their efforts became more difficult with each day that passed, and by July 26, a force of more than 1,300 soldiers marched after the Indian band. The two groups finally met on the banks of the Mississippi, just south of the mouth of the Bad Axe River. The Indians faced the soldiers on the land and an armed steamboat on the river. On the morning of August 2, the American assault from land and water led to the deaths of approximately 300 men, women, and children. Based on eyewitness reports of both soldiers and Indians, the episode might be more accurately designated a massacre than a battle.

Within only a few weeks of the violence on the riverbank, American soldiers had moved most of the surviving Sauks and Mesquakies to the western territories. Only the alleged leaders of the Black Hawk band, including Black Hawk himself, were imprisoned at the Jefferson Barracks in St. Louis.

The conclusion of the Black Hawk War had consequences beyond the bloodshed at the Bad Axe River. Black Hawk and four of the other prisoners were sent via steamboat to the nation's capital in Washington, D.C. Although President Andrew **Jackson** initially intended to keep these men in jail for several years, he decided to send them to rejoin their relatives in present-day Iowa. But their return journey was directed through several American cities in an effort to show them the uselessness of any further resistance to the powerful and populous United States. The impact of the war on the Sauk Indians as a whole was even more dramatic. Federal treaty commissioners visited the Sauks west of the Mississippi shortly after Black Hawk's capture and pushed for further land cessions west of the Mississippi River. This 1832 treaty was followed a decade later by another accord that removed the Sauks from Iowa completely and moved them to present-day Kansas.

But other tribes in the Great Lakes region also felt the repercussions of the Black Hawk War. The violence occurred two years after the passage of the **Indian Removal Act**, and Americans in Ohio, Indiana, and Illinois saw the violence as further affirmation of their desire to remove Indians from the region. Throughout the mid-1830s treaty commissioners visited the villages of **Potawatomis**, **Miamis**, **Ottawas**, and others in efforts to gain land cessions and agreements to relocate to the western territories.

FURTHER READING: "The Black Hawk War." At www.wisconsinhistory.org/turn ingpoints/tp-012/; Bowes, John P. *Black Hawk and the War of 1832*. New York: Chelsea House Publishers, 2007; Jackson, Donald, ed. *Black Hawk: An Autobiography*. Urbana–Champaign: University of Illinois Press, 1987; Trask, Kerry A. *Black Hawk: The Battle for the Heart of America*. New York: Henry Holt and Company, 2006; Whitney, Ellen M., comp. and ed. *The Black Hawk War 1831–1832*. 3 vols. Springfield: Illinois State Historical Library, 1973.

JOHN P. BOWES

Boudinot, Elias (c. 1804–1839)

Elias Boudinot was a rising young star in the Cherokee Nation when the government's removal policy threatened his people. Educated at mission schools in the Nation and later at the Cornwall School in Connecticut, Buck Watie (Galligena) had adopted the name of a white benefactor, the president of the American Bible Society and former president of the Continental Congress. A colleague of missionary Samuel A. **Worcester**, in 1828 he became the first editor of the *Cherokee Phoenix*, the bilingual newspaper that was the first newspaper publication by tribal people in America. The threat of removal was one of the catalysts for the founding of the newspaper, which had a large readership in eastern cities and in the pages of which the Cherokees sought to convince readers of their advanced degree of "civilization." This was in reaction to the Jeffersonian idea that the Indians needed to be separated from white society until such time as they became acculturated. The Cherokees attempted to argue that since they were already civilized, there was no need of separation and, indeed, removal.

Boudinot argued this and other points in his newspaper until 1831. At that time, Samuel A. Worcester and another missionary to the Cherokees were arrested by the Georgia authorities. Convicted of violating the Georgia legislature's prohibition of whites living in the Cherokee Nation without a permit, Worcester appealed the case to the U.S. Supreme Court. As the appeal was pending in early 1832, Boudinot, his cousin John **Ridge**, and a large delegation were sent by the tribe to Washington to offer arguments against removal and to inform officials there about depredation by intruders from Georgia. They did not meet with much success. Lewis **Cass**, when told about intruders, replied that if conditions were that bad, the Cherokees should move to the West. Ridge and Boudinot then traveled to New York, Boston, and Philadelphia to garner support for the *Phoenix* and for the Cherokee anti-removal position. On their journey, they heard about the

Supreme Court's decision in *Worcester v. Georgia* and took heart in the decision. John Ridge returned to Washington, where he met President Andrew **Jackson**, by whom he was told that he had no intention of enforcing the Court's decision and suggested he return to the Cherokee Nation to convince the people to remove. When Boudinot and Ridge got much the same message from congressmen who had previously supported them, they thought the Supreme Court victory a hollow one.

Boudinot returned to the Nation in 1833 with Ridge following soon after. By this time both were convinced that removal was the only course open to them. They determined to make the best of the situation and to negotiate the best terms for their people they could get. The pair, along with others who agreed with them, tried to convince the majority of Cherokees to take action along these lines. They were opposed by John **Ross** and other leaders; when Boudinot tried to argue for removal in the pages of the *Phoenix*, he was called a traitor and removed as editor. Boudinot, along with the Ridges and other Treaty Party members, registered for emigration to the West in 1833, thus making their break with the Ross faction complete. Widespread anger between the groups erupted, and violent incidences were reported.

The Ridge-Boudinot group persevered, however, and at a council in 1834 at New Echota, they drew up a message to Congress in which they announced their conviction that removal was the only course left to the Cherokee people. This message made it clear to the government that one faction, at least, was ready to enter into a new treaty. As a result, John F. **Schermerhorn** and William **Carroll** were appointed in the spring of 1835 to treat with that group. They reached an agreement with the faction which provided that the Cherokee people would exchange their lands in the East for 13.8 million acres as well as a payment of $4.5 million and an annuity to support schools in the Nation. Only a few hundred Cherokees out of about 16,000 attended the negotiation. Twenty members of what came to be known as the Treaty Party met in Boudinot's house in the Cherokee capital on December 29, 1835, to sign the **Treaty of New Echota**. After adding his mark to the other signatures, John Ridge's father, Major **Ridge**, reportedly said, "I have signed my death warrant."

The Boudinots and John Ridge's family left for the West together, Major Ridge and his wife having preceded them. They took the northern, overland route through Kentucky, crossing the Ohio River into Illinois and then crossing the Mississippi River into Missouri. They rode across southern Missouri until they angled through northwestern Arkansas to the new land. Boudinot and his family left the Ridges at Honey Creek and traveled southward to Park Hill, where Worcester had already settled. He began to build a house near Worcester's, as the Cherokee had been admitted to the clergy of the Congregationalist faith. His plans were to continue working with Worcester in translating and publishing the scriptures in Cherokee and to preach to the Cherokees in their language.

However, when the main body of Cherokees arrived from Georgia after traveling through the winter of 1838–1839, Ross took steps to assert his authority over both the Old Settlers and the Treaty Party. Just over two weeks after he announced his intentions at a council held at Takatoka on June 3, 1839, assassination parties set upon the Ridges and Boudinot. Boudinot was called away from his work at building a house by a Cherokee feigning sickness, whereupon he was stabbed from behind and his head split open with an axe. Members of the Ross party bragged about their actions in the weeks to come, but the murderers were never brought to justice. The Ridge and Boudinot families fled to Arkansas to save themselves from further reprisals.

FURTHER READING: McLoughlin, William. *Cherokee Renascence, 1794–1833.* Princeton, NJ: Princeton University Press, 1987; Perdue, Theda, ed. *Cherokee Editor: The Writings of Elias Boudinot.* Knoxville: University of Tennessee Press, 1983; Wilkins, Thurman. *Cherokee Tragedy: The Story of the Ridge Family and the Formation of a People.* New York: Macmillan, 1970.

JAMES W. PARINS

Bowlegs, Billy

See Hulbutta Micco

Brotherton Removal

The Brotherton (Brothertown) Indians are descendants of the Pequots and Mohegans from southern New England, who became a tribe in 1769 when seven scattered Christian settlements banded together and moved to upper New York State under Samson Occom and Joseph Johnson. They established a community that they called Brotherton and lived there until the 1820s, when, feeling pressure from land speculators, settlers, and state government officials, they decided to move to the West. They joined members of neighboring tribes, the Oneidas and Stockbridge-Munsees, and in 1821 and 1822 purchased land from the Wisconsin Indians, with the Brothertons taking a tract along the Fox River at present-day Kaukauna. However, the Menominees and Winnebagos who had relinquished the land had misunderstood the transaction, believing that they had agreed to share the land, not sell it. In the three treaties that followed in 1831 and 1832, the Stockbridge-Munsees were removed to two townships on the eastern side of Lake Winnebago, while the Brothertons received an adjacent township in present-day Calumet County.

The tribe liked the land along Lake Winnebago, but as the white settlers flowed into Wisconsin, the federal government was forcing the original tribes to remove west of the Mississippi. The Brothertons believed that it was just a matter of time before they would be removed as well. To defend themselves against removal, in 1834 the tribe petitioned the federal government for individual titles to their lands, offering to give up communal ownership by the tribe. As the tribe seemed well on its way to acculturation in the eyes of the government, Congress granted their request in 1839, giving Brotherton individuals full U.S. citizenship and title to their own farms.

While the tribal government still functioned under a tribal council, individual Brothertons began to drift away from the area, some seeking employment in nearby towns, others marrying into other Wisconsin Indian nations, especially the nearby Stockbridge-Munsees and Oneidas. Since the 1990s, the Brothertons have tried to reestablish their federal recognition as a sovereign Nation, having retained their tribal identity and maintained tribal rolls. However, according to federal regulations, once a tribe has lost federal recognition through congressional legislation, it cannot be reinstated. Nevertheless, the Brothertons have kept alive their fight for sovereignty.

FURTHER READING: "Brotherton Indian Nation." At www.brothertownindians.org; "Brothertown History." At www.mpm.edu/wirp/ICW-157.html; "The Brothertown Indians." At http://home.earthlink.net/~herblst/indians.htm; Ellis, Albert G. "The Advent of the New York Indians into Wisconsin." *Collections of the State Historical Society of Wisconsin* 2 (1855): 415–449; Loew, Patty. *Indian Nations of Wisconsin.* Madison: Wisconsin State Historical Society Press, 2001.

JAMES W. PARINS

Butrick, Daniel S. (1789–1847)

Daniel Sabine Butrick was a missionary to the Cherokees for twenty-nine years beginning in 1818. Born at Windsor, Massachusetts, he was educated at Cooperstown Academy and ordained a Congregationalist minister in 1817. Two months later, he left for the Cherokee Nation, arriving at Brainerd Mission in January 1818. Later, his work took him to Carmel, Willstown, and elsewhere in the Nation.

Along with Samuel A. **Worcester** and others, Butrick was convinced that the best way to convert the Cherokees to Christianity and to hold them was to learn the Cherokee language and preach in that tongue. While he worked mightily at the task, he was never able to learn the language well enough to preach in it. He did, however, contribute to the translation work done by Worcester, Evan **Jones**, and others. In later years, he wrote extensively on Cherokee history, relying on people he had interviewed, and compiled a number of manuscripts, many of which were lost during the Civil War. Butrick was convinced that the Indians were a lost tribe of Hebrews, so he spent much of his linguistic endeavors comparing the Hebrew language with the Cherokee. His oral history was published as *Antiquities of the Cherokee Indians* in 1884.

Individual missionaries were guided by their governing boards, in Butrick's case the American Board of Commissioners for Foreign Missions and its secretariat, the Prudential Committee, headed by anti-removal activist Jeremiah Evarts. The composition of the board was predominantly **Whigs** who opposed Andrew **Jackson** and his aggressive removal policy. In addition, board members saw the removal policy as being antithetical to its theoretical underpinning, the civilization policy that had long governed federal relations with the Indians in the Southeast. Butrick agreed with his superiors, opposing removal as best he could. He was one of the signers of a manifesto drafted by a group of missionaries from four denominations who gathered at Samuel A. Worcester's house in 1830. This document set out an explicit argument against removal.

After the so-called "Oath Act" passed by the Georgia legislature in 1830 required whites in the Cherokee Nation to swear allegiance to the state of Georgia, Butrick refused, left Georgia, and went to Tennessee to avoid imprisonment. After 1832, missionaries from all the denominations as well as their governing boards refrained from active opposition to removal. This mirrored a shift in public opinion among the whites living on the eastern seaboard. Settlers in the West, obviously, supported the policy from the beginning.

Butrick was a diarist whose journals give the modern reader some of the most graphic descriptions of Cherokee suffering in the prison camps in Tennessee between May 1838, when they were imprisoned, and the time they departed in October over the removal trails to the West. Butrick and his family rode in their carryall with the Taylor Contingent of removing Cherokees. His diary offers detailed insights into not only events but also conditions of travel on the trail that took them through Tennessee, Kentucky, southern Illinois, Missouri, and northwestern Arkansas into the Cherokee Nation. Butrick's diary also reflects his spiritual angst as he questioned whether he could take communion with pro-removal, or Treaty Party, Cherokees when he arrived in the West. Unfortunately for him, through the efforts of Worcester, the Congregationalists had made Elias **Boudinot** a lay missionary for the church in the West. Although Butrick remained with the Cherokees after removal, reestablishing his church in Indian Territory, the Congregationalists lost ground as the majority of Cherokees, particularly the followers of John **Ross**, turned to the Baptist teachings of Evan Jones. Butrick died at Dwight Mission, Cherokee Nation, on August 3, 1847.

FURTHER READING: Bass, Athea. *Cherokee Messenger.* Norman: University of Oklahoma Press, 1936; McLoughlin, William C. *The Cherokees and Christianity, 1794–1870: Essays on Acculturation and Cultural Persistence.* Athens: University of Georgia Press, 1994; McLoughlin, William C. *Cherokees and Missionaries, 1789–1839.* New Haven, CT: Yale University Press, 1984; Sequoyah National Research Center. "Antiquities of the Cherokees." At http://anpa.ualr.edu/digital_library/Antiquities%20of%20the%20Cherokee%20Indians.htm.

JAMES W. PARINS

C

Caddo Removal

The early European explorers found Caddo villages in what is now Louisiana, Arkansas, and Texas, but by the time of the Louisiana Purchase, the tribe seems to have been centered near the Red River about 120 miles northwest of Natchitoches. Caddo hunters, however, ranged widely throughout the area, including the lands north of the river, soon to become **Indian Territory**. Once the **Indian Removal Act** was put into effect, however, they were compelled to give up their lands in Louisiana. The 1835 Caddo treaty called for the tribe to move beyond the borders of the United States within two years; to compensate them, the government offered $40,000 in goods, horses, and annuities to be paid over five years. The Caddo people now found themselves homeless.

The tribe split into three groups: some bands went to Texas to be near relatives, others briefly migrated to Mexico, and still others went to Indian Territory, where they settled on land on the Red River near the Wichita Mountains. This last contingent, however, had settled on land claimed by the Choctaws, who regarded them as "foreign" Indians. The Caddos who went to Mexico were struck with smallpox, which killed a great number of them. The survivors joined the Texas and Indian Territory groups.

In Texas, things did not go well for the Caddos. Texans and Mexicans were engaged in a struggle in which the Indians became embroiled, mainly because each side sought to involve them against the other. The result was that both the Texans and the Mexicans regarded the Indians as hostile and treated them as enemies. In January 1837, for example, Capt. George Erath, commanding fourteen Texas Rangers, encountered more than one hundred Caddos at Elm Creek west of the Brazos. Texas Rangers were an irregular body first authorized in 1835 to protect the frontier, primarily from Indians, while the regular army and the militia carried on the revolution. Erath's Rangers were defeated, but this was only one such skirmish in a long-running, smoldering war. At one point, the Caddos were forced to take refuge on an island in the Red River, where they gazed warily at the Texas shore for marauding Texan war parties. After Texas's independence, the republic's official policy was annihilation of the Indians. In time, however, cooler heads prevailed, and Sam Houston, among others, pursued a peace policy toward the tribes.

After the Mexican War, the Caddos and other tribes, including Wichitas and Comanches, were gathered together on land set aside for them on the Brazos River Reserve. Although the Indians lived peacefully, following several years of back-and-forth raids of settlers and Indians, resentment among the whites was still high. Texans, especially those who lived close to the Brazos Reserve and a similar reserve at Clear Fork, called for the removal of all the Indians from the state. And actions against hostile Indians in Texas and elsewhere fed the settlers' fears, in spite of the fact that many of the Brazos Reserve Indians served as scouts for U.S. and Texas troops fighting the Comanches. In 1859, whites attacked camps on the Brazos, killing and scalping several Indians. Following this, J. R. Baylor led a force of 250 whites in an attack on the reserve, intending to kill all the inhabitants and then move on to Clear Fork and do the same. This time, however, the Indians rose up against the whites and forced Baylor and his men into a position from which they were rescued by the U.S. Army.

Responding to the situation, Texas and federal officials created a new reserve in Indian Territory in the area known as the Leased District, west of the ninety-eighth meridian and of the Choctaw and Chickasaw lands (*see* **Chickasaw Removal**; **Choctaw Removal**). In the summer of 1859, as the time approached for the removal of the Indians to the new reserve, officials received word that the whites had set a date to attack the Brazos encampments and were intent on slaughtering all who lived there. The departure was moved up, and the Indians left for Indian Territory on August 1, without military protection. A new reserve was set up just north of the Washita River called the Wichita Agency, and it was here that the Caddos settled. Fort Cobb was constructed near the Wichita Agency to protect the Indians from attack from both Comanches and the Texans, who were still very much feared.

FURTHER READING: "Caddos." *The Encyclopedia of Arkansas History and Culture.* At http://encyclopediaofarkansas.net/encyclopedia/; Carter, Cecile Elkins. *Caddo Indians: Where We Come From.* Norman: University of Oklahoma Press, 1995; LaVere, David. *Contrary Neighbors: Southern Plains and Removed Indians in Indian Territory.* Norman: University of Oklahoma Press, 2000; Wright, Muriel. *Indian Tribes of Oklahoma.* Norman: University of Oklahoma Press, 1977.

JAMES W. PARINS

Caldwell, Billy (Sauganash) (1780–1841)

Thomas "Billy" Caldwell was a metis born near Fort Niagara in Canada. His childhood was spent with the Mohawks, his mother's tribe, but he was reconciled with his white father when, at age 10, he was sent to live with him. He entered the fur trade, moved to Chicago to clerk in the Forsyth and Kinzie trading firm, and then joined the British Indian Department. He was discharged for incompetence in 1816 and returned to Chicago to work for the Kinzie operation.

The federal government appointed Caldwell a Potawatomi "chief" in 1829 so he could take part in removal treaty negotiations. His name among the Potawatomis was *Sauganash*, or "The Englishman" (*see* **Potawatomi Removal**). As "chief," he was given two and a half sections of land on the north branch of the Chicago River, a site earmarked for future settlement, and a frame house on the corner of Chicago and State streets. He also opened the Sauganash, Chicago's first hotel, at Lake Street and what is now Wacker Drive.

Caldwell was a principal to the Treaty of Chicago of 1833, which ceded the Potawatomi lands in Illinois, and he facilitated the tribe's move to Iowa. Under treaty provisions, he received a grant of $5,000 as well as a stipend of $400 annually; the Kinzie and Forsyth families received over $30,000. When the tribe removed to the Council Bluffs, Iowa, area in 1837, Caldwell moved with them after selling his land and other interests in Chicago. When the government later tried to move the Potawatomis again from Iowa to Kansas, Caldwell was among those who resisted. The people who gathered around him in Iowa became known as "Caldwell's Band of Potawatomis." Before the Potawatomis moved to Kansas and **Indian Territory**, Council Bluffs was known as "Caldwell's Village." Caldwell died of cholera in 1841.

FURTHER READING: "Thomas 'Billy' Caldwell." At www.encyclopedia.chicagohistory.org; Murphy, Joseph. *Potamatomi of the West: Origins of the Citizens Band.* Shawnee, OK: Citizen Band Potatwatomi Tribe, 1988.

JAMES W. PARINS

Carroll, William (1788–1844)

William Carroll, a native of Pennsylvania, moved to Nashville, Tennessee, in 1810, carrying a letter of introduction to Andrew **Jackson** from Albert Gallatin, his father's associate, and one of the architects of the Georgia Compact of 1802. Carroll established a nail factory, which he ran until the Panic of 1819, when he went bankrupt. During the War of 1812, he joined the militia and served under Jackson, making a reputation for himself as a soldier. He was wounded at the Battle of Horseshoe Bend in 1813, and his wound and bravery endeared him to Jackson, whom he replaced as commander of the Tennessee militia. He later again served under Jackson, then commanding the regular U.S. Army forces at the Battle of New Orleans.

Carroll's association with Gallatin and Jackson meant a promising career in politics. Blaming the banks for his bankruptcy, Carroll ran for governor of Tennessee, winning and serving from 1821 to 1827 and then again from 1829 to 1835. However, his politics created a strain on his relation with Jackson. The focus of the anger that spurred Carroll to run for governor was the control over Tennessee banking held by John Overton, Jackson's good friend and land speculation partner, so when Jackson first ran for the presidency in 1824, Carroll served as political advisor to Henry Clay, Jackson's opponent. However, his strong support for Jackson in 1828 and 1832 and Jackson's ultimate loyalty to the men who had fought bravely under him brought Carroll back into the fold, not far enough, though, to get him the national appointment in the Jackson administration that he hoped for.

Carroll's association with Jackson also meant that he would play a role in Indian removal. While the Indian removal bill (*see* **Indian Removal Act**) was being debated, Secretary of War John **Eaton** sent Carroll and John **Coffee** on a mission to the Creek and Cherokee country. Coffee's task was to determine the boundary line between the Cherokees and Creeks, and Carroll's was to try to convince the tribes of the inevitability of removal. Acting on Carroll's belief that some of the chiefs could be bribed into supporting removal, Eaton specifically instructed him to hide his real motives, to avoid meeting the Indians in council, and to meet privately with the chiefs in their homes. He was to stress how the tribes had declined from their former days and had become degraded, to stress the inability of the United States to prevent the states from assuming jurisdiction over them, and to argue that their only hope for survival lay west of the Mississippi. Although Carroll failed in his mission, he made clear the tactics the Jackson administration routinely practiced on the tribes.

Carroll was a strong advocate for removal and played an important part in **Cherokee removal.** When, on June 3, 1830, Governor George R. Gilmer issued edicts announcing that Georgia's laws would be enforced in Cherokee country and that the land that contained gold mines belonged to the state, Carroll, as governor of Tennessee, endorsed Gilmer's action. Prevented in 1834 from running for governor again by Tennessee constitutional term limits, Carroll received an appointment from the secretary of war to accompany John F. **Schermerhorn** to Georgia to negotiate a removal treaty with the Cherokees. In December 1835, the two men negotiated the infamous **Treaty of New Echota** with a small faction of Treaty Party Cherokees. Signed on December 29, the Cherokee treaty ceded all their lands in Georgia, North Carolina, Tennessee, and Alabama, and the Cherokees agreed to move west and join the Western Cherokees in **Indian Territory**. The treaty's validity, though questionable and protested against by a large majority of the Cherokee people, was upheld by the Jackson administration.

Carroll's last major role in Indian removal was service as land commissioner to oversee the liquidation of the Chickasaw domain in Mississippi and Alabama preceding **Chickasaw removal**. From his land office at Pontotoc, he coordinated the transfer of deeds to Chickasaw allotments from Chickasaws to whites beginning in 1836. Sale of the allotments set off a flurry of **land speculation** much like the speculation that had followed allotment of Choctaw lands after the **Treaty of Dancing Rabbit Creek** in 1830 and of Creek lands after the **Treaty of Washington** in 1832. Land speculation had begun as soon as the survey of the land had been completed, and Carroll cooperated with the speculators when disputes over deeds arose, working to privately settle them so as not to cause criticism of himself or Jackson. Carroll, a businessman, could not pass up such a promising opportunity. He was said to have become wealthy, holding speculative entries on 10,605 acres of Chickasaw land.

FURTHER READING: Atkins, Jonathan M. "William Carroll." *Tennessee Encyclopedia.* At http://tennesseeencyclopedia.net/imagegallery.php?EntryID:C037; Ratner, Loren A. *Andrew Jackson and His Tennessee Lieutenants.* Westport, CT: Greenwood Publishing Group, 1997; Young, Mary E. *Redskins, Ruffleshirts and Rednecks: Indian Allotments in Alabama and Mississippi, 1830–1860.* Norman: University of Oklahoma Press, 1961.

DANIEL F. LITTLEFIELD, JR.

Cass, Lewis (1782–1866)

Born in Exeter, New Hampshire, Lewis Cass attended Exeter Academy, where he was a friend of Daniel Webster. He taught school briefly in 1799, but he left that year to go to Marietta, Ohio, where he established a law practice. In 1802, he was elected to the Ohio legislature, where he supported Thomas Jefferson's policies. In the War of 1812, Cass enlisted and was made colonel of the Ohio regiment, serving at the battle of Malden. However, he was with Gen. William Hull's forces at Detroit when that commander surrendered, bringing down Cass's wrath that took shape in official reports addressing Hull's incompetency. He commanded forces in Kentucky, Ohio, Indiana, Michigan, Illinois, and Missouri in 1813, traveling extensively in these areas. In that year, he was appointed territorial governor of Michigan.

In 1817, Cass was appointed negotiator with various Indian groups in Indiana, Michigan, and Ohio to wrest land cessions from the tribes. In 1820, he undertook a 5,000-mile journey, mostly by canoe, to visit the Indian nations under his jurisdiction, setting the stage for several treaties. In 1825, he and Governor William **Clark** of Missouri met with several tribes at Prairie du Chien, in present-day Wisconsin, to make land cession treaties.

Under President Andrew **Jackson,** Cass became secretary of war upon John H. **Eaton**'s resignation and in that position was a strong supporter of the removal policy, involving himself in most aspects of the removal process,

Lewis Cass, a Democratic politician known as the "Father of Popular Sovereignty," served as President Andrew Jackson's secretary of war during the removal period. (Library of Congress)

including the **Black Hawk War** and the hostilities between Georgia and the Cherokees. His influence on the removal process was profound. As secretary, he followed Jackson's hard line on removal. He told tribal delegates who appealed to him to prevent their removal or to protect them from white intruders that the government was helpless to act. He gave orders to remove tribes by force if necessary. And he approved whatever tactics his commissioners used to obtain signatures on treaties. He served as secretary from 1831 to 1836 before his tenure ended, and he was appointed ambassador to France, where he served until 1842. His old animosity toward the British, dating from the War of 1812 and his skirmishes with pro-British Indians, surfaced in this position. In 1845, Cass was elected senator from Michigan, and in 1848 he was a candidate for president. He served as secretary of state under Buchanan from 1847 to 1860 and wrote essays on Indian subjects for the *North American Review* and other publications. Although he held a number of other appointed and elected offices from 1836 until his death, Cass's years as territorial governor and secretary of war gave him tremendous influence over the enforcement of the **Indian Removal Act**.

FURTHER READING: Klunder, Willard Carl. *Lewis Cass and the Politics of Moderation.* Kent, OH: Kent State University Press, 1996; "Lewis Cass." *Dictionary of American Biography.* Vol. 3. New York: Charles Scribner's Sons, 1929, pp. 562–564; Satz, Ronald N. *American Indian Policy in the Jacksonian Era.* Norman: University of Oklahoma Press, 2002; Woodford, Frank B. *Lewis Cass: The Last Jeffersonian.* New Brunswick, NJ: Rutgers University Press, 1950.

JOHN P. BOWES

Cavallo, John (c. 1812–1882)

John Cavallo, also known as John Cowaya, John Horse, and Gopher John, was of African-Seminole descent and had served the Americans as an interpreter for a number of years before the **Second Seminole War** and **Seminole removal**. When Fort Brooke was established at Tampa Bay, his family was living nearby. As a youth, he became a familiar face around the post. When the war broke out in late 1835, he seems to have played no role, but by early 1837, when he was about 25, he had apparently earned a place as a warrior and was recognized as a subchief.

On March 6, 1837, Cavallo was a signer on an agreement with some of the Seminole leaders to assemble their people to remove. He was among those, including **Miconopy**, **Coacoochee**, and others, who agreed to remain as hostages with the army to guarantee Seminole compliance with the agreement. The plan fell apart, and the hostages made good their escape.

In October of that year, he was a negotiator representing Miconopy and other leaders in a meeting with Gen. Joseph M. Hernandez under a flag of truce. Following orders from Gen. Thomas S. **Jesup**, Hernandez violated the truce and seized the Seminoles, including Oceola, Coacoochee, **Coe Hadjo**, and Cavallo. They were sent to St. Augustine, from which he, Coacoochee, Coacoochee's two brothers, and two women escaped.

Back in the field, he resumed his role as a warrior allied with **Hulbutta Tustenuggee** (Alligator). In December 1837, he commanded warriors at the Battle of Lake Okeechobee, the largest battle of the Second Seminole War. In April 1838, he surrendered with Hulbutta Tustenuggee, and he and his family along with 305 Seminoles and 30 blacks left Florida in June. But his stay in the West did not last long. In May 1839, he was sent back to Florida to encourage others to remove.

Cavallo's authority among the Seminoles made him a valuable agent for the army, and he became an interpreter and go-between. He urged the army to send a delegation of Seminoles from the **Indian Territory** to attempt to persuade the remaining Seminoles to remove. The first of a number of such delegations arrived in Florida in the summer of 1840. Perhaps Cavallo's greatest achievement in his role

John Cavallo, a Black Seminole interpreter, as illustrated in *The Exiles of Florida* by Joshua Reed Giddings (1795–1864), a congressman representing Ohio and an opponent of slavery. (Giddings, Joshua R. *The Exiles of Florida*, 1858)

as negotiator was his helping to persuade Coacoochee to surrender in early 1841 and getting **Halleck Tustenuggee** to come in in 1842.

Cavallo and his wife and child removed with Halleck Tustenuggee's band in the summer of 1842. Because of low water, the steamboat carrying them and Halleck Tustenuggee's band ran aground in the Arkansas River below Little Rock, Arkansas, and they were forced to go overland to Indian Territory, the longest distance traveled overland by any Seminole removal group. Lt. E. R. S. Canby (later general in the Civil War), who was accompanying the Seminoles, had no funds to hire wagons and was forced to borrow money from John Cavallo. Cavallo and his followers remained in the Indian Territory until 1849, when they went to Mexico with Coacoochee and remained, serving the Mexican government as a buffer against the tribes in the north and west. In the late 19th century, some of the descendants of his people played important roles as scouts in the U.S. Army during the Indian wars in the Southwest.

FURTHER READING: Mahon, John K. *History of the Second Seminole War, 1835–1842.* Gainesville: University Press of Florida, 1967; Miller, Susan A. *Coacoochee's Bones: A Seminole Saga.* Lawrence: University of Kansas Press, 2003; Porter, Kenneth W. *Black Seminoles: History of a Freedom-Seeking Poeple.* Revised and edited by Alcione M. Amos and Thomas P. Senter. Gainesville: University Press of Florida, 1996; Rivers, Larry E. "'The Indispensable Man': John Horse and Florida's Second Seminole War." *Journal of the Georgia Association of Historians* 18 (1997): 1–23.

DANIEL F. LITTLEFIELD, JR.

Cherokee Nation v. Georgia (1831)

In 1828 and 1829, the state of Georgia passed laws that added the territory held by the Cherokees to the surrounding Georgia counties, extended the laws of Georgia over Cherokee land, and annulled Cherokee laws. The Cherokees held their land through a series of treaties, including the Treaties of Holston and Hopewell, and had passed laws to govern themselves (*see* **Cherokee Removal**). The effect of the Georgia laws would have been to abolish the Cherokee Nation as a self-governing and sovereign nation. The Cherokees asked President Andrew **Jackson** to intervene to uphold the Cherokee treaty rights, and he refused.

The Cherokees filed a writ to the U.S. Supreme Court seeking an injunction to prevent Georgia from enforcing its laws and a declaration that the Georgia laws were void. The Supreme Court, under the Constitution, had original jurisdiction over controversies between a state and foreign nations. The Cherokees, through their attorney William **Wirt**, a former U.S. attorney general under President Monroe and President John Quincy Adams, argued that they were a foreign nation. When the case was argued before the Supreme Court, Georgia did not appear or argue its case.

Chief Justice John Marshall wrote the opinion of the Court, which is considered the second case of the Marshall Trilogy (including *Worcester v. Georgia* and *Johnson v. M'Intosh*). Marshall framed the issue as one of jurisdiction. Was the Cherokee Nation a "foreign nation" as provided by the Constitution?

Marshall examined the relationship of the Indians generally to the federal government. Indian nations were physically located within the boundaries of the United States. Indian nations could not enter into treaties with other foreign nations. The treaties with the Cherokees stated that the Indians were under the protection of the United States. The relationship of the Indians to the United States was not one of equal nations. Marshall wrote,

> They may, more correctly, perhaps, be denominated domestic dependent nations. They occupy a territory to which we assert a title independent of their will, which must take effect in point of possession when their right of possession ceases. Meanwhile they are in a state of pupilage. Their relation to the United States resembles that of a ward to his guardian.

Marshall determined that the framers of the Constitution did not intend to include Indian nations as foreign nations when they wrote the Constitution. He commented upon the status of the Indians as follows:

> At the time the constitution was framed, the idea of appealing to an American court of justice for an assertion of right or a redress of wrong, had perhaps never entered the mind of an Indian or of his tribe. Their appeal was to the tomahawk, or to the government. This was well understood by the statesmen who framed the constitution of

the United States, and might furnish some reason for omitting to enumerate them among the parties who might sue in the courts of the union.

Marshall also pointed out Section 8 of Article I of the Constitution, where the federal government was given the power to "regulate commerce with foreign nations, and among the several states, and with the Indian tribes." As foreign nations and Indian tribes were both mentioned, the inference was made that they were different and distinct entities. So the Cherokees' argument that they were a foreign nation did not make sense.

The Court decided that "an Indian tribe or nation within the United States is not a foreign state in the sense of the constitution, and cannot maintain an action in the courts of the United States." In other words, the Supreme Court had no jurisdiction over the matter. The Court never reached a discussion of the merits of the case. If there was no jurisdiction, the Court had no authority to decide the case, so it did not consider the underlying legal question of whether the Georgia laws were valid.

The case has been cited repeatedly for finding the Cherokees to be "a domestic dependent nation" and for stating that their relationship to the federal government "resembles that of a ward to his guardian." These phrases have been used by the courts to limit the rights of Indians in self-governance. The Court actually split 2–2–2 in its decision, with one justice absent. There were ideological differences on the issue of tribal sovereignty among the jurists. Four justices believed that the Court did not have jurisdiction, but Marshall's opinion recognized the Cherokees' sovereignty. Two justices believed the Cherokees had no sovereignty at all. Two believed that the Cherokee Nation was a foreign nation and that the court did have jurisdiction. The practical effect of the decision was that there was no one who would stop the Georgia legislature from acting. The Cherokees would lose their government and identity if they were incorporated into Georgia towns and counties.

FURTHER READING: Berutti, Ronald A. "The Cherokee Case: The Fight to Save the Supreme Court and the Cherokee Indians." *American Indian Law Review* 17 (1992): 291–308; *Cherokee Nation v. Georgia*. 30 U.S. (5 Pet.) 1 (1831); Garrison, Tim Alan. *The Legal Ideology of Removal: The Southern Judiciary and the Sovereignty of Native American Nations*. Athens: University of Georgia Press, 2002; Norgren, Jill. "Lawyers and the Legal Business of the Cherokee Republic in Courts of the United States, 1829–1835." *Law and History Review* 10 (1992): 253–314; Swindler, William F. "Politics as Law: The Cherokee Cases." *American Indian Law Review* 3 (1975): 7–20.

JILL E. MARTIN

Cherokee Removal

Serious talk of removing not only the Cherokees but also other tribes had begun in the early years of the American nation. The abandonment of any hope that the Cherokees could be sufficiently "civilized" to become "Americans," the pressure for more land to accommodate the growing populations of the southern states, and the threat of some of those states to nullify federal authority over Indian affairs within their borders created a national political and economic atmosphere in which removal became a possibility, if not probability. However, it was not until the third decade of the 19th century that Indian removal as policy became the center of national public debate.

By that time the Cherokees occupied only a small portion of their former domain in southeastern Tennessee, western North Carolina, northwestern Georgia, and northeastern Alabama. As their territory had shrunk in the late 18th and early 19th centuries, many Cherokees had chosen to remove voluntarily. Small groups began to migrate to what is now Arkansas in the 1790s, and larger groups moved and formed the Western Cherokee Nation following the treaties of 1817 and 1819.

During the 1820s the Cherokee Nation mounted an effort to establish their sovereignty, which provided their right to remain, and at the same time demonstrate their "civilization," which provided evidence of their ability to survive in the East. They had written laws for years, and in 1827, they wrote a constitution, under which they passed laws forbidding the sale of Cherokee land, revoking citizenship of those who voluntarily removed, and securing private property. Many Cherokees invested in slaves and adopted a for-profit agricultural economy. Fortuitously for the Nation, Sequoyah had perfected his syllabary early in the decade, and in 1828, the Cherokee Nation began publishing the *Cherokee Phoenix*, touting Cherokee "civilization" and opposing Georgia's actions and the push for removal. Finally, the first principal chief elected under the new constitution was John **Ross**, who would provide leadership opposing removal during the following decade.

Angered in general by Cherokee resistance to removal and in particular by the Cherokee constitution, Georgians responded by exercising what they determined were their rights to control the inhabitants within their borders. The election of Andrew **Jackson** in 1828 boosted Georgians' hopes, especially when he spoke out in favor of Indian removal and showed no inclination to defend the Cherokees' rights. Late that year, the Georgia legislature passed a law extending the state's jurisdiction over Cherokee lands, to become effective in June 1830. The **Indian Removal Act** of May 1830 further emboldened the Georgians, and late that year they outlawed the Cherokee government, requiring whites living in the Cherokee Nation to obtain permits from Georgia, and established a unit called the Georgia Guard to enforce the Georgia laws. In 1830, Georgia also provided for a survey of Cherokee lands and claimed authority over gold mining in the Cherokee country, denying the Cherokees' right to mine their own gold.

The Cherokee Nation and others challenged these actions in two historic Supreme Court cases. In *Cherokee Nation v. Georgia* in 1831, the Court avoided the constitutional questions of Georgia's jurisdiction over Cherokees, saying the Cherokee Nation could not sue for relief in the Supreme Court because it was not a foreign power according to the Constitution, calling the Cherokees a "domestic dependent nation." In 1832 in *Worcester v. Georgia*, the Court heard the case because Samuel Austin **Worcester** and others arrested by Georgia were American citizens. Although the Court was split, Chief Justice John Marshall ruled that Georgia had no legal jurisdiction over the Cherokee Nation.

Georgians ignored Marshall's ruling, and President Jackson supported them by inaction. They opened Cherokee lands to American settlement by lottery. In 1833, Georgia began confiscating the reservations taken by Cherokees under the treaties of 1817 and 1819, including that of Chief John Ross. American intruders entered the Cherokee Nation, rousted Cherokees from their homes, and stole property.

The Cherokees moved their council to Red Clay, Tennessee, and during the early 1830s continued their opposition to Georgia's actions. Delegations frequently went to Washington to plead the Nation's case. In time, the Cherokee leadership began to split over the question of removal, with sympathy growing for removal. In June 1834, the United States negotiated a removal treaty with the Cherokee delegation, but it was repudiated by the Cherokee council. In early 1835, rival delegations of Ross's National Party and the Ridge or Treaty Party went to Washington. John F. **Schermerhorn** negotiated a treaty with the Treaty Party delegation, but the Cherokee council rejected it that fall.

The Cherokees were then directed to meet in December at New Echota, where Schermerhorn and William **Carroll** drafted the **Treaty of New Echota**, and the Treaty Party Cherokees signed it. Ross Party adherents boycotted the meeting even though Schermerhorn had warned them that absence would be interpreted as tacit agreement, and the small number of Treaty Party followers who signed thus committed the entire Nation to removal. Although approximately 16,000 Cherokees called the treaty fraudulent, the U.S. government called it valid and gave the Cherokees somewhat more than two years to remove.

By the time the New Echota treaty was signed, many Cherokees had given up hope of remaining in the east and had removed to the West. Following passage of the Indian Removal Act in May 1830, some small groups began to remove to join the Western Cherokees, who, under the Treaty of 1828, had given up their Arkansas lands and removed to **Indian Territory**. About 400 reached the West in January 1830. In March, 70 to 80 more arrived, followed by about 80 in April. They were all destitute, with little means to sustain themselves.

In addition, the federal government and Georgia combined efforts to force even larger numbers to remove. Andrew Jackson stopped the enrollment of small parties. In 1831, Georgians began to use the state law forbidding Cherokees to testify in court as a way to extort and steal Cherokee property. Some Cherokees removed to Alabama and Tennessee to escape persecution.

Despite these actions, the government was unsuccessful in enrolling large groups for removal. Some Cherokees who had removed came back to the old Nation with bad reports about the country in the West. The Cherokee majority resisted removal, and some intimidated those who gave up and agreed to leave. Agent Benjamin Currey worked hard to enroll Cherokees, but Governor George Gilmer of Georgia had selected most of Currey's assistants, whom the Cherokees did not trust. By the end of 1831, Currey had enrolled only 366 people. Those Currey had enrolled remained in squalid camps for months, awaiting transportation.

By April 1832, only 380, primarily from Georgia, were ready to go, including 108 blacks and 40 whites. On April 10, they started on flatboats down the Tennessee River to Waterloo, Alabama. From there they traveled by steamboat down the Tennessee, Ohio, and Mississippi rivers and up the Arkansas River to the Cherokee Agency above Fort Smith. Like those who had arrived earlier, they were destitute. The Cherokee agent issued rations to the Cherokees but denied subsistence to the slaves and the intermarried whites. The government later ruled that the slaves and whites belonging to the Cherokees should receive rations equal to those issued to the Cherokees.

The next major removal party of more than 450 left in March 1834, led by Lt. Joseph W. Harris. Made up primarily of Cherokees from the Valley Towns and from towns along the Hiwassee and Tennessee, they traveled by flatboats down the Tennessee and then transferred to a steamboat towing three flatboats, arriving at Little Rock on April 6. By then, measles had broken out, and the number of cases was growing. Water in the Arkansas was low, and the group was forced to stop at Cadron and go into camp. Cholera struck the group, a number died within 24 hours, and the outbreak raged for days. The party had to go overland the remainder of the journey, many barefoot. Their horses and other property were stolen by Arkansans. Before they reached their final destination at Dwight Mission, Cherokee Nation, in May, more had died. Of the 81 who had died since they left the Tennessee River, 45 were children under 10 years old, who succumbed primarily to measles. Of those who survived the journey, nearly half died within the next year.

In normal times of debate, this ill-fated party would have provided strong arguments in opposition to removal. However, by the time Harris's party reached the West, the Cherokee leaders in the East were deeply divided and antagonistic to each other, an antagonism that led to the fraudulent Treaty of New Echota in December 1835, which set a deadline of somewhat more than two years for the Cherokees to remove. After the treaty and before the deadline, large numbers, primarily Treaty Party followers, went west by steamboat or traveled overland. However, they delayed departing as long as possible.

It was not until early 1837 that a group, including most of the Ridges and Waties, removed to the West under Dr. John S. Young. The group's movements were chronicled by the attending physician, Dr. Clark Lillybridge. Some 466 strong, the group left Ross's Landing, Tennessee, in March on flatboats and descended the Tennessee to Gunter's Landing. They were towed from there by a steamboat to Decatur, Alabama, where they were put aboard railroad cars, which took them to Tuscumbia. There they boarded a steamboat towing two keelboats, which took them down the Tennessee, Ohio, and Mississippi to the mouth of the Arkansas. They arrived at Little Rock on March 21, having been plagued by whiskey sellers and illnesses of all sorts along the way. They arrived at Fort Coffee in the Indian Territory on March 28.

A second group of Treaty Party adherents left the Cherokee Agency in Tennessee in October 1837. Consisting of 365 Cherokees led by B. B. Cannon, the party took an overland route through McMinnville, Mufreesboro, and Nashville, Tennessee, and Hopkinsville, Princeton, and Salem, Kentucky, crossing the Ohio at Golconda, Illinois. From Golconda, they crossed southern Illinois, ferrying across the Mississippi near Cape Girardeau, Missouri. From Jackson, Missouri, they traveled west to Waynesville, then southwest to Springfield, and on to the Arkansas line north of Fayetteville. From there they traveled to Fayetteville and west to the Cherokee Nation. Cannon's diary records the illnesses, the cold temperatures, and the bad roads endured by the people and chronicles the death and burial of a number of the party. They arrived in late December.

The next party to leave for the West was a party of 250 conducted by Lt. Edward **Deas**. They left Waterloo, Alabama, on April 6, 1838, by steamboat and traveled down the Tennessee, Ohio, and Mississippi to the Arkansas River. They reached Little Rock on April 11, but from that point on were slowed down by low water. They finally were forced to disembark at McLean's Landing and continue overland, reaching their final destination on May 1.

When the deadline for voluntary removal came in May, an estimated 14,000 Cherokees remained in the East. Andrew Jackson ordered the U.S. Army to remove the Cherokees by force if necessary. Because of a troop shortage, Gen. Winfield **Scott**'s regulars were delayed in arriving in the Cherokee Nation. Scott ordered the Cherokees to assemble for removal and ordered the state militias under his command to carry out his edict. Militias from the four states began to arrest Cherokees in the late spring of 1838. The soldiers spread out through the country, forcing Cherokees from their homes and marching them to holding camps in Tennessee, Georgia, and Alabama in preparation for departure. Wealthy Cherokees, especially slaveholders, were exempt from the arrests. Throughout the summer, the less fortunate Cherokees suffered in the sweltering heat in the overcrowded camps, which were unsanitary and disease-ridden. Death from disease and violence was common.

Deas conducted the first party of Cherokees to remove after the deadline for voluntary removal had passed and the roundup had begun. He left Ross's Landing on June 6 with about 650 people, primarily poorer Cherokees who had been rousted from their homes in Georgia. They had few personal possessions and were poorly clothed, so Deas had to purchase clothing for them. They were forced aboard a steamboat and six keelboats by guards posted to keep them from escaping. At Decatur, they took the rail cars to Tuscumbia, where they were put aboard a steamboat for the West. By that time, a large number had escaped so that Deas counted only 489. They arrived opposite Fort Coffee on June 23.

The next party, consisting of about 875, was directed by Lt. R. H. K. Whiteley. They started from Ross's Landing on June 12 aboard flatboats and went down the Tennessee to Waterloo, where they were put aboard a steamboat. By that time, nearly 100 had escaped. Whiteley could not enroll them because the Cherokees would not give their names. They also refused the clothing he bought for them. The party stopped at Little Rock on July 6, when Whiteley forced the Cherokees to walk a gangplank from the boat to the shore opposite Little Rock to count them. There were 722. The boat could go no farther than Lewisburg, Arkansas, where the people were put ashore and began their overland trek to the Cherokee Nation, arriving about August 1. Sickness prevailed in this part of the journey, and a number died.

Difficulty with water levels resulted from a drought that gripped the South. The government's plan was to remove the Cherokees on steamboats as Deas and Whiteley had done. The low water and the illnesses that the parties had encountered, however, caused the plan to fall apart. In July, John Ross and other Cherokee leaders persuaded the War Department to allow the Cherokees to postpone removal until the fall and to permit the Cherokee government to conduct the removal.

By that time, however, another party had been organized under the direction of Capt. G. S. Drane. They started overland from Ross's Landing on June 25, numbering 1,072. At Bellefont, Alabama, word came that the removal had been delayed until fall, and the Cherokees began to escape. Drane called out a local militia unit to escort them and prevent further escapes, but about 225 escaped nevertheless. At Waterloo, the party boarded a steamboat that took them to within 30 miles of Little Rock. From there, their journey was difficult because of low water, and they did not reach the Cherokee Nation until September 4. Along the way, 293 escaped before they reached Waterloo, and 141 died on the trip.

By fall, separated from their homes and bereft of their property, those still to be removed—the vast majority of the Nation—were less rebellious than the spring removal parties had been. A contingent left the East in early October headed by John A. Bell, a Treaty Party leader who refused to remove under John Ross. With Edward Deas as the official to oversee their removal, this group traveled through southern Tennessee to Memphis. Their plan was to go the rest of the way by boat, but on learning that the Mississippi Swamp was passable, they traveled overland to Little Rock. Illness and death slowed their movement down so that they did not reach Little Rock until early December. From there, they followed the Military Road to Indian Territory, arriving in early January.

The Cherokee government organized the nearly 13,000 remaining Cherokees into 12 detachments that would travel overland. They were led by Elijah Hicks, Daniel Colston, John Benge, Jesse Bushyhead, Situwakee, Old Fields, Moses Daniel, Chuwalookee, James Brown, Richard Taylor, George Hicks, and Peter Hilderbrand, with assistant conductors, wagon masters, teamsters, physicians, and other necessary employees. The Cherokee Nation awarded a contract to the chief's brother, Lewis Ross, for supplying the people and animals with rations along the route. The detachments took up the line of march, one after the other, during October and November 1838. All but one group followed the route the Cannon party had taken in 1837. By the time they reached the Mississippi River in southern Illinois, winter had set in, and they were held up by cold weather and ice floating in the river, which made the crossing dangerous. Once across the river, they followed the Cannon route to Springfield, Missouri, except for the Hilderbrand contingent, which took an alternate route through part of central Missouri.

The Benge contingent, which started from Fort Payne, Alabama, in October, took a different route from the others. They traveled to Gunter's Landing and Huntsville and then to Columbia, Tennessee, where they turned west-northwest, crossed into western Kentucky, and crossed the Mississippi at Iron Banks. From the Mississippi, they turned north to Jackson, Missouri, and then south along the old Southwest Trail and into Arkansas northwest of Batesville. From there, they continued on the north side of the White River, through the Ozarks to present-day Gassville, where they crossed and traveled southwest to Fayetteville and then west to the Cherokee Nation.

The last major party of Cherokees to leave the old Nation was led by John Drew and included John Ross and his family. They left the Cherokee Agency in Tennessee on December 5, 1838, aboard four flatboats. They floated down the Hiwassee and the Tennessee to Muscle Shoals, where they took the newly constructed canal around the Shoals and stopped in Tuscumbia. There Ross bought the steamboat *Victoria*, which took them to the mouth of the Illinois River in the Western Cherokee Nation. The journey was halted at Cairo, Illinois; here, Ross had to leave the boat and go to the Mississippi River crossing in Illinois, where the overland contingents had been held up for some time by ice in the river. Some of the teamsters in one contingent were on the point of rebellion. Ross resolved the issue and rejoined his family at Cairo. Mrs. Ross was desperately ill at the time. Her condition worsened as they continued, and she died aboard the *Victoria* shortly before the party reached Little Rock, where she was buried in the city's cemetery. Ross arrived in the West in February 1839.

The land contingents continued to arrive as late as early March. Cherokee removal, which had gone on for more than 20 years, was officially over, although small groups continued to make their way to the West for years to come. In the early 20th century, the Cherokees began to refer to the ordeal of removal as their "**Trail of Tears**."

FURTHER READING: Anderson, William L., ed. *Cherokee Removal Before and After.* Athens: University of Georgia Press, 1991; Foreman, Grant. *Indian Removal: The Emigration of the Five Civilized Tribes of Indians.* Norman: University of Oklahoma Press, 1989; Littlefield, Daniel F., Jr. *The John Drew Detachment.* Resources on Indian Removal No. 2. Little Rock, AR: Sequoyah National Research Center, 2006; McLoughlin, William G. *Champions of the Cherokees: Evan and John B. Jones.* Princeton, NJ: Princeton University Press, 1990; Perdue, Theda, and Michael D. Green, ed. *The Cherokee Removal: A Brief History with Documents.* Boston: St. Martin's Press, 1995; Satz, Ronald N. *American Indian Policy in the Jacksonian Era.* Lincoln: University of Nebraska Press, 1975; Sturgis, Amy H. *The Trail of Tears and Indian Removal.* Westport, CT: Greenwood Press, 2007; "Treaty with the Cherokee, 1835." At http://digital.library.okstate.edu/kappler/Vol2/treaties/che0439.htm.

DANIEL F. LITTLEFIELD, JR.

Chickasaw Removal

The last of the southeastern tribes to agree to remove, the Chickasaws chose to pay for their own removal, experienced a removal that differed greatly from the hardships endured by other tribes, and remained unified throughout the period, ensuring the survival of their Nation.

Between 1830 and 1837, the Chickasaws negotiated four removal treaties and agreements. Ratification of the Treaty of Franklin (1830), the **Treaty of Pontotoc** (1832), and the Articles of Convention and Agreement (1834) at Washington, which amended the latter, depended on the Chickasaws finding land in the West that suited them. Their searches were unsuccessful until 1837, when, in the Treaty of Doaksville, they agreed to remove and occupy the westernmost district of the Choctaw Nation in present-day south-central Oklahoma.

Terms of removal were set down in the Treaty of Pontotoc and the Washington Articles. While the Doaksville document confirmed removal, the Treaty of Pontotoc ceded all Chickasaw land east of the Mississippi and provided for allotments of land to heads of households, according to the number of people in the household, and to single men and orphan girls. Money from sale of surplus land would be used to pay expenses of land survey and sales, removal, and subsistence of the people for one year after removal. The treaty also provided for compensation for abandoned improvements on their homesteads when they removed. Land sales were to be public in an effort to prevent **land speculation**. Two years later, the Articles of Convention and Agreement at Washington addressed Chickasaw objections to some provisions of the Pontotoc treaty. They adjusted the size of allotments for households, provided more generous allotments for orphans, and called for investing the money generated from sales of land that had not been allotted and use of the earnings from investments to pay for land survey and sales and removal. Individuals were to receive title to their allotments in fee simple, and when the allotments were sold at removal, the money would go to the individuals. The Articles also established a commission of seven Chickasaw leaders to oversee land sales and determine the competency of individuals to do business and therefore receive their money.

While Chickasaw exploring parties searched for lands in the West, the Chickasaws received their allotments and awaited removal. Living under the civil and criminal laws of Mississippi and Alabama, which the states began to press in late 1828 and early 1829, they suffered from a loss of their tribal government, which was forbidden, and the social disruption that followed the influx of whites into their lands and the actions of American merchants, who encouraged the whisky trade and sought to get the Chickasaws in debt.

Removal began in the summer of 1837. Insistence on paying for their own removal gave the Chickasaws a good deal of independence that other tribes did not experience during removal. A good example is the first party of more than 400 Chickasaws, who removed for Sealey's District of the Chickasaw Nation in June and July 1837. Traveling overland to Memphis, the Chickasaws were supposed to take steamboats from there to **Indian Territory**. However, at Memphis they decided to travel through the Mississippi Swamp to Little Rock. There the government agent had assumed that they would travel up the Military Road to Fort Gibson and beyond. However, about 300 chose to cross the Arkansas River at Little Rock and go to Fort Towson. They traveled at leisure, going only 35 miles in two weeks, hunting and supplying their own needs. Summer was the "sickly" season in Arkansas, and some became ill, suffering primarily from fevers, but only a few died. The people were beset by horse thieves and whiskey dealers from the time they left Little Rock until they entered the Choctaw Nation near present-day De Queen, Arkansas. Although government agents threatened and cajoled them into a faster pace from time to time, the Chickasaws clearly controlled their own movements.

The largest removal occurred in the fall of 1837, when an estimated 4,000 Chickasaws converged on Memphis. They, too, were supposed to go by steamboat from that point, but a majority of them chose, instead, to go overland. Water levels were good, and those who traveled by water reached Fort Coffee in about a week. Those who went by land passed through the Mississippi Swamp, crossed the St. Francis, and turned southwest to Mouth of Cache, known today as Clarendon. From there they crossed the Grand Prairie to Little Rock. From that point, most went up the Military Road to the Choctaw Agency and Fort Coffee while others took to the boats.

No other large-scale removals occurred. Small groups removed in early 1838, choosing for the most part to travel by land, with other small parties following in 1838 and 1839. An estimated 1,000 Chickasaws moved on their own resources. By the fall of 1839, the vast majority of Chickasaws and their slaves (some 7,968) were in the West. The government "officially" closed Chickasaw removal in 1839, but Chickasaws continued to arrive in the West as late as 1850.

Unlike the other tribes, many of whose members were reduced to poverty by removal, the Chickasaws were deemed wealthy because of the money received from the sale of their land and because of their determination to take their personal property with them. Although government regulations allowed each person in other tribes to take only 30 pounds of personal property on the removal trail, the Chickasaws averaged more than 450 pounds. In addition, the Chickasaws drove great herds of livestock, including more than 7,000 horses. Thus they escaped many of the rigors of overland travel. Few Chickasaws walked. Nearly all rode horses or traveled in wagons or other vehicles.

The Chickasaws also experienced low mortality rates. They avoided epidemic diseases such as cholera that attacked other tribes and were vaccinated either on the trail or upon their arrival against smallpox, which was raging in the West at the time of their removal.

For many Chickasaws, the most difficult times followed their arrival in the West. The subsistence rations system, established to help them during their first year, at times failed. The Chickasaws hoped that proceeds from land sales would benefit individuals by helping them bear the expenses of removal and reestablish themselves in the West, but many saw no immediate benefits. The federal government held the money of the so-called "incompetents" and orphans, who spent years attempting to obtain what was due them. The Chickasaw commissioners extended the ration period an extra seven months. Still, the people experienced hard economic times that led to a highly inflated credit economy, based on IOUs known as "due bills" issued by merchants in the Choctaw Nation.

Throughout the removal period, the Chickasaw people maintained a remarkable sense of unity that the other southeastern tribes did not. For more than 20 years following 1834, the Chickasaw Commission acted as a de facto government for the Chickasaws. Consisting of the hereditary minko **Ishtehotopa** and six others, the body resembled the old Chickasaw hereditary form of government, preferred by most Chickasaws to the Choctaw system, under which they lived. Although the Chickasaws had a district chief and council members who represented them in the Choctaw national council, they considered the society and laws of the Choctaws too Americanized and sought a separation from them, which they achieved in a treaty in 1855.

The Chickasaws were determined to reunite their people in the West. From 1839 onward, the Chickasaw Commission encouraged those Chickasaws who had remained east of the Mississippi to join them in the West, paying $30 per person to defray their expenses. Chickasaw removals on those terms continued at least until 1850. As a result, the Chickasaws were the only major tribe from the Southeast who left no remnant tribe east of the Mississippi.

FURTHER READING: Atkinson, James. *Splendid Land, Splendid People*. Tuscaloosa: University of Alabama, 2004; Foreman, Grant. *Indian Removal*. Norman: University of Oklahoma Press, 1972; Gibson, Arrell. *The Chickasaws*. Norman: University of Oklahoma Press, 1971; Hitchcock, Ethan. *A Traveler in Indian Territory*. Grant Foreman, ed. Cedar Rapids, IA: Torch Press, 1930; Paige, Amanda, et al. *Chickasaw Removal*. Ada, OK: Chickasaw Press, 2010; "Treaty with the Chickasaw, 1832." At http://digital.library.okstate.edu/kappler/Vol2/treaties/chi0356.htm.

DANIEL F. LITTLEFIELD, JR.

Choctaw Removal

Since they were the first of the so-called Five Civilized Tribes (the Choctaws, **Chickasaws**, **Muscogee [Creeks]**, **Cherokees**, and **Seminoles**) to give up their southern homeland for a section of Indian Territory, the U.S. government planned to make their relocation as agreeable as possible. That way, other tribes would be less reluctant to sign removal treaties and move west. However, a combination of factors, including inclement weather, cholera, dysentery, transportation problems, whiskey peddlers, and government cutbacks, made their 500-mile march to the West fatal for some and mournful for others.

From 1818, U.S. policymakers targeted the Choctaws for removal from the South. They were a large, peaceful tribe who were enthusiastic about educating their youth. In addition, they were the westernmost of the so-called Five Civilized Tribes and already hunted in Arkansas territory, a prospective site for their relocation.

Beginning in 1818, during President James Monroe's administration, Secretary of War John C. Calhoun tried to induce the Choctaws to immigrate to the West. A proponent of education and fair dealings, Calhoun wanted the decision to be the Choctaws' and refused to employ the threat of force to secure their cooperation. However, in 1818 Choctaw chiefs refused to consider westward migration when Calhoun's commissioners first proposed it to them. White Mississippians badgered Calhoun to obtain for them the Choctaws' fertile cotton lands. In 1819, Calhoun appointed Andrew **Jackson** a commissioner, and the frontier general determined to bring Choctaws to the negotiation table. After Jackson's opening address, Choctaw chief Pushmataha answered that his people were unwilling to move and that, furthermore, they knew the land in the West to be greatly inferior. Having failed to get a removal treaty signed, Jackson ridiculed Calhoun for his lenient Indian policy. He also accused the Choctaws' missionaries of interfering with his efforts to buy the Indians' remaining lands. Later, missionaries were barred from treaty grounds.

In 1820 at Doak's Stand, Jackson headed another treaty conference. This time he proposed that the Choctaws exchange one-third of their prime delta land (more than 5 million acres) for a larger tract of undeveloped land in western Arkansas and what was later eastern **Indian Territory**. Despite the Choctaws' distrust of the general, they reluctantly signed the Treaty of Doak's Stand to maintain friendly relations with the United States. While white Mississippians cheered Jackson's triumph in obtaining a huge land cession, Arkansans denounced the treaty because some whites were already settled on the lands in the territory that the treaty assigned to the Choctaws. In 1824, Pushmataha died of croup in Washington, D.C., during negotiations leading up to the Treaty of Washington City (1825), which moved the boundaries of the Choctaws' newly acquired Arkansas lands further to the west. Apuckshunnubbee, another great hereditary chief, died on this treaty mission, and the deaths stunned the Choctaw Nation. The only remaining traditional chief was **Mushulatubbee**.

In his first annual address to Congress (1829), President Andrew Jackson announced that he was going to get tough on the Choctaws and other southern Indians who refused to move west. Encouraged by Jackson's election, in late 1828 and early 1829, the state of Mississippi extended its civil and criminal laws over the Choctaws and the Chickasaws and outlawed tribal governments; it strengthened these laws in 1830. Indians were to expect no protection from the federal government, which wanted to break down their resistance to moving west. Jackson's treaty commissioners warned that the whites could summon thousands of soldiers to compel the Indians to submit to Mississippi's laws. Convinced of the inevitability of removal, Choctaw chief Greenwood **LeFlore** and his supporters began talks with the commissioners. These Choctaws were Christianized and materially better off than their countrymen. In the final removal treaty, they awarded themselves valuable tracts of lands that they selected themselves. Although the other district chiefs Mushulatubbee and Nitakechi (spelled variously) resented LeFlore's leadership in U.S. negotiations, they too realized that the United States could force their exodus.

On September 27, 1830, the three district chiefs signed the **Treaty of Dancing Rabbit Creek**. The older chiefs may have signed because they feared losing their influence and a chance to profit from the proceedings. LeFlore had promised to deliver a removal treaty in exchange for a guarantee of sufficient land reserves to set himself up as a planter, for he had long intended to remain in Mississippi. With the treaty of 1830, the chiefs exchanged the remaining Choctaw lands in Mississippi with lands in Indian Territory. For the most part, it was an unfavorable treaty that left the Choctaws vulnerable to a forced, military-directed march. The Treaty of Dancing Rabbit Creek's articles included provisions for one blanket per family, which they were to receive at the end of the trail; removal within three years; and Article 14, which permitted Choctaws to remain in Mississippi on small, individually owned allotments. However, U.S. Indian agent William Ward failed to uphold this provision. He bullied most Choctaws into making the western trek and made it impossible for all but a sprinkling of Choctaws to obtain homesteads.

In each of the districts, the Choctaw people protested the treaty and tried to replace the treaty signers by voting in chiefs who would fight government efforts to force their relocation. LeFlore was reportedly obliged to "fly the country" until resistance turned passive. The U.S. government, which controlled the Choctaws' annuity funds and a standing army, refused to recognize any leaders other than the ones who signed the treaty. It also sent a company of cavalry into the Choctaw Nation to guard against a potential Choctaw uprising.

Even before the Senate ratified the Treaty of Dancing Rabbit Creek, white squatters poured into the Choctaws' homeland and drove some unfortunate tribal members out of their homes. LeFlore played real estate agent, selling off individual Choctaws' homes to whites, and then he organized a large, nonofficial removal party himself. While profiting from this role, LeFlore prevented whites from defrauding his clients of their lands, which was usually the case for Choctaws who negotiated with whites unaided by him or another literate Choctaw. LeFlore never moved to Indian Territory. Instead, he carved out a cotton plantation on the land he received for expediting the removal treaty and went on to serve as a Mississippi state senator.

In November, Choctaws began to assemble near Greenwood LeFlore's home in preparation for removal. Their plan was to cross the Mississippi at Vicksburg and travel through Louisiana and southwestern Arkansas to Ecore Fabre, now Camden, Arkansas, and then west to the Choctaw Nation. Few, however, could be convinced to remove voluntarily. Government officials wrangled over the best routes and the logistics of removal, effectively delaying removal a year. Francis Armstrong, a close acquaintance of Andrew Jackson, became Choctaw removal agent east of the Mississippi, and Capt. Jacob

Brown became agent west of the river. Finally, in the fall of 1831, the Choctaws became the first of the southeastern tribes to move west under government-directed relocation.

Traveling by wagons, horseback, and foot, some went overland to Memphis, but most went to Vicksburg. At Vicksburg some crossed the river and took the route small parties had traveled earlier. Others took steamboats up the river to Arkansas Post. Still others went downstream and then up the Red and Ouachita Rivers to Ecore Fabre. That year was one of the coldest on record, and many early emigrants lacked footwear and adequate clothing. Exposure weakened and killed many of the barely clad, poorly provisioned, and inadequately sheltered people on the march. The groups at Arkansas Post huddled in camps with nighttime temperatures near zero. Some traveled overland to Little Rock in extremely cold temperatures. Others took boats to Little Rock. From there, most crossed the Arkansas River and traveled down the Southwest Trail to Washington, Arkansas, and then turned west to the Choctaw Nation.

Despite the weather, those who went through central Arkansas fared better than those who went across southern Arkansas. Those who took steamboats to Ecore Fabre found no supplies awaiting them when they arrived. The group that had crossed the Mississippi at Vicksburg became bogged down in the swamps near Lake Providence, Louisiana, and had to be rescued, taken to Monroe, and then brought by boat to Ecore Fabre. Like those who had arrived there before them, they were hungry, and their conductor had to buy supplies on credit from local suppliers, who charged exorbitant prices. From Ecore Fabre, the parties traveled west to Washington and then to the Choctaw Nation.

In 1832, emigrating parties departed earlier in the year, but then cholera presented even a greater threat and made Choctaws fearful of crowded steamboat passage. Again, parties were taken first to Vicksburg and Memphis. Those who left Vicksburg went up the Mississippi and White River to Rock Roe, Arkansas, from which point they traveled overland to Little Rock and then to Indian Territory. Those who went to Memphis were supposed to take boats to Little Rock, but the cholera epidemic had reached Memphis, and many Choctaws refused to board the boats because they feared the disease. Most chose to brave the Mississippi Swamp and the other rigors of overland travel, going by way of Mouth of Cache, now Clarendon, Arkansas, crossing the White River and joining those who had gone to Rock Roe. From there, all traveled across the Grand Prairie to Little Rock. In November 1832, a major outbreak of cholera occurred at Rock Roe, causing a large number of deaths. Most of the survivors did not reach their destination until January 1833.

Choctaw removal was physically more difficult than the removals of any of the other large tribes in the Southeast. Those who separated from large, government-conducted parties often got bogged down in swamps and cut off from necessary supplies. Emigrant parties suffered from dysentery as well as cholera because good water had become scarce along the emigration routes. To make matters worse, thieves stole emigrants' horses and livestock and peddled whiskey to desperate souls. Many of the difficulties were due to the government's lack of organization during the first year of Choctaw removal. It was the first removal of a large mass of population, and there was a good bit of trial and error in the process.

In 1836, there were still upwards of 6,000 to 7,000 Choctaws in Mississippi, and whites clamored for their forced relocation elsewhere. The Choctaw holdouts faced legal battles, intimidation, and sometimes violence. Congress passed an act in July of that year to allow for more government-organized Choctaw Indian removal, fearful that the Choctaws might join Creek resistance. In all, nearly 15,000 Choctaws made the move to what would be called Indian Territory. Others remained on private tracts or church lands, and today their descendants constitute the federally recognized **Mississippi Band of Choctaws**.

FURTHER READING: Akers, Donna. *Living in the Land of Death: The Choctaw Nation, 1830–1860.* East Lansing: Michigan State University Press, 2004; Debo, Angie. *The Rise and Fall of the Choctaw Republic.* Norman: University of Oklahoma Press, 1924; DeRosier, Arthur. *The Removal of the Choctaw Indians.* Knoxville: University of Tennessee Press, 1970; Kidwell, Clara Sue. *Choctaws and Missionaries in Mississippi, 1818–1918.* Norman: University of Oklahoma Press, 1995; Stahl, Mary Lou. *The Ones That Got Away, A Choctaw Trail of Tears.* Angleton, TX: Biotech Publishing, 1996; "Treaty of Dancing Rabbit Creek." At http://digital.library.okstate.edu/kappler/Vol2/treaties/cho0310.htm.

WENDY ST. JEAN

Clark, William (1770–1838)

William Clark was born on a Virginia plantation, the son and brother of soldiers. When he was 15 years old, Clark's family moved to Kentucky, where his parents died shortly thereafter. As a young man, he joined the army and served as a cadet under Gen. Charles Clark on the frontier, fighting Indians in Kentucky, Ohio, and Indiana. In 1792, he was commissioned a lieutenant in the infantry and served under Gen. Anthony Wayne, fighting under him at Fallen Timbers, the site of a decisive victory over several allied tribes. Clark resigned from the army in 1796 and turned to family matters, including the tangled finances of his brother, George Rogers Clark.

In 1803, Clark was contacted by Capt. Meriwether Lewis and asked to undertake an expedition sponsored by President Thomas Jefferson to explore the area that was newly acquired through the Louisiana Purchase. Clark accepted this commission and set out with a party in 1804, returning in 1806. He was appointed brigidier general of militia for Missouri Territory in 1807 and superintendent of Indian affairs with headquarters at St. Louis. He became governor of Missouri Territory in 1806.

During the War of 1812, many of the Indian Nations were allies of the British, attacking American towns and settlements. The governors of Illinois, Indiana, and Missouri were charged with the protection of the settlers in their territories, and Clark actively carried out campaigns against the

Indians. In 1814, he led a party against the tribes of northern Illinois and southern Wisconsin, establishing a fort at Prairie du Chien in present-day Wisconsin, a long-time outpost of the French and, later, the British. The British and their Indian allies shortly took back the fort. Clark later used his knowledge of the tribes of that region when he negotiated a series of land cession treaties with them.

In later years, Clark became the superintendent of Indian affairs for the St. Louis Superintendency. Heavily involved in Indian affairs and removal, he was an invaluable coordinator for the relocation of removed Indian peoples on the western side of the Mississippi River from 1820 to 1838. In 1825, he and Lewis **Cass** set down terms for the removal of several Nations in the important Treaty of Prairie du Chien. He negotiated treaties with tribes in the West to open land for removed Indians and supervised the movement of eastern Indians through St. Louis and into the western territories.

A capable and energetic soldier, William Clark became one of the United States' ablest Indian agents after his exploration of the Louisiana Purchase with Meriwether Lewis. (Library of Congress)

FURTHER READING: Buckley, Jay H. *William Clark: Indian Diplomat*. Norman: University of Oklahoma Press, 2008; Foley, William E. *Wilderness Journey: The Life of William Clark*. Columbia: University of Missouri Press, 2006; Jones, Landon Y. *William Clark and the Shaping of the West*. New York: Hill and Wang, 2005; "William Clark." *Dictionary of American Biography*. Vol. 4. New York: Charles Scribner's Sons, 1930, pp. 141–144.

JOHN P. BOWES

Coacoochee (d. 1857)

Coacoochee, or Wildcat, was the best-known warrior, after Osceola, who opposed **Seminole removal**. Even though he was young at the beginning of the **Second Seminole War**, he commanded authority in the field because his mother was **Miconopy**'s sister and his father Philip (Emathla) was a respected Mikasuki leader. By early 1837, he was active in the field, fighting with his father. At the head of several hundred warriors, they engaged a detachment under Col. Alexander Fanning in early February at Lake Monroe. At Fort Dade later that month, some chiefs signed a capitulation agreement, and the army expected the Seminoles to report to Tampa Bay for removal. Although some complied, Coacoochee was among those who held back.

In September, Philip, Coacoochee, and a number of other leaders were captured. In the following month, Osceola and **Coe Hadjo** met Gen. Joseph

Coacoochee, a major Seminole leader who resisted removal. (Giddings, Joshua R. *The Exiles of Florida*, 1858)

Hernandez under a flag of truce. On the orders of Gen. Thomas S. **Jesup**, Hernandez violated the flag of truce and took the leaders captive, a notorious act that Jesup would repeat again and again. The captives were held in prison at St. Augustine. On November 29, 1837, Coacoochee, John **Cavallo**, and eighteen others escaped.

Back in the field, Coacoochee figured prominently in the Battle of Lake Okeechobee in December, leading about 80 warriors. After the engagement, he remained at large for many months. In May 1840, he and more than 80 warriors attacked a unit under Lt. James S. Sanderson near Miconopy, killing Sanderson and five of his men. He also attacked a theatrical troupe on the road from Picolata to St. Augustine, killing three actors and plundering their baggage wagon.

By early 1840, the U.S. Army had instituted a policy of using bribery to entice the Seminoles to surrender for removal. In March, Coacoochee appeared at Fort Cummings, dressed in one of the Shakespearean costumes he had taken from the actors. He agreed to bring in his followers in May. He appeared at Fort Pierce, escorted by Lt. William T. Sherman, and was given 30 days to get his band ready to remove. Coacoochee was seized, and Col. William Gates, in charge of the post, ordered that he be shackled and sent immediately to New Orleans and the West. Whether Coacoochee's willingness to come in had to do with money is not certain. He may have been convinced to surrender by his favorite brother, who was among a delegation of Seminoles who had returned to Florida in the summer of 1840 and remained several months, attempting to persuade others to surrender and remove.

Col. William J. Worth, commanding the army in Florida, ordered Coacoochee's return to Tampa Bay, for he had plans for the young chief. He ordered Coacoochee to bring in all of his people or be hanged. This event was a turning point. Coacoochee, who was held by the army, sent out emissaries with his personal message, appealing to other leaders to surrender. He worked diligently on behalf of the army, earning about $8,000 for his efforts.

His usefulness past, Coacoochee was sent to the West in the fall of 1841 with the band of Hospitakee, one of the chiefs he had convinced to surrender. They left Tampa Bay on October 12 and traveled by brig to New Orleans and from there by steamboat, arriving at Fort Gibson on November 12. His family and other followers left Florida the following April but did not arrive at Fort Gibson until June. Coacoochee settled near **Hulbutta Tustenuggee** (Alligator) in the Cherokee Nation near Fort Gibson, unwilling to settle in the Creek Nation, where they were supposed to settle according to the treaties.

Coacoochee was sometimes at odds with the Seminole leadership during the next few years. He and Hulbutta Tustenuggee led an unauthorized delegation to Washington in an attempt to adjust their affairs. His dissatisfaction with Seminole affairs led to his idea for emigration to Mexico. He and other Seminoles made several trips to the Southwest during the late 1840s, taking the first steps to carry out his emigration plan. When he was passed over as chief upon Miconopy's death in 1849, he migrated to Mexico with John **Cavallo** and a number of Creeks and Seminole blacks. However, he made a trip back to the Seminole Nation in 1850 in a futile attempt to persuade the entire Seminole Nation to emigrate. He returned to Mexico and remained there, where he died in 1857.

FURTHER READING: Mahon, John K. *History of the Second Seminole War, 1835–1842.* Gainesville: University Press of Florida, 1967; Miller, Susan A. *Coacoochee's Bones: A Seminole Saga.* Lawrence: University of Kansas Press, 2003; Mulroy, Keven. *Freedom on the Border: The Seminole Maroons in Florida, the Indian Territory, Coahuila, and Texas.* Lubbock: Texas Tech University, 1993.

DANIEL F. LITTLEFIELD, JR.

Coe Hadjo (dates unknown)

Coe Hadjo was one of the exploring party who went west in 1832 to look at possible locations for settlement of the Seminoles in **Indian Territory**. The Treaty of Payne's Landing earlier that year had provided for **Seminole removal** under certain circumstances. A delegation of seven chiefs was to go west to find a suitable land for the Seminoles. If they found such a land, the Seminoles would remove in stages over a period of years. The delegation arrived in Indian Territory during the visit of the Stokes Commission, composed of Montfort Stokes, Henry **Ellsworth**, and John F. **Schermerhorn**, who were there to assess the relations between local and recently removed tribes.

The commissioners were able to get the seven delegates to sign an agreement testifying that they liked the land. It was the common practice of Andrew **Jackson**'s negotiators to cajole or coerce chiefs without authority to sign papers that the United States claimed were binding to entire tribes. The government applied that tactic in the Seminoles' case. The United States claimed that the agreement signed at Fort Gibson bound all of the Seminole bands to remove to the West. Coe Hadjo, Holata Emathla, and Jumper denied that they had signed the document, and the Seminoles generally denied that the seven delegates had decision-making authority for all.

Coe Hadjo, a Seminole chief. Oil painting by George Catlin, 1838. (Smithsonian American Art Museum, Washington, DC / Art Resource, NY)

Disagreement over interpretation of the treaty among Seminole leaders and between the Seminoles and U.S. officials led to the **Second Seminole War**. In April 1835, Seminole agent Wiley Thompson convinced 16 headmen to sign a paper attesting to the validity of the Treaty of Payne's Landing. He struck the names of those who were absent or who refused to sign from his "official" list of chiefs. Coe Hadjo was among them. When the war broke out, he was a major figure. In October 1837, he and Osceola indicated they were willing to come in under a flag of truce to talk with Gen. Joseph M. Hernandez, not knowing that Gen. Thomas S. **Jesup** had directed Hernandez to violate the flag of truce, as Jesup had done before, and seize the leaders if he could. According to Dr. Nathan Jarvis, who accompanied Hernandez and his force, Osceola was so emotional he could not speak and asked Coe Hadjo to talk for the Seminoles. He told the general that they had been urged to negotiate by Philip (Emathla), through his son and emissary **Coacoochee**. Hernandez said he took them prisoners because the army had been deceived by the Seminoles too often.

Surrounded by troops, they were disarmed, and the two leaders with 71 warriors, six women, and four blacks were marched off to St. Augustine and imprisoned at Fort Marion. Later that year, a delegation of Cherokees led by John **Ross** arrived in Florida to try to convince the Seminoles to remove to the West. Jesup allowed Coe Hadjo to guide the Cherokees and gave them six days to complete their mission. The Cherokee delegation sought out and brought in **Miconopy**, Yaholoochee, Tuskegee, Nocose Yahola, and other subchiefs to Fort Mellon. To the dismay and anger of the Cherokees, who were there to attempt to negotiate a peaceful end to the war, Jesup once more violated the flag of truce and had the chiefs seized and promptly shipped to St. Augustine and prison. In early January 1838, Coe Hadjo, Osceola, Miconopy, Philip, and other leaders were sent to prison at Fort Moultrie at Charleston, South Carolina.

Coe Hadjo remained in prison until he removed. He and the other Fort Moultrie prisoners were transported to New Orleans in May 1838. Coe Hadjo traveled to Indian Territory in Miconopy's party, arriving in June. His band went west a year later. That group arrived at Fort Jackson in March 1839; they numbered about 200 and included, in addition to his band, **Abraham**, Tom, Cudjo, and Tony Barnett, free blacks who had interpreted and scouted for the U.S. Army. Other free blacks and slaves were also in the party. They arrived at Fort Gibson on April 13, 1839.

In October 1842, Coe Hadjo and other Seminole leaders wrote a letter to the War Department asking for Seminole self-rule in Indian Territory, which had been promised them in 1840 if they would send a delegation back to Florida to encourage the remaining Seminoles to remove. The granting of self-rule was one of the first steps toward the establishment of a separate Seminole Nation in the West.

FURTHER READING: Littlefield, Daniel F., Jr. *Africans and Seminoles: From Removal to Emancipation*. Westport, CT: Greenwood Press, 1977; Mahon, John K. *History of the Second Seminole War, 1835–1842.* Gainesville: University Press of Florida, 1967; McReynolds, Edwin C. *The Seminoles.* Norman: University of Oklahoma Press, 1957; Paige, Amanda L., et al. "The North Little Rock Site on the Trail of Tears National Historic Trail: Historical Contexts Report." http://anpa.ualr.edu/trail_of_tears/indian_removal_project/site_reports/site_reports.html.

AMANDA L. PAIGE

Coffee, John (1772–1833)

John Coffee, a Virginian by birth and one-time business partner of Andrew **Jackson**, was married to Rachel Jackson's niece and was, therefore, perhaps Jackson's closest friend and advocate. He fought under Jackson against the Creeks in 1813 and was one of the commissioners appointed to survey the treaty boundary between the Creeks and the United States following the Treaty of Franklin in 1814. Along with Jackson, Coffee speculated in Indian land that was opened following land cessions in the early 19th century. A strong proponent of Indian removal, he was Jackson's most trusted negotiator with the Chickasaws and Choctaws. In 1816, Coffee had been one of the commissioners appointed to negotiate with the Choctaws. Jackson pressed upon him the necessity of the Americans occupying the lower Mississippi Valley as a bulwark against foreign invasion, and he urged Coffee to be firm with the Choctaws, taking his stand and holding to it. He was appointed to treat with the Choctaws and Chickasaws in 1826. Although he was unsuccessful, the arguments he and his friend Jackson had devised to use with the Indians became clear: stress the inevitability of white invasion of their lands, using Georgia's treatment of the Cherokees and Creeks as an example, and encourage them to move west of the Mississippi, where they would no longer be bothered by whites.

After the election of Andrew Jackson, the two friends had an opportunity to put the tactics they had earlier devised to use against the tribes. Shortly after passage of the **Indian Removal Act**, in the summer of 1830 Coffee joined Secretary of War John H. **Eaton** at Franklin, Tennessee, where Eaton had invited the Choctaws and Chickasaws to meet to discuss removal (*see* **Chickasaw Removal**; **Choctaw Removal**). Only the Chickasaws attended, the Choctaws refusing to negotiate outside the boundaries of their own Nation. Coffee was single-minded in following Jackson's orders and told the tribes that they had only two options: to remove or break up their tribes and live under state law. He assisted Eaton and Jackson, who also came to Franklin, in negotiating the Treaty of Franklin with the Chickasaws. The treaty ultimately failed because its validity depended on the Chickasaws finding lands they liked in the West, which they failed to do. Nevertheless, it showed the Chickasaws' willingness to negotiate removal.

In September 1830, Coffee and Eaton turned to the Choctaws. In their negotiation of the **Treaty of Dancing Rabbit Creek**, Coffee and Eaton resorted to bribery as they had done with the Chickasaws, including large land grants to the principal tribal negotiators. And, as with the Chickasaws, they raised the specter of tribal destruction and submission to Mississippi state laws. Although the treaty was not popular among many Choctaws, it was ratified by the Senate.

In 1832, Coffee was the principal U.S. negotiator of the **Treaty of Pontotoc** with the Chickasaws. When Chickasaw leaders rejected his attempts at bribery, he ejected the friends and advisors of Levi **Colbert** and the chiefs from the treaty grounds and attempted to create dissension by pitting Colbert and the chiefs against a handful of mixed bloods and whites, including several land speculators. He threatened the Chickasaws, delayed the payment of an annuity that was due the people, and ultimately resorted to lies to get the chiefs to sign. When a delegation of Chickasaws went to Washington the next year to protest the treaty and attempt to renegotiate it, Coffee felt that their actions were a personal attack upon him, and he withdrew from further negotiation. Coffee engaged in no more removal activities. He died in the summer of 1833.

FURTHER READING: DeRosier, Arthur H., Jr. *The Removal of the Choctaw Indians.* Knoxville: University of Tennessee Press, 1970; Paige, Amanda L., et al. *Chickasaw Removal.* Ada, OK: Chickasaw Nation Press, 2010; Ratner, Lorman W. *Andrew Jackson and His Tennessee Lieutenants: A Study in Political Culture.* Westport, CT: Greenwood Press, 1997; Remini, Robert V. *Andrew Jackson and His Indian Wars.* New York: Viking, 2001; Satz, Ronald. N. *American Indian Policy in the Jacksonian Era.* Lincoln: University of Nebraska Press, 1975.

DANIEL F. LITTLEFIELD, JR.

Colbert, Levi (c. 1764–1834)

One of four sons of Noe and James Logan Colbert, a Georgia trader, Levi Colbert lacked a formal Christian education but was traditionally raised by his Chickasaw mother. His father's main influence may have been teaching him how white men think and do business. Colbert owned hundreds of horses, livestock, slaves, and a wide array of farming implements, which he obtained through inheritance, trade, military service, and gifts from U.S. agents. He had more than one wife and defended the Chickasaws' traditional social structure.

Levi Colbert distinguished himself in the political sector, following his brothers William and George as appointed "chief" under the hereditary minko or highest leader. In 1812, Levi Colbert came to power, succeeding George as chief counselor to the minko Chinnubbee. Colbert's Indian name Itawamba, which is clouded in folklore, translates as "bench chief," a reference to the honor of sitting on a bench rather than the ground during councils.

Levi Colbert's position enriched not only him but his brothers as well. He signed successive treaties in 1816, 1818, and 1830. The Treaty of 1816 paid him $4,500 for redistribution to those Chickasaws who lost valuable improvements on the lands ceded to the United States and provided him and his brother George land reserves on the Tennessee and Tombigbee Rivers and cash payments of $150 and $100, respectively. The Treaty of 1818 paid off William Colbert's debt of $1,115 and reserved a salt lick to Levi Colbert, as trustee for his Nation; it also provided for cash payments to the Colbert brothers. Colbert became wealthy by the standards of the day. His home in Cotton Gin Port (in present-day Monroe Country, Mississippi) was filled with the comforts of life, as was the inn that he ran for travelers near Buzzard Roost Spring on the Natchez Trace.

U.S. officials tried to manipulate Colbert. Granting cash payments, reserves, and other favors to chiefs and other signatories typified Indian treaties at this time and served as a way for U.S. commissioners to simultaneously "soften" the chiefs' resistance and compromise their reputations among their people. In 1827, Indian commissioner Thomas McKenney met privately with Levi as "Speaker of the Nation" to discuss the tribe's removal to **Indian Territory**. Colbert made no commitment to removal at this meeting, but he agreed to send a party to view the lands in the West. In an abortive attempt to turn the Chickasaws against Colbert, U.S. Indian agent Benjamin Smith spread rumors that Colbert had sold the Chickasaw homeland (*see* **Chickasaw Removal**). Colbert had to call a special assembly to allay his people's fears. In 1828, the Chickasaw people chose Levi to lead an exploring party to view a potential new site for settlement west of Arkansas. They found no satisfactory lands.

No outright cash payments were made in the Franklin Treaty of 1830, or in later treaties, because of the vigilance of the Chickasaw people. The Franklin Treaty, of which Colbert was the lead Chickasaw negotiator, provided for the cession of all remaining Chickasaw lands in exchange for a tract west of the Mississippi. The United States was to pay for the tribe's traveling costs, provide the Chickasaws with food for one year after their emigration, and give them a $15,000 annuity for 20 years. The treaty contained a clause stating that if the Chickasaws did not find satisfactory lands, they would not have to leave their homeland. Their failure to do so nullified the Treaty of Franklin.

Aging and ill, Colbert was present during negotiation of the **Treaty of Pontotoc** in 1832. He and the chiefs frustrated John **Coffee**'s efforts to give him and others large reservations of land. Coffee, supported by whites and mixed bloods, whom Colbert called "half people," pushed for investment of Chickasaw funds by the United States and division of the land into reservations based on household size, both points that Colbert and the chiefs found unsatisfactory. Their dissatisfaction led to further negotiations with the Chickasaws. In 1834, Colbert died on his way to Washington, D.C., to negotiate a supplemental treaty, which overcame their objections regarding reservations. He did not live to see the Chickasaws' removal to Indian Territory. They remained on their reservations until they were sold and removal began under provisions of the Treaty of Doaksville (1837), which settled the Chickasaws in the Choctaws' new country and required the Chickasaws to forfeit their independent government until the Treaty of 1855 restored the Chickasaw Nation's self-governance.

FURTHER READING: Champagne, Duane. *Social Order and Political Change: Constitutional Governments Among the Cherokee, the Choctaw, the Chickasaw, and the Creek.* Stanford, CA: Stanford University Press, 1992; Craig, Ronald Eugene. "The Colberts in Chickasaw History, 1783–1818: A Study in Internal Tribal Dynamics." PhD diss., University of New Mexico, 1998; Foreman, Grant. *Indian Removal; the Emigration of the Five Civilized Tribes of Indians.* Norman: University of Oklahoma Press, 1989; Hawkins, Benjamin, and C. L. Grant. *Letters, Journals, and Writings of Benjamin Hawkins.* Savannah, GA: Beehive Press, 1980; McKenney, Thomas. *Reports and Proceedings of Colonel Thomas McKenney on the subject of his recent tour among the Southern Indians, as submitted to Congress with the message of the President U.S.* Washington, DC: Gale & Seaton, 1828.

WENDY ST. JEAN

Cowaya, John

See Cavallo, John

Creek Removal

See Muscogee (Creek) Removal

D

Deas, Edward (1812–1849)

Lt. Edward Deas, a native of South Carolina and a West Point graduate, was only 23 when he was attached to the War Department for Indian services. Between 1835 and 1839, he accompanied more removal parties of the southeastern tribes to **Indian Territory** than any other military officer assigned to Indian removal. Deas paid close attention to details and followed regulations. He was a prolific writer, and his journals of occurrences and other correspondence pertaining to the groups he accompanied give valuable information about removal experiences. He was well thought of by the Indians for his humane considerations and his attention to their welfare and comfort.

Muscogee (Creek) removal began in 1835 under civilian contractors, the John W. A. **Sanford** Company. Each party removed under contract had a military officer attached to see that the contractors lived up to the letter of the contract and a physician to see to the health of the party and determine how far the Indians could go each day. Deas was assigned to the first party of 511 Muscogees, who left Wetumpka, Alabama, on December 6, 1835, and reached Fort Gibson, Indian Territory, on February 4, 1836. The Creeks traveled by a combination of steamboat and land travel.

By the fall of 1836, the Alabama Emigrating Company, which consisted primarily of Sanford company members, had the contract to remove the remaining Muscogees from Alabama. Five companies of more than 2,000 each left in September 1836, Deas accompanying the last party to Memphis. From there, many traveled by steamboat. Others with horses traveled overland on the Memphis to Little Rock Road. At Rock Roe, Arkansas, Deas reported that the civilian contractors were not doing a good job. Thousands of Muscogees, many from other parties, were scattered all across the state of Arkansas from west of the Mississippi River crossing to Fort Smith on the western edge of the state. At one point, Arkansas's governor ordered Deas to remove all Muscogees from the state immediately. Deas refused on humanitarian grounds until more of the scattered Indians had arrived at his encampment across the river from Little Rock. Deas backtracked over the route to pick up stragglers, and when he was satisfied that most had caught up, he left the Little Rock area.

Deas made one more trip with emigrating Muscogees in May 1837. This party of 543 Muscogees had tried to avoid removal by hiding in the Cherokee country. They left Gunter's Landing in Alabama and arrived at Fort Gibson on June 4, 1837. In the spring of 1838, Deas was assigned to **Cherokee removal**. He accompanied two parties of Cherokees that traveled mostly by boat to Indian Territory. He was disbursement agent for these parties and as such purchased all supplies and food rations and arranged for transportation. Deas accompanied and served as disbursement agent for one more Cherokee party in 1838. This group, led by Cherokee John A. Bell, included supporters of the **Treaty of New Echota**. They traveled overland from east Tennessee to Memphis and, from there, across Arkansas to the Western Cherokee Nation. Deas was authorized to spend $1,000 for clothes, shoes, blankets, and other items for the poor in the detachment.

After his duties with Indian removal, Deas continued in the military. He served in Texas in 1845 and in the war with Mexico from 1846 to 1848. On May 16, 1849, he drowned in the Rio Grande River.

FURTHER READING: Gibson, Wayne. "Cherokee Treaty Party Moves West." *Chronicles of Oklahoma* 79 (2001): 314–335; Littlefield, Daniel F., Jr., ed. *Lieut Edward Deas' Journal of Occurrences, April–May 1838.* Resources on Indian Removal No. 3. Little Rock, AR: Sequoyah National Research Center, 2006; Litton, Gaston, ed. "The Journal of a Party of Emigrating Creek Indians, 1835–1836." *Journal of Southern History* 7(2) (1941): 225–242; Sequoyah National Research Center. RG 217, Indian Affairs, Settled Accounts & Claims, Edward Deas Files.

CAROLYN YANCEY KENT

Delaware Removal

Delaware removal began in the early 18th century and ended in 1868. The Delawares, dispossessed of their historic homelands situated along the Delaware River, eventually found permanent settlements in Ontario and **Indian Territory**. The Delawares collectively experienced 150 years of dispossession, removal, and relocation, both voluntary and involuntary. Despite the cultural, political, economic, and spiritual trauma caused by a century and a half of uncertainty, the Delawares remain a distinct and vibrant people.

The processes and programs of colonization led to the loss of Delaware lands. Treaties, the encroachment of European and American settlements, and the decisions of Delaware leaders explain most of these relocations. As white settlers moved onto Delaware lands, they impacted the ability of the Delaware peoples to live successfully in their homelands. White settlements interfered with access to hunting lands, fishing waters, and the fertile bottomlands required to sustain their towns. Increased white settlement also inevitably led to conflicts and violence, despite the Delawares' traditional expertise at negotiating peaceful coexistence with neighbors. As a result, town leaders and sachems made decisions to distance themselves from white settlements, and kin-based groups elected to follow or remain. Delaware treaties ceded lands to the English and later American colonists in exchange for money, other lands, or various goods and services.

The Delawares experienced no single large-scale removal comparable to that of the **Cherokees**. Unlike them, the Delawares were not organized as a single national entity that allowed for a unified response of resistance or conciliation to removal. Delaware communities and families most often relocated in relation to leadership decisions, missionary communities, or other tribes. The Delawares historically lived in small kin-based towns scattered along river tributaries. In the second half of the 18th century, there was a brief period of centralized Delaware authority in response to the French and Indian War (1754–1763) and the American Revolution (1775–1783). Apart from this brief attempt at unification, most Delawares adhered to a pattern of removal organized around community leadership and kin-based decisions. By the end of the 18th century, many Delaware communities were also relocating relative to Moravian missionary communities and in alliance with other tribes, particularly the Shawnees.

From 1730 to 1795, Delaware communities were dispossessed of lands from generation to generation. The first major removal and diaspora of Delaware Indians began with a series of treaties that ceded the majority of their ancestral homelands by the 1740s. The most infamous, the Walking Purchase Treaty in 1737, was an intentionally fraudulent treaty signed by William Penn's heirs and Delaware leaders, including Lappawinsoe. By the 1770s, war and a new wave of white settlement led many Delawares to move into the Ohio Territory. In the 1770s, the Delawares were divided between their alliances to the British and the Americans. The Continental Congress signed a treaty with the Delawares in 1775 that designated the Ohio River as a border between Indian and white settlements. This treaty led most Delawares to relocate to several major Delaware towns in Ohio. The treaty was quickly abandoned by the new American government, and frontier violence devastated Delaware communities, disintegrating any remaining unified leadership. During this same period, many Delaware families relocated to Moravian mission towns in Ohio and Indiana. Delawares also resisted removal from their lands in Ohio territory by uniting with other tribes to fight American forces. Despite numerous victories, the Delawares, along with their allies, were forced out of their Ohio homelands by the Treaty of Greenville in 1795.

The Treaty of Greenville marks the beginning of a second major wave of removal that found Delawares who previously shared a historic homeland reorganizing in towns in Indiana, Missouri, Kansas, and Ontario, Canada, with the majority living in Indiana Territory. Their futures were uncertain, and their communities had been ravaged by decades of removal and warfare. The Delawares established 9 to 11 towns along the White River. Kikthawenund, Buckongahelas, Hockingpomska, and Tetepachksit were among the leaders who relocated to the lands and built towns. During this same period, Moravian Delawares relocated with the Munsees to the province of Ontario and settled on a reserve near the Thames River.

Jefferson's presidency, beginning in 1801, ushered in a new era of Indian policy that was realized differently in the Northwest Territories than in the Southeast. In the Northwest Territory, federal and local agents used the factory system to create debt that forced tribal leaders to sell lands. Jefferson's "civilization" program demanded that Indian peoples, to survive the expansion of American settlement, abandon their lifeways for a western European–American model. The civilization program required that Indian peoples adopt American farming techniques, gendered divisions of labor, and domestic production. Delawares and many other tribes facing removal were historically agriculturalists. European and Indian peoples had exchanged agricultural knowledge for decades, each selectively choosing what to adopt into their mode of living. Despite external pressures from missionaries, territorial representatives, and other agents of the civilization program, Delawares selectively resisted abandoning their Delaware way of life.

Delawares responded to the civilization programs in a variety of ways, but ultimately most made voluntary decisions to move west of the Mississippi before Andrew **Jackson** implemented the **Indian Removal Act** in the 1830s. As early as 1789, family-based groups of Delawares chose Cape Girardeau, Missouri, as their new home. Many were enticed by Spanish invitations to settle there and the welcome distance between Delaware towns and American expansion. The greatest diaspora of Delawares across the Mississippi River occurred between 1800 and 1818. During this period, Indiana territorial governor William Henry Harrison oversaw Indian affairs in the Old Northwest and implemented the ideology of the Jeffersonian civilization policy. He negotiated 11 of the 12 treaties signed in Indiana Territory securing all Delaware lands in the process. In 1818, the Delawares signed a treaty at St. Mary's that ceded their entire claim to lands in Indiana in exchange for lands west of the Mississippi. The Delawares were given three years to prepare for relocation. Kikthawenund and other Delaware leaders prepared to make the journey that many of their relatives made decades earlier.

The majority of Delawares did not travel together, but many passed through Illinois during the winter of 1820. The federal government did little to organize the Delaware removal in Indiana, and as a result there are few records to provide details of their experience. It is difficult to estimate how many Delawares died on their 300-mile route from their villages along the White River through Illinois. However, more than 1,300 Delawares and their 1,500 horses crossed the Mississippi River at the close of 1820. By 1830, most Delawares, including those in Missouri, were generally located in eastern Kansas. For the next 40 years, Delaware families adjusted to their new homelands. This period may have been one of the most challenging episodes in the long history of the Delaware peoples. Both the climate and environment demanded that the Delawares adopt new strategies for their continued survival. The deciduous forests of the eastern woodlands and lower Great Lakes were replaced by prairie lands. Sources of food, lodging, fuel, and trade altered Delaware lifeways. Despite their eventual successful adaptation to the new lands, relocation led to the death of many Delaware people from starvation, violence, and illness.

In 1854, the Kansas-Nebraska Act organized Kansas into a territory and initiated an assault on Indian landownership west of the Mississippi (*see* **Kansas Territory and Removal**). Delaware lands were inundated with illegal American squatters. Divisions within the federal government over slavery provide some explanation for the failure of the federal government to respond to Delaware demands for protection and eviction of illegal claimants. In 1854, Delaware leaders signed a treaty in Kansas that ceded more than 1 million acres and retained a reserve 10 miles wide and 40 miles long. By 1861, Delaware lands guaranteed by the federal government had been invaded and preempted, stolen and sold. By 1868, the Delaware relocated one final time to **Indian Territory** in Oklahoma.

The story of removal and relocation for the Delaware people is not a story bound or directed by the implementation of the federal Indian policies in the early 19th century. The Delawares' decisions were determined by their leadership, their kinship, and the desire to remain a distinct and unique people. It is a complex and protracted story that demands a closer look to understand the patterns of their relocation and removal as well as the changes caused by their dispossession. It is also critical to understand that Delaware peoples today continue to live at many places along the trails of their removals and relocations, from the Delaware River Valley to Oklahoma.

FURTHER READING: Bowes, John P. *Exiles and Pioneers: Eastern Indians in the Trans-Mississippi West.* New York: Cambridge University Press, 2007; Dowd, Gregory Evans. *A Spirited Resistance: The North American Struggle for Unity, 1745–1815.* Baltimore: Johns Hopkins University Press, 1992; McConnell, Michael. *A Country Between: The Upper Ohio Valley and Its Peoples, 1724–1774.* Lincoln: University of Nebraska Press, 1992; "Treaty with the Delawares, 1829." At http://digital.library.okstate.edu/kappler/Vol2/treaties/del0304.htm; Warren, Stephen. *The Shawnee and Their Neighbors, 1795–1870.* Urbana: University of Illinois Press, 2005.

DAWN G. MARSH

E

Eastern Cherokees

Prior to removal, the Cherokee confederation was arguably the largest of the southeastern Native American organizations. The confederation occupied the Allegheny region and ranged from the Iroquois lands in the north to the Creek lands around what is now the Atlanta area and from the Blue Ridge to the Cumberland Range. According to James Mooney, the groups that made up the Cherokees referred to themselves as Yun'wiya ("real people") or Ani'-Kitu'hwagi ("people of the Kituhwa" or Cuttawa), indicating their origin on the Tuckasegee River. Their language was Iroquoian but consisted of differing dialects.

The history of the Cherokees indicates a people who were willing to embrace culturally divergent individuals and tribes. However, the history also indicates wars and disagreements with Native American cultures such as the Shawnees and Creeks. The significance of these differing historical events is that these same divergent inclinations came to define factions that were formed during the time of the removal. While John **Ross** led the majority of Cherokees to the West, a more culturally conservative group avoided capture by hiding in the mountains. Those who stayed in the mountains pledged to never leave the land of their ancestors, which contained both the spiritual and physical aspects of their culture. Still other Cherokee factions created the Chickamauga resistance and scattered at the time of removal.

Both spiritual and territorial differences contributed to the existence of Cherokee factions. The main point of contention was non-Native incursion into Native lands and the acceptance or denial of assimilation. The events leading to the split between Western and Eastern Cherokees were caused by attempts to assimilate the Cherokees into the American government and culture. The adoption of the national constitution at New Echota in 1827 attempted to organize the Cherokee into an "American style" government system. The creation of the syllabary by Sequoyah, on the one hand, was hailed by some Cherokees as an effective communications tool and a means of perpetuating their language. However, the creation of the *Cherokee Phoenix,* a weekly paper published in both Cherokee and English, followed by the introduction of the Bible in Cherokee, set the stage for cultural division. For many of the traditional communities, these elements of assimilation represented the destruction of the Cherokee culture. The newspaper's role as a demonstration of Cherokee acculturation was resented, as were the Bible translations, which were seen to undermine the old traditions. The traditional communities tied their cultural identification and their existence to the land of their ancestors, so leaving the land of their ancestors was not an option. The final severing of the union came in the form of the removal treaty signed in New Echota on December 29, 1835 (see **Treaty of New Echota**). While a small faction of Cherokees signed this document, the American government held it to be binding on the entire Nation. For those who wished to avoid removal in 1829 and again in 1835–1839, the mountains offered refuge. The number of refugees is estimated to be from 1,000 to more than 2,000, depending on the source.

The struggle and cost to capture the dispersed Cherokees led Gen. Winfield **Scott** to seek the assistance of William H. Thomas to achieve a compromise. Their proposition required any Cherokees involved in earlier violent attacks to be surrendered. Those specified to be turned over were Charley (Tsali) and others associated with an earlier raid, including his sons. Accounts of this event vary, but many indicate that Charley and his sons surrendered and, with the exception of one son, were subsequently shot. After this event, Thomas assisted in the acquisition of land that would later become part of the Cherokee reservation in North Carolina. Thomas, although not a Native American, was instrumental in ensuring a continued Cherokee presence in the East. His efforts as an agent and advocate for the Cherokees would ultimately lead to his adoption as a citizen into the Eastern Cherokees. He later served in the U.S. Senate and commanded a unit in the Civil War.

The struggle for recognition and reservation was not without legal, political, and social battles. Although the U.S. Congress acknowledged and recognized the rights of the Eastern Cherokees, questions of sovereignty remained. The issue is addressed in *Rollins v. Cherokees* (1882) and in *Eastern Band of Cherokees v. The United States and the Cherokee Nation* (1885). These cases, separated by only three years, did not lend clarity to the question of sovereignty, so the status of the tribe was not settled for many years. The Eastern Cherokees incorporated under North Carolina law in the 1880s. The band has maintained a continuous political and social presence that has survived the ebbs and flows of state and federal policy and remains an autonomous body today.

FURTHER READING: Cotterill, R. S. *The Southern Indians: The Story of the Civilized Tribes Before Removal.* Norman: University of Oklahoma Press, 1954; Foreman, Grant. *The Five Civilized Tribes: Cherokee, Chickasaw, Choctaw, Creek, Seminole.* Norman: University of Oklahoma Press, 1934; Foreman, Grant. *Indian Removal: The Emigration of the Five Civilized Tribes of Indians.* Norman: University of Oklahoma Press, 1989; McLoughlin, William G. *Cherokee Renascence in the New Republic.* Princeton, NJ: Princeton University Press, 1986; McLoughlin, William G. *Cherokees and Missionaries, 1789–1839.* Norman: University of Oklahoma Press, 1995; Mooney, James. *History, Myths, and Sacred Formulas of the Cherokee.* Asheville, NC: Historical Images, 1992.

LAVONNA LOVERN

Eaton, John Henry (1790–1856)

John Henry Eaton was one of Andrew **Jackson**'s inner circle and thus played a major role in removal of the southern Indians. A native of North Carolina, Eaton studied law and moved to Franklin, Tennessee, where he married a ward of Jackson, creating a close tie between the men. He served in the Tennessee state house and in 1818 was appointed to fill a vacant U.S. Senate seat, to which he was elected in 1821, serving until 1829.

Upon Jackson taking office, Eaton became secretary of war in early 1829. Eaton was a strong proponent of Indian removal. He wanted Congress to establish an **Indian Territory** in the West with a government established by the United States and a military force sufficient to enforce its boundaries. As secretary of war and a personal friend of Jackson, he worked for passage of the **Indian Removal Act** and took direct part in negotiating removal treaties.

In the summer of 1830, Eaton invited the Choctaws and Chickasaws to Franklin, Tennessee, to talk about removal (*see* **Chickasaw Removal**; **Choctaw Removal**). Only the Chickasaws sent delegations, the Choctaws refusing to negotiate outside their Nation. The Chickasaws, however, were willing to negotiate. Eaton and John **Coffee**, along with Jackson himself who joined them in Franklin, negotiated the Treaty of Franklin in August 1830. This removal treaty was the first negotiated under the Indian Removal Act, but it would be valid only if the Chickasaws found land in the West that suited them. This they failed to do, and the treaty was null and void.

The next month, Eaton and Coffee then went to the Choctaw Nation. As a negotiator, Eaton followed Jackson's explicit orders to promise nothing the government could not deliver and to threaten the Indians with the specter of domination by state laws. He and Coffee negotiated the **Treaty of Dancing Rabbit Creek** with Greenwood **LeFlore** and other Choctaws of questionable authority. When Choctaw opposition arose

John Henry Eaton, Andrew Jackson's first secretary of war and proponent of Indian removal. (Florida Photographic Collection)

against the treaty, Eaton refused to recognize any Choctaw leaders, except those who had signed the treaty, until the Choctaws removed to the West.

As secretary of war, Eaton helped carry out the tactics devised by Jackson to obtain signatures on removal treaties. For example, he sent William **Carroll** and John Coffee to visit the **Muscogees (Creeks)** and **Cherokees** and promote removal. However, they were directed to hide their true motives and talk to chiefs individually in an effort to divide and conquer and to find who might be prone to take bribes. If persuasion did not work, Eaton directed them to bribe the chiefs. Eaton also promoted administration efforts to consolidate tribes with similar histories or cultures. Early on, Eaton helped engineer Georgia's assault on the Cherokees, encouraging the governor to temper the state's harsh treatment of the Cherokees. He viewed *Cherokee Nation v. Georgia* as the fatal blow to not only Cherokees' but also all southern tribes' resistance to removal. To all tribes' appeals that they be spared removal, he gave Jackson's standard response: it was not within the power of the federal government to prevent it.

In 1829, Eaton sought congressional establishment of an Indian Territory west of the organized states and territories, with a governor appointed by the president and with guarantees of federal protections from white intrusion. His vision was supported by Isaac **McCoy**, who continued to work for such a territory after Eaton left office.

With the power of office behind him, Eaton was vindictive toward opponents of Indian removal. A week following passage of the Indian Removal Act, he cut off federal funding to the American Board of Commissioners for Foreign Missions, headed by Jeremiah Evarts, who had been a strong opponent of the bill. As a result, he set back educational efforts among the Cherokees and other tribes. Eaton resigned as secretary of war in 1831 as the result of a scandal involving his second wife.

In April 1834, Jackson appointed Eaton governor of Florida Territory. Surprisingly, he questioned the validity of the **Seminole removal** treaty because of the Senate's delay in ratifying it. When the **Second Seminole War** broke out, he accurately predicted a long war because of stiff resistance by the Seminoles. The only way to subdue them, he believed, was to send a strong force of regular troops against them, not militia as Jackson had suggested. The number of troops Eaton had considered necessary would have taken too much of the nation's army manpower, which Jackson considered risky.

Eaton also engaged in an effort to negotiate an act of union between the Choctaws and Chickasaws. Such a union was agreed upon in 1837, but on the tribes' terms, not Eaton's and Jackson's. His service as governor of Florida was Eaton's last service in Indian removal. In 1836, Jackson appointed him minister to Spain.

FURTHER READING: Abernethy, Thomas P. "John Henry Eaton." *Dictionary of American Biography.* Vol. 5. New York: Charles Scribner's Sons, 1930; DeRosier, Arthur H., Jr. *The Removal of the Choctaw Indians.* Knoxville: University of Tennessee

Press, 1970; Ratner, Lorman W. *Andrew Jackson and His Tennessee Lieutenants: A Study in Political Culture.* Westport, CT: Greenwood Press, 1997; Remini, Robert V. *Andrew Jackson and His Indian Wars.* New York: Viking, 2001; Satz, Ronald. N. *American Indian Policy in the Jacksonian Era.* Lincoln: University of Nebraska Press, 1975.

DANIEL F. LITTLEFIELD, JR.

Ellsworth, Henry L. (1791–1858)

Native of Connecticut, son of a Supreme Court chief justice, attorney, land speculator, traveler, and author, Henry L. Ellsworth was appointed to a commission created by the U.S. House in July 1832 to study conditions among the tribes in **Indian Territory** and to lay the groundwork for further removals under the **Indian Removal Act** of 1830. The other commissioners were John F. **Schermerhorn** and Montfort Stokes, chairman. Specifically, Secretary of War Lewis **Cass** directed them to attempt to settle any grievances still existing among removed tribes, make provisions for "civilization" of the people, and seek agreements to unify tribal groups of similar lifestyles and cultures as they negotiated with the tribes. They were to report back to the House at the conclusion of their work. Ellsworth arrived in the Southwest before the others, and, in company with the well-known writer Washington Irving, went with a military escort on a tour of the western Creek country and the plains beyond the Cross Timbers. After Schermerhorn and Stokes arrived, the commission remained for months.

Ellsworth was party to several treaties. In December 1832, he and Schermerhorn concluded a treaty with the recently removed Senecas of Lewistown, Ohio, and mixed Shawnees, adjusting their boundaries and guaranteeing title to the land in fee simple (*see* **Seneca Removal**; **Shawnee Removal**). They and Stokes negotiated similar articles of agreement with the Western Cherokees in February 1833, settling their boundaries and guaranteeing them a perpetual hunting outlet to the West. The same day, they negotiated articles of agreement with the McIntosh Creeks, clarifying boundaries, attempting to smooth political differences that grew out of early Creek removal (*see* **Muscogee [Creek] Removal**), and providing for a union of Seminoles and Creeks after **Seminole removal**.

That same month, the three commissioners negotiated what has become known as one of the most notorious treaties of the removal period. At Fort Gibson they negotiated with a delegation of Seminoles who had been sent west to see if suitable lands could be found for the Florida Indians. In the Treaty of Payne's Landing, signed the year before, the Seminoles had agreed to remove on the condition that the delegation found a suitable land. Although the party had no authority to negotiate a treaty, they were nevertheless persuaded to sign the document. Despite the questionable authority of the negotiators, the United States claimed the document was binding upon the entire body of tribes that made up the Seminoles. This document was the first major step toward the outbreak of the **Second Seminole War**. In the fall of 1833, Ellsworth attended a peace conference at Fort

Leavenworth. He negotiated a convention with the Otoes and Missourias of the Platte on September 21 and a treaty with the Pawnees on October 9.

The commission's report to the secretary of war contained a number of recommendations. Perhaps the most significant was the establishment of a territorial government of the western Indian Territory to preserve peace among the tribes. After the commission completed its work, Ellsworth returned to the East, where he pursued his business interests and served in public official capacities, including head of the U.S. Patent Office for a number of years.

FURTHER READING: Ellsworth, Henry L. *Washington Irving on the Prairies: Or a Narrative of a Tour of the Southwest in the Year 1832.* New York: American Book Company, 1937; Foreman, Grant. *Advancing the Frontier, 1830–1860.* Norman: University of Oklahoma Press, 1933; Foreman, Grant. *Indian Removal: The Emigration of the Five Civilized Tribes of Indians.* Norman: University of Oklahoma Press, 1989; Satz, Ronald. *American Indian Policy in the Jacksonian Era.* Lincoln: University of Nebraska Press, 1975; U.S. Congress. House. *Regulating the Indian Department.* 23rd Cong., 1st sess., 1834. H. Rept. 474.

DANIEL F. LITTLEFIELD, JR.

Eneah Emathla (Neamathla) (c. 1750s–1830s)

When the **Indian Removal Act** was signed, Eneah Emathla was approaching 80 years old and had been known as an active opponent of the Americans for twenty years, fighting against them in the Red Stick War. In the second decade of the 19th century, Eneah Emathla was a person of note among the Florida Indians, to whom he had fled after the war. When the First Seminole War broke out, he was chief of the Hichiti band at Hichiti Fowl Towns near Fort Scott and was instrumental in preventing the Americans from crossing the Flint River. In 1836, once more at war with the Americans, he contributed directly to Andrew **Jackson**'s decision to remove the Creeks by force.

The United States's annexation of Florida in 1821 did not bode well for him and his people. After the First Seminole War, Eneah Emathla had settled at Tallahassee, where he was apparently a trader. In 1823, he was chief of the Miccosukees. The various tribes of Florida Indians named him chief of all the Seminoles for the purpose of negotiation with the United States at Moultrie Creek. In the Treaty of Moultrie Creek, the Seminoles agreed to remove to central Florida, giving up most of the northern areas. The United States considered concentration of the tribes into a smaller region the

An engraving from a portrait of Eneah Emathla, a Muscogee (Creek) chief, by American painter Charles Bird King, from *The Indian Tribes of North America.* (McKenney, Thomas L. and James Hall. *The Indian Tribes of North America,* 1836–1844)

first step to removal. An exception was made for the bands led by six leaders, including Eneah Emathla, who were permitted to settle on reserves on the Apalachicola River in the panhandle of Florida. But he found life less and less tolerable when whites began to move into the area and made Tallahassee the territorial capital. His people were beset by whites who raided their lands, stealing slaves and other property.

In 1824, Eneah Emathla left Florida with his Hichiti band. Seminole agent Gad Humphreys had believed that giving him a separate reservation was a mistake because he was the only leader capable of controlling all of the bands. The Seminoles were not preparing to move from northern Florida to lands to the south. Believing Eneah Emathla's influence was the cause of inaction, Governor William DuVal deposed him as chief of the Seminoles and replaced him with Tukose Emathla (John Hicks), a Miccosukee. The United States let his action stand. Whether it was his being deposed or the increasingly intolerable conditions that caused the move, Eneah Emathla moved his people into southern Alabama, where they established their town square on Hatchechubbee Creek northwest of Columbus, Georgia. However, in 1826, he accompanied Tukose Emathla and other delegates to Washington to plead for adjustments of the Treaty of Moultrie Creek and to protest against removal.

At Hatchechubbee, the Hichitis again suffered from incursions by whites as the pressure built for Creek removal (*see* **Muscogee [Creek] Removal**). The infamous Treaty of 1825 signed by William McIntosh forced some 7,000 Creeks across Georgia's western border into the Creek Country in 1826. The Treaty of 1832 at Washington, signed by the Upper Creeks, led to the survey of Creek lands, allotment of land to individuals, and an orgy of **land speculation** and fraud that resulted in the loss of much Creek land and other property, leaving many homeless. Alabama (*see* **Alabama and Indian Removal**) extended its laws over the Creeks and outlawed their government. White intruders came into the Creek lands, destroying crops, stealing property, selling whiskey, and committing other crimes. Many Creeks verged on starvation. Tensions and hostilities grew between the Creeks and whites until war broke out in the spring of 1836.

The so-called Creek War of 1836 was led by the Hichitis, who were joined by Yuchis, Eufaulas, Chiahas, and Kasihtas (Cussetas). The main leaders were **Eneah Micco**, chief of the Hichitis; Jim **Henry**; and Eneah Emathla, the latter two apparently the main strategists. From all accounts, Eneah Emathla's concern since the First Seminole War had been preservation of the Hichiti homeland. The warfare of 1836 was another attempt to do that. Warriors under these leaders raided farms and towns alike, killing whites and destroying property in both Alabama and Georgia. By the middle of July 1836, however, combined forces of the U.S. Army under Gen. Thomas S. **Jesup** and nearly 2,000 Upper Creeks led by **Opothleyohola**, **Tustenuggee Emathla** (Jim Boy) and others had brought the hostilities to an end. The Hichiti towns on the Hatchechubbee were destroyed, and the three leaders and their followers were captured and collected for immediate removal to the West.

By September, the three Hitchiti leaders and most of their followers were in the **Indian Territory**. From prison camps near Fort Mitchell and Tuskegee, 300 men and boys considered the most "hostile" were handcuffed and chained together, including the 84-year-old Eneah Emathla and Eneah Micco, and marched about 90 miles to Montgomery, followed by wagons containing children, old women, and the sick. Jim Henry was placed in jail at Montgomery, where he was held on murder charges. When the Creeks were unfettered to be loaded on boats, fifteen revolted. Troops shot one and bayoneted another, one committed suicide, and some escaped. From Montgomery 2,498 went by boat to Mobile, where 2,300 were transferred to steamboats bound for New Orleans, under the charge of the J. W. A. **Sanford** Emigrating Company. From there, they were sent by steamboat to Rock Roe on the White River. On the night of July 29, the day they arrived, in a last act of defiance the Yuchis slipped out of camp and rolled the barrels containing their shackles into the White River in Arkansas. From Rock Roe, the group had to travel overland to Indian Territory. Because only 20 wagons could be procured, many of the children, old women, and infirm had to walk, traveling at night because of the intense heat during the day. They reached Fort Gibson on September 3. The remaining "hostiles" in Alabama followed in a second contingent.

The people were destitute. Rounded up as prisoners of "war," they had no time to prepare for their march. Those who had meager personal effects were obliged to carry them from Rock Roe westward because adequate transportation had not been arranged. The Yuchis had been sent on their way with practically nothing. Foods to which they were unaccustomed led to dysentery and diarrhea. Fevers and cholera infantum killed 50 children as well as others who were old and infirm. Collapse of the rotten deck of a barge on which they were being towed killed one and injured several others. Though aged, Eneah Emathla survived the ordeal. When asked his intentions by Roley McIntosh, brother of William and chief of the Lower Creeks in the West, Eneah Emathla submitted his people to the laws of the Lower Creeks. How much longer he lived is not known.

FURTHER READING: Debo, Angie. *The Road to Disappearance: A History of the Creek Indians.* Norman: University of Oklahoma Press, 1979; Foreman, Grant. *Indian Removal: The Emigration of the Five Civilized Tribes of Indians.* Norman: University of Oklahoma, 1989; Mahon, John K. *History of the Second Seminole War, 1835–1842.* Gainesville: University Press of Florida, 1967; Paige, Amanda L., et al. "The North Little Rock Site on the Trail of Tears. National Historic Trail: Historical Contexts Report." At http://anpa.ualr.edu/trail_of_tears/indian_removal_project/site_reports/north_little_rock/northlittlerockreport.htm; Wright, J. Leitch, Jr. *Creeks and Seminoles: The Destruction and Regeneration of the Muscogulge People.* Lincoln: University of Nebraska Press, 1986.

DANIEL F. LITTLEFIELD, JR.

Eneah Micco (Neamicco) (c. 1780–1836)

When the **Indian Removal Act** became law, Eneah Micco, a Hichiti, was head chief of the Lower Creek towns, and Tuskeneah Thlocco was chief of the Upper Creek towns, although **Opothleyohola** had emerged as leader there. In 1831, Eneah Micco and other leaders of the Lower Creek towns sent a delegation to Washington to petition Secretary of War John H. **Eaton** to support their wishes to remain in their home country and to relieve them of the difficulties that beset them. They complained of murders by both Creeks and whites. Although the Creeks were punished, the whites went free. Their word was not accepted in Alabama courts, whiskey was brought into their country, and their property was confiscated for alleged debts. The Creeks received the standard reply that they must remove because the government could not prevent the application of Alabama laws in the Creek country (*see* **Alabama and Indian Removal**). Later that year they appealed to Secretary Lewis **Cass** and received the same response. In December 1831, Eneah Micco sent a list of names of some 1,500 intruders in the Lower Creek country to the Creek agent and asked for their removal, but once more he received the standard answer.

By 1832, the Lower and Upper Creeks were at odds over Creek removal (*see* **Muscogee [Creek] Removal**). In the wake of William McIntosh's assassination for signing the Treaty of Indian Springs, significant numbers of Lower Creeks had removed to the western lands provided by the treaty. The Lower Creek leadership tried to prevent others from removing by threatening their lives, destroying their crops, killing their livestock, and burning their property. On the other hand, sympathy for removal grew among the Upper Creeks.

In early 1832, a delegation from the Upper towns, led by Opothleyohola, signed a treaty at Washington. It provided for a survey of the Creek lands, allotment of land to Creek households, removal of intruders, and voluntary emigration of the Creeks to the West. Apparently as a sop to the Lower Creek leaders, the treaty provided an annuity for life for Eneah Micco and two others. Compensation was provided for those who had lost improvements under the Treaty of 1826 or had lost property as a result of being prevented from removing. Although the treaty provided monetary and other incentives for the Creeks to remove, those opposed to removal took heart in the language of Article 11: "This article shall not be construed so as to compel any Creek Indian to emigrate, but they shall be free to go or stay, as they please."

Of course, most Creeks took the article to mean what its language said and opted to remain in Alabama. But life became intolerable. Individual Creeks could not maintain the integrity of the boundaries of their allotments. Intruders squatted on their land, took their property, destroyed their homes, and committed acts of violence. The Creeks became demoralized. The Creek country was also beset by an orgy of **land speculation** that further disrupted Creek life. By theft, intimidation, and fraud, speculators gained control of most Creek land. Secretary Cass finally undertook an investigation in the spring of 1835.

The investigation was destined to go nowhere because Cass appointed J. W. A. **Sanford** to do it. Sanford, of Columbus, Georgia, was one of the leading speculators, and the Indians distrusted him. The speculators used their distrust to prevent the Creeks from going to Columbus to deliver their complaints. They circulated word that the request was a ruse to get them into Georgia, where they would be captured and sent to the West. Eneah Micco asked Sanford to meet the Creeks in Alabama, but he refused. John B. Hogan, whom the Creeks trusted, assumed the investigation and denounced the fraud for what it was.

However, the investigation was dropped when the so-called Creek War of 1836 broke out in May. Dispossessed and harassed by whites, the Lower Creeks struck back. Although some Alabamians claimed that the war was merely a sham conjured up by the whites, the government responded with force. Led by Eneah Micco, who was about 60; Jim **Henry**, who was just past 20; and **Eneah Emathla**, who was past 80, the Lower Creeks were soon subdued by U.S. Army troops under Gen. Thomas S. **Jesup** and almost 2,000 Upper Creek warriors under Opothleyohola, **Tustenuggee Emathla**, and others. By mid-July the leaders had been captured along with most of their followers. Eneah Micco was captured in early July and the remnants of his people about two weeks later.

About 2,300 Eufaulas, Chiahas, Hichitis, Kasihtas (Cussetas), and Yuchis were rounded up and sent to the West immediately. From staging camps at Fort Mitchell and near Tuskegee, where Eneah Micco was held, about 300 men and boys considered the most "hostile," including Eneah Micco, were handcuffed and chained and marched about ninety miles to Montgomery. Wagons followed with children, old women, and the sick. At Montgomery, the chains were removed as the people were boarding boats, and 15 revolted, resulting in some escaping, one shot by troops, one bayoneted by troops, and one committing suicide. They traveled down to Mobile, where their military escort left them and where they boarded steamboats bound for New Orleans. At New Orleans they were transferred to boats bound for Rock Roe on the White River in Arkansas, which they reached on July 29. Their manacles had been stored in barrels and were unloaded with the provisions at Rock Roe. In one final act of defiance, on the night of their arrival, the Yuchis slipped out of camp and rolled the barrels into the White River.

At Rock Roe, the J. W. A. Sanford Emigrating Company, which was in charge of the party, made arrangements for an overland trek from there to Fort Gibson in **Indian Territory**. Because only 20 wagons could be procured, many of the children, old women, and infirm had to walk, traveling at night because of the intense heat during the day. They arrived at Fort Gibson on September 3.

They were without question the most destitute Indians to arrive in the West. Rounded up and dealt with as prisoners, they had no time to prepare for their march. Most who had meager personal effects were obliged to carry them from Rock Roe westward. The Yuchis had been sent on their way with practically nothing. Diet to which they were unaccustomed resulted in dysentery and diarrhea. In the summer season, fevers and cholera infantum were common. Fifty of those who died were children, and most of the others were the old and infirm. Between New Orleans and Rock Roe, the rotten deck of a barge on which they were being towed collapsed, killing one and injuring several others. Eneah Micco died near Fort Gibson in December 1836. Although he was a stalwart opponent of Creek removal, his leadership in the hostilities of 1836 led directly to the government's orders for the forced removal of all the Creeks from Alabama.

FURTHER READING: Debo, Angie. *The Road to Disappearance: A History of the Creek Indians.* Norman: University of Oklahoma Press, 1979; Foreman, Grant. *Indian Removal: The Emigration of the Five Civilized Tribes of Indians.* Norman: University of Oklahoma Press, 1989; Paige, Amanda L., et al. "The North Little Rock Site on the Trail of Tears National Historic Trail: Historical Contexts Report." At http://anpa.ualr.edu/trail_of_tears/indian_removal_project/site_reports/north_little_rock/northlittlerock report.htm; Wright, J. Leitch, Jr. *Creeks and Seminoles: The Destruction and Regeneration of the Muscogulge People.* Lincoln: University of Nebraska Press, 1986.

DANIEL F. LITTLEFIELD, JR.

F

Florida and Indian Removal

The federal policy of removal of American Indians in Florida was aimed at the Seminoles in the aftermath of the Seminole Wars (*see* **Second Seminole War**; **Third Seminole War**) and in response to southern expansion. The relationship between the Seminoles and the U.S. government was, and remains, a complex and convoluted thing. Removal would not be the end of difficulties, as significant numbers of Seminoles would remain in Florida even after years of concentrated efforts to move the population to the West.

Some have argued that the Seminole identity was born in response to European and white American incursion. Early 20th-century scholars argued that the Seminoles descended from Creeks, including absorbed peoples, who moved south into Florida as life in Georgia and Alabama became untenable because of white incursion. These separatists filled a void in the indigenous population that was left by the interactions of the Spanish with previous inhabitants. The Seminoles began to become identified as a people separate and distinct from their Creek brethren in about 1775. In dealing with the Indian question, the federal government used the definitions that best suited its motives. If configuring the Seminoles and Creeks as one entity allowed a stronger position for the government, then the parties were defined collectively. If separating the two was deemed useful, severance was used.

The issue of slavery was a primary sticking point in the development of policy toward the Seminoles. In a 1790 treaty with the Creeks, in the interest of placating the citizens of Georgia in their claims of deprivations at the hands of the Creeks, the federal government held the Creek Nation accountable for slaves who ran away and settled with the Seminoles. This was not an insignificant number of slaves, and the point would prove to be of primary importance in undercutting cohesion between the Creeks and Seminoles. The issue of slavery would also serve as an underlying reason for the Seminole Wars.

The First Seminole War (1816–1818) began with Col. D. L. Clinch joining forces with the Creek chief William McIntosh and engaging the Seminoles at Fort Apalachicola in Spanish Florida. The fort was said to have harbored escaped slaves, and McIntosh's stated mission involved the location of runaway slaves and their return to their "lawful" owners. This engagement made clear the formal governmental approval and a militarization of what were previously civilian "slave raids" into north Florida. It is important to understand that the first two of three Seminole Wars and the Creek involvement were greatly influenced by the Red Stick War (1813–1814) within the Creek Nation. Through that conflict, McIntosh came to prominence and the conditions of the relationship between the Lower Creeks and the federal government were forged.

The First Seminole War ended in 1818, and the next year Florida was purchased from Spain. This eliminated any legal misgivings regarding incursion into the territory of a sovereign European power. The problems of runaway slaves and complaints of perceived deprivations could be more conveniently solved with Florida as a U.S. territory. In addition to the recovery of lost slaves, which meant in many cases the return of the descendants of runaway slaves to the descendants of the original owners, efforts began in earnest to move the Seminoles southward.

The Treaty of Moultrie Creek (1823) called for the relocation of the Seminoles from northern to central Florida, and from the areas of the Apalachicola and Suwannee Rivers south to below Tampa Bay. It also required the return of runaway slaves. Many chiefs refused to turn over the sought-after "slaves" and also refused to move, as the land in central Florida was considerably poorer than the cultivated land that they were being required to leave. Slaves continued to escape servitude in Georgia and seek haven in Florida. Obviously and predictably, slave raids recurred, although now apparently without military mandate or assistance. In the aftermath of the Treaty of Moultrie Creek, the subject of relocation to places west of the Mississippi River was broached. Immediately, the Seminoles were suspicious, and some, especially the freed and assimilated blacks, feared enslavement by the Creeks upon their own relocation. The wedge between the Creeks and Seminoles was driven deep and used to best advantage by the federal government. The focus of federal policy shifted from removal southward to removal westward.

The 1830 **Indian Removal Act** mandated the removal of all Native Americans to locations west of the Mississippi River. The old nemesis of the Creeks and Seminoles, Andrew **Jackson**, was now president, an office to which he had been elected in part because of his espousal of a removal policy. Pursuant to the new law, in 1832 Col. James Gadsden began negotiation with the Seminoles for western removal. Gadsden found the Seminoles in desperate conditions. A drought had decimated their crops, and Gadsden reported that the Seminoles were "naked and starving." Whether this was the true condition of the Seminoles or not, those who met with Gadsden seemed amenable to removal only if the federal government would provide for a party of Seminoles to go to the West and to report back their findings on a proposed settlement site. The Seminoles were told that, upon relocation, they would be required to reaffiliate with the Creeks and that annuity payments for them would be made to the Creeks to then be distributed to them. Again, fears of subservience to the Creeks arose. This uneasy accord was formalized by the Treaty of Payne's Landing in 1832.

The exploratory delegation traveled to Little Rock, Arkansas, via steamboat and then on to Fort Gibson by horseback. At Fort Gibson, after viewing the site for relocation, the delegation signed agreements to the effect that it had found the site suitable. The government held that the delegation spoke for the entirety of the Seminole leadership and that its approval satisfied the requirements of the Treaty of Payne's Landing, subsequently binding the Seminoles to removal. The Seminoles disagreed, holding that the delegation was advisory and was not charged with the authority to act on a larger mandate. Further, the delegation was not pleased with the site because it was adjacent to the Comanches, Wichitas, and Kiowas, who were given to raids for the purpose of stealing horses, so the delegation had not intended to approve the relocation without tribal authority. This disagreement was a primary cause of the Second Seminole War.

January 1, 1836, was the date for the Seminoles to report to Tampa to be shipped west. Gen. Clinch, who had as a colonel attacked the Seminoles at Fort Apalachicola twenty years earlier, mustered a body of 200 troops to force the removal if it was not undertaken voluntarily. A few days prior to the appointed date for compliance, the Seminoles attacked Fort King and on the same day intercepted Major Dade's force moving from Fort Brooke in Tampa to Fort King, near present-day Dade City. These engagements serve as testimony to the rising prominence of Osceola as a leader within the Seminole people. He had personal grievances with a government-appointed agent to the Seminoles, one of the casualties at Fort King, for having contributed to the abduction of his wife and for placing him under arrest at a previous meeting.

By the end of February, overtures were made so that an agreement seemed to be in the offing. A conference was held at which the government proposed that the Seminoles relocate south of the Withlacoochee River in central Florida and cease raids and hostilities. In return, the troops would not follow them. Agreement was reached on these terms, but then Gen. Clinch, apparently unaware of the agreement, arrived and assailed the Seminole party at the conference. The Seminoles fled, convinced that they had been betrayed yet again.

In April 1836, a party of 407 under Holata Emathla left Tampa Bay en route to Little Rock. Eighty-seven of that party, including Holata Emathla, would die. Despite this development, hostilities continued, culminating with the surrender of **Miconopy** in 1837. Deputies of Miconopy treated with Gen. Thomas S. **Jesup**, agreeing to the relocation of their party under the condition that they could take their "slaves" with them to the West, thus protecting them from being sent or sold to white slave owners. Jesup agreed, and on March 18 Miconopy surrendered himself to be used as a hostage to ensure compliance with the treaty. With Miconopy came Jumper, Alligator (**Hulbutta Tustenuggee**), and **Abraham**. Missing from Miconopy's party was Osceola. In time, those represented by the parties to the agreement assembled near Tampa Bay and were staged for removal. Pressure began to mount on Jesup to give over the blacks amongst the Indians, and eventually he succumbed to the sentiment. This was an obvious violation of the underlying conditions, and Miconopy, Jumper, and others took their people and left the vicinity. The ongoing effort to round up other Seminoles continued in the aftermath of this failed agreement, with the Creek presence being supplemented by other Indian tribes, including the Shawnees, Delawares, and Choctaws. Ongoing negotiation led to Miconopy, Alligator, and Jumper again bringing their people in for removal. Through a violation of a flag of truce and treaty protocol orchestrated under Jesup's command, Wildcat (**Coacoochee**) and then Osceola were captured. Many soldiers, army officers, and citizens of the time were very much disappointed and chagrined by the dishonorable means by which Osceola was captured and subsequently treated.

As the military campaign continued, the Seminoles moved further south into areas for which army tactics were ill designed. Defeats and hollow victories against what was an essentially nebulous foe added to the already low morale and confidence in leadership. From above, Jesup was burdened by a damaged reputation and a loss of political will for further prosecution of what many considered an unwinnable war. These factors led the superior officers within Jesup's command to advocate striking a truce with the Seminoles, leaving them all of southern Florida. Jesup approached the secretary of war, who would only allow a temporary truce and insisted on continuing the push for removal. In 1838, Jesup was recalled from the command of the army in Florida. His own estimates were that in the approximate year previous to his recall from command, 1,978 Seminoles were captured and staged for removal, of which 23 escaped.

Gen. Zachary Taylor replaced Jesup in command. Taylor's primary effort appeared to be not so much prosecuting a war against the Seminoles as facilitating the shipment of immigrants to the West. In April 1839, Taylor was replaced by Gen. Alexander Macomb, who was assigned specifically to negotiate a peace. In May, a peace was negotiated, the agreement of which was similar to what Jesup had suggested. The agreement met with wide approval from policymakers and citizens outside of Florida. However, citizens of Florida wanted nothing less than annihilation or removal and pressed on with provocative actions and hostilities. Through their actions, the agreement was not allowed to succeed.

Removal typically followed a water route from Tampa to New Orleans, up the Mississippi River to the Arkansas River, then up the river to Fort Gibson. From Fort Gibson, the trip was overland into **Indian Territory** (*see* **Seminole Removal**). Covington (1993) says that it is "estimated that some 2,968 Seminoles were shipped out from 1836 to March 1841 and 934 from April 1841 to April 1842, a total of 3,902." Adding the aforementioned parties cited by Wright, which totaled more than 300, a conservative estimate is that more than 4,200 began the journey, although some died along the way.

In late 1842, Col. E. A. Hitchcock was charged with reopening the war that, by his estimation, "had been closed so often heretofore." Through evenhanded dealing and patience, he gained the respect of the Seminole leaders and eventually succeeded where others had failed in brokering a peace that terminated involuntary removal, although intimidation and other influence continued to be used toward the goal of total removal. The citizens of Florida still wished for relocation, and incentives were offered for voluntary removal in 1849, 1851, and 1856. Wright (1986) reports that the brief Third Seminole War (1855–1858) resulted in almost 300 immigrants to the West. He goes on to say that Seminole tradition suggests that several other small family groups of Seminoles left Florida after the Civil War ended in 1865.

In 1881, again the federal government took up the policy of removal and sent Clay McCauley to Florida to investigate the Seminole presence there. As a result of McCauley's report, the notion of removal was overturned, and Congress, in 1884, began appropriating annual sums for disbursement to the Seminoles in Florida, thereby establishing a relationship with the Seminoles remaining in Florida that was similar to that reached with Native Americans who had been relocated to what would become Oklahoma.

FURTHER READING: Covington, James W. *The Seminoles of Florida.* Gainesville: University Press of Florida, 1993; Deloria, V., Jr. "The Application of the Constitution to American Indians." In *Exiled in the Land of the Free: Democracy, Indian Nations and the U.S. Constitution,* ed. Oren Lyons et al. Santa Fe, NM: Clear Light Publishers, 1992; Foreman, Grant. *Indian Removal.* Norman: University of Oklahoma Press, 1989; Wright, J. Leitch, Jr. *Creeks and Seminoles.* Lincoln: University of Nebraska Press, 1986.

FRED E. KNOWLES, JR.

Folsom, David (1791–1847)

David Folsom's role in **Choctaw removal** was dictated in part by Choctaw factionalism, which arose when Mississippi extended its laws over the Choctaws in January 1830, outlawing tribal government. At the time, Greenwood **LeFlore** was chief of the northwestern district, Folsom of the northeastern district, and John Garland of the southern district. Determined to remove the Choctaws to the West, LeFlore called a council, persuaded Folsom and Garland to resign, and drafted a removal treaty. In the political strife that followed, the Choctaws came close to civil war.

English-speaking and with a rudimentary American education, Folsom was well liked and was one of the first chiefs elected by vote of the Choctaws from his district. In 1826 he, LeFlore, and Garland replaced district chief **Mushulatubbee**, Robert Cole, and Tapanahoma, and stood firm against negotiations with the United States. The election of Andrew **Jackson** and passage of Mississippi laws extending state jurisdiction over the Choctaws made some of the older chiefs willing to discuss removal, but Folsom and LeFlore remained opposed. Shortly after Mississippi extended its laws over

David Folsom, pro-removal Choctaw chief. (Research Division of the Oklahoma Historical Society)

the Choctaws, the Choctaws deposed Folsom and Garland and replaced them with Mushulatubbee and Nitakechi. Without authority, LeFlore began negotiating with the United States, even writing a removal treaty. Mushulatubbee put the treaty before the Choctaw council, and LeFlore swayed the Choctaws so that they made him chief of the whole Nation, an office that had not existed before. As chief, he sent the treaty to Washington, but the Senate failed to ratify it. These events laid the groundwork for removal talks only a few months after passage of the **Indian Removal Act** of 1830.

Into a charged political atmosphere, U.S. officials came to negotiate the **Treaty of Dancing Rabbit Creek** on September 15, 1830. The Choctaws opposed the treaty and negotiations almost failed, but LeFlore, who had a monetary interest in getting the Choctaws to remove, helped engineer a treaty that Mushulatubbee, Nitakechi, and others would sign. The treaty was ratified by Congress on February 25, 1831. On hearing of the ratification of the treaty, Folsom wrote, "Our Doom is sealed. There is no other course for us but to turn our faces to our new homes toward the setting sun."

When removal began, Folsom and his followers decided to remove to the Choctaw lands on the Red River. Weather made travel conditions harsh. Folsom's 594 Choctaws reached Arkansas Post by steamboat from Vicksburg, Mississippi, on November 26, 1831. The weather was bitterly cold, with temperatures reaching zero and the ground covered with ice and snow. While they were on the road from the Post to Little Rock, the temperature averaged 12°F. On December 21, 1831, they reached the north side of the Arkansas River at Little Rock, where they crossed the river and went south on the Southwest Trail to Washington, Arkansas; turned west on the Fort Towson road; and reached their destination on January 29, 1832. Folsom set up his home, assisted his people to get settled, and planted corn in the spring of 1832.

Folsom then returned to Mississippi to lead another party of 800 to 900 that reached the camping grounds opposite Little Rock on November 14. The trip was difficult because of the cholera epidemic that had developed in the region, and a number of the group died. Folsom made a quick economic recovery following removal. He and his slaves built a fine home, and he was so proficient at growing corn that he became a well-known merchant and supplied rations to Chickasaws who arrived in the West during **Chickasaw removal** from 1837 through 1839. Folsom died at the age of 56 on September 24, 1847.

FURTHER READING: Conlon, Czarina C. "David Folsom." *Chronicles of Oklahoma* 4 (1926): 340–355; U.S. Congress. Senate. *Correspondence on the Emigration of Indians, 1831–1833.* 23rd Cong., 1st sess., S. Exec. Doc. 512. Serial 244–248.

CAROLYN YANCEY KENT

Food

By act of Congress in 1832, a U.S. soldier's daily rations were set at $1^1/_4$ pounds of beef, $1^1/_8$ pounds of flour, and 2 quarts of salt per hundred rations, as well as a small amount of soap, sugar, coffee, and candles. This had been the ration since the War of 1812, when rum was included instead of sugar and coffee. The army ration was used as the basis for the rations issued to American Indians during removal. At the commencement of removal in December 1830, Gen. George Gibson, the commander of the commissary general for subsistence, ordered Lt. J. R. Stephenson at Cantonment Gibson to supply the Choctaws who had already arrived in the Kiamichi area daily rations consisting of $1^1/_2$ pounds of fresh beef or pork, 1 pound of cornmeal or flour, and 2 quarts of salt per hundred rations.

Commodities were procured from private contractors, usually at a cost of between $6^1/_2$ and $12^1/_2$ cents per ration, and warehoused along removal routes. When necessary, due to scheduling or long delays, the military disbursing officers accompanying the Indians made local purchases. The War Department insisted that the provision be of good quality. On at least one occasion during **Choctaw removal**, beef rations supplied by civilian contractors were rejected by the disbursing agents as spoiled.

Distribution of rations varied with the tribe, the disbursing agent, and the immediate circumstances. For instance, forgoing white distributing agents with roll sheets and measuring cups, the Shawnees chose their distribution agents from among themselves and distributed by necessity rather than numbers (*see* **Shawnee Removal**). Rations could be distributed daily, every other day, every four days, or according to some other practical pattern. Substitutions were sometimes necessary; for instance, dried peas or pork was issued instead of beef or, as occurred quite often in the South where corn was a staple crop, corn or cornmeal was substituted for flour.

During Choctaw removal, the Choctaws generally refused pork, preferring beef. In light of this preference, Gen. Gibson suggested to the disbursing agent for removal of the Ohio Indians, Lt. J. F. Lane, that he solicit the preferences of the Senecas and the Shawnees regarding their meat rations as their removal was begun in 1832 (*see* **Seneca Removal**). The Shawnees took their full meat ration as steers and pigs rather than as butchered meat. On arrival at Indianapolis in the winter of 1832–1833, they butchered the beef, dried and salted the meat, and sold the hides and tallow, using the proceeds to purchase coffee, sugar, spices, and other items not included in their rations. The **Cherokee removal**, beginning in 1838, was organized and conducted by the Cherokees themselves, and the daily rations, as stipulated by Cherokee negotiators, included large quantities of hand soap and those sorts of items that were purchased by the Shawnees.

The usual form in which corn was consumed by the southeastern tribes was as hominy, in which a lye treatment made corn less liable to spoilage by germination and made the niacin in the corn available for digestion by humans. The change from hominy to ground, dried corn no doubt contributed to vitamin deficiencies and generally increased the stress levels of the Indians, leading to illness.

During the Winnebago removal (*see* **Ho-Chunk Removal**), in the fall and winter of 1832, rations were used as an enticement and then as a powerful motivator to encourage the Winnebagos to move west. The terms of their treaty allowed the Winnebagos to remove west of the Mississippi or to remove to lands they held between the Mississippi and the Wisconsin River. White settlers desiring the former pressured the federal government to withhold rations from those Indians who did not move west of the Mississippi. Additionally, the treaty, unlike other removal treaties, stipulated half-rations for children under 10 years of age. The Winnebagos initially refused to go west and were soon on the verge of starvation. When they were told that rations had been deposited for them west of the Mississippi, the majority capitulated and made the required removal.

FURTHER READING: U.S. Congress. Senate. *Correspondence on the Emigration of Indians, 1831–1833*. 23rd Cong., 1st sess., S. Exec. Doc. 512. Serial 244–248; "Rations: Conference Notes Prepared by the Quartermaster School for the Quartermaster General, January 1949." At www.qmfound.com/history_of_rations.htm.

TONY R. ROSE

Fox Removal

See Sauk and Mesquakie (Fox) Removal

G

Gardiner, James B. (1789–1837)

James B. Gardiner, one of the early settlers of Greene County, Ohio, served as the special agent and commissioner negotiating the **Shawnee removal from Ohio**. In 1812 he started the *Freeman's Chronicle,* the second newspaper in Franklinton (Columbus), Ohio. At the same time he served on the town's council. In 1823, he returned to Greene County and became involved in local government. His election to the lower house of the Ohio legislature in 1825 was contested because of improper campaign promises, and Gardiner was denied his seat. He edited and published the *People's Press and Impartial Expositor* and served two terms in the Ohio Senate, 1826 and 1827, representing Greene and Clinton Counties. During the 1828 presidential campaign he published the *Ohio People's Press,* a pro-Jackson paper. After Andrew **Jackson**'s election, Gardiner was nominated for a position at the U.S. Land Office in Tiffin, Ohio, but his appointment, opposed by several leading Ohio politicians on the grounds of his frequent intoxication, was not confirmed.

Gardiner sought a position in the Indian affairs division of the War Department and was appointed a commissioner to the Ohio tribes. During this time the leaders of the Senecas of Sandusky River were in Washington attempting to gain permission to relocate west of the Mississippi. On February 28, 1831, Gardiner negotiated a treaty with the Senecas for removal under the guidelines of the **Indian Removal Act** of 1830. On March 29, 1831, he was appointed special agent to the Ohio Indians by John H. **Eaton**, secretary of war. Gardiner successfully negotiated treaties with the Senecas–Shawnees of Lewistown, the Shawnees of Hog Creek and Wapakoneta, and the Ottawas of Blanchard's Fork and Oquanoxa's Village in the summer of 1831. In June 1832, Gardiner was appointed head of the emigration of these tribes but was dismissed in October 1832.

Gardiner's dismissal from office was based on slow travel (the emigration had progressed only as far as central Illinois after forty-two days of travel), money expenditure, and reports of his alcohol problem. Washington was aware of the lack of confidence in Gardiner among the Indian leaders as well as his staff. Open hostility between Gardiner and his disbursement officer, Lt. J. F. Lane, over authorization to spend government funds created a situation in which Gardiner had to borrow money from the chiefs for supplies for the people and their livestock. When concern grew in Washington over these issues, Col. J. J. Abert joined the emigration to resolve the problems. Abert's solution was to assign Lane to the Seneca–Shawnee group and to dismiss Gardiner. Gardiner was asked to remain with the emigration until the Indians reached the Mississippi River.

Returning to Ohio, Gardiner sent a detailed letter to the War Department regarding his actions in the Indian removal. He again became involved in publishing, securing an appointment as official printer for the state of Ohio. In 1836, he started another campaign paper supporting Whig candidates (*see* **Whig Party**).

FURTHER READING: Buchman, Randall. *A Sorrowful Journey*. Defiance, OH: Defiance College Press, 2008.

RANDALL L. BUCHMAN

Georgia and Indian Removal

At the core of Georgia's relations with the Indians, both colonially and nationally, was the acquisition of land. Like the other original colonies, Georgia took Indian land either by agreement or by an aggressive intrusion that overwhelmed the tribes and forced them farther west. After the Revolutionary War, the citizens of Georgia were singleminded in their intent to remove all of the Indians from within the state's territorial boundaries. Their intent became a part of federal Indian policy in a document known as the Georgia Compact of 1802. In it, Georgia ceded to the United States the territory it claimed in what are now the states of Alabama and Mississippi, for which the United States agreed to pay $1.25 million. The United States gave up its claim to any rights or titles to lands within the chartered boundaries of Georgia east of the line with Alabama and also agreed to extinguish the Indian titles to all lands within those limits. During succeeding decades, the compact and the government's promises served as the core of Georgia's Indian policy and provided the major political impetus for development of a federal Indian removal policy. Georgia's insistence on Indian removal focused on two tribes: Creeks and Cherokees.

Of first concern to Georgia was the land occupied by the Creeks, for it contained excellent farmland. True to its word during the decade and a half after 1802, the United States negotiated treaties and agreements with the Creeks in which they gave up more and more of their lands. Believing, however, that the government was not moving fast enough and displeased with its policy of voluntary removal, by the early 1820s Georgia had become more strident in its demands and more devious in its tactics.

Georgia began an earnest campaign in the early 1820s to force the Creeks out of the state. Beginning with the Treaty of Indian Springs in 1821, the Georgians began divide-and-conquer tactics that were effective in generating Indian treaties in the removal period. The treaty was signed by William McIntosh, who was speaker for the Lower Creeks, and other Lower Creek chiefs. They ceded the land between the Ocmulgee and Flint rivers to pay off the Creeks' debts.

In response, the Creek council passed a law against the sale of Creek land, but it failed to stop McIntosh, who was set on enriching himself at the Creeks' expense. His actions, however, led to his downfall. He held a high position in the tribe, representing it in the Cherokee councils. The Cherokees, in turn, sent Major **Ridge** to the Creek councils. At a Cherokee meeting with U.S. commissioners in 1823, McIntosh urged the Cherokees to cede their land and remove to the West and attempted to bribe John **Ross** to use his authority to get the Cherokees to agree to remove. The Cherokees expelled McIntosh from their meeting and warned the Creek council about his machinations. In July, the Creek council adopted a resolution stating their refusal to cede any more land. The council's act should have been warning enough for McIntosh.

Engraving from a portrait of Creek chief William McIntosh by 19th-century American painter Charles Bird King, from *The Indian Tribes of North America*. McIntosh was a strong proponent of Creek removal and was assassinated for signing away Creek lands in Georgia. (McKenney, Thomas L. and James Hall. *The Indian Tribes of North America*, 1836–1844)

Nevertheless, in December of that year, U.S. commissioners met with the Creeks to attempt to reach a removal agreement, relying on McIntosh to help them. The Americans argued that the Creeks were foreigners who had migrated into the lands and that they had forfeited any right to the land by siding with England during the Revolutionary War. The Creeks stood by the Treaty of New York (1790) and the Treaty of Fort Jackson (1814). The Americans then resorted to bribery, using McIntosh, who worked with the Creeks in council and with the Americans behind the scene. Learning of his actions, the council removed him as speaker for the Lower Towns.

The Americans relied on McIntosh to deliver them a treaty. But McIntosh was afraid to push for a treaty as long as the negotiations took place in Alabama. If they were removed to Indian Springs in Georgia, he would sign, for he believed that the Georgians would protect him from retribution by the Nation. The Americans went back to Washington with word that a treaty could be made, ceding the Creek land in Georgia, if the government would move the proceedings. The Creek council put McIntosh on notice. Georgia governor George Troup, McIntosh's cousin, rabid in his intent to rid Georgia of

Indians, had helped hatch the scheme and promised to protect McIntosh from the Creek law if he signed the treaty.

Negotiators met with McIntosh and other Creek chiefs and headmen at Indian Springs in February 1825, where a treaty was signed. **Opothleyohola**, speaker for the Upper Towns, spoke against the treaty and said that those who signed did not have the authority to speak for the whole Nation. Nevertheless, the treaty ceded all of the Creeks' land in Georgia and much of the northern two-thirds of their Alabama lands. The Creeks protested the treaty as invalid, and as Creek sentiment rose against McIntosh, Troup threatened to call out the militia and invade the Creek country in Alabama, if necessary, if the Creeks tried to harm McIntosh. The treaty was ratified in March 1825. Secretary of War James Barbour set about carrying out the treaty provisions immediately. Although the treaty gave the Creeks until September 1 to remove from the limits of Georgia, Troup issued a proclamation announcing a survey of the ceded land in Georgia in preparation for a land lottery by which the state could distribute the land to its citizens.

In April, a group of Okfuskees executed McIntosh and some of his family and close friends, resulting in an "Indian scare." Troup mobilized the Georgia militia and threatened to invade the Creeks to seek retribution. Barbour and President John Quincy Adams, knowing that Troup was a hothead, nevertheless ordered an investigation and sent the army under Gen. Edmund P. Gaines to Georgia to protect Georgians from the Creeks. The Georgia assembly ordered its own investigation, authorized the survey to begin, and placed Georgia laws over the Creek lands, attaching them to five adjoining counties.

Gen. Gaines's actions angered Troup, whom the general came to despise. First, Gaines announced that the $400,000 promised for the land in the treaty would be distributed to all Creeks in the ceded area, not just McIntosh's followers. Second, he stopped the McIntosh Creeks from seeking revenge for the death of McIntosh. Third, Gaines developed a good rapport with the Alabama Creeks, who promised to welcome the McIntosh Creeks into their lands, causing some of the latter to denounce the treaty as fraudulent. President Adams ordered Troup not to send surveyors into the ceded land and gave Gaines authority to stop him if he tried.

Adams also directed Gaines to negotiate a new treaty, this time with the whole Nation, if he could not persuade the Creeks to vacate the ceded lands in Georgia. He was to promise them an equal-size tract in the West if they would agree to remove. With Opothleyohola at its head, a delegation of Creeks went to Washington with authority to negotiate. On January 26, 1826, a new treaty ceded all Creek lands that were claimed to be in Georgia, admitted the McIntosh Creeks into the Creek Nation, and provided for exploration of land in the West, and if suitable land could be found, the Creeks in the ceded area could remove. A new date of January 1, 1827, was set for the Creeks to vacate the land.

Troup maintained that the Treaty of Indian Springs of 1825 was the valid treaty. Because it called for a removal date of September 1, 1826, he ordered the survey to begin. The Creeks protested his action. The situation was tense, but U.S. officials were finally able to convince the Creeks that they should not oppose the early survey.

It was discovered that some 192,000 acres of Creek land had been left in Georgia by the boundaries drawn by the **Treaty of Washington**. Troup made plans to send surveyors into the unceded lands. Adams warned him that the United States would prevent it, and Troup mobilized the Georgia militia. There was talk of civil war, but the Adams administration worked out a solution. A treaty with the Creeks was negotiated at Fort Mitchell on November 15, 1827, in which they gave up all their remaining lands in Georgia.

The Creeks who had remained in Georgia found life difficult. A large number of the McIntosh faction removed to the West. The Creeks intimidated others who wished to enroll for removal. About 7,000 were forced to move across the Alabama line and reside among the Creeks there. Through the years, many became displaced and impoverished, and their desperate condition contributed in large measure to the outbreak of the Creek War of 1836 and the immediate forced removal of a large number of Creeks to the West.

With the Creeks out of the way, Georgia turned its full attention to the Cherokees, intent on driving them out as well. During their attack on the Creeks, the Georgians had learned a valuable lesson. They could defy the United States, push the country to the brink of war, and through threats, intimidation, and underhanded tactics do what was necessary to rid the state of Indians. In 1826 and 1827, the state's general assembly had reaffirmed the state's claim to Cherokee lands as its own. Unwilling to tolerate a state or nation, sovereign or pretending to be, within their state's borders, Georgians were angered by the Cherokees' adoption of a constitution in 1827. In a response that was emboldened by the election of Andrew **Jackson** in the fall of 1828, the state passed legislation that attached the Cherokee land to five adjoining counties. The law would go into effect in 1830, at which time the state's laws would be enforced in the Cherokee lands and the laws passed by the Cherokee council would become null and void. Georgians hoped that fear of subjection to state law would persuade the Cherokees to remove.

The Cherokees responded to these pressures first by appealing to the U.S. government to intervene in their behalf and then, in 1829, by attempting to take away the citizenship of any Cherokee who gave in to Georgia's pressures and enrolled to remove to the West. The Georgians took heart in Washington's response. Jackson was unwilling to confront either the Georgians' argument that the state had a right to nullify federal law or their flagrant violation of the Constitution, which gave sole authority in Indian affairs to the federal government. Instead, he fell back on the Compact of 1802, saying there was nothing the government could do. Angered by the Cherokees' threatening those who wanted to remove, the Georgia assembly passed another, much stronger, bill on December 19, 1829, reasserting the state's authority over the Cherokees and their land.

The 1829 act encompassed earlier laws, expanded them, and applied them as well to any Creeks still residing within Georgia. First, it attached the

Cherokee lands to Carroll, DeKalb, Gwinnett, Hall, and Habersham counties. Second, on June 1, 1830, criminal and civil laws of the state applied to those lands. Third, officers were to be compensated for carrying out the laws. Fourth, laws enacted by the Cherokees were declared null and void after June 1, 1830, and carried no validity in Georgia courts. Fifth, attempts to prohibit Cherokees from leaving Georgia or punishing them for trying to leave were punishable by four years at hard labor in the Georgia penitentiary. Sixth, attempts to prevent Cherokees from selling or ceding Cherokee lands to the United States were punishable by four to six years at hard labor. Seventh, killing Cherokees for attempting to emigrate or to sell land or to meet U.S. negotiators was punishable by hanging. Eighth, judges of counties were empowered to call out militia to protect officers who were executing the laws. Ninth, testimony by Cherokees or Creeks was not valid against whites unless the whites resided in the Indian country.

Passage of the **Indian Removal Act** in May 1830 further strengthened Georgia's hand. The question, then, was not whether removal would take place but when. Georgia's goal now was to make the Cherokees' lives as miserable as possible and make them embrace the idea of removal as relief. Georgians used the gold fields to justify their next major move. Gold had been discovered in the Cherokee lands in 1828, and by 1829 a full-fledged gold rush was underway. By 1830, there were thousands of miners, both Cherokee and non-Cherokee, working the fields. Having asserted that the Cherokee lands were Georgia lands, the Georgia assembly in late 1830 set out to take charge of the gold fields and further outlaw Cherokee control over their land.

Legislation was passed December 22, 1830, to prevent the exercise of powers by anyone whose pretext to authority came from the Cherokees and their laws; to prevent whites from living in Georgia lands "occupied" by Cherokees; and to create a guard to protect the gold fields and to enforce the state laws inside the lands claimed by the Cherokees. The law, which became effective February 1, 1831, forbade Cherokee headmen, chiefs, and warriors to assemble for any purpose, to pass laws, to hold court, or to punish Cherokees who enrolled to remove. All violations were punishable by four years in the Georgia penitentiary. Cherokees could, however, meet with U.S. commissioners. Whites within the limits of the Cherokee lands were forbidden to remain after March 1, 1831, without a license or a permit issued by the governor or his agent, except authorized agents of the federal government or Georgia or any white who was renting or occupying improvements abandoned by Cherokees who had moved to the West. All whites with permits to stay were required to swear a loyalty oath to Georgia. The law struck a blow at some of the wealthy Cherokees by forbidding them to collect tolls on turnpikes or bridges. Finally, the governor was authorized to establish a guard of citizens under the command of a commissioner. They were specifically charged with guarding the gold fields and arresting any person charged with a violation of the law.

Despite evidence to the contrary, the Cherokees continued to trust the legal process as a way out of their dilemma. They challenged Georgia's jurisdiction over Cherokees by filing an injunction in the case of George Tassle. Tassle had killed another Cherokee inside the Cherokee lands and in 1830 had been arrested by Georgia officials, tried, and sentenced to hang. With William **Wirt** as their attorney, in 1831 the Cherokees argued their case before the U.S. Supreme Court in *Cherokee Nation v. Georgia*, in which the judges evaded the constitutional question. They ruled that the Cherokee Nation could not sue for relief before the Court because it was not a foreign country according to the language of the Constitution. In his brief, Chief Justice John Marshall called the Cherokees a "domestic dependent nation," a term that tribes have used since in arguing their cases for sovereignty. The outcome, unfortunately, meant nothing to Tassle, for Georgia had already hanged him.

The Cherokees fared better with their next major test of Georgia's claim to jurisdiction over them. After the law took effect in 1831, requiring whites residing in the Cherokee lands to acquire a license and swear allegiance to Georgia, the Georgia Guard under John W. A. **Sanford** arrested Samuel A. **Worcester**, Elizur Butler, and nine others. The latter took the oath or left the state. Worcester and Butler refused to take the oath and claimed illness in their families as their reason for not leaving. They were tried and convicted and sentenced to four years at hard labor. Worcester appealed his conviction, which the U.S. Supreme Court heard because Worcester was a U.S. citizen. In March 1832 in *Worcester v. Georgia*, the Court ruled that the Georgia laws extending their jurisdiction over the Cherokees were null and void, calling the laws hostile to U.S. constitutional authority, the treaties, and the laws of Congress. The Court reversed and nullified Worcester's conviction and, by application, Butler's.

Imbued with a strong belief that the state had a right to nullify federal law, Georgia officials cared little what the Supreme Court said. They refused to release Worcester and Butler. In November 1832, Governor Wilson Lumpkin—demagogue that he was—published a lengthy diatribe against the Court's decision. Seeing no use in continuing their legal battle for release, Worcester and Butler ended their legal battle the following month. In January 1833, they capitulated and appealed to Lumpkin to pardon them. Exulting in his victory, he did.

Having successfully faced down the federal government once more, Georgians set about tightening their grip on the Cherokee people and, apparently with no moral sense, making their lives as miserable as possible. White intruders in the Cherokee lands had been a problem for years. The federal government refused to force them out as it had agreed to do. Georgia, of course, supported the intruders and set about legitimizing their presence on Cherokee land. In 1830, the state legislature had ordered the survey of Cherokee lands in preparation for white occupancy. In 1832, male, widowed, and orphaned citizens of Georgia registered for a lottery that turned plots of Cherokee land over to whites, who moved in and dispossessed the Cherokees whose homes were on their allotted plots. In 1833, Georgia made a legal assault primarily upon the wealthy class of Cherokees, hoping to demoralize them and encourage them to remove. Because some of them had taken reserves under the treaties of 1817 and 1819, Georgia argued that they had no right to property that they had thereafter claimed in the Cherokee Nation. In December 1833, the state assembly ordered the confiscation of the property of the wealthiest, among whom were the political leaders of the Nation. The next year, the Georgia Guard evicted the Cherokees, including men like John Ross, John Martin, Richard Taylor, and Joseph Vann, and turned their property over to Georgians.

The Georgia Guard harassed the Cherokees in other ways. Created by the Georgia assembly in 1830, the men who made up the unit, according to Governor George Gilmer, were not responsible to anyone for their actions. They evicted Cherokee citizens; shut down the *Cherokee Phoenix*, the national newspaper; and even invaded Tennessee in 1834 and arrested Chief John Ross.

The actions taken by the Georgians slowly but certainly had their desired effect. By 1834, the Cherokees were split over the question of removal. Those who followed Ross and opposed removal far outnumbered those who favored it. The latter, who came to be known as the Treaty Party, were willing to negotiate a removal treaty and did so, but the Cherokee council rejected it. In 1835, Secretary of War Lewis **Cass** sent John F. **Schermerhorn** and William **Carroll** to Georgia to negotiate with the Treaty Party. The commissioners met with a few hundred Treaty Party Cherokees and drafted the **Treaty of New Echota** in December 1835. The United States ratified the treaty and applied its provisions to all the Cherokees. The treaty ceded their eastern lands and called for their removal by early 1838 (*see* **Cherokee Removal**).

During the 1830s the government condoned Georgia's assault on Cherokee sovereignty, either by openly supporting it or by conveniently looking the other way. Secretary John H. **Eaton**, following Andrew Jackson's lead, had consistently argued that the government had no authority to intervene in Georgia's affairs. His successor, Lewis Cass, placed his support behind the Treaty Party Cherokees and ordered his agents to do what they must to get signatures on a removal treaty. Andrew Jackson, president until early 1837, did not believe in the states' right to nullify federal law, but nullifiers were less important to him than Indian removal. The civil war he avoided by refusing to confront the nullifiers was simply delayed for two and a half decades, long enough for small-arms manufacturers to improve the technology of their products to make them more deadly.

FURTHER READING: Berutti, Ronald A. "The Cherokee Cases: The Fight to Save the Supreme Court and the Cherokee Nation." *American Indian Law Review* 17(1992): 291–308; Garrison, Tim Alan. *The Legal Ideology of Removal: The Southern Judiciary and the Sovereignty of Native American Nations.* Athens: University of Georgia Press, 2002; Green, Michael D. *The Politics of Indian Removal: Creek Government and Society in Crisis.* Lincoln: University of Nebraska Press, 1982; Haveman, Christopher D. "The Removal of the Creek Indians from the Southeast, 1825–1838." PhD diss., Auburn University, 2009; Morris, Michel; "Georgia and the Conversation over Indian Removal." *Georgia Historical Quarterly* 91(2007): 403–423; Norgren, Jill. "Lawyers and the Legal Business of the Cherokee Republic in Courts of the United

States, 1829–1835." *Law and History Review* 10(1992): 253–314; Perdue, Theda, and Michael D. Green. *The Cherokee Removal: A Brief History with Documents.* Boston: Bedford Books of St. Martin's Press, 1995; Swindler, William F. "Politics as Law: The Cherokee Cases." *American Indian Law Review* 3(1975): 7–20.

DANIEL F. LITTLEFIELD, JR.

Gopher John

See Cavallo, John

H

Halleck Tustenuggee (dates unknown)

Halleck Tustenuggee, a Miccosukee, was described by Lt. John T. **Sprague** as crafty, indomitable, and fearless. A volatile character and intensely opposed to removal, he emerged as a strong leader in Florida during the later years of the **Second Seminole War.**

Although he was intensely opposed to removal, Halleck Tustenuggee often seemed willing to talk peace, always with the belief that his followers could avoid removal. In May 1839, he met in council with Gen. Alexander Macomb at Fort King, where the general promised the Seminoles that they could remain in Florida if they withdrew south of Peace Creek. The agreement angered Floridians, who wanted the Seminoles removed. However, the point became moot in July when Indians in southwestern Florida attacked American troops under Col. William S. Harney. Sprague blamed the attack on Halleck Tustenuggee. In November 1840, Halleck Tustenuggee and Tiger Tail, a Tallahassee, met with Gen. Walker K. Armistead, again to talk peace. Armistead offered each $5,000 to bring in their bands and remove; however, he did not allow them time enough to come in and resumed troop movements that once more stymied the peace process.

The failure of the peace effort led to an extended period of warfare involving Halleck Tustenuggee. In December 1840, in retaliation for the army's attack on the Spanish Indians in southwestern Florida, the Miccosukees attacked a detail that was escorting an officer's wife from Fort Miconopy to Fort Wacahoota, killing Mrs. Alexander Montgomery, Lt. Walker Sherwood, and three others. Halleck Tustenuggee was believed to be the leader in the attack. In March 1841, he and his warriors attacked troops on the Oklawaha. In May, he sent word that he was ready to surrender his band, but in June he and other leaders made a pact to kill any messengers sent by the Americans. In December 1841, he and his warriors attacked Mandarin northwest of St. Augustine, killing four people, burning buildings, and looting. The army counterattacked, but the Miccosukees escaped. They fought again in April southeast of Peliklakaha, but the Miccosukees again escaped.

Finding it more and more difficult to carry the war further, Halleck Tustenuggee met Col. Jenkins Worth near Warm Springs shortly after the last-mentioned fight, bringing with him his two wives and his family. He was given free movement in the camp, and Worth persuaded him to accompany him to Fort King, secretly leaving orders with his subordinates to seize Halleck Tustenuggee's family. The troops held a feast to lure 114 additional warriors, women, and children into the camp, where they took them captive as well. Then Worth seized Halleck Tustenuggee. The Miccosukee leader was reported to have become so enraged at Worth's treachery that he fainted. Nevertheless, he accepted Worth's offer of $1,000 for the capture of his band. When some of his warriors openly criticized him for having done so, he flew into a rage, knocking them down, kicking them, biting off the ear of one of them, and yelling that he was still their chief whether a prisoner or not.

Worth used Halleck Tustenuggee to send messages that those Indians still free could remain in Florida if they withdrew south of Peace Creek, and on May 10, 1842, the War Department unilaterally declared that the Second Seminole War was over.

In July 1842, Halleck Tustenugeee with his band of 120 left Florida. He supposedly said, "I have been hunted like a wolf, and now I am sent away like a dog." The man who had once killed his own sister for urging his people's surrender was now removing. The contingent, accompanied by Lt. E. R. S. Canby, reached New Orleans on July 21 and embarked by steamboat the following day for **Indian Territory**. The Arkansas River was at a particularly low level, and the party was forced to abandon its boat six miles below Little Rock and march overland to Fort Smith and the Choctaw Agency. Canby had no authority to requisition land transportation and, not having money, had to borrow enough from the well-known black Tustenuggee John **Cavallo** (Gopher John), who was with the contingent, to pay for the trip from Little Rock to the Choctaw Agency. Although they suffered much sickness on the way, only one died. They met the western Seminole agent at the Creek council ground on September 6.

Details of Halleck Tustenuggee's postremoval life are sketchy. In 1845, he was one of the signers of the agreement between the Seminoles and Creeks that ultimately led to a separate Seminole Nation in the West. The following year, he accompanied **Coacoochee** on an expedition to Mexico, where Coacoochee was apparently thinking of settling. In 1861 he was one of the three main pro-Union Seminole leaders who, with their followers, engaged in the battles of Round Mountain, Chusto Talasah, and Chustenalah in the northern Creek Nation during the flight of pro-Union Creeks and Seminoles from the Indian Territory to Kansas under **Opothleyohola**. Halleck Tustenuggee and his warriors were credited with having inflicted the high number of casualties suffered by the Confederate Indian forces.

FURTHER READING: Littlefield, Daniel F., Jr. *Africans and Seminoles: From Removal to Emancipation*. Westport, CT: Greenwood Press, 1977; Mahon, John K. *History of the Second Seminole War, 1835–1842*. Gainesville: University Press of Florida, 1967; McReynolds, Edwin C. *The Seminoles*. Norman: University of Oklahoma Press, 1957.

AMANDA L. PAIGE

Heckaton (d. 1842)

Heckaton was a leader of the Quapaws and as such was a party to land cessions beginning in 1818, so much so that his story closely follows the narrative of **Quapaw removal**. After the War of 1812, settlers began to enter Quapaw lands in Arkansas, setting up farms and building roads. At the same time, as U.S. removal policy was being developed, it became apparent to some in Washington that lands the Quapaws occupied were desirable for the settlement of eastern tribes that had been removed west of the Mississippi. In 1816, the Quapaws under Heckaton were called to St. Louis for talks aimed at land cessions. Although these negotiations ended with an agreement, the pact was vetoed by U.S. officials in Washington, so in 1818, Heckaton and the other negotiators returned to St. Louis for further talks.

The result was the Quapaw treaty of 1818, in which the tribe agreed to cede their land bounded on the north by the Arkansas River from its mouth to the Canadian River, up that river to its source, and from there south to the Red River, then down the Red River to the Big Raft. From the Big Raft on the Red River (near present-day Shreveport, Louisiana), a line was drawn to 30 leagues below the mouth of the Arkansas River at the Mississippi River, which served as the southern boundary. The tribe had formerly relinquished its claim to lands north of the Arkansas River and east of the Mississippi River. A triangle of land was left to the Quapaws, with the apex at Little Rock and the base a line running from Arkansas Post to the Saline River. The lands thus ceded were to be occupied by Cherokees, who had been migrating west for at least a decade (*see* **Cherokee Removal**). However, white settlers entered the area first and soon were clamoring for more land.

Robert Crittenden, territorial secretary for Arkansas, led the movement to rid the region of Indians. He was instrumental in getting the Arkansas General Assembly to send a memorial urging Congress to acquire the lands still held by the Quapaws. Once again, Heckaton was pressured into treating with the government, this time at Arkansas Post, deep in the Quapaws' former domains. Under the terms of the 1824 treaty, the Quapaws relinquished their remaining lands in Arkansas, thus becoming, for all practical purposes, landless. The ever-helpful Arkansans suggested that they go and live among the Osages or the Cherokees; however, they were afraid they would lose their tribal identity with the Osages, and the Cherokee culture was vastly different from that of the Quapaws. It was decided, finally, to send the tribe to live on Caddo land along the Red River.

For his part, Heckaton petitioned the whites to allow the Quapaws to purchase cheap land in Arkansas, their hereditary homelands. This proposal was ignored, and Heckaton made an impassioned speech, recorded by the *Arkansas Gazette* on May 4, 1824, in which he traced the step-by-step loss of homelands, recounted the broken promises of earlier treaties, and included a plea for some land in Arkansas upon which the Quapaws could continue their lives and maintain their society. Nonetheless, Heckaton led his people into the Caddo country, where they found the living difficult.

The Quapaws planted their crops as they had since time immemorial, but flooding on the Red River, largely a result of the Big Raft, a jam in the river made up of logs and other debris that persisted for years, destroyed what they had planted. To make matters worse, the Caddos did not welcome them, regarding them as intruders. A group under **Sarasin** returned to Arkansas and were treated well by Governor George Izard and other whites sympathetic to their plight. The rest of the tribe remained in Louisiana under Heckaton, until, family by family, they, too, returned to Arkansas. Here, however, they were landless, and the annuities they were to receive under the cession treaty were discontinued. Excluded from their former plots, most of the Quapaws lived in the swamps of southeastern Arkansas. In 1830, Heckaton went to Washington in an attempt to regain some land in Arkansas and the resumption of payments. Nothing came of his petition, so in 1833, he appeared before the Stokes Commission, a group empowered to resolve problems incurred by the removed tribes, and once again pleaded for a tract of land in Arkansas. However, John F. **Schermerhorn**, member of the commission, flatly rejected his proposal, substituting the draft of another treaty, this one reserving a tract of land west of Missouri for the tribe. Reluctantly and without further recourse, Heckaton agreed to its terms.

This treaty was not implemented until 1834, but by that time, some of the Quapaws decided to return to the Red River country and others decided to move to Mexico, present-day east Texas. As the Quapaws prepared to move to Kansas, the situation there changed, and lands in northeastern **Indian Territory** were acquired for the tribe. However, when Heckaton's people arrived there and planted crops, they found that land surveys determined that they had settled on the wrong tract, so once again, they moved to new lands. Heckaton died there in 1842.

FURTHER READING: Baird, W. David. *The Quapaw Indians: A History of the Downstream People.* Norman: University of Oklahoma Press, 1980; "Heckaton." The Encyclopedia of Arkansas History and Culture. At www.encyclopediaofarkansas.net/encyclopedia/; Nieberding, Velma Seamster. *The Quapaws.* Wyandotte, OK: Gregarth Publishing Company, 1999; Quapaw Tribe of Oklahoma. 2009. At www.quapawtribe .com/site/view/12817_TribalHistory.pml.

JAMES W. PARINS

Henry (McHenry), Jim (c. 1815–1883)

Jim Henry was the son of Antonio Rea, whose European ancestry is uncertain, and a Hichiti mother. He was estimated to be 20 to 23 years old and had worked for three years as a clerk in a mercantile business in the booming town of Columbus, Georgia, when the so-called Creek War erupted in May of 1836. His views on Creek removal are unknown (*see* **Muscogee [Creek] Removal**), but Henry left his job and joined **Eneah Micco** and **Eneah Emathla**, Hichitis of the Lower Creek town of Hatchechubbee, as one of the three main leaders in the war.

At the head of 300 Hichiti and Yuchi warriors, Henry helped burn Alabama and Georgia plantations, steal slaves and other property, and kill American occupiers of Creek land. He was most noted for leading his warriors in an attack on the town of Roanoke. In the surprise dawn attack, they killed 15, wounded 20, burned houses, and sent people from miles around fleeing to the larger towns. Hichitis and Yuchis occupied Roanoke until they were finally forced to retreat by Georgia and Alabama militias.

By mid-July 1836, the war was brought to a close by the combined forces of the U.S. Army under Gen. Thomas S. **Jesup** and about 2,000 Upper Creeks under **Opothleyohola** and **Tustenuggee Emathla** (Jim Boy). The Hichitis and Yuchis were the last of the Creeks in the field. When many of Henry's followers were captured, he escaped and remained at large for a few more days, becoming the last of the three main leaders to be captured.

Henry was held at Tuskegee with Eneah Micco and others only a few days before they were started on their way to the West. About 300 men and boys who were considered the most "hostile" were handcuffed, chained together, and marched from holding camps at Fort Mitchell and Tuskegee to Montgomery, followed by a train of women, children, and the elderly and infirm.

But Henry did not go to the West with the estimated 2,300 Chiaha, Eufaula, Kasihta, Hichiti, and Yuchi captives. They boarded steamboats and barges and were taken under guard to Mobile and sent from there to New Orleans and then up the Mississippi to Arkansas. Henry said goodbye to his wife and was then lodged in jail with others at Montgomery to await trial for murder. Georgia wanted him taken back to that state to stand trial for his attack on Roanoke, but Alabama wanted to hang him and so refused, arguing that he was a citizen of Alabama. Henry went to trial in January 1838. Probably to his surprise, he and David Hardage were acquitted. The local people were angered at the verdict, and Capt. John Page of the U.S. Army kept the two in his quarters to prevent their being murdered until the U.S. Creek interpreter could take them to the West.

In the West, Henry followed a much different lifestyle under the name Jim or James McHenry. By 1853, he had become a Methodist minister, and after the Civil War, he was a member of the committee that wrote the constitution for the Muscogee Nation. He was active in tribal politics, serving as a member of the House of Kings and judge of Coweta District. He died at Broken Arrow town on May 1, 1883.

FURTHER READING: Debo, Angie. *The Road to Disappearance: A History of the Creek Indians.* Norman: University of Oklahoma Press, 1979; Foreman, Grant. *Indian Removal: The Emigration of the Five Civilized Tribes of Indians.* Norman: University of

Oklahoma Press, 1989; Wright, J. Leitch, Jr. *Creeks and Seminoles: The Destruction and Regeneration of the Muscogulge People.* Lincoln: University of Nebraska Press, 1986.

DANIEL F. LITTLEFIELD, JR.

Ho-Chunk Removal

Ho-Chunk (or Winnebago, as the people were called at the time) removal is an interesting case because this group experienced the process in its several manifestations: they were moved to a smaller portion of their ancestral lands, they were removed outright to another region west of the Mississippi, and individuals were offered a choice between removal with the tribe and accepting an "allotment" on their original soil. All told, the Ho-Chunk Nation underwent 11 separate removals. In addition, Winnebago removal illustrates how the process was shaped not only by national policy but also by local whites envious of Indian lands.

The Winnebagos, like the other Great Lakes tribes, experienced social and political upheaval well before the **Indian Removal Act** was passed. Indian peoples were being forced westward from the 17th century onward because of wars between tribes, competition due to the fur trade among Indian groups, war and rivalry among the French, Dutch, and English colonizers, and later, the Americans. As Indian tribes such as the Ojibwes, Potawatomis, and Ottawas pressed to the West, the Winnebagos and Menominees, the original inhabitants of Wisconsin, were forced to share land and resources. Inevitably, arguments and battles broke out, often abetted by French and English traders, trappers, and military personnel.

By the end of the War of 1812, the tribe had settled into an area that stretched from Green Bay south to north-central Illinois to the Mississippi River. When Illinois achieved statehood in 1818, white settlers began to challenge the Winnebagos for land in that state and southern Wisconsin. At the same time, the lead mines in southwestern Wisconsin and northwestern Illinois were being exploited, and miners flooded into the area, pressuring not only the Winnebagos, but the Sauks and Foxes as well. In 1815, American forces replaced the British at Green Bay, and another threat from the East now unfolded, the arrival of Indians from New York, largely backed by the U.S. government.

In 1821, the Oneidas, Stockbridges, and Brothertons approached the Menominees and the Winnebagos about purchasing land near the Fox River, adjacent to Winnebago territory. This initial contact was followed by other proposals by the New York Indians and the federal government; in the end, 6,720,000 acres were sold to eastern tribes. Although the Winnebagos were not party to the final treaties involving the eastern Indians, the latter's arrival had an immediate impact on the Ho-Chunks, as the lands they formerly shared with other Wisconsin tribes shrank. After reliable translations were furnished the tribes, the Menominees and Winnebagos rejected the treaties, saying that their interpretation of them was that the New York and Wisconsin tribes would share the land, rather than take outright owner-ship of it. Sharing had been common practice among the tribes of the west-ern Great Lakes from time immemorial. The argument was rejected by the U.S. government.

After passage of the Indian Removal Act, the federal government deter-mined to move the tribe west of the Mississippi River. The Winnebagos resisted, knowing the difficulties a woodland culture would face in being transported to the western plains. After the **Black Hawk War** ended in 1832, they were forced to cede their lands in southwestern Wisconsin and north-ern Illinois and were given the Neutral Ground or Turkey River reservation in western Iowa; some Winnebagos held out, however, and remained in Wis-consin. The Iowa area was being contested by the Sauks and the Sioux, so in 1837 the Winnebagos were removed from Iowa to northern Minnesota, near Long Prairie. Here, the government wanted to use them as a buffer between the Dakotas and Ojibwes, who were traditional enemies. Only when they received a written copy of the treaty did the Winnebagos discover that they had not been given eight years to remove, but only eight months. Many refused to leave Iowa, and others returned to Wisconsin. By 1847, however, the Ho-Chunks had left Iowa for northern Minnesota.

In 1855, the tribe was moved once again from northern to south-central Minnesota near Blue Earth, where they remained, growing their crops and living peacefully. However, when the Civil War began and many of the young Winnebagos joined the Union Army, the white settlers in the vicinity of their reservation began to complain about their presence, especially after the Sioux Uprising in 1862. In response, Abraham Lincoln issued an execu-tive order for the tribe to remove again, this time to South Dakota. They were forced to move in the dead of winter, and they reached their reserva-tion in 1863. On the way, many of the people died. In 1865, most of the tribe left South Dakota, which they found inhospitable, for Nebraska, where a reservation was created for them adjacent to Omaha lands.

All through the middle of the century, individual and small groups of Ho-Chunks returned to Wisconsin, where the federal government attempted to round them up and return them to the Nebraska reservation. Many individuals returned to their northern homelands only to find white settlers living where they had resided for centuries. In 1874, the government extended the Homestead Act to Indians, and many Winnebagos took home-steads in Wisconsin, mostly in central Wisconsin. Today, the Ho-Chunk peo-ple reside in both Nebraska and Wisconsin.

FURTHER READING: "Ho-Chunk History." At www.mpm.edu/wirp/ICW-150.html; "Ho-Chunk Nation: People of the Big Voice." At www.hochunknation .com/AboutUs.aspx; Loew, Patty. *Indian Nations in Wisconsin: Histories of Endurance and Removal.* Madison: Wisconsin Historical Society, 2001; "Treaty with the Winne-bago, 1837." Indian Affairs: Laws and Treaties. At http://digital.library.okstate .edu/kappler/Vol2/treaties/win0498.htm.

JAMES W. PARINS

Hulbutta Micco (dates unknown)

Hulbutta Micco, or Alligator King, was best known to Americans as Billy Bowlegs, the recognized Miccosukee leader in the **Third Seminole War**, and was the last hereditary chief of the Florida tribes to remove to the West. He had survived the **Second Seminole War** that ended in 1842 and, in the ensuing years, became accepted by Americans as the undisputed leader of the remaining Seminoles in Florida.

Descended from Cowkeeper, a Creek considered the founder of the Seminole tribe, he was also kin to **Miconopy**, King Payne, and King Bowlegs, all recognized leaders of the Florida Indians. However, it was not until 1839 that his leadership became known. After the major leaders of Seminole resistance had been captured or had surrendered and gone west, Hulbutta Micco along with Sam Jones and other leaders withdrew to the Big Cypress. There remnant Seminoles, Miccosukees, Creeks, and Tallahassees tried to pursue their old lifeways. In 1839, Hulbutta Micco with his warriors, along with Spanish Indians under Chekika and Hospitake, attacked troops under Col. W. S. Harney on their way to Charlotte Harbor. Harney attacked Chekika's settlement the next year, killing the chief. Sam Jones, who was a spiritual leader with great influence among the Seminoles, led them into the Everglades. There, during the next few years, Hulbutta Micco, known by then as Billy Bowlegs, grew in stature.

Engraving from a portrait of Hulbutta Micco, a Seminole chief, by 19th-century American painter Charles Bird King, from *The Indian Tribes of North America.* (McKenney, Thomas L. and James Hall. *The Indian Tribes of North America,* 1836–1844)

In 1842, Col. W. J. Worth announced the end of hostilities in the Second Seminole War and said that those who did not wish to remove could remain on lands assigned to them temporarily. The Seminoles settled on the north side of Lake Okeechobee, where they farmed and raised livestock unmolested for the next seven years (*see* **Seminole Removal**).

By 1849, Americans were beginning to encroach on the Seminoles once more. Clashes between whites and Indians became more common. For several years, Bowlegs attempted to keep the warriors in check and tried to cooperate with the Americans. Then, in 1855, when his property was destroyed by an American surveying crew, a guerilla war began that lasted until 1858.

With his followers reduced in numbers, Bowlegs finally agreed to remove to the West in the spring of 1858. He and his family and about 140 followers left Florida by steamboat on May 5 and three weeks later arrived in **Indian Territory**. While at New Orleans, he sat for a photograph and became the only major Indian leader to be photographed during removal. In December 1858, he returned to Florida and persuaded another 75 Seminoles to go to the West with him in 1859. Their arrival ended Seminole removal. By then the public sentiment supporting Indian removal had subsided. The *Arkansas*

Gazette at Little Rock not only hailed Bowlegs as a hero but also praised the Seminoles' long years of resistance against removal as a historic episode.

FURTHER READING: Covington, James W. "An Episode in the Third Seminole War." *Florida Historical Quarterly* 45 (July 1966–April 1967): 45–59; Covington, James W. "Billy Bowlegs, Sam Jones, and the Crisis of 1849." *Florida Historical Quarterly* 68, no. 3 (1990): 299–311; Foreman, Carolyn Thomas. "Billy Bowlegs." *Chronicles of Oklahoma* 33 (1955–1956): 512–532; *Harper's Weekly Magazine,* June 12, 1858; Paige, Amanda L., et al. The North Little Rock Site on the Trail of Tears National Historic Trail: Historical Contexts Report. 2003. At http://anpa.ualr.edu/trail_of_tears/ indian_removal_project/site_reports/site_reports.html; Porter, Kenneth W. "Billy Bowlegs (Halata Micco) in the Seminole Wars." *Florida Historical Quarterly* 45, no. 3 (1967): 219–242.

DANIEL F. LITTLEFIELD, JR.

Hulbutta Tustenuggee (c. 1795–?)

Hulbutta Tustenuggee, an Alachua, was sometimes called Halpatter Tustenuggee and sometimes Alligator by the whites. He has been described as a funny fellow, "a natural comedian," creating laughter even in council, yet recognized as intelligent and shrewd in dealing with the whites. Only five feet tall, his size belied his ability as a leader in Seminole resistance to removal and, after removal, as an emissary sent to encourage others to remove.

Hulbutta Tustenuggee's leadership as a resister began in 1835 in the early stages of the **Second Seminole War**. He was apparently one of the leaders who helped plan, over a period of several months, the events that set off the war: the simultaneous killing of Agent Wiley Thompson and the strike on the U.S. Army. On December 28, 1835, he led his warriors in the attack that annihilated Maj. Francis Dade's command as it marched from Fort Brook to Fort King, leaving only one survivor. A few days later, he was a leader in the attack by 250 Seminoles on Gen. D. L. Clinch's troops in the Battle of the Withlacoochee. He later engaged Gen. Edmund P. Gaines's forces on the Withlacoochee and helped hold them under siege for over a week. On March 5, 1836, he along with Jumper and Osceola tried unsuccessfully to arrange a peace by offering to retire across the Withlacoochee if the army would not molest them.

In February 1837, Alligator, **Miconopy**, and **Abraham** negotiated a truce until further talks could be held. On March 6, twenty Seminole leaders signed a surrender agreement. Although Hulbutta Tustenugee did not sign the agreement, by the following May he was among the several hundred who had gone to Fort Brooke at Tampa. In early June, however, Seminoles under Osceola and Sam Jones raided the camp and released all of the prisoners.

In December 1837, Hulbutta Tustenuggee, back in the field, commanded 120 warriors against Gen. Zachary Taylor and his troops at the Battle of Okeechobee, in which 26 Americans were killed and 112 were wounded. The Seminoles had 11 killed and 14 wounded. In March 1838, Hulbutta Tustenuggee sent word to Gen. Thomas S. **Jesup** that he wanted peace. He surrendered after Jesup guaranteed that he could retain his property, including his blacks, who had already surrendered, as well as those who were still with him. Acting as Jesup's emissaries, Abraham and Holatoochee brought in **Halleck Tustenuggee** and 88 others. Among them were John **Cavallo** and 27 other blacks.

In July 1838, Hulbutta Tustenuggee and his party of 67 left Florida for the West by way of New Orleans. From there they traveled by steamboat and experienced no difficulty until they reached Fort Coffee in **Indian Territory**, where low water on the Arkansas River forced them to travel overland to Fort Gibson. The extreme heat caused the people to suffer, but they arrived without casualties in early August.

Hulbutta Tustenuggee and his band refused to settle in the Creek Nation as the Treaty of Payne's Landing called for, but remained near Fort Gibson in the Cherokee Nation. He tried unsuccessfully to get the United States to give him a new rifle that had been promised him and farming tools that had been promised his people. As time wore on, the Cherokees began to lodge complaints against his village of nearly 500 people and its occupation of Cherokee land.

In 1841, Hulbutta Tustenuggee returned to Florida. There he headed a delegation of five other Seminoles and an interpreter whose mission was to try to convince the remaining Seminoles to remove. They convinced Tiger Tail, his brother, and 162 women and children to surrender.

In 1844, Hulbutta Tustenuggee, **Coacoochee**, and two others went to Washington to pursue their claims. His property had not been restored as promised, and the Seminoles had not been given a separate land of their own even though the military officers had assured them it was awaiting their arrival in the West. Hulbutta Tustenuggee and Coacoochee complained bitterly that slave hunters from the Cherokee and Creek Nations and the United States had made repeated attempts to take the Seminoles' blacks, many of whom had been promised freedom in the West by Jesup. The visit of the Seminole leaders to Washington resulted in orders directing negotiation of a treaty between the Seminoles and Creeks to lay the groundwork for a separate land for the Seminoles. The negotiations came to fruition in early 1845. Although **Seminole removal** was far from over, those Seminoles in the West could at least look forward to a time when they could live unmolested, a condition that most of them had never experienced.

FURTHER READING: Littlefield, Daniel F., Jr. *Africans and Seminoles: From Removal to Emancipation.* Westport, CT: Greenwood Press, 1977; Mahon, John K. *History of the Second Seminole War, 1835–1842.* Gainesville: University Press of Florida, 1967; McReynolds, Edwin C. *The Seminoles.* Norman: University of Oklahoma Press, 1957.

AMANDA L. PAIGE

Indian Removal Act (1830)

The Indian Removal Act was the culmination of political debate during the first two and a half decades of the 19th century, a divisive debate that pitted the nation's moral obligations to the Indian tribes against nationalism, greed, and racism. An agreement that the Georgians called the Georgia Compact of 1802 was the first major step toward removal, made during the administration of Thomas Jefferson. In the agreement, the United States promised to extinguish Indian land titles within the state. In exchange, Georgia sold its claims to lands that became the states of Alabama and Mississippi. Asserting its right to control affairs within its boundaries, Georgia began to push for fulfillment of the government's promise. Jefferson proposed in 1803 that Indians be encouraged to move voluntarily to the newly acquired Louisiana Purchase west of the Mississippi River. During the next two decades, some Indians did so, but the majority of tribes remained east of the river.

By the mid-1820s, Indian removal had become a hotly debated issue. Americans generally thought of Indians as "cumberers" of the earth, and the American population and economy needed room to expand in the early 19th century. Alabama and Mississippi had been admitted to the Union, and their legislatures began to exert their claim to states' rights over Indian affairs and to make stronger calls for removal of the tribes from their states. President James Monroe asked Congress for legislation to carry out Jefferson's plan, believing, like Jefferson, that the Indians faced extinction if they remained in the East and could survive only if they removed to the West. There they could have time to become "civilized" enough to live alongside Americans. Monroe's plan of voluntary removal was followed by John Quincy Adams. Forced removal policy would be left to Andrew **Jackson**.

The election of Andrew Jackson in the fall of 1828 gave the pro-removal adherents encouragement. A southerner, Jackson focused on removal of the southern tribes. The southern states gave him the support he needed to formulate a national plan. Between his election and inauguration, the legislatures of Georgia, Alabama, and Mississippi took action to extend their states' criminal and civil laws over the Indians within their borders. Jackson refused to respond to the appeals of the tribes to have the states desist. Instead, unwilling to confront the states and create a constitutional conflict concerning jurisdiction in Indian affairs, Jackson used the states' actions to push his national removal agenda forward.

The declaration by the Georgia legislature in December 1828, extending Georgia civil and criminal law over the Indians within Georgia's borders, prompted newly elected President Andrew Jackson to urge the leaders of the Cherokees and Creeks, the two largest tribes, to move their people west of the Mississippi. In a letter to them, he warned that there could be no appeal of Georgia's decision to the federal government because "the arms of this country can never be employed, to stay any state of this Union, from the exercise of [its] legitimate powers."

Rising to the aid of the southern tribes were numerous northern humanitarian groups, foremost among them the American Board of Commissioners for Foreign Missions, perhaps not coincidently the primary recipient of federal funds allocated for "civilizing" the Indians. Having been supported in his election by a large number of church groups, Jackson feared the defection of those groups and moved quickly to shore up his coalition by developing public support for Indian removal.

With the convening of the Twenty-first Congress in early December 1829, Jackson was ready to push for the enactment of legislation enabling Indian removal. In his State of the Union message of December 8, 1829, Jackson reiterated his position that the federal government could not bar the states from applying their laws to all residents within their borders, including Indians; it was a matter of sovereignty. Further, he said that it would be in the interests of the Indians to remove themselves: "Surrounded by the whites with their arts of civilization, which by destroying the resources of the savage doom him to weakness and decay, the fate of the Mohegan, the Narragansett, and the Delaware is fast overtaking the Choctaw, the Cherokee, and the Creek. That this fate surely awaits them if they remain within the limits of the States does not admit of a doubt." Jackson asked Congress for unorganized territory west of the Mississippi that would "be guaranteed to the Indian tribes as long as they shall occupy it," with each tribe having its own district to govern as it saw fit.

Each congressional chamber referred the president's requests to its committee on Indian affairs. Both of those committees were chaired by Jackson supporters from his home state of Tennessee, Senator Hugh L. White and Representative John Bell. The Senate bill was reported out on February 22, 1830, with an appropriation of $500,000, and debate was taken up on April 6. Senator Theodore Frelinghuysen of New Jersey, past president of the American Board of Commissioners for Foreign Missions, led the opposition to the bill. He began a speech on April 7 that he presented, in parts, over three days, taking six hours to deliver it. With eloquence, Frelinghuysen

Theodore Frelinghuysen, senator from New Jersey and opponent of the Indian Removal Act. (Library of Congress)

approached the proposed bill on several fronts, initially taking exception to Jacksonian Indian policy in general, branding it as corrupt in its use of bribery and intimidation against people who, through treaty obligation, were, in effect, wards of the United States. He decried the desire of the Jackson administration to "rescind, modify, or explain away, our public treaties," outlining several treaty obligations of the United States that contradicted the spirit of the proposed bill. He countered Jackson's statement that the United States could not support the Cherokees against Georgia by pointing out that President Washington had established the precedent of federal intervention under the Treaty of Hopewell in 1791. Frelinghuysen urged his fellow senators to uphold the ideals of common decency and fairness and to reject the removal of the Indians. Anti-Jackson senators Peleg Sprague of Maine and Ascher Robbins of Rhode Island both attacked the bill, pointing out that no provisions were being made for creating a hospitable home for the Indians in the West.

Senator John Forsyth, a former governor of Georgia, defended the actions of the Georgia legislature and declared the divisions over the matter of Indian removal to derive from sectionalism and the long-standing northern disregard for the individual sovereignty of the southern states. Robert Adams of Mississippi rejected the idea that the removal bill was aimed at forcibly removing the Indians, stressing that the removal was to be purely voluntary.

The Senate vote on April 24 was 28 to 19 in favor of the removal bill, with both the Jackson supporters and the anti-Jacksonians holding fast to their party lines. The Senate bill was sent to the House of Representatives on April 26, and Representative Bell withdrew his bill in favor of the Senate version. House debate began on May 14. Bell was assisted in his argument for the bill by Dixon Lewis of Alabama and Georgia congressmen Wilson Lumpkin, Richard H. Wilde, and James M. Wayne. The proponents of the bill argued that it would merely enshrine in law the accepted policy of the United States toward the Indians; they charged that the opponents of the bill were merely engaging in anti-Jackson politics. They reiterated Jackson's proposition that to let the Indians remain east of the Mississippi would result in their extinction and that removal was, in that sense, the most humane policy that could be described. The Georgia congressmen took the position that the sovereignty of Georgia could not be denied and that, regardless of the outcome of the removal bill vote, Georgia would extend its laws to cover the Cherokees and their lands. It was pointed out that the New England states had long ago dealt with their Indian "problems" and the southern and western states could not be denied the same right.

The opponents of the bill were led by William Storrs of Connecticut, Samuel F. Vinton of Ohio, and Massachusetts congressmen Edward Everett and Isaac Bates. The critics of the bill repeated the arguments made in the Senate: treaties entered into with the various Indian tribes must be upheld as the supreme law of the land and the obligations of those treaties contravened the idea of removing the Indians to the West. Bates questioned the habitability of the "Great American Desert" in the West and accused the Jackson administration of "nefarious" designs. And, although the opponents of the bill denied they were engaged in partisan grandstanding, the fact remained that Henry Clay had designs on the White House in 1832 and hoped that a prolonged and fierce debate would weaken Jackson's support in the mid-Atlantic states, where public opinion was divided.

A late amendment by Joseph Hemphill of Pennsylvania, a Jackson supporter placed in a difficult position by his anti-removal Quaker constituents, proposed that the matter of implementation of removal be delayed by a year to allow a commission time to clarify the manner of removal and the disposition of the tribes in the West. The vote on the amendment ended in a 98–98 tie with Speaker of the House Andrew Stevenson, a Jackson man, breaking the tie in opposition to the amendment.

The vote was called on May 26 with a result of 102 to 97 in favor of the bill, and it was returned to the Senate for reconciliation. Certain of victory, the Senate supporters of Jackson refused to yield to late assaults on the bill, including an amendment to restrict its application to Georgia, and the bill was sent to President Jackson for his signature on May 28, 1830.

Georgia's aggressive assault on Cherokee sovereignty had resulted in legislation that was potentially destructive to all tribes east of the Mississippi. Titled "An Act to provide for an exchange of lands with the Indians residing in any of the states or territories, and for their removal west of the river Mississippi," the Indian Removal Act, as it came to be called, gave the president authority to assign districts west of the Mississippi, not included in any state or territory, to tribes who chose to exchange their present lands and move there. The United States was obligated to extinguish any claims of western tribes to the established districts. The act guaranteed any removed tribe the right to its new lands; the government would issue a patent to any tribe that preferred one, provided that the land revert to the United States if the tribe became extinct or left it. The Indians were to be reimbursed for the improvements they lost in moving, and the government would provide aid during removal and subsistence during the year following removal. The act guaranteed the tribes protection from other tribes or individuals who might intrude upon them, and it continued the superintendence of Indian affairs as practiced in the East. Finally, the act appropriated $500,000 to carry out the provisions of the law.

Although the Indian Removal Act called for voluntary removal, Jackson used it as a device to coerce tribes into negotiating removal agreements and as a justification of the forced removal of tribes who resisted, such as the Sauks and Foxes, the Creeks, the Seminoles, and the Cherokees. A brief, simple piece of legislation, the Indian Removal Act ranks with the General Allotment Act of 1887 and Public Law 280 of 1953 as one of the three most devastating legislative assaults on Indian society passed by Congress.

FURTHER READING: *Register of Debates in Congress*. Vol. 6, pts. 1 and 2. Washington, DC: Gales and Seaton, 1830; Satz, Ronald L. *American Indian Policy in the Jacksonian Era*. Lincoln: University of Nebraska Press, 1975.

TONY R. ROSE

Indian Territory

"Indian Territory" is a term that gained currency after the removal period and today is used almost exclusively to refer to lands occupied in the 19th century by the so-called Five Civilized Tribes in the eastern half of present-day Oklahoma. By 1830, when the **Indian Removal Act** became law, areas west of Missouri and Arkansas were widely accepted as the region to which tribes would be removed. As early as 1823, Baptist missionary Isaac **McCoy** had advocated such a territory specifically for removed tribes, who could be organized into a territory of their own, and published a tract on the subject in 1827. A late amendment during debate on the Indian Removal Act had called for a commission to clarify the manner of removal and the disposition of the tribes in the West. In 1832, the House of Representatives created a commission to travel among the tribes, study their condition, and make recommendations for changes. The commission consisted of Montfort Stokes, chair, John F. **Schermerhorn**, and Henry L. **Ellsworth**, who recommended, among other things, that an Indian Territory be created under a governmental structure to ensure peace among the tribes, especially in the wake of removal. A bill for creating the western territory was introduced in Congress but failed to pass. The Indian Intercourse Act of 1834 officially designated all of the lands west of the Mississippi and not in the states of Missouri and Louisiana or the Territory of Arkansas as "Indian Country," in which removed tribes would settle. The act sought to safeguard against some of the evils that had plagued the tribes prior to removal: intrusion by whites, unregulated trade, whiskey traffic, and others. In 1849, Ojibwe Methodist minister George Copway proposed an Indian state between the Big Sioux and Missouri Rivers where the remnant tribes of the Old Northwest, especially Michigan, Wisconsin, and Iowa, could be placed. But Indian Territory would shrink rather than expand. **Kansas** and Nebraska Territories were established in 1854, and the term no longer applied to them but referred to Indian lands in what is now Oklahoma.

FURTHER READING: Abel, Annie Heloise. "The History of Events Resulting in Indian Consolidation West of the Mississippi." In *Annual Report of the American Historical Association for the Year 1906*. Vol. 1. Washington, DC, 1908, pp. 233–450; Copway, George. *Organization of a New Indian Territory, East of the Missouri River*.

Arguments and Reasons Submitted to the Honorable Members of the Senate and House of Representatives of the 31st Congress of the United States. New York, 1850; Everett, Dianna. "McCoy, Isaac (1784–1846)." 2009. At http://digital.library.okstate.edu/ency clopedia/entries/M/MC014.html; Satz, Ronald N. *American Indian Policy in the Jacksonian Era.* Lincoln: University of Nebraska Press, 1975; Schultz, George A. *An Indian Canaan: Isaac McCoy and the Vision of an Indian State.* Norman: University of Oklahoma Press, 1972.

DANIEL F. LITTLEFIELD, JR.

Indiana and Indian Removal

Indiana Territory was established in 1800. At that time the lands were controlled by various tribes, with the majority held by the Potawatomis and Miamis. The Shawnees and Delawares also established a large presence in the state after the Treaty of Greenville in 1795 (*see* **Delaware Removal**; **Miami Removal**; **Potawatomi Removal**). At the beginning of the 19th century, the American settlements were limited to the southern part of the territory, close to the Ohio River. William Henry Harrison, as territorial governor, also served as the U.S. commissioner plenipotentiary to the Indian tribes north of the Ohio River and chief land cession negotiator. During his term as territorial and state governor, Harrison efficiently implemented Jefferson's removal plans.

In 1818, Indiana achieved statehood. The new governor of the state, Jonathan Jennings, quickly negotiated the Treaty of St. Mary's in 1818. This treaty is significant because it identified and granted private reserves for individual Miami leaders. The private landholdings were a reward for their loyalties to the United States against Tecumseh and Tenskwatawa as well as their allegiance to the United States in the War of 1812. The Miamis cited the Treaty of St. Mary's and their acceptance of the federal civilization programs to avoid removal after 1832.

By 1822, the federal government had abandoned the factory system, and the last agency in the state at Fort Wayne transitioned into a land office. At that time the Miami and Potawatomi tribes together claimed over 6 million acres of land in northern Indiana. In the absence of the federal factory system, private traders moved into the area and transformed the Indian trade. After the War of 1812, the fur trade decreased dramatically. Trade based on credit quickly increased, and both the Miamis and Potawatomis were drawn into an economic system backed by the federal government. Indian traders confidently extended credit to the tribes, knowing that their debts were secured by the federal government.

As a result of increasing pressures from settlers and the accrued debts, the Miamis ceded most of their lands and were restricted to the private reserves previously negotiated. The Potawatomis also ceded a majority of their lands in the state. The 1826 treaties are particularly significant because they set a precedent for the treaties that followed. The treaties specifically set aside specific amounts for payment of debts. The debts were to be paid to the federal government, using the purchase monies for the Potawatomi and Miami lands. This gave the private traders incredible leverage over the tribes and the federal government. As long as they profited from Indian trade and indebtedness, they attempted to subvert the removal of the Miamis and Potawatomis. When federal legislation left no doubt that the Indians would be removed, the traders acquiesced to the terms of the debt repayments. The federal government allowed the traders to encourage indebtedness with the land cessions as the desired end. The merchants were unscrupulous in their dealings with the tribes, selling goods at greatly inflated prices. Although the federal government did make some weak attempts to investigate some of their fraudulent practices, it generally endorsed the results. Between 1834 and 1846, the Potawatomis and Miamis signed treaties that traded all of their tribally held lands for reservations in Kansas, paid their debts to the traders at Fort Wayne, and provided annual annuities in goods, services, and cash.

The **Indian Removal Act** of 1830 was a relatively anticlimactic event in the state of Indiana. Removal as experienced by Indian peoples in Indiana can be better characterized by the federal government's economic policies toward Indians, rather than by the legal policies used to justify the better-known removal of the southeastern tribes. By the removal period, the majority of Indians living in the state's boundaries had voluntarily left the state for Missouri, Canada, and Kansas. The questionably voluntary motivation of the majority of removals was due to land cessions made through treaties prior to the enactment of the federal legislation. The majority of tribes that signed land cession treaties before 1830 did so to pay off debts to private traders and the federal government. The Indians incurred the debts as a direct result of Thomas Jefferson's scheme to encourage the federal control and consolidation of all trade with the Indians in the Northwest Territory through the factory system and the appointment of Indian agents.

The plan to force a peaceable cession of Indian lands and encourage relocation in the West was largely enacted by the territorial governor William Henry Harrison. Between 1803 and 1826, the majority of lands claimed by the Indian tribes in Indiana were ceded to the federal government. Most of the Wea, Kickapoo, Delaware, and Shawnee peoples had voluntarily relocated before the Indian Removal Act (*see* **Kickapoo Removal**; **Peoria-Kaskaskia-Piankeshaw-Wea Removal**; **Shawnee Removal from Ohio**). Only the Miamis and Potawatomis living in the northern part of the state remained when the legislation was signed into law. By 1846, the federal government had gained control of all Indian lands in the state. The majority of Miamis relocated voluntarily, but only the Potawatomis were forcibly removed by the army in what is now known as the Trail of Death. Many Miami families were allowed to stay on lands privately owned and negotiated through treaties. Eventually these lands were all lost over subsequent generations.

The Trail of Death story of the Potawatomis in Indiana is the only story of federally enforced removal in the state. Potawatomi leaders negotiated two treaties in October 1832, ceding most of their remaining lands in exchange for reserves and annual annuities. American agent A. C. Pepper negotiated a series of treaties with the individual bands (four in 1834 and eight in 1836) to cede their reserves and agree to removal. Once this was done, a collective agreement with five bands was signed in February 1837 at Washington, D.C. The chiefs signed, but there was widespread resistance to this agreement. Menominee and his band at Twin Lakes, Indiana, refused to sign any of the treaties. He traveled to Washington to protest the treaty he never signed, but President Van Buren refused to see him. Confronted by government agents at a meeting in July 1838, he still refused to sign or leave Indiana.

In 1838, Indiana governor David Wallace sent Gen. John Tipton to force removal. He arrived at Menominee's village on August 30 and arrested every Potawatomi at the site. Menominee was thrown into a caged wagon. The soldiers burned the village, and on September 4, 859 Potawatomis departed on what is now commemorated as the "Trail of Death." Fewer than 700 Potawatomis arrived at Osawatomie, Kansas, in November.

FURTHER READING: Cayton, Andrew R. L. *Frontier Indiana.* Bloomington: Indiana University Press, 1996; Gernhardt, Phyllis. "Justice and Public Policy: Indian Trade, Treaties, and Removal from Northern Indiana, 1826–1846." In *The Boundaries between Us: Natives and Newcomers along the Frontiers of the Old Northwest Territory, 1750–1850.* Ed. Daniel P. Barr. Kent, OH: Kent State University Press, 2007, pp. 178–195; Horsman, Reginald. *Expansion and American Indian Policy, 1783–1812.* East Lansing: Michigan State University Press, 1967; Owens, Robert M. *Mr. Jefferson's Hammer: William Henry Harrison and the Origin of American Indian Policy.* Norman: University of Oklahoma Press, 2007; Wallace, Anthony F. C. *Jefferson and the Indians: The Tragic Fate of the First Americans.* Cambridge, MA: Harvard University Press, 1999.

DAWN G. MARSH

Ishtehotopa (c. 1800–c. 1850)

The last hereditary Chickasaw minko, Ishtehotopa played a major role in preserving unity among the Chickasaws during the removal period. Traditionally, the minko, whom Europeans called "king," was the ranking leader, chosen from the beloved family, or hereditary ruling clan. Succession was matrilineal: brother to brother or maternal uncle to nephew. Ishtehotopa became minko in 1820, succeeding Chehopistee.

By then pressure for removal was mounting, and Chickasaw government had changed. Much authority of government rested with Levi **Colbert** and, before him, his brothers William and George. Ishtehotopa was minko for only a decade before Mississippi and Alabama extended their laws over Chickasaw lands and forbade the exercise of tribal government (*see* **Alabama and Removal**; **Mississippi and Removal**).

After 1834, Ishtehotopa and other Chickasaw leaders governed through the seven-member Chickasaw Commission, created by the Washington Articles of Convention and Agreement, which adjusted the **Treaty of Pontotoc** (*see* **Chickasaw Removal**). They oversaw the survey of Chickasaw land and its allotment preparatory to removal. At removal, they oversaw the sale of individual allotments and determined if the holders were competent to do business and, therefore, to manage the money they received for their allotments. From 1834 until removal, the commission, headed by Ishtehotopa, managed Chickasaw affairs: overseeing the liquidation of their tribal estate, handling the Nation's financial affairs, and dealing with the federal government regarding removal to the West. After a majority of the Chickasaws had removed, beginning in 1837, Ishtehotopa removed in 1838 at the head of a party of 129 people, traveling overland by way of Memphis, Tennessee; Little Rock, Arkansas; and Fort Towson in the Choctaw Nation. His wife, known at the time as "Queen of the Chickasaws," died on the trail at Little Rock.

The Chickasaw Commission continued as the de facto government until the Chickasaws began electing a district chief to represent them in the Choctaw national council in 1841. Besides dealing with the federal government and handling financial affairs, the commission worked to unify their people in the West, encouraging those who had remained behind to remove and paying their removal expenses out of the national coffers.

As the Chickasaws began to reestablish themselves, the beginnings of a political rift emerged. Many Chickasaws sought a revival of the traditional government led by the hereditary minko and chiefs. Others leaned toward the election of public officials. In 1845, to avoid a rift, Ishtehotopa and the other six commissioners resigned, a major factor in preserving unity in the Nation. With the authority of the commission gone, sentiment for a constitutional government grew during the following decade, leading to the establishment of an elected government in 1856.

Decline of the minko's role in society became evident. From 1845 until 1848, Ishtehotopa's name as "king" appeared at the top of the list of signers on documents. In 1848, however, his name began to appear lower in the list, signed as "captain." His name did not appear on public documents in subsequent years.

FURTHER READING: Atkinson, James. *Splendid Land, Splendid People.* Tuscaloosa: University of Alabama Press, 2004; Childers, Gary, ed. "The Last of the Chickasaw Kings." 2008. At www.chickasaw.net.

DANIEL F. LITTLEFIELD, JR.

J

Jackson, Andrew (1767–1845)

During his two terms as president, Andrew Jackson and his administration oversaw the majority of removals that were carried out under provisions of the **Indian Removal Act** of 1830. On the one hand, Jackson has been glorified as an American hero for his military campaigns against Indians and the British; on the other hand, he has been vilified for his execution of Indian removal policy. In recent decades, scholars have attempted to rehabilitate his tarnished image by dubbing him a humanitarian who saved the Indians from certain extinction or a man who was simply following the will of the people. Although his intent may be debated, there is no question that he condoned, or abetted through inaction, a process of removal that could hardly be called humane.

Indian removal was in many ways the capstone event of Jackson's public career. During his early years as a solicitor, Tennessee state senator, U.S. congressman and senator, judge, commander of Tennessee troops in the Creek war of 1813, commander of the U.S. Army at the Battle of New Orleans in 1815, invader of Florida in 1817, territorial governor of Florida, and U.S. senator once more in 1823–1825, Jackson established a political base that led to his election as president in 1828. He served from 1829 to 1837, a majority of the years often called the "removal period." Along the way, Jackson acquired an army of political allies who proved useful to him in executing the Indian Removal Act.

Indian removal was a divisive public issue when Jackson took office. Steps toward removal had progressed through every administration from Jefferson on. President James Monroe, through his secretary of war John C. Calhoun, formulated a plan for removal based on voluntary emigration of the tribes. The policy had some successes with parties of Choctaws, Cherokees, Creeks, New York tribes, and others who voluntarily went to the West. The southern states looked at Jackson's election as a chance to rid their lands of

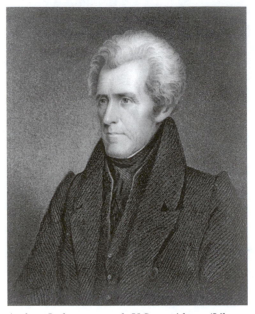

Andrew Jackson, seventh U.S. president. (Library of Congress)

Indians. To force the issue, Georgia, Alabama, and Mississippi extended their jurisdiction over the Indian tribes within their boundaries before he took office.

As sentiment built for Indian removal, Americans were split over the issue, but Andrew Jackson was not conflicted. He entered the presidency with a single-minded focus on removal and with the intent to achieve it. In his first annual message to Congress in late 1829, he urged legislation to establish an **Indian Territory** west of the Mississippi, and although he argued that removal should be voluntary, he insisted that those tribes who refused to leave the states east of the Mississippi should be subjected to the laws of the states. Congress was also divided over the issue. Jackson worked hard in behalf of removal legislation, which passed by a narrow margin in May 1830. Nevertheless, Jackson considered the act a mandate, and he quickly abandoned previous administrations' encouragement of voluntary emigration and endorsed a policy of aggressive execution of the **Indian Removal Act**, by force if necessary. However, because anti-removal politicians and others argued that removal would violate existing treaties, Jackson adopted the tactic of negotiating new treaties that included the removal provisions. During the 1830s about 70 such treaties were negotiated.

Jackson's obsession with preserving the Union and blunting **nullification** arguments in the southern states resulted in many of the atrocities associated with removal. He agreed with the states' desire to remove all of the Indians from within their boundaries, and he was willing to ignore or violate treaty promises to achieve this removal. He refused to give the Indians any relief from the extension of state laws over their territories and to remove intruders from their lands, despite treaty promises to do so. He chose to ignore the tribes' pleas and to violate treaty stipulations rather than to risk angering the states. His administration's inaction led to mounting debts, civil claims, loss of property, criminal activity, and displacement of tribal people, often creating a chaotic scene in which the Indians were demoralized and at times resorted to arms, as the Seminoles did in Florida in 1835 and the Creeks did in Alabama in 1836. Perhaps Jackson's best-known attempt to blunt a nullification movement was his siding with Georgia in the Cherokee cases in the early 1830s.

Jackson's concerns for national security caused his administration to ignore the unabated, large-scale **land speculation** with its fraud and graft that attended Indian removal. He wanted Americans to populate the southern states as a bulwark against possible invasion or intrigue by foreign powers, as had occurred during the Revolutionary War and the War of 1812. If speculation ultimately led to farmers' acquisition of Indian lands, Jackson could condone any evils that attended it. Of course, speculation in Indian land in Tennessee and Alabama had contributed significantly to Jackson's wealth before he reached the presidency, and he continued to speculate in land during and after his presidency.

The widespread political patronage that attended Jackson's administration contributed to many of the hardships and much of the victimization experienced by Indian people during their removals to the West. Jackson's close friends, political allies, and relatives such as John H. **Eaton** and John **Coffee** negotiated removal treaties, and his orders were to use what was necessary to get a treaty: exaggeration, threats, or bribes. From Secretary Eaton and Commissioner of Indian Affairs Carey Harris in the War Department down to local agents, suppliers of goods and services, and removal conductors, Jackson's friends, their associates and relatives, and his political supporters oversaw the day-to-day business of removal as exemplified by the brothers of Robert Armstrong, the apple of Jackson's eye. This kind of patronage created an atmosphere in which corruption and fraud could, and did, blossom, like that involving rations for newly arrived Indians in the Indian Territory.

Finally, Jackson was not hesitant to call out the army to enforce removal, as he did with **Black Hawk** and his followers, the Creeks, the Seminoles, and the Cherokees. Jackson's preference was to use regular troops rather than local militias in the removal process. A strong argument might be made that removal created a reason for enlarging the army, which had low enlistments at the beginning of the removal period. For the most part, however, removal was carried out by state militias, sometimes under army command and sometimes not. In general, such units were made up of men who cared little for Indians, and these men perpetrated most of the atrocities commonly cited regarding removal.

Andrew Jackson was not an Indian hater as he is often depicted. He used Indian removal as a way of not only satisfying his constituents but also addressing some of his larger national concerns, such as averting nullification and providing national security. Whatever his personal motives, Jackson's actions or lack of action and his political patronage left removed tribes with a legacy of violence, deprivation, and social discontinuity that looms large in tribal histories. Even a cursory knowledge of the process of removal leaves little room to argue that Jackson was a humanitarian.

FURTHER READING: Jackson, Andrew. *Correspondence of Andrew Jackson.* Ed. John Spencer Bassett. Washington, DC: Carnegie Institution of Washington, 1926–1935; Reprint, Kraus, 1969; Remini, Robert V. *Andrew Jackson and His Indian Wars.* New York: Viking, 2001; Satz, Ronald N. *American Indian Policy in the Jacksonian Era.* Lincoln: University of Nebraska Press, 1975.

DANIEL F. LITTLEFIELD, JR.

Jesup, Thomas S. (1788–1860)

Brigadier Gen. Thomas S. Jesup had been quartermaster general of the United States for 12 years when the **Indian Removal Act** became law. A master at military logistics, he was less than stellar when he was dealing directly with Indians in a war setting. When some of the Creeks rebelled against Creek removal in 1836 (*see* **Muscogee [Creek] Removal**), Andrew **Jackson** dispatched him to take command of troops in Alabama. After the collapse of the Creek rebellion in the summer of 1836, Jesup moved on to Florida to engage the Seminoles, who were resisting removal.

During the two years of his Florida command, Jesup brought in hundreds of Seminoles and their black allies for removal to Creek lands in the West. Struck early on by the large number of African-descended warriors in the field with the Seminoles—slaves of the Indians, free blacks, and runaways from the states—Jesup concluded that he was fighting a "negro" and not an Indian war. Because much of the American pro-removal argument in Florida was based on fear of the large number of enclaves of blacks in Seminole country, Jesup saw an opportunity to solve two problems at once. In early 1838, he promised to send those blacks who surrendered to the West to be settled as free people in a village of their own. Large numbers surrendered. Deprived of much of their support in the field and at home, the Seminoles' ability to make war was much diminished.

Jesup's methods of bringing in Seminoles were questionable. On three occasions he invited tribal leaders to come in for talks under flags of truce. On all these occasions he violated the rules of war by taking the leaders captive, including Philip, **Coacoochee** (Wildcat), Osceola, **Coe Hadjo**, John **Cavallo**, **Miconopy**, Cloud, Tuskegee, and Nocose Yohola. The last four had come in under a truce arranged by a delegation of Cherokees, led by Chief John **Ross**, who were outraged by Jesup's actions. The well-known Osceola died in prison, but Coacoochee and John Cavallo escaped to continue the fight.

By his acts of treachery, Jesup shares a large measure of blame for the continued resistance by the Seminoles. An investigation of his behavior was launched by Congress in 1838. His reputation survived it, but the issue dogged him for two decades. After his command ended in Florida, Jesup returned to his quartermaster general's post and served there until his death.

FURTHER READING: "Brigadier General Thomas S. Jesup." 2009. At www.qmfound .com/BG_Thomas_Jesup.htm; Littlefield, Daniel F., Jr. *Africans and Seminoles: From Removal to Emancipation.* Westport, CT: Greenwood Press, 1977; Mahon, John K. *History of the Second Seminole War, 1835–1842.* Gainesville: University Press of Florida, 1967; U.S. Congress. House. *Captured Negroes.* 25th Cong., 3rd sess., 1839. H. Doc. 225. Serial 348; U.S. Congress. House. *Jesup's Conduct of the War.* 25th Cong., 2d sess., 1838. H. Doc. 219. Serial 328; U.S. Congress. House. *Memorial of the Cherokee Mediators.* 25th Cong., 2d sess., 1838. H. Doc. 285. Serial 328.

DANIEL F. LITTLEFIELD, JR.

Jim Boy

See Tustenuggee Emathla

John Horse

See Cavallo, John

Jones, Evan (1788–1872)

Evan Jones, born in Wales and educated in London, had immigrated to the United States at age 33 and settled in Philadelphia. He became a teacher and was well versed in several languages, including his native Welsh and the clergyman's staples, Latin, Greek, and Hebrew. Jones and his wife Elizabeth were members of a Baptist church whose pastor, Thomas Roberts, was recruited by the Baptist Foreign Mission Board to become a missionary to the Cherokees at their newly established outpost at Valley Towns. Roberts, in turn, enlisted several of his parishioners, including the Joneses, to accompany him, and the group traveled to the Cherokee Nation in September 1821. Jones remained with the Cherokees for the rest of his life.

From the beginning of his missionary work, Jones recognized that he and his colleagues would never reach the full bloods until they had learned their language. Accordingly, he set about learning it from his Cherokee neighbors. Finding the language very difficult, he was further hampered in his effort by the lack of teachers and any kind of learning materials. With the conversion of bilingual Cherokee John Timson in 1823, however, he gained a tutor and began to make significant progress. Jones went on to translate the Bible and other tracts into Cherokee over his long career with the Indians, setting up a press and publishing a newspaper for a time in **Indian Territory** after **Cherokee removal**. While in the eastern Nation, Jones was posted by the American Baptist Foreign Mission Board to work among the mainly full-blood communities in the Valley Towns of North Carolina. He maintained contact with his fellow missionaries in Georgia, however, linked by their joint interest in linguistic study as well as missionary work.

As the threat of removal for the Cherokees increased in the late 1820s, Jones was adamantly opposed to the imposition of this policy. Jones joined the missionary group gathered at Samuel A. **Worcester**'s house in 1830 to draft and sign a manifesto denouncing removal policy and continued to express his view vocally after that time. In this, he took an opposing line to that of the Baptist mission board, an unusual stance for an individual missionary, who, after all, relied on the board's financial support to carry out his work. The board, influenced by Isaac **McCoy** and others sympathetic to Andrew **Jackson**'s plans to drive the tribes into lands west of the Mississippi, argued with Jones, but after a trip to the East on which the missionary appeared before its members, the board came around to his way of thinking.

The anti-removal position that Jones defended with vigor in the early 1830s continued unabated until the Cherokees were forced to leave their lands in the Southeast in 1838. Jones acted as assistant conductor of Situwakee's contingent of an estimated 1,300 Cherokees who traveled overland to the West in the fall of 1838. Their journey took them through Tennessee, Kentucky, southern Illinois, Missouri, and northwestern Arkansas to Indian Territory. Jones apparently did much of the work as leader, for the group was often referred to as Jones's party. Jones's stance against removal earned the respect and gratitude of Principal Chief John **Ross** and his followers, and the two men had a close relationship until Ross's death. Even after Ross's passing, Jones and his son John continued to have influence in the Cherokee Nation, especially among the full bloods. Jones died in the Cherokee Nation in 1872.

FURTHER READING: Faught, Herry L., III. "Evan Jones." Encyclopedia of Oklahoma. 2009. At http://digital.libary.okstate.edu/encyclopedia/entries/J/JO019.html; McLoughlin, William C. *Champions of the Cherokees: Evan and John B. Jones.* Princeton, NJ: Princeton University Press, 1990; McLoughlin, William C. *The Cherokees and Christianity, 1794–1870: Essays on Acculturation and Cultural Persistence.* Athens: University of Georgia Press. 1994; McLoughlin, William C. *Cherokees and Missionaries, 1789–1839.* New Haven, CT: Yale University Press, 1984.

JAMES W. PARINS

K

Kansas Territory and Indian Removal

With passage of the Kansas-Nebraska Act in May 1854, Congress established borders around a territory that for almost three decades had become the destination for eastern Indians removed from the Old Northwest. Although Kansas Territory became the center of a dramatic struggle between pro- and antislavery forces from 1854 to 1861, it was also home to thousands of Indians who then faced the possibility of another removal. Kansas was a territory for nearly seven years before it became a state, and during that short period the Indian residents of the territory faced tremendous pressure to give up their lands and relocate south to Indian Territory.

The congressional legislation that created Kansas Territory was largely the work of Stephen Douglas, an Illinois senator who hoped to encourage the construction of railroad routes to the West Coast. Because debates over the western territories had begun well before 1854, bureaucrats in the Office of Indian Affairs knew that it would be necessary to obtain Indian land cessions from those Native communities living in the region along the western border of Missouri. In 1853, Commissioner of Indian Affairs George Manypenny sent word to the Delawares, Shawnees, Wyandots, and others that they would need to send delegates to Washington, D.C., to talk to American officials about their reserves. Despite some initial protests, most tribes sent representatives to negotiate with Manypenny and his subordinates. The treaties that followed these talks eventually resulted in other Indian removals and opened up millions of acres of land to white settlers.

Although the Indians living in Kansas Territory did not cede all of their lands in the treaties signed in 1854 and 1855, they still had a difficult time holding on to their homes. Under their 1854 accord, two bands of Shawnees retained a communal reserve, even as other Shawnees received small sections of land through allotment. The Delawares surrendered 1 million acres located north of the Kansas River but still held on to a communal reserve that measured 10 miles by 40 miles. Within six years, however, so many non-Indians had ignored the reservation boundaries and established homes on the Delaware lands that Delaware leaders requested a new treaty that would divide their lands into individual plots for tribal members. Many Shawnee people had lost their allotments to squatters or through fraudulent land deals.

Thousands of white settlers had rushed into Kansas Territory both to claim land and to support the efforts to make Kansas a slave or free state. Delawares, Shawnees, and other Indians were caught in the middle of an ideological and geographical battle. For example, Reverend Thomas Johnson, the head of the Methodist mission on the Shawnee reserve, turned the Indian Manual Labor School into a headquarters for the pro-slavery side. Abelard Guthrie, a white man married to a Wyandot woman, helped found the town of Quindaro to provide a landing point on the Kansas River for abolitionists. But the Indians did not stay out of these battles. Among the Wyandots the debates over slavery led to attacks on both the Southern and Northern Methodist Episcopal Churches on their reserve. Several Shawnees wrote letters to the Office of Indian Affairs protesting the presence of slaves in a territory located north of the Missouri Compromise line.

Despite the prominence of this battle over slavery, however, the Indian residents of Kansas Territory ultimately had to fight over ownership of their land. Through a variety of means, hundreds of thousands of acres of Indian lands, beyond those ceded in the official treaties, changed hands. Indian Rings—loose affiliations of businessmen, private citizens, Indian agents, and territorial officials—facilitated this exchange in an effort to promote the growth of the territory and the removal of Indians. In addition, some wealthier Indians became involved in real estate speculation to profit from these same circumstances.

The creation of Kansas Territory opened up a new chapter in the national debate over slavery in the mid-19th century. But it also initiated another episode of American expansion that placed tremendous pressure on the Indians who only decades earlier had been removed from their homes in the Great Lakes region. As a result of these developments, by the time Kansas became a state, thousands of Indians who had lived in the territory had either moved south to **Indian Territory** or were on the verge of losing their lands in the region.

FURTHER READING: Bowes, John P. *Exiles and Pioneers: Eastern Indians in the Trans-Mississippi West.* New York: Cambridge University Press, 2007; Herring, Joseph B. *The Enduring Indians of Kansas: A Century and a Half of Acculturation.* Lawrence: University Press of Kansas, 1990; Miner, Craig, and William Unrau. *The End of Indian Kansas: A Study of Cultural Revolution, 1854–1871.* Reprint ed. Lawrence: University Press of Kansas, 1990; Unrau, William E. *The Rise and Fall of Indian Country, 1825–1855.* Lawrence: University Press of Kansas, 2007.

JOHN P. BOWES

Kaskaskia Removal

See Peoria-Kaskaskia-Piankeshaw-Wea Removal

Kennekuk (dates unknown)

Kennekuk, or the Kickapoo Prophet, was a spiritual leader of the tribe who, because of his pacifist views and willingness to assimilate the white practices he saw as useful, was disliked by many of his Nation and was, to some extent, ostracized. He claimed to be a mystic with supernatural powers and as such was revered by about 250 followers from the Indiana and Illinois Kickapoos whom he led into exile. He established a village on the Vermillion River in Illinois, where he taught his people the tenets of his religion. This creed advocated a virtuous life, promising that those who avoided conflict and obeyed the laws, remained sober, and abandoned their tribal religious practices would live in peace and harmony in an abundant land.

The Kickapoo Treaty of 1819 provided for land cessions in Illinois and Indiana and removal of the Nation to southwestern Missouri and later to Kansas (*see* **Kickapoo Removal**). Kennekuk and his band, however, did not move; they chose a path of passive resistance, meeting the government's insistence that they remove with polite excuses. Kennekuk and William **Clark** carried on a correspondence during this time, and at least once a year the Prophet visited the official at St. Louis, where they discussed the band's removal.

In 1832, after the **Black Hawk War**, Clark became more insistent. White settlers were lobbying local, state, and federal officials for the removal of all the Indians to lands west of the Mississippi and were demanding enforcement of the recently enacted **Indian Removal Act**. Although Kennekuk had maintained peaceful relations with his white neighbors, his band was included in the blanket call for removal. Finally, in 1833, Kennekuk saw that removal was inevitable and led his band west out of Illinois.

Kennekuk and his followers settled in Kansas, establishing their own village separate from that of Kishko, the Kickapoo chief who had formerly lived with his people on Kickapoo land on the Osage River in Missouri. With the Treaty of Castor Hill of 1832, the tribe had ceded its lands in Illinois and Missouri for land in Kansas. The two Kickapoo villages went in distinctly different directions, with Kennekuk preaching his assimilationist message, while Kishko's larger contingent resisted most things white. The treaty had promised farming implements and the services of a blacksmith, and whereas these were rejected by Kishko and his "Southern Kickapoos," Kennekuk's village of "Northern Kickapoos" embraced them. Kennekuk continued to preach his religion, attracting the attention of Isaac **McCoy**, who called him a "fraud" because he didn't embrace traditional Christianity. However, McCoy tolerated Kennekuk because of the "progress" his people were making. Kennekuk conducted meetings in surrounding Indian communities that resembled Baptist and Methodist revival gatherings, and in time, his religion attracted the attention of a number of Potawatomis and people from other tribes. By 1844, so many Potawatomis had intermarried with the Kickapoos that Kennekuk proposed to the commissioner of Indian affairs that they come together as one nation. As the federal government had no objection, articles of agreement were drawn up in 1851 in which annuities and other resources were to be shared. This merger drove a deeper wedge between the "Northern" and "Southern" Kickapoos because the former resented the Potawatomis sharing in their annuities, income from land sales, and other resources.

FURTHER READING: Gibson, Arrell M. *The Kickapoos: Lords of the Middle Border.* Norman: University of Oklahoma Press, 1963; "Kiikaapoi (Kickapoo) History." Kansas Kickapoo Tribe. 2009. At http://ktik-nsn.gov/history.htm; Wright, Muriel. *A Guide to the Indian Tribes of Oklahoma.* Norman: University of Oklahoma Press, 1951.

JAMES W. PARINS

Keokuk (c. 1780–1848)

Keokuk was a leader of the Sauks and Mesquakies (Foxes) during the time leading up to and following their removal from their lands in Illinois and Iowa (*see* **Sauk and Mesquakie [Fox] Removal**). Groomed as a leader by William **Clark**, Keokuk rose to prominence in 1821 when he went with a delegation to deliver to the white authorities at St. Louis two Indian prisoners accused of killing a Frenchman. Keokuk had years before established himself as an orator in his councils and was known as a crafty politician. At St. Louis, he lived up to his reputation by entering into an agreement beforehand with Clark that Keokuk would turn the prisoners over voluntarily without being ordered to do so by the white man. Keokuk thus saved face for himself and his people and increased his own political stock among the Indians. After this incident, he became one of the chief negotiators with the Americans. Recognizing his cupidity, Clark gave Keokuk gifts of money and goods.

Animosity grew between Keokuk and the older Sauk leader and hero **Black Hawk** as pressure to remove increased. Black Hawk adamantly refused to remove or to enter into talks concerning such a possibility, whereas Keokuk was more accommodating to the whites. This was true in part because Keokuk had become close to the whites, had traveled far in their country to the east, and understood the strength that lay in their numbers and wealth. However, Keokuk angered many of his people when, during the 1832 treaty negotiations under Winfield **Scott**, the Americans made him a "chief" even though Keokuk did not belong to a clan from

Sauk chief Keokuk, 1780–1848. (Smithsonian American Art Museum, Washington, DC / Art Resource, NY)

which the Sauks and Mesquakies traditionally chose their headmen. The Americans were employing a tactic they used repeatedly in dealing with the Indians: taking a friendly or compliant tribal member and elevating him to a powerful position in which he was not recognized by his people. These "treaty chiefs," as they became known, often signed away the lands and rights of the people they putatively represented. Keokuk was instrumental in ceding Sauk and Mesquakie lands east of the Mississippi.

After the **Black Hawk War**, Keokuk, true to form, delivered Neapope, one of Black Hawk's lieutenants, and several other warriors from the band, to the Americans. After Black Hawk's capture at the Bad Axe River in Wisconsin, he and his chief followers were led as captives to Jefferson Barracks in St. Louis. When they returned to Illinois, custody of Black Hawk was turned over to Keokuk, and the older man resented it bitterly.

After the tribe's removal to Iowa, Keokuk was in the seat of power. Because this fact was resented by many of his people, the chief selected a group of 30 to 40 warriors to serve as his private "army" and to protect him against any hostile individuals, giving them special privileges, clothing, and money in payment for their services. The private army led to further resentment against the chief. In 1837, Keokuk was ordered to Washington to negotiate a land dispute between the Sioux tribes and the Sauks and Mesquakies. Shrewdly, Keokuk made Black Hawk a member of the delegation so that he did not plot against Keokuk while the chief was gone from Iowa. Secretary of War Joel R. Poinsett was pleased at this development, hoping to parade Black Hawk through the streets of the eastern cities as a vanquished enemy. However, the American crowds cheered Black Hawk as they came out in throngs to greet him. Keokuk, on the other hand, was ignored by the public. Having seen the Americans' might on his journey, Black Hawk refrained from further hostilities against the whites upon his return to his people.

In Iowa, despite being despised by many of the tribe, Keokuk continued his maneuverings, thanks to the recognition accorded him by the U.S. government. In 1836, he sold his "reserve" to the whites, with a good portion of the proceeds going to him personally. In 1842, after much pressure by the whites and negotiations in which Keokuk took a role, the Sauks and Mesquakies ceded all their lands in Iowa for a tract in Kansas on the Missouri River. This treaty led to a breakup in the alliance between the Nations and a subsequent separation of various segments of the former population. Black Hawk did not live to witness the breakup, having died in 1838. Ten years later, Keokuk followed his old nemesis in death. Ironically, in 1883, Keokuk was removed one final time. His remains were moved from Kansas and reburied in the city park at Keokuk, Iowa, and a statue of him was raised by the citizens of the town.

FURTHER READING: Bowes, John P. *Black Hawk and the War of 1832.* New York: Chelsea House Publishers, 2007; Fixico, Donald. "The Black Hawk-Keokuk Controversy." In *Indian Leaders: Oklahoma's First Statesmen.* Ed. H. Glenn Jordan and Thomas M. Holm. Oklahoma City: Oklahoma Historical Society, 1979; Hagan,

William T. *The Sac and Fox Indians.* Norman: University of Oklahoma Press, 1958; Jackson, Donald, ed. *Black Hawk: An Autobiography.* Urbana-Champaign: University of Illinois Press, 1987.

JAMES W. PARINS

Kickapoo Removal

French missionaries in the 17th century came upon the Kickapoos first in present-day Wisconsin, where they lived between the Fox and Wisconsin Rivers. They moved south following the French and Indian War into present-day Illinois, then east along the Wabash River. They were members of Tecumseh's confederation in 1811–1812 and in 1832 supported **Black Hawk** in his resistance to removal. Kickapoo warriors were recruited by the U.S. Army to fight the Seminoles in 1837.

The Kickapoos had signed a treaty in 1819 with the United States that ceded all their land in Illinois in exchange for land in Missouri. However, for more than a decade, a group under **Mecina** remained in western Illinois and harassed the settlers, and in 1832 a number of Mecina's band joined Black Hawk, despite Mecina's protestations. He, with the remnants of his band, joined the followers of **Kennekuk**, who were still in Illinois. The U.S. government used the **Indian Removal Act** to force tribes west of the Mississippi to remove farther west. Thus, in 1832, the Missouri Kickapoos were removed to a reservation along the Missouri River farther west near Fort Leavenworth in Kansas. Members of Mecina's band who survived the **Black Hawk War** under **Panoahah** joined the Kickapoos in Missouri, just as they were about to depart to their new reserve. Late in 1833, Kennekuk, along with some of his band who had remained in Illinois, joined the Kickapoos in Kansas. Then, in 1834, the remaining members of his band, led by Wabanim, crossed the Mississippi and joined the Kickapoos on the Kansas reserve. This reservation was reduced in 1854 to make way for white settlement, and, in 1862, an allotment treaty was ratified that assigned land to individual Indians. The "surplus" lands were sold to a railroad company.

A large contingent of Kickapoos had rejected the 1819 cessions and removed to Missouri and subsequently to Texas, where they joined forces with the Texas Cherokees. When Texans ejected both groups in 1839, they moved to **Indian Territory**, one band of Kickapoos settling in the Choctaw Nation on Wild Horse Creek, the other with the Creeks on the Canadian River. In 1850–1851, the Wild Horse Creek band left for Mexico with Seminole leader Wildcat (**Coacoochee**). When the Civil War began, the Canadian River Kickapoos joined the others in Mexico. The Kickapoos were persuaded to return to Indian Territory in the 1870s. In 1893, their lands were allotted, but two-thirds of the tribe rejected their allotments and refused to accept any payment. Nonetheless, their lands became a part of Oklahoma Territory in 1895 and were opened to white settlement. Today, the Kickapoos are divided into four separate bands, the Kickapoo Tribe in

Kansas, the Kickapoo Tribe in Oklahoma, the Texas Band of Kickapoo, and the Mexican-Kickapoos.

FURTHER READING: Gibson, Arrell M. *The Kickapoos: Lords of the Middle Border.* Norman: University of Oklahoma Press, 1963; "Kiikaapoi (Kickapoo) History." Kansas Kickapoo Tribe. 2009. At http://ktik-nsn.gov/history.htm; "Treaty with the Kickapoo, 1832." Indian Affairs: Laws and Treaties. At http://digital.library.okstate.edu/kappler/Vol2/treaties/kic0365.htm; Wright, Muriel. *A Guide to the Indian Tribes of Oklahoma.* Norman: University of Oklahoma Press, 1951.

JAMES W. PARINS

L

Land Speculation and Indian Removal

Perhaps no issue has been more central to American Indian affairs than land and the resources it contains. Entrepreneurial speculation in Indian lands played a major role in the expansion of the Euro-based society from the 17th century until the so-called closing of the frontier with the opening of the Indian lands in Oklahoma and **Indian Territory** in the late 19th and early 20th centuries.

By the advent of the removal period, speculation had become commonplace. Whether it was in Essex County, Maine, in the late 17th century; Pennsylvania, Tennessee, or Ohio in the 18th century; Georgia speculation that led to the Georgia Compact of 1802; or the **Ogden Land Company** claim in New York, speculation was backed by the social philosophy that Indians were "cumberers" of the earth. All earlier speculation ventures had an indirect bearing on removal policy. For example, the Ogden claim still loomed over the New York tribes in 1830. In Ohio, the Virginia Military District, Symmes Purchase, and the Ohio Associates speculation ventures of the 1780s led to the Indian wars that culminated in the Battle of Fallen Timbers in 1794 and forced the Shawnees and other remnant tribes who remained north of the Ohio River onto small landholdings, which removal treaties in the 1830s sought to liquidate. And the Georgia Compact of 1802 became the authority under which the state of Georgia extended its laws over the Creeks and Cherokees, setting off the national debate over Indian removal.

Although speculation occurred in Indiana, Illinois, Michigan, and Wisconsin during the removal period, the large landholdings of some of the southeastern tribes were prime targets. The land lottery in Georgia blunted speculation in Cherokee lands, and the lingering **Second Seminole War** and lack of prime agricultural land provided insufficient incentive for speculators in Florida. In contrast, Choctaw, Creek, and Chickasaw domains held out the promise of rich cotton lands and thus became the focus of speculators on a large scale.

The Choctaw **Treaty of Dancing Rabbit Creek**, signed only a few months after the **Indian Removal Act** in 1830, provided for Choctaw removal under terms that attracted land speculators. It created three basic types of land allotments for Choctaws: allotments containing homesteads of individual households, allotments that Choctaws could select elsewhere, and allotments for those who wished to remain in Mississippi. In theory, the allotment system would ensure the Choctaws a home until they removed and would provide a homestead for those who wished to remain under Mississippi law.

Assuming the Choctaws were ready to remove, government officials allowed land transactions to begin immediately. Some Choctaws sold their allotment claims to the United States and left for the West. Others sold their claims to local speculators, primarily local businessmen and government agents. Whites settled promiscuously on Choctaw lands, and the government began to hold public sales of unallotted land, even before all of the Choctaws had made their selections. These sales attracted other speculators. The poorly planned and hurried process of disposing of Choctaw land resulted in conflicting claims to tracts of land and legal battles between speculators that went on for years. Andrew **Jackson** used his influence to settle the claims of his appointees and friends who were among the speculators.

Speculation continued long after most Choctaws had reached the West. Matters were confused by government actions. The Preemption Law of 1838 called for setting aside enough land to provide allotments for Choctaws who had not selected theirs. However, preemption claims by whites continued and ultimately took precedence over Choctaw claims. In 1842, scrip was introduced. If land surrounding a Choctaw's improvements had been sold and there was not enough adjoining land for an allotment, the Choctaw received scrip, good for a certain number of acres in Alabama, Mississippi, Arkansas, and Louisiana. Although scrip helped clear land titles, it was useless to most Choctaws, who had no desire to settle in those states away from their tribe. Speculators bought up scrip claims and set off another round of speculation.

Legal disputes among speculators clouded the titles of thousands of acres for years. Local operators sold their claims to land agents and capitalists such as the New York and Mississippi Land Company, a number of whom were also engaged in speculation in Chickasaw lands in the late 1830s. The years of clouded titles delayed Choctaw removal, forced the Choctaws to go into debt with local traders, and made paupers of those who chose to remain in Mississippi.

Liquidation of the Creek domain, like the sale of Choctaw and Chickasaw land, in the short run benefited primarily land speculators. Allotments were assigned by the beginning of 1834, but speculators had been hard at work since the **Treaty of Washington** was ratified in 1832. Unlike speculation in other tribes, capital came in this case from Georgia and Alabama sources. Although there was a large number of small companies and combinations, two dominated the field: the Columbus Land Company of Georgia and Ware, Dougherty, and Company of Alabama. These companies used ruthless and fraudulent tactics. Their agents assisted Creeks in selecting allotments, thereby locating the best lands, and sold goods and whiskey to Creeks on credit in return for agreements to sell their allotments. In dealing with Creek men, who were not considered property owners in their society, they used black slaves as interpreters, who followed and harassed allotment holders until they committed suicide or agreed to sell, usually at low prices. They hired Creeks to impersonate others and to sell allotments they did not own. By 1835, the Columbus company had control of the Lower Creek allotments, and Alabama speculators had become the advisors of **Opothleyohola**, the Upper Creek leader who had opposed removal. Ultimately, 87 percent of Creek land went to speculators.

Government officials not only tolerated the speculators' activities but also aided their work. Extension of Alabama laws over the Creeks in 1832 brought an onslaught of intruders onto Creek lands. Instead of removing them as the treaty called for, the government encouraged legal settlement and also encouraged Creeks to lease their improvements. When violence erupted between intruders and Creeks, the speculators supported the intruders, and the government turned expulsion of them over to local officials, who took no action. Public sale of land began in 1834 amid rumors of fraud, but members of the speculation companies and their agents were appointed to verify the sales. Agents investigating fraud were ordered to tone down their reports, and members of Congress came to the defense of the companies whenever their actions came into question.

Rather than delay removal as they did in the Choctaw and Chickasaw lands, speculators speeded up Creek removal (*see* **Muscogee [Creek] Removal**). They disrupted Creek society, and the people became demoralized. In the spring of 1836, some Creeks struck back at intruders out of frustration resulting from their displacement and the failure of their crops. The army under Gen. Thomas S. **Jesup** was sent to end hostilities and to send the Lower Creeks to the West. The Upper Creeks became resigned to removal. Sadly, the civilian company hired to remove the Creeks was made up of speculators who had committed fraud upon the Creeks.

Chickasaw removal provided the last major opportunity for large-scale land speculation during the removal period. The **Treaty of Pontotoc** in 1832 provided for allotments to heads of households and orphans to provide them homes until they left for the West, at which time they could sell their land. As soon as the treaty was signed, local merchants assisted Chickasaws in selecting allotments; they chose the best land in return for an agreement to sell the land to the merchant when it came up for sale. The thousands of acres garnered in this fashion were sold to capitalist-backed companies such as the New York and Mississippi Land Company, the Chickasaw Company, and the Pontotoc and Holly Springs Land Company. These companies did not engage in the fraud that marked the Creek speculation or the contention and clouded titles of the Choctaw speculation.

Neither did speculation ventures in the Chickasaw country prove as profitable as the speculators had hoped. Because the price of cotton was rapidly rising during the middle years of the 1830s and capital was available, speculators paid the Chickasaws a fair price for their land. However, the Panic of 1837 in the banking industry, the rapid decline of the cotton market after 1837, and the availability of cheaper land in Arkansas and Texas left Mississippi speculators with large holdings that took them years to sell. Companies faltered, and individual speculators went bankrupt.

Whatever the disposition of the land in the wake of the speculation-based boom in any given region, the result was the same: large tracts of Indian land passed into non-Indian hands. Without question, U.S. government action or inaction abetted the process. The foremost concerns of the Andrew Jackson administration were to remove the tribes and transfer their lands to American settlers. Jackson himself had long speculated in land before he became president and had many close friends and appointees among the speculators. They were ostensibly vehicles through which the transfer of land could be achieved. However, because of muddled titles, contention and contests between speculators, and the banking crisis of the late 1830s, legal settlement in some areas was delayed for years. The federal government for the most part gave the speculators in the Southeast free rein, for over it all loomed the specter of **nullification**, which Jackson had hoped to avoid by carrying out the Georgia Compact of 1802. When federal officials mustered enough moral fortitude to attempt to expel the speculators' intruder allies from Indian lands, the speculators and state officials sided with the intruders in the Choctaw, Creek, and Chickasaw lands, hinting that an attempt to remove them would result in armed rebellion and nullification of federal law.

FURTHER READING: Feight, Andrew Lee. "Land Speculation and Lawlessness." 2009. At http://lowerscioto.blogspot.com/2009/09/land-speculation-and-lawlessness.html; Paige, Amanda, et al. *Chickasaw Removal.* Ada, OK: Chickasaw Press, 2010; Silver, James W. "Land Speculation Profits in the Chickasaw Cession." *Journal of Southern History* 10 (1944): 84–92; Young, Mary. *Redskins, Ruffleshirts and Rednecks: Indian Allotments in Alabama and Mississippi, 1830–1860.* Norman: University of Oklahoma Press, 1961.

DANIEL F. LITTLEFIELD, JR.

LeFlore, Greenwood (1800–1865)

Greenwood LeFlore used his upbringing by his Choctaw mother and the American-style education insisted on by his French father to fulfill his political ambitions and enrich himself during the **Choctaw removal** period. Vain and devious, he was willing to subvert the Choctaw people's desires to serve himself.

LeFlore was at first strongly anti-removal. In the wake of the Treaty of Doak's Stand (1820), he emerged on the Choctaw political scene in the mid-1820s as the United States exerted pressure on the Choctaws to cede more land. In 1826, he, David **Folsom**, and Samuel Garland replaced

Greenwood LeFlore, pro-removal Choctaw chief, enriched himself by supporting removal. (Courtesy of Mississippi Department of Archives and History)

Mushulatubbee, Robert Cole, and Tapanahoma as district chiefs and helped defeat the treaty negotiations then going on between the Choctaws and U.S. agents William **Clark**, Thomas Hinds, and John **Coffee**. That summer, LeFlore called a council to draft a constitution that established a council with power to adopt laws. One law it passed forbade the sale of Choctaw land.

Apparently understanding LeFlore's nature, Secretary of War Thomas McKenney set about undermining the young chief's anti-removal stand. In 1828, he appointed LeFlore to lead a Choctaw delegation to look at lands in the West. McKenney flattered him, comparing him to Moses. However, the promised land LeFlore expected to find was disagreeable to him, and he apparently determined to find a way to remain in Mississippi even if the rest of the nation removed.

The pressure for removal resulted in continued political shifts in the Choctaw Nation. The election of Andrew **Jackson**, followed by his aggressive removal policy, made some of the older chiefs more willing to talk, whereas leaders like LeFlore and Folsom remained opposed. Shortly after Mississippi extended state law over the Choctaws in early 1830, the Choctaws deposed Folsom and Garland and put Mushulatubbee and Nitakechi in their place. LeFlore threatened to send an armed force against them, but instead he took advantage of the unsettled state of affairs. Without authority, he began to negotiate with Commissioner McKenney, developing a removal treaty he hoped the Choctaws would accept and that would motivate them to retain him as chief. In April, he asked Mushulatubbee to put the proposed treaty before the council. At the council, LeFlore defended the treaty so eloquently and persuasively that the Choctaws believed that he may have found a way out of their dilemma. Recognizing him as their leader, they made him chief of the whole Nation, an office that the Choctaws had not had before. When LeFlore sent the treaty to Washington, Jackson thought the document was too generous to the Choctaws; however, in early May he recommended it to the Senate, which rejected it.

Passage of the **Indian Removal Act** later that month forced the Choctaws to act. Those who favored removal were angry at rejection of their treaty offer, those who opposed it were angry at the chiefs, and some made threats against them. That summer, Secretary John H. **Eaton** and President Jackson invited the Choctaws to meet them at Franklin, Tennessee, to discuss removal, but LeFlore, still chief of the Nation, refused to negotiate outside its boundaries. However, earlier that year, he had let it be known that if the

United States would allow him to stay in Mississippi and give him the land and resources necessary to set himself up as a planter when the Choctaws removed, he would guarantee Choctaw removal. Thus, he invited War Department officials to go to the Choctaw Nation for negotiations.

Eaton and John Coffee arrived in the Choctaw Nation in September 1830 and negotiated the **Treaty of Dancing Rabbit Creek**. The chiefs and captains of the Nation wanted to select 20 delegates representing all districts, but LeFlore wanted to appoint all of the delegates. Ultimately they agreed that the chiefs could select ten and LeFlore could select 10. The treaty ceded the Choctaw lands in return for lands west of the Mississippi and called for an early removal of the Nation. It also provided allotments for Choctaws who wished to remain in Mississippi and live under state law, as well as grants of four sections of land and generous pensions to LeFlore, Mushulatubbee, and Nitakechi, the three district chiefs. Some 17 sections went to LeFlore and his relatives.

The Choctaws were angry at the removal provisions of the treaty and at the signers. They questioned the authority of some of the signers and believed some had taken bribes. In October they deposed the sitting district chiefs. George W. Harkins defeated LeFlore in the northwestern district, Joel H. Nail replaced Nitakechi in the southern district, and Peter Pitchlynn replaced Mushulatubbee in the northeastern district. However, the United States refused to recognize any chiefs except those who had signed the treaty,

Meanwhile, LeFlore worked to push the removal process forward. In November 1830, he refused to accompany an exploring party, led by Nitakechi and including Mushulatubbee, that was to look at the western lands. He was already deeply involved in the removal process. He sent a number of removal parties to the West across southern Arkansas by way of Ecore Fabre and Washington. It was a hard winter, they were poorly organized and outfitted, they had insufficient provisions, and they were destitute when they arrived in the West. LeFlore, on the other hand, had fared well. As the agent responsible for disposing of the property of Choctaws he had sent west, he had enriched himself in the process.

LeFlore had reached his goal: to remove his tribe but to remain in Mississippi with an economic base to establish his plantation. His Malmaison became well known for its opulence, paid for by the labor of his large number of slaves. LeFlore lived the life of a wealthy planter and was elected to the Mississippi State Legislature, while the majority of his fellow Choctaws hacked out a new life for themselves in the West.

FURTHER READING: DeRosier, Arthur H., Jr. *The Removal of the Choctaw Indians.* Knoxville: University of Tennessee Press, 1970; Kidwell, Clara S. *Choctaws and Missionaries in Mississippi, 1818–1918.* Norman: University of Oklahoma Press, 1995; Satz, Ronald N. *American Indian Policy in the Jacksonian Era.* Lincoln: University of Nebraska Press, 1975; Young, Mary E. *Redskins, Ruffleshirts and Rednecks: Indian Allotments in Alabama and Mississippi, 1830–1860.* Norman: University of Oklahoma Press, 1961.

DANIEL F. LITTLEFIELD, JR.

Little Rock Office of Removal and Subsistence

When the Choctaw **Treaty of Dancing Rabbit Creek** was ratified by Congress on February 24, 1831, the U.S. government began to get ready for **Choctaw removal**. Capt. John B. Clark of the U.S. Army was named superintendent of removal and subsistence west of the Mississippi River and was stationed at Fort Smith, Arkansas, but was soon ordered to move his office to Little Rock.

The U.S. government assigned two superintendents the responsibilities of removing the Choctaws. The eastern superintendent started them on their way, saw them across the Mississippi River, or, if they were transported on steamboats, stayed with them until they landed in Arkansas. The western superintendent and his agents took over at that point. Although designed for Choctaw removal, this administrative structure remained intact for the remainder of the period during which all the southeastern tribes removed.

Capt. Jacob Brown was the first superintendent to occupy the Little Rock office. His responsibilities included fulfilling treaty promises to the Indians. Primarily, he was to provide subsistence for a year after the Indians arrived in **Indian Territory** as well as provide other goods and services, such as building blacksmith shops and providing blacksmiths, delivering blankets and looms, and paying annuities to the tribes.

By 1834, Brown had responsibility of the Choctaws who had removed during the past three years and two parties of Senecas and Shawnees who had arrived in Indian Territory from Ohio (*see* **Seneca Removal**; **Shawnee Removal from Ohio**). He was also responsible for the Osages and the second **Quapaw removal** from Arkansas. At the same time, the U.S. government was in the process of making plans for **Muscogee (Creek) removal**, **Seminole removal**, **Chickasaw removal**, and **Cherokee removal**.

Because Arkansas Territory had no banks, Brown's biggest challenge was to keep funds on hand to pay expenses. He or one of his clerks made frequent trips to New Orleans for funds. At other times he had to wait for some other officer to bring him money. He frequently complained about not having money and even considered asking to be relieved of his duties over this issue. After Arkansas became a state in 1836, Brown engaged in other economic ventures that overshadowed his Indian removal work.

Brown was replaced by Capt. Richard D. C. Collins, who assumed the duties of the Little Rock office in March 1837. As superintendent of subsistence and removal, he oversaw removal of Creeks, Seminoles, Chickasaws, and Cherokees. Unfortunately, his association with local entrepreneurs and politicians resulted in questionable decisions. While keeping his military rank and performing the duties of superintendent of removal and subsistence west, Collins accepted the position of cashier of the newly established Real Estate Bank of Arkansas and engaged in other business ventures. By 1839, his accounts were in arrears, and he was relieved of his duties. Investigation later revealed that more than $200,000 of federal money was missing. Collins's malfeasance resulted in the closing of the Little Rock office. His duties were assigned to the Western Superintendency at the Choctaw Agency, Indian Territory.

During the nine years the office was in operation, almost $4.5 million passed through the hands of the officers charged with its operations. The office was vital to the subsistence of the removing Indians and was an economic windfall for Arkansas. When Indian removal started in 1831, Little Rock's population was 250 to 300. By 1838, jobs and employment connected with removal had helped the population grow to 1,500. In 1831, there were no banks in Arkansas and cash was in very short supply. By the end of the decade, several banks had been established in the new state.

FURTHER READING: Foreman, Grant. *A Traveler in Indian Territory, the Journal of Ethan Allen Green*. Norman: University of Oklahoma Press, 1996; Paige, Amanda L. *Chickasaw Removal*. Ada, OK: Chickasaw Press, 2010; U.S. Congress. Senate. *Correspondence on the Emigration of Indians, 1831–33*. 23rd Cong., 1st sess., 1834. S. Doc. 512. Serial 244–248.

CAROLYN YANCEY KENT

M

Makataimeshekiakiak

See Black Hawk

McCoy, Isaac (1784–1846)

Born in Uniontown, Pennsylvania, Isaac McCoy left there for Vincennes, Indiana, in 1804, where he was licensed to preach by the Baptist Church. Ordained as a pastor, he served a church in Indiana for several years before being appointed a missionary to Indians living in the Wabash Valley in 1817. McCoy first worked as a missionary among the Native residents of Indiana in the 1810s and established the Carey Baptist Mission in present-day southern Michigan in 1822. Because of his personal observations of white encroachment upon the Indians and its negative impact on Potawatomi and Ottawa lives during that time, McCoy believed that Indian survival depended on their removal to the western territories. Because of his belief that proximity to whites was degrading them, he was appointed to a commission set up to facilitate the removal of the Miamis and Ottawas from the area in 1828. This conviction also led him to formulate a plan to remove all Indians west of the Mississippi to an area where an Indian state would be formed. He published his ideas on the subject in a publication, *Remarks on the Practicability of Indian Reform,* in 1827.

McCoy was appointed surveyor and removal agent for the midwestern tribes in 1828, and he traveled west of the Mississippi to Missouri and Kansas to examine the land there and its suitability for Indian habitation. He surveyed some areas to be used as reservations for the Indiana and Ohio tribes, with an eye toward creating an Indian state, and was assisted in this endeavor by his sons Rice and John Calvin. McCoy lobbied for passage of the Indian Removal Act as well as for establishment of an **Indian Territory**. It appeared that he might achieve his goal after the report of the Stokes

Commission, appointed by Congress in 1832. Montfort Stokes, John F. **Schermerhorn**, and Henry L. **Ellsworth** recommended the establishment of such a territory, but a bill creating the western territory failed. The Indian Intercourse Act of 1834 included some of the safeguards for the Indians that McCoy had sought.

Later, McCoy wrote pamphlets for the *Annual Register of Indian Affairs within the Indian Territory* (1835–1838). He also published the *History of the Baptist Indian Missions* in 1840. In 1842, he became the first corresponding secretary of the Indian Mission Association at Louisville, Kentucky, where he lived for the rest of his life.

FURTHER READING: McCoy, Isaac. *History of Baptist Indian Missions.* Washington, DC: William H. Morrison, 1840; Schultz, George A. *An Indian Canaan: Isaac McCoy and the Vision of an Indian State.* Norman: University of Oklahoma Press, 1972.

JOHN P. BOWES

McHenry, Jim

See Henry, Jim

Mecina (dates unknown)

After many of the Kickapoos removed from lands in Illinois and Indiana to southwestern Missouri and points south of there (*see* **Kickapoo Removal**), two bands remained in Illinois. Mecina led one band that was vehement that the Kickapoos had not, in fact, ceded their ancestral homelands and who vowed to remain where they were. William **Clark** and various government officials argued with the chief, who invoked the name of his old ally Tecumseh, yet Mecina's people continued to resist. They lived at Peoria Lake, raising corn, beans, and squash and hunting the local wildlife for 10 years after the 1819 removal of the main body of Kickapoos.

As white settlers arrived in increasing numbers, Mecina's band, as well as Potawatomis and some whites who lived in the area, were accused of raiding farms to steal livestock and anything else of value. The settlers raised an alarm, saying that they feared for their lives and property, and demanded that the federal government remove the Indians to more remote locations in the West. The resulting uproar somewhat abated with a new threat to the settlements, the refusal of Sauk and Fox leader **Black Hawk** to remove west of the Mississippi.

Although Mecina cautioned his people not to enter the ensuing **Black Hawk War**, many of his warriors did under the younger war chief **Panoahah**. With his band split, Mecina and his followers joined the other Kickapoo band that had remained in Illinois, the group under **Kennekuk**, or the Kickapoo Prophet. When Black Hawk was defeated and captured at Bad Axe, Panoahah and those Kickapoos who accompanied him joined the other members of the Nation in Missouri. This left Mecina and his people with the Kennekuk band as the only Kickapoos left in Illinois.

Through all this, Kennekuk had remained friends with William Clark and had carried on a correspondence in which Clark had tried to persuade the Kickapoo chief to remove west. Finally, after Black Hawk's defeat in 1832, Clark informed Kennekuk that if he did not vacate his lands in Illinois, he and his people would be regarded as an enemy by the United States, and the military would move against him. As a man who had always followed peaceful ways, Kennekuk, along with Mecina and his band, reluctantly left Illinois forever.

FURTHER READING: Gibson, Arrell M. *The Kickapoos: Lords of the Middle Border.* Norman: University of Oklahoma Press, 1963; "Kiikaapoi (Kickapoo) History." Kansas Kickapoo Tribe. 2009. At http://ktik-nsn.gov/history.htm; Wright, Muriel. *A Guide to the Indian Tribes of Oklahoma.* Norman: University of Oklahoma Press, 1951.

JAMES W. PARINS

Medicine and Disease

At the beginning of the removal period, American medicine, particularly on the frontier, was still very much in the thrall of the theories of Benjamin Rush (1745–1813). Rush had maintained that all disease was a manifestation of fever and that fever was caused by tension in the body's fluids. As there was only one underlying disease, only one course of treatment was needed: large doses of mercurial compounds, usually in the form of calomel (often in combination with jalop), to relieve tension in the bowels, followed by opiates to relieve nervous tension, and then a combination of bleeding and blistering to relieve vascular tensions. The results were often disastrous for the patient, leading to painful death through mercury poisoning and/or dehydration.

Through lack of experience and foresight perhaps, the War Department did not provide medical assistance for the **Choctaw removal**, the first major removal following the **Indian Removal Act**, in the fall of 1831. It quickly became apparent to the government agents that, if only for injuries, doctors would need to accompany all large removal contingents. Frequently equipped with little more than opium, doctors set up infirmary tents and attempted to treat the sick and injured. Some groups, such as the Seminoles, were accompanied by army medical personnel.

As government agents, both military and civilian, became more experienced with removal, the quantities and varieties of medical supplies increased. At least one **Cherokee removal** contingent's physician was equipped with then state-of-the-art gynecological and obstetric equipment and medications for treatment of venereal diseases.

For tribal people being interned in camps while awaiting removal, the crowding, new and often poor diets, and high levels of stress produced a raft of ailments, mostly diarrheal. Many were serious, and many were also made so by the conventional treatments. Common amoebic dysentery and other bacterial diarrheal conditions were frequent because of contaminated water supplies and were worsened by physical and emotional stress. Once local game supplies near the camps were exhausted, various dietary deficiencies began to have an impact on the camp occupants; one of the first symptoms of pellagra is diarrhea.

Physicians of the period lumped many of the diarrheal conditions together under the names "summer complaint" and "cholera." Children and the elderly were particularly vulnerable to these illnesses, and it is in those two groups that most of the deaths associated with removal occurred. The 1832 arrival of epidemic cholera in the Great Lakes region and fear of it spreading to the Southeast greatly impacted removal operations in those areas, resulting in route changes and frequent delays.

Those groups that were quickly assembled and moved were far less likely to suffer from the medical conditions that afflicted the Cherokees, Choctaws, and other larger tribes that were collected in the large camps. However, a group of 860 Potawatomis, assembled in northern Indiana in less than a week and put on the road in early September 1838, suffered tremendously from heat exhaustion and dehydration, experiencing more than 40 deaths before they crossed the Mississippi in the first week of November.

One early 19th-century medical practice that was effective was inoculation of Indians against smallpox. In 1832, Congress passed the Indian Vaccination Act, authorizing funds for the inoculation of Indians on the frontier by the War Department. Some 40,000 inoculations were carried out during the removal years under this legislation, with some of the removal groups being inoculated before their removal, some after, and, as in the case of the Chickasaws and Seminoles, some while on the road to their new homes. Those Indians who had removed before the outbreak of the smallpox epidemic of 1838 suffered high casualties, whereas those who were vaccinated during their removal suffered low mortality rates.

FURTHER READING: D'Elia, D. J. "Dr. Benjamin Rush and the American Medical Revolution." *Proceedings of the American Philosophical Society* 110 (1966): 227–234; Douglas, Jesse C. "Journal of an Emigrating Party of Pottawattomie Indians, 1838." *Indiana Magazine of History* 21, no. 4 (1925): 315–336; Gillet, Mary C. *The Army Medical Department 1818–1865*. Washington, DC: Center of Military History, United States Army, 1987; Pearson, J. Diane. "Lewis Cass and the Politics of Disease: The Indian Vaccination Act of 1832." *Wicazo Sa Review* 18, no. 3 (2003): 9–35; U.S. Congress. Senate. *Correspondence on the Emigration of Indians, 1831–33*. 23rd Cong., 1st sess., 1834. S. Doc. 512. Serial 244–248.

TONY R. ROSE

Menominee Removal

Much of Menominee history in the early 19th century was determined by other tribes as well as by actions of white U.S., British, and French citizens. In 1804, for example, the Sauks and Mesquakies signed a treaty with the U.S. government surrendering their claim to lands south of the Fox River. Since the Menominee lands were situated north of there—along the river, on both sides of Green Bay, and extending northward into the northern

Wisconsin forests—the threat of increased white settlements put their position at risk. Although the French, British, and, after 1815, the Americans had occupied a settlement at Green Bay dating into the 17th century, the Menominees, Potawatomis, Sauks, Mesquakies, and Winnebagos had used the lands of central and northeastern Wisconsin for centuries (*see* **Ho-Chunk Removal**).

By 1817, the **Ogden Land Company** planned to remove three New York tribes to the Northwest Territory, including the Oneidas, Stockbridges, and Munsees (*see* **Stockbridge-Munsee Removal**). Governor of Michigan Territory Lewis **Cass** agreed, and he promised government backing to the venture to remove the Indians to west of Lake Michigan. A treaty was signed by a few Menominee leaders, some Winnebagos, and representatives of the New York Indians in 1821 that ceded a small tract of land along the Fox River. In 1822, a vast land grant was made by John C. Calhoun, secretary of war, and Governor Lewis Cass; under its terms, a tract of 6,720,000 acres of land lying between Green Bay, Sturgeon Bay, and the Fox River was sold to the New York Indians for $3,950 in goods. The Brothertons were included in this transaction, along with the St. Regis, Tuscaroras, Oneidas, and Munsees. Shortly thereafter, the eastern tribes began their migration to Wisconsin. The Menominees and Winnebagos contested the grant after receiving accurate translations of the 1821 and 1822 treaties, asserting that the agreements said they were to share the land with the New York tribes rather than to cede it to them outright. This kind of arrangement was familiar to the Indians but was rejected by U.S. authorities.

Confusing the issue was the fact that the French and mixed-blood traders at Green Bay had attempted a major land grab involving a fertile tract 75 miles along the Fox River south of Green Bay. The issue came to a head in 1830, just after the **Indian Removal Act** was passed. The Menominees sent a delegation to Washington to resolve the matter, but the result was the Treaty of 1831 in which Andrew **Jackson** insisted on the president's right to set the limits of tribal land. This treaty was abridged somewhat in 1832, when another pact was signed, this one reserving for the Menominees 500,000 acres in northeastern Wisconsin and ceding a similar amount of land southwest of the Fox to the New York Indians.

However, Jackson and Cass were determined to move the tribes west of the Mississippi, pursuant to the Removal Act. In 1836, Cass as secretary of war began to plan for the removal of the Menominees to Missouri; at a meeting in August, the Indians were reminded that the president had the power to determine the limits of Indian lands. Faced with removal, the tribe negotiated the sale of some of their land east of the Wolf River and along the Wisconsin River for $700,000, one of the largest settlements made to date for Indian land, but yielding the Menominees only about $17\frac{1}{2}$ cents an acre. After the 1836 Treaty of the Cedars was ratified, the tribe removed to their lands in northeastern Wisconsin. They were still threatened with removal to Missouri as late as 1841 by territorial governor Henry Dodge, but Dodge's efforts were thwarted, mostly by the leadership of the Menominee chief Oshkosh. However,

Dodge and other white officials' efforts were not futile, for another treaty in 1854 reduced the size of the Menominee reservation by half.

FURTHER READING: Ellis, Albert G. "The Advent of the New York Indians into Wisconsin." *Collections of the State Historical Society of Wisconsin* 2 (1855): 415–449; Loew, Patty. *Indian Nations of Wisconsin.* Madison: Wisconsin State Historical Society Press, 2001; Ourada, Patricia K. *The Menominee Indians. A History.* Norman: University of Oklahoma Press, 1979; "Treaty with the Menominee, 1854." Indian Affairs: Laws and Treaties. At http://digital.library.okstate.edu/kappler/Vol2/treaties/men0626.htm#mn3.

JAMES W. PARINS

Metoxin, John (1770–1858)

John Metoxin was a Stockbridge-Munsee leader born in Stockbridge, Massachusetts. As a young man, he went to Bethlehem, Pennsylvania, where he was educated by the Moravians. He rejoined his tribe after their removal from Massachusetts to New York in 1785. When the Stockbridge-Munsees were pressured in 1817 by the **Ogden Land Company**, supported by the U.S. government, to remove from their lands in the Oneida Nation, Metoxin led some of the tribe in 1818–1819 to new land in Indiana that was ostensibly set aside for them. However, soon the Indians of this area also came under pressure to cede the land to white settlers; subsequently, in 1822, some Stockbridge-Munsees left for southwestern Missouri, from where they were forced to move again, this time to Kansas. Settlers and land speculators flooding into Kansas soon demanded their removal, at which point they moved to **Indian Territory** and settled on land provided by the Cherokee Nation. A significant number of tribal members, however, chose to leave Indiana for Wisconsin, where the main body of the Nation had moved from New York. These migrations took place in the period 1822 through 1829.

Metoxin was a leader among the Wisconsin Stockbridge-Munsees once they settled on the eastern shore of Lake Winnebago, southeast of Green Bay (*see* **Stockbridge-Munsee Removal**). According to contemporary sources, he was a leading orator and translator, earning the nickname "Old Man Eloquent." He was also a leader in the Presbyterian Church in the Stockbridge community, where he died in 1858.

FURTHER READING: *Collections of the State Historical Society of Wisconsin*, 4. 1859; *Collections of the State Historical Society of Wisconsin*, 15. 1900; "Metoxin, John." *Dictionary of Wisconsin Biography*. Madison: State Historical Society of Wisconsin, 1960.

JAMES W. PARINS

Miami Removal

Miami removal from Indiana in 1846 constituted one of the last Indian removals to the West. Because of the effective political leadership of Jean Baptiste **Richardville** (Peshewa, 1761–1841) and various sociopolitical

Miami chief Jean Baptiste Richardville (1761–1841), painted at the Treaty of Fort Wayne in 1827 by J. O. Lewis. (New York Public Library)

strategies from other leaders and community members, the greater Miami community thwarted removal for 16 years after passage of the **Indian Removal Act** of 1830. Although removal to Kansas became an inevitable reality for the Miamis, through skillful diplomacy and accommodation, half the community was able to remain in Indiana.

The Miamis, American settlers, Indian traders, missionaries, and bureaucrats were major players during the removal period, and each operated from self-interest. Miami lifeways were intrinsically linked to the landscape. Their lands included many important rivers, such as the Wabash, which proved useful for travel and commerce, but perhaps even more important was soil fertility throughout the region. The Miami landscape was coveted by American settlers and bureaucrats, and an aggressive bureaucratic strategy for American expansionism involving numerous treaty negotiations ensued. Prior to Indiana statehood in 1816, six treaties were signed between the Miamis and the federal government, diminishing their land base, and six subsequent treaties ceded the majority of their remaining land base thereafter. Although significant acreage was ceded in each of these treaties, Miami leadership successfully secured various stipulations, including sizeable annuity payments to the community, individual land grants, agricultural supplies, commodity goods, and ready access to formal education.

Indian traders were nervous about Indian removal because they relied on the Miamis for their exploitative enterprise. Inflated pricing of commodity goods and alcohol kept the Miamis indebted to traders and kept the traders' pockets lined. Missionaries, however, were morally divided over Indian removal. Although Catholic and Baptist missionaries were successful in converting many Miamis, other Protestant leaders were frustrated by rampant alcoholism and violence in the community, and therefore desired their removal west. Protestant missionaries hoped that those who stayed behind, including any exempt non-Christian Miamis and American settlers, would be far more receptive to conversion. Although many traders advocated for the Miamis to stay in Indiana and missionaries differed in their opinions about removal, settlers' attitudes rarely wavered. Their persistent demands for land cessions required removal of all Indian peoples from within Indiana's borders.

The Treaty of 1834 opened discussions for Miami removal, but it was not secured until the Treaty of 1840 was ratified. Chief Richardville, who was bicultural with Miami-French parentage, literate in French and English, and trilingual in Miami, French, and English, intentionally avoided the terms for removal in the Treaties of 1834 and 1838. However, pressures for removal, coupled with insurmountable tribal debt and alcoholism, nudged Richardville to treaty discussions one last time, and he ultimately acquiesced. Although the Treaty of 1840 ensured Miami removal, Richardville also secured several exemptions from removal, including one for his family and for the Godfroy and Matosinia families.

Many tactics were engaged to delay removal. Some Miamis, such as Maconaquah (1771–1847) and her Miami and American families, secured exemptions from removal through congressional appeal. Maconaquah, formerly a white captive known as Frances Slocum, lived her life as a Miami woman. With the support of her Miami family and recently confirmed American family, Maconaquah used her whiteness and advanced age to plea for the right for her and her Miami family to remain in Indiana. She along with 21 family members, constituting her entire village, received congressional exemption from removal on March 3, 1845. Others, including Meaquah (1790–1856), Rivarre (Shapenemah, c. 1816–1853), Coesse (c. 1819–c. 1856), and White Loon (Wapamungwah, c. 1804–1876), secured de facto rights to remain in Indiana by demonstrating their assimilation through successful adoption of agriculture and entrepreneurship.

Traders and some settlers also lobbied and petitioned the state government more than once for the Miamis' right to remain in Indiana. Furthermore, federal investigations dealing with excessive tribal debt delayed removal for over a year, as did a Miami delegation that inspected their reserved lands in the West as guaranteed by the 1838 treaty. Physical evasion of removal occurred more than once as several Miami families, such as the Papkeechis, Eel Rivers, and Wauwasees, left the region and headed north to Michigan and Canada. However, resistance to an oppressive bureaucracy during the removal era was sometimes less subtle, such as Richardville's decision to wear only Miami dress, speak only the Miami language, and mark all correspondence, including treaties, with only his mark. Whether resistance was physical or ideological, several Miamis felt that community integrity was threatened with impending removal.

In spite of numerous, albeit successful, delays, federal pressures to remove were insurmountable, and the Miamis were forced to assemble for removal at gunpoint by a detachment of U.S. soldiers from Cincinnati, Ohio, in Peru on October 6, 1846. Whereas some families had fled previously and others refused to assemble that fateful autumn day, several Miami families did not fare so well. Removal began with a caravan of five canal boats that took the Miamis east to Ohio on the Wabash-Erie Canal and then south on the Miami-Erie Canal until they reached the Ohio River, a six-day journey altogether. From there, they boarded a steamboat and journeyed for eight days down the Ohio River and up the Mississippi River until they reached St. Louis, Missouri. At the port of St. Louis, the Miamis stayed at Bloody Island for three days until they boarded a second steamboat, the *Clermont No. 2*, that took them up the Missouri River. Finally, the Miami caravan arrived in Kanza Landing, Missouri, on November 1 and from there walked to their new reserve at Sugar Creek, Kansas, a journey of 50 miles. Approximately 325 Miamis reported to their new Indian subagent at the Osage River.

Although removal took only a month to complete, several Miamis were sickly or injured and died en route, and upon their arrival in Kansas, survivors were grief-stricken and disheartened over their new lands. Those who remained in Indiana and elsewhere, both officially and otherwise, were equally saddened over the departure of so many community members. Removal demographically split the greater Miami community, therefore splintering familial and clan relations, and it fractured cultural and linguistic continuity thereafter. Consequently, the migration of many Miamis between western and Indiana communities continued well into the 20th century.

The western Miamis were removed a final time to **Indian Territory** during the 1870s and have since retained their status as a federally recognized Indian tribe. Those who remained in Indiana lost their status in 1897 by an unfounded administrative decision by Attorney General Willis Van Devanter and have not since successfully regained recognition from the federal government. Although both communities have come together in the past for various legal matters and more recently for cultural events, including powwows and language and cultural revitalization activities, both western and eastern Miamis remain a persistent people who are steadfastly committed to maintaining a distinctive Miami identity in their respective historical and ancestral landscapes.

FURTHER READING: Anson, Bert. *The Miami Indians.* Norman: University of Oklahoma Press, 1970; Berry, Kate, and Melissa Rinehart. "A Legacy of Forced Migration: The Removal of the Miami Tribe in 1846." *International Journal of Population Geography* 9 (2003): 93–112; Rafert, Stewart. *The Miami Indians of Indiana: A Persistent People, 1654–1994.* Indianapolis: Indiana Historical Society, 1996; "Treaty with the Miami, 1840." Indian Affairs: Laws and Treaties. At http://digital.library.okstate.edu/kappler/Vol2/treaties/mia0531.htm.

MELISSA A. RINEHART

Miccosukee Seminole Nation

The people of the Miccosukee Seminole Nation and the **Seminole Tribe of Florida**, both descendants of the last resisters to removal, shared a common history from the end of **Seminole removal** until the early 20th century. At that time, their economies and political goals began to diverge, as did their attitudes toward occupation of reservations set aside for them by the state and federal government.

In the 1930s, few members of either group embraced the Indian Reorganization Act. However, when Congress and the Eisenhower administration enacted and executed tribal termination legislation in 1953, there was a revived interest in reorganization, which had its support primarily among the Seminoles who resided on reservations. In 1957 the Seminoles organized as the Seminole Tribe of Florida.

By then, the Miccosukees had taken a different direction. In 1954, they hand-delivered a Buckskin Declaration of Independence to Washington and in 1957 wrote a constitution. In July of that year, the state of Florida recognized their tribal status, and in early 1958, the United Sates followed suit. In 1959, a delegation traveled to Cuba, where the delegates and the Cuban government signed a Treaty of Recognition, Friendship, and Mutual Assistance, achieving international recognition.

The Miccosukee Seminole Nation continued to take steps in exercising its sovereignty. By 1971, it had become the first tribal nation to contract all of the services formerly provided by the federal government, and the federal Indian agency closed its doors. The Miccosukees take pride in their history of resistance to removal and other policies of the American nation that encroached upon their sovereignty.

FURTHER READING: Covington, James W. *The Seminoles of Florida.* Gainesville: University Press of Florida, 1993; Kersey, Harry A., Jr. "Those Left Behind: The Seminole Indians of Florida." In *Southeastern Indians since the Removal Era.* Ed. Walter L. Williams. Athens: University of Georgia Press, 1979, pp. 174–190; Miccosukee Seminole Nation. At www.miccosukeeseminolenation.com; Sturtevant, William C., and Jessica R. Cattelino. "Florida Seminole and Miccosukee." In *Handbook of North American Indians.* Vol. 14: *Southeast.* Gen. ed. William C. Sturtevant, vol. ed. Raymond D. Fogelson. Washington, DC; Smithsonian Institution, 2004, pp. 429–449.

DANIEL F. LITTLEFIELD, JR.

Miconopy (c. 1800–1849)

Miconopy, whose name has been variously spelled, was also known as Sint-Chahkee and Pond Chief. He was present at the Treaty of Moultrie Creek in 1823, but he claimed later that he had not signed the document even though his name appears on it. In 1826, the United States wanted a delegation of influential chiefs to visit Washington to see firsthand the power of the United States. Miconopy was among those who went, and he joined the others in opposition to removal and education. Later that year, the United States engineered a plan for the Seminoles to elect a head chief to make it easier for the government to deal with them. The process pitted the Aluchuas, who favored Miconopy, against the Miccosukees and Tallahassees, who favored Tukose Emathla who was elected.

As chief of the Aluchuas, Miconopy still held authority as the head chief of the Seminoles in the 1830s because of his descent from Cowkeeper, who has been called the founder of the Seminole tribe. He was allied with the Miccosukees because of the marriage of his sister to King Philip (Emathla). American military officers had little respect for Miconopy as a leader. Corpulent and apparently truly lacking in leadership skills, he was easily maneuvered by others like **Abraham** and Osceola into the conflict with the United States in the **Second Seminole War**, caused by opposition to **Seminole removal**. He was a reluctant participant in the annihilation of Maj. Francis Dade's command in 1835 and also engaged in later battles. Convinced by a Cherokee delegation to meet with army officials in 1838, he went to Fort Mellon under a flag of truce. He was nevertheless taken prisoner by Gen.

Thomas S. **Jesup**, imprisoned at Fort Marion, and later transferred to Fort Moultrie near Charleston, South Carolina, where he was sketched and painted by George Catlin.

Miconopy was sent west by steamboat, arriving in 1838. He was among some 878 Seminoles and 257 "Negro Indians" aboard two boats that left New Orleans in May. Claims to many of the blacks followed the party from Florida. At Little Rock, the army asked assistance from the governor of Arkansas to take the blacks who were claimed by whites from the Seminoles, but the governor refused to intervene. The party continued to the **Indian Territory**, arriving in early June. Miconopy remained head chief of the Seminoles until his death in 1849.

FURTHER READING: Mahon, John K. *History of the Second Seminole War, 1835–1842.* Gainesville: University Press of Florida, 1967; Miller, Susan A. *Coacoochee's Bones: A Seminole Saga.* Lawrence: University of Kansas Press, 2003; Paige, Amanda L., et al. The North Little Rock Site on the Trail of Tears National Historic Trail: Historical Contexts Report. 2003. At http://anpa.ualr.edu/trail_of_tears/indian_removal_project/site_reports.html.

DANIEL F. LITTLEFIELD, JR.

Mississippi and Indian Removal

Groundwork for removal of the Choctaws and Chickasaws from Mississippi was laid in the first two decades of the 19th century. In the Treaty of Fort Adams in 1802, the Choctaws ceded an area in southwestern Mississippi. This was followed by the Treaty of Hoe Buckintoopa in 1802, the Treaty of Mount Dexter in 1805, and the Treaty of Fort St. Stephen in 1816. In the last-mentioned year, the Chickasaws ceded their land east of the Tombigbee River. By those treaties, the tribes had ceded some 13 million acres of Mississippi land. Still, when Mississippi was admitted to the Union in 1817, more than two-thirds of the land within its borders was occupied by the tribes.

The lands ceded by the tribes filled rapidly with Americans, who converted the land to cotton culture and demanded even more. In 1818 and 1819, government negotiations failed with the Choctaws. By 1820, a strong pro-removal feeling began to emerge in Mississippians. That year Governor George Poindexter publicly urged the government to remove the Indians. In response, Secretary of War John C. Calhoun appointed Andrew **Jackson** and Jackson's friend Thomas Hinds to negotiate with the Choctaws. By use of gifts and threats, they convinced the Choctaws to sign the Treaty of Doak's Stand, in which the Choctaws gave up about a third of their land in exchange for lands between the Arkansas and Red Rivers in the West. The Treaty of Doak's Stand was the first removal treaty signed by the Choctaws. However, few Choctaws were willing to remove, and in the West controversies arose over the location of the boundary between Arkansas and the Choctaws.

With the election of Governor Gerard C. Brandon in 1827, Mississippians became strong advocates for forced removal. The voluntary removal called for in the Treaty of Doak's Stand had been ineffective. Mississippians found support in Andrew Jackson, elected in 1828, who also favored forced removal. In anticipation of government action, only weeks before Jackson took office, under Brandon's leadership the Mississippi General Assembly extended the state's laws over the Choctaws and Chickasaws. As expected, Jackson aggressively lobbied for Indian removal in the national debate then going on concerning the issue. He received the authority he sought in the **Indian Removal Act** of May 1830. The Mississippi law and the congressional act were sufficiently threatening to the tribes to make them more willing to entertain removal.

Shortly after passage of the removal bill, Jackson invited the tribes to meet at Franklin, Tennessee, to discuss removal. Jackson focused on the Choctaws and Chickasaws first because he wanted to secure the American presence in the lower Mississippi Valley by settling it with American farmers. To his disappointment, only the Chickasaws sent a negotiating delegation to Franklin, where they negotiated the Treaty of Franklin, their first removal treaty. Its execution, however, depended on the Chickasaws finding a suitable land to settle in the West. They failed to do so, and the Treaty of Franklin was null. The Choctaws, who had refused to go to Franklin, invited the government to send negotiators to them. In September 1830, they signed the **Treaty of Dancing Rabbit Creek**, which called for **Choctaw removal**. By the end of 1834, most Choctaws had removed to the West. **Chickasaw removal** was guaranteed by the **Treaty of Pontotoc** in 1832, adjusted in a treaty at Washington in 1834.

It would take several years more for Mississippi to reach its goal of removing the tribes from within its boundaries. The Chickasaw treaty's execution depended on the Chickasaws finding a suitable land in the West. It was not until early 1837 that they agreed to settle with the Choctaws. Removal itself took two years more. Finally, in 1839, Mississippi reached its goal when the War Department officially closed Chickasaw removal.

Unfortunately for Mississippi, removal did not bring the rapid agricultural development its leaders expected. Both Choctaw and Chickasaw treaties provided for allotments of land to heads of households to ensure the Indians a home until they removed, at which time the land could be sold. **Land speculation** was rampant. Speculators secured options on most of the best land, leading to years of legal maneuvering before the lands could be sold to individual farmers and titles could be cleared. Transfer of land to individuals was also delayed by the money crisis that led to the banking panic of 1837 and decline of the cotton market during the same period.

FURTHER READING: DeRosier, Arthur H., Jr. *The Removal of the Choctaw Indians.* Knoxville: University of Tennessee Press, 1970; Fortune, Porter L., Jr. "The Formative Period." In *A History of Mississippi.* Ed. Richard Aubrey McLemore. Vol. 1. Hattiesburg: University and College Press of Mississippi, 1973; Young, Mary E. *Redskins, Ruffleshirts and Rednecks: Indian Allotments in Alabama and Mississippi, 1830–1860.* Norman: University of Oklahoma Press, 1961.

DANIEL F. LITTLEFIELD, JR.

Mississippi Band of Choctaw Indians

Article 14 of the **Treaty of Dancing Rabbit Creek** provided for the creation of allotments for those Choctaws who wished to remain in Mississippi rather than go west during **Choctaw removal**. Approximately 5,000 remained. Unfortunately, the government failed to safeguard the reserves that were supposed to provide the Choctaws their homesteads. Agent William Ward, who received applications for allotments, denied many of them, so that patents were granted to fewer than 10 percent of the claims that had been laid out by the government surveyor by 1842. By that time, the frenzy of **land speculation** that had engulfed the Choctaw lands after Choctaw removal had affected the remaining Choctaws. With much of the land tied up by speculators, white farmers in search of land encroached on the Choctaws, stealing their livestock, destroying crops, and harassing the people, forcing them ever deeper into the hill country of central Mississippi. Land speculators hounded the Choctaws for decades to come, making them the only remnant of the large southeastern tribes to experience a second removal in the 20th century and to be threatened with a third.

Details of the Choctaws' condition between removal and the Civil War are limited. As a third racial group, they did not fit into Mississippi society and lived by subsistence farming. The Choctaw Nation sent emissaries to encourage them to join the tribe in **Indian Territory** and appropriated funds to support them after removal. One such emissary was Chief Nitakechi, who died while on a mission to Mississippi in 1845. In 1846, about 1,000 went west, 388 left in 1853, and 300 others left in 1854.

The Choctaws took advantage of white farmers' need for labor in the 1870s and ensuing years. Land that had been kept out of the market by speculators became available to white farmers who needed laborers. The Choctaws became sharecroppers, their society became stable, and they developed systems of schools and churches in several communities.

Unfortunately, the land speculators were not finished with them. The Commission to the Five Civilized Tribes had been established by Congress in 1893 to negotiate with the Choctaws and other tribes of Indian Territory to allot their land in preparation for statehood. Failing at negotiation, the Dawes Commission, as it was called, urged Congress to pass the Curtis Act in 1898, which provided for allotment of tribal land with or without the tribes' consent. The allotment process, in which the Mississippi Choctaws would share, began in 1899. In 1903 Congress confirmed the Mississippi Choctaws' right to land in Indian Territory. The Dawes Commission enrolled 1,660 Mississippi Choctaws, 1,357 of whom were full bloods. The speculators saw allotment as another opportunity for them to acquire Indian land.

Congress appropriated $20,000 to transport those Mississippi Choctaws who wished to remove to the West. Special trains were used to transport them to camps that were established in areas where allotments were available. They were furnished with food, tents, and tools and were encouraged to build houses on their allotments. Many who went to Indian Territory were "sponsored" by land speculators. One land company loaded them like cattle in boxcars in Mississippi and shipped them to the Choctaw Nation, put them into unsanitary housing, and saw to it that they were allotted the best land in the area, the speculators hoping that they would soon become owners of the land.

In the wake of this second Choctaw removal, the land speculators were not as successful as they had hoped to be. Most of the Mississippi Choctaws who had removed were full bloods whose allotments were restricted from alienation for 25 years. The land speculators who had taken large numbers of Choctaws to Indian Territory obtained their signatures on wills that assigned most of their allotments to the land dealers. U.S. attorneys instigated suits in the Choctaws' behalf, and in 1906 the court for the southern district of Indian Territory refused to admit the wills to probate, nullifying approximately 1,000 of them.

Then members of Congress from Mississippi attempted to instigate another removal of the 1,250 Choctaws still remaining in Mississippi. They introduced legislation in 1911 to reopen the Dawes rolls. Failing that, in 1912, they began attempts to enroll the Mississippi Choctaws without requiring them to remove and tried to establish their right to share in per capita payments to the western Choctaws or permit them to receive cash instead of allotments. Although the Mississippi politicians failed, they managed to hold up the Choctaw per capita payments in the West for years.

In 1916, apparently convinced that the Choctaws would remain in Mississippi, the politicians then turned to obtaining federal appropriations for their education and economic improvement. By that time, the condition of the Choctaws was widely known in political circles. In 1918, Congress appropriated $75,000 for schools and social work for them. Thus, recognizing that they qualified for services under the Bureau of Indian Affairs, the government also established a Choctaw agency at Philadelphia, Mississippi, that year.

During the next two decades, conditions improved for the Choctaws. Schools and a hospital were built. The government instituted a land acquisitions program that resulted in the base of the Choctaws' present reservation. In 1935, they organized under the Indian Reorganization Act, and in 1944, their reservation of more than 15,000 acres was declared trust land. In 1945, they adopted a constitution.

Taking advantage of their status as a federally recognized tribe and of Great Society legislation in the 1960s, the Choctaws began their rise socially and economically to their present state. During the past four decades they have enjoyed a stable government and have become one of the most economically self-sufficient tribes in the United States.

FURTHER READING: Debo, Angie. *And Still the Waters Run: The Betrayal of the Five Civilized Tribes.* Princeton, NJ: Princeton University Press, 1972; Galloway, Patricia, and Clara Sue Kidwell. "Choctaw in the East." In *Handbook of North American Indians.* Vol. 14: *Southeast.* Gen. ed. William C. Sturtevant, vol. ed. Raymond D. Fogelson. Washington, DC: Smithsonian Institution, 2004; Mississippi Band of Choctaw Indians. 2010. At www.choctaw.org; Peterson, John L., Jr. "The Choctaws of

Mississippi." In *Southeastern Indians since the Removal Era*. Ed. Walter L. Williams. Athens: University of Georgia Press, 1979, pp. 142–153.

DANIEL F. LITTLEFIELD, JR.

Muscogee (Creek) Removal

The Creek removal era began on February 12, 1825, when the Coweta chief William McIntosh signed the Treaty of Indian Springs, which ceded large portions of Creek land to the federal government in exchange for a large sum of money and an equal amount of land in present-day Oklahoma. McIntosh was later executed for his role in the treaty signing. The Treaty of Indian Springs created great hardship for the Creeks, who were forced off their land, and a number suffered from hunger and even starvation. The Treaty of Indian Springs also commenced the period of voluntary Creek removal. Between 1827 and 1836, approximately 3,500 Creeks voluntarily moved west. Voluntary Creek emigration ended in 1836 when a small band of Lower Creeks initiated a war in response to the continued encroachment of white squatters onto their land. As a result of the war, Andrew **Jackson** ordered all Creeks to move west.

In late 1827, approximately 700 friends and followers of the late William McIntosh, along with their slaves, packed their belongings into wagons and traveled westward. The party walked from Harpersville, Alabama, to Tuscumbia, where a portion of the party took boats down the Tennessee, Ohio, and Mississippi Rivers before ascending the Arkansas River and arriving at Cantonment Gibson in late January or early February 1828. The balance of the party walked overland. Almost a year after the first McIntosh party left Alabama, a second McIntosh party traveled approximately the same route and arrived at the Western Creek Agency in late 1828.

Whereas the first two emigrating parties were composed largely of Creeks who were friends and followers of McIntosh, the third voluntary emigrating party included Creeks who had decided to leave the dire conditions found in the eastern Creek Nation. White settlers not only squatted illegally on Creek land but also, in many cases, had become brazen enough to forcibly evict Creeks from their homes. Many Creeks had their livestock and crops stolen. Approximately 1,400 Creeks, constituting the third voluntary emigrating party, left Alabama in June 1829 and, like the first two parties, either walked or boarded boats at the Tennessee River. While on the Arkansas River, east of Little Rock, the steamboat *Virginia* ran aground, and the Creeks on board were forced to either walk the rest of the way or take keelboats that drafted less water. Disease also ravaged the party, and a number of emigrants died along the route.

The emigrants of the third voluntary party arrived at the Western Creek Agency amidst a sea of discontent involving the emigrants of the earlier parties. Western Indians raided the Creek settlers, and the government was slow in distributing the rifles and agricultural utensils necessary for survival in the West. Disease was also so prevalent that many Creeks packed their bags and returned eastward. But life was little better for the Creeks in the East. Many Lower Creeks had been unable to reestablish their lives after being forced from Georgia in 1826, and starvation became a looming threat. The Alabama legislature compounded the Creeks' misery by extending legal jurisdiction over the Creek Nation between 1827 and 1829. And white squatters continued to settle illegally on the Creeks' land. In response to these problems, a number of prominent headmen traveled to Washington to negotiate an agreement that would salvage the Creek Nation. The 1832 **Treaty of Washington**, signed that March, ceded all sovereign Creek land to the federal government in exchange for parcels of 320 acres for each Creek head-of-family or 640 acres for each Creek headman. The Creeks could sell their parcels and emigrate west or remain on their land for as long as they wished. But many Creeks who tried to sell were quickly cheated out of their land outright or had their land devalued by unscrupulous land speculators. Moreover, the Alabama state government and federal officials did not enforce the articles of the treaty to the Creeks' satisfaction.

Two more voluntary emigrating parties left Alabama in 1834 and 1835. More than 500 Creeks left Centreville, Alabama, in December 1834 and traveled through Tuscaloosa and Columbus, Mississippi, to Memphis. At Memphis, a number of emigrants boarded steamboats while the balance walked. Both parties suffered from the cold, and the Creeks experienced rain or hail during much of their journey. Government agents conducting the Creeks wrapped the children in tents to keep them warm, and the party was forced to stop often to build fires along the route. The land party struggled over the frozen ground through the Mississippi Swamp in the Arkansas Territory. At times they had to tie ropes to their horses' legs and pull them over the ice. The water party was also delayed by ice on the Arkansas River. The emigrants arrived at Fort Gibson in March 1835. In an attempt to save money on the next emigration, the federal government entered into a contract with the **Sanford** Emigrating Company to emigrate 5,000 Creeks at $20 per person. By December 1835, the Sanford company had collected approximately 500 Creeks. The party traveled north to the Tennessee River, where a portion of the party boarded the steamboat *Alpha* with two keelboats in tow at Waterloo, Alabama, while the remainder walked. The land party marched long distances over difficult roads, and 15 percent of the Creeks' horses died before they reached Memphis. The journey was also, at times, hazardous for the water party. As the *Alpha* approached Lewisburg, Arkansas Territory, one of the keelboats hit a snag on the Arkansas River and sank with 250 Creeks on board. The emigrants arrived in February 1836.

Back in Alabama, the land frauds associated with the 1832 Treaty of Washington drove the Creeks to distraction. Although the government investigated the frauds, justice seemed to elude many Creeks. In May 1836, a small band of Lower Creeks lashed out at white settlers and started a war in eastern Alabama. The Second Creek War, as it came to be called, was the last, desperate act of a number of Creeks who had been victimized by the Treaty of Indian Springs and the 1826 and 1832 Treaties of Washington.

Many had lived on the edge of starvation for almost a decade and had had their reserves stolen by white land speculators. The violence gave Andrew Jackson an excuse to forcibly remove the remaining 16,000 Creeks to the West. Military agents quickly rounded up captured Creek warriors, placed them in chains, and marched them to Montgomery, where they were placed on steamboats. In July 1836, the detachment of approximately 2,300 Creek prisoners descended the Alabama River to Mobile before traveling by boat to New Orleans and then ascending the Mississippi River to Rock Roe, Arkansas. From Rock Roe, the prisoners marched the remainder of the way to Fort Gibson. A second, smaller detachment of Creeks, following the same approximate route as the first, left Montgomery in early August 1836.

Even before the Creek prisoners arrived at Fort Gibson, the government collected the remaining "friendly" Creeks. Five detachments left from various locations in the former Creek Nation and marched, along different routes, to Memphis. From Memphis, the detachments took land and water routes to Rock Roe or Little Rock, before marching the remainder of the way to Fort Gibson. During their journey, the Creeks experienced a scarcity of potable water and torrents of rainfall. A severe snowstorm hit as the detachments approached Fort Gibson, and the Creeks were forced to walk in as much as eight inches of snow. The Creeks arrived at Fort Gibson in December 1836 and January 1837. The Alabama Emigrating Company, which contracted to remove the Creeks, tallied the number of deaths. They reported that they removed 2,318 Creeks of detachment one with 78 deaths; 3,095 Creeks of detachment two with 37 deaths; 2,818 Creeks of detachment three with 12 deaths; 2,330 Creeks of detachment four with 36 deaths; and 2,087 Creeks of detachment five with 25 deaths.

Despite the removal of approximately 15,000 emigrants in 1836, many Creeks remained in the Southeast. Most were family members of Creek warriors commissioned to fight the Seminoles in Florida. In exchange for their service, the family members of the Creek warriors were allowed to remain in Alabama until their tour of duty was over. But local whites terrorized the emigrants as they waited in camps for their relatives to return from Florida. In a move designed to protect the Creeks from local settlers, government agents removed the Creek families from east-central Alabama to Mobile Point on the Gulf Coast in March 1837. By the summer of 1837, disease had become so prevalent at Mobile Point that agents again moved the Creeks to a healthier location at Pass Christian, Mississippi.

While the Creeks waited at Pass Christian, government agents rounded up the refugee Creeks who had fled to live among the Cherokee and Chickasaw people. In May 1837, 543 refugee Creeks living among the Cherokees traveled by boat from Gunter's Landing, Alabama, to Fort Gibson entirely by water. A number of these Creek refugees were captured as far away as North Carolina. Eighty Creeks died or deserted the party during the journey, and they arrived in the West in June 1837. Agents also traveled to Mississippi to round up the Creeks living among the Chickasaws. Enrollment camps were established near Memphis and Pontotoc. In November 1837, approximately

300 Creeks marched to Memphis. There the party was divided, and a portion boarded the steamboat *Itasca* while the balance walked to Fort Gibson. The Creeks arrived in late December 1837.

In mid-October 1837, the Creeks waiting at Pass Christian, along with their reunited relatives from Florida, boarded a number of steamboats to continue their journey west. Over 600 Creeks ascended the Mississippi River in the *Monmouth,* an aging steamboat scheduled to be dismantled. As the boat passed Profit Island, it was cut in half by the steamboat *Trenton.* Approximately 300 Creeks were killed in the accident. The recovery effort took a number of days, and the party continued westward after burying their dead on the west side of the river. The Creeks did not arrive in the West until sometime in early 1838.

Many Creeks continued to trickle into the Indian Territory from Alabama into the 1840s and 1850s. These Creeks traveled individually or in small family groups. Other Creeks, entrenched among other southeastern Indian nations, were removed with the **Cherokee removal**, **Chickasaw removal**, or **Seminole removal**. Those who remained under the Treaty of Fort Jackson in 1814 were the ancestors of the **Poarch Band of Creek Indians** in Alabama today.

FURTHER READING: Foreman, Grant. *Indian Removal: The Emigration of the Five Civilized Tribes of Indians.* Norman: University of Oklahoma Press, 1989; Green, Michael G. *The Politics of Indian Removal: Creek Government and Society in Crisis.* Lincoln: University of Nebraska Press, 1982; Haveman, Christopher D. "The Removal of the Creek Indians from the Southeast, 1825–1838." PhD diss., Auburn University, 2009; "Treaty with the Creeks, 1832." Indian Affairs: Laws and Treaties. At http://digital.library.okstate.edu/kappler/Vol2/treaties/cre0341.htm.

CHRISTOPHER D. HAVEMAN

Mushulatubbee (d. 1838)

Mushulatubbee was chief of the northeastern district of the Choctaw Nation at the time of **Choctaw removal**. He had become chief in 1809 after the death of Mingo Homastubbee, his uncle. Mushulatubbee had been a well-respected warrior and leader in his early days for his part in raids on the Osages and Caddos west of the Mississippi.

As the pressure for removal mounted against the Choctaws, Mushulatubbee and other old chiefs were opposed politically by nontraditional Choctaws like David **Folsom** and Greenwood **LeFlore**, the latter an ambitious and ruthless politician who, in the spring of 1830, managed to have himself named chief of the entire Choctaw Nation while at the same time serving as a district chief. Although Mushulatubbee had at first opposed removal, he began to lend support to the idea in an effort to retain his position as chief, and he was not opposed to accepting bribes offered by American negotiators. He was one of the signers of the **Treaty of Dancing Rabbit Creek** in 1830. The Choctaw people were angry about the treaty, and in the October 1830 elections, they defeated all of the old chiefs: Mushulatubbee, Greenwood LeFlore, and Nitakechi. However, because the United States needed

Mushulatubbee, "He Who Puts Out and Kills," a district chief of the Choctaw Tribe, painted in 1834 by George Catlin. (Smithsonian American Art Museum, Washington, DC / Art Resource, NY)

the support of the old chiefs who had signed the treaty a month earlier, the government refused to recognize the newly elected chiefs George Harkins, Joel Nail, and Peter Pitchlynn and recognized only the district chiefs who had signed the treaty.

When Mushulatubbee and his Choctaw followers removed to the **Indian Territory**, they settled in the northern part of the Choctaw Nation along the Arkansas watershed. Thus they distanced themselves from the less traditional Choctaws, who, along with the missionaries who greatly influenced them, settled along the Red River in the southern Choctaw Nation. Mushulatubbee fell victim to the smallpox during the great epidemic that swept the trans-Mississippi West in 1838.

FURTHER READING: Akers, Donna, L. *Living in the Land of Death: The Choctaw Nation, 1830–1860.* East Lansing: Michigan State University Press, 2004; DeRosier, Arthur H., Jr. *The Removal of the Choctaw Indians.* Knoxville: University of Tennessee Press, 1970; Kidwell, Clara S. *Choctaw and Missionaries in Mississippi, 1818–1918.* Norman: University of Oklahoma Press, 1995; O'Brien, Greg. "Mushulatubbee and Choctaw Removal: Chiefs Confront a Changing World." Mississippi History Now. 2003. At http://mshistory.k12.ms.us; Paige, Amanda L., et al. The North Little Rock Site on the Trail of Tears National Historic Trail: Historical Contexts Report. 2003. At http://anpa.ualr.edu/trail_of_tears/indian_removal _project/site_reports/north_little_rock.

DANIEL F. LITTLEFIELD, JR.

N

Neamathla

See Eneah Emathla

Neamicco

See Eneah Micco

Northwest Ordinance (1787)

In 1787, shortly before drafting the Constitution of the United States, the Confederation Congress passed "An Ordinance for the Government of the Territory of the United States North West of the River Ohio," which created the Northwest Territory, composed of the modern states of Ohio, Indiana, Illinois, Michigan, and Wisconsin. The Northwest Ordinance initiated the first great wave of settlement into the region by establishing a plan for creating territorial governments and providing for a system whereby territories could apply for statehood.

The idea for the Northwest Ordinance had begun several years earlier, as the Continental Congress pushed eastern states to relinquish their claims to western lands. By 1780, states like Virginia, New York, and Pennsylvania agreed to cede their massive claims to the federal government. By 1784, Congress decided that a plan was necessary to create western governments in an effort to encourage settlement. In March of that year, it appointed Thomas Jefferson to lead a committee charged with the responsibility of drafting a report outlining such a process. The committee recommended the creation of a survey system that would divide the territory into square tracts and a bureaucratic process of issuing warrants and deeds to potential buyers that would encourage land sales. Later that year, the committee expanded upon its report with a system for establishing temporary governments in the West to initiate peaceful and orderly settlement. Congress adopted the recommendations and passed the Land Ordinance of 1784, which laid the groundwork for the later Northwest Ordinance. The following year, Congress passed an additional Land Ordinance that outlined a specific system of disbursing western lands via a system of public land auctions.

The need for further legislation outlining the process by which territories would become states was precipitated by Congress's sale of nearly 5 million acres of land in the modern state of Ohio to two groups of land speculators—the Ohio Company of Associates and the Scioto Land Company. As these organizations prepared to move west, Congress sought to forge an expedited process for creating governments in the West. The Northwest Ordinance provided a solution.

The opening sections of the Ordinance outlined a system of territorial governance centered on the appointment of a territorial governor, secretary, and panel of three judges. The territorial governor was granted broad powers to administer the government, lead western militias, and administer public land sales. He also was charged with protecting the white settlers in the region and often acted as superintendent of Indian affairs. The Northwest Ordinance proclaimed that "utmost good faith shall always be observed towards the Indians." It also guaranteed Indian tribes legal title to lands occupied by them throughout the Northwest Territories. Still, the territorial governor's responsibility to protect the territory's white population often overshadowed his obligation to protect the region's Native residents.

The promise of future states being carved from the Northwest Territories and the settlement of former Revolutionary War officers at Marietta, in the southeastern corner of Ohio, emboldened many Americans to pack their belongings and move west. White settlers often ignored the boundaries between public and Indian lands in the Northwest Territories. Conflicts ensued and the federal government responded. In 1790, President George Washington ordered Gen. Josiah Harmar to lead an army into Indian country to pacify the tribes of the Northwest Territories who had killed nearly 1,500 Americans along the Ohio River in retaliation for aggressive white settlement in the West. Harmar and his troops attacked a confederation of Indians, led by Miami chief Little Turtle, near modern-day Fort Wayne, Indiana. Native warriors routed the Americans, and Harmar led his beleaguered army back to Cincinnati.

The following year, territorial governor Arthur St. Clair personally led American soldiers into Indian country to avenge Harmar's loss. The battle, which took place near modern-day Fort Recovery, Ohio, ended in disaster for the Americans, as St. Clair lost nearly two-thirds of his army. In all, over 800 Americans (including several hundred camp followers) lost their lives. Finally, in 1794, Gen. Anthony Wayne led an army of well-trained troops north from Cincinnati and defeated the Indian confederacy in the Battle of Fallen Timbers. The next summer, he led a treaty council at Greenville, Ohio, whereby the tribes of the lower Great Lakes agreed to cede additional lands and cease killing as a means of retribution for the wrongs of white settlers.

The Northwest Ordinance initiated the first large wave of settlement into the area of the lower and western Great Lakes by assuring American settlers that the government's aim was to encourage development and ensure white settlement in the region. Thus it laid the groundwork for the economic and social pressure that led to Indian removal from the region in the 19th century.

FURTHER READING: Linklater, Andro. *Measuring America: How an Untamed Wilderness Shaped the United States and Fulfilled the Promise of Democracy.* New York: Walker and Company, 2002; Onuf, Peter. *Statehood and Union: A History of the Northwest Ordinance.* Bloomington: Indiana University Press, 1987; Taylor, Robert, Jr., ed. *The Northwest Ordinance, 1787: A Bicentennial Handbook.* Indianapolis: Indiana Historical Society, 1987.

JIM J. BUSS

Nullification and Removal

The national debate over nullification, the constitutional theory positing a state-centered vision of sovereignty, provides an important political context through which the removal policies of the Andrew **Jackson** administration should be viewed.

The roots of the doctrine of nullification reach back to the second Kentucky Resolution of 1799, written by Thomas Jefferson. Jefferson argued that the sovereign states alone possess the right and authority to determine the constitutionality of actions taken by the legislative and executive branches of the federal government. The principle of state nullification of federal law, in this regard, stands at the heart of the struggle between Jeffersonian (and later Jacksonian) democrats and the strong federalist view of government and judicial review championed by the Marshall Court. That struggle intersects most directly with the history of Indian removal in the Cherokee cases of the 1830s, especially *Worcester v. Georgia* (1832).

Nullification progressed from a mere theory in 1799 to a major, national political problem by the 1820s, with South Carolina as the focal point. During the 1820s, leaders in that state began to expand the Jeffersonian doctrine and argue that, under the U.S. Constitution, the states remained, in fact, independent sovereigns. In the view of the nullifiers, the U.S. Congress possessed only very limited, delegated powers.

By the 1830s, John C. Calhoun had become the most sophisticated theorist and advocate of this more radical strain of nullification; his 1831 *Address on the Relation of the States to the Federal Government* may be regarded as a culminating expression of the principles involved. The crucial test of Calhoun's articulation of the theory came in the Nullification Crisis of 1832, which looms in the background of the controversies and court challenges surrounding the **Indian Removal Act** of 1830 that were occurring simultaneously.

The Nullification Crisis represents the culmination of a decade-long battle between South Carolinians and Congress over protective tariffs and federal spending on internal improvements in the states (both of which were viewed in South Carolina as vehicles for undermining state sovereignty).

The adoption of an ordinance "nullifying" the 1832 Tariff Act by a South Carolina convention triggered a forceful response from President Andrew Jackson and the Congress. No zealous champion of centralized state power (as evidence by his assault on the national banking system), Jackson nevertheless saw South Carolina's nullification effort as an untenable threat to the Union. He denounced the ordinance in his 1832 "Proclamation to the People of South Carolina" as an illegal act of secession, and he subsequently supported the passage by Congress of the Force Act of 1833 (which provided alternate means of collecting the tariff without the cooperation of state authorities, while giving Jackson other, coercive military options if needed). At the same time, though, not wanting to trigger an irreconcilable confrontation with South Carolina (or other southern states), Jackson and Congress (including some of his political enemies in the North) moved to weaken the tariff and defuse the crisis through political, rather than legal or military, means.

The political balancing act and heated rhetoric surrounding the Nullification Crisis clearly influenced key events during the removal of the southeastern tribes, particularly **Cherokee removal**. The Indian Removal Act, it should be remembered, was driven in part by another enduring state-federal conflict (between Georgia and the U.S. government), and the concern that Indian policy could add to the destabilization of the Union was part of the political calculus of the 1830s. President Jackson's refusal or, as some more generous commentators would have it, inability to enforce the Marshall Court's invalidation of the Georgia law banning white missionaries from Indian lands in *Worcester v. Georgia* was tied, in part, to his reluctance to widen the Nullification Crisis. Even many northern politicians who were sympathetic to the situation of the Cherokees and opposed to Jackson's Indian policy were reluctant to risk a broader political confrontation. The Nullification Crisis with South Carolina sapped the national political will for federal-state conflict in ways that could not possibly help the Cherokees or their supporters. In this regard, the legality and practical implementation of removal were contested against a background of simmering sectional tensions and fears over the durability of the Union itself.

This complex weave of sectional and national politics may explain a final, intriguing intersection between "nullification" and Indian affairs in the 1830s: the use of the rhetoric of nullification by a northern Indian community as part of their own, rather different political struggle. In 1835, William Apess, an itinerant Pequot Methodist minister and activist, published *Indian Nullification, of the Unconstitutional Laws of Massachusetts Relative to the Marsphee Tribe; or, The Pretended Riot Explained*. This text, possibly coauthored with attorney Benjamin Hallett and writer William G. Snelling, recounts the so-called Mashpee Revolt of 1833–1834 through a variety of testimonials, newspaper stories, and autobiographical reflections. During the "Revolt," the members of the Mashpee community, led by Apess, challenged the governing authority of a state-appointed board of overseers and demanded full control of their property and religious affairs. Apess's pamphlet employs the language of nullification as one of its strategies for demanding that the Mashpees (heretofore almost completely disregarded by the government of Massachusetts) be recognized as a political entity. *Indian Nullification* demands for the residents of Mashpee the same protections of rights and property afforded to any citizen of Massachusetts, and Apess's references to "nullification" represent a strategic move to link this relatively small, local political conflict to the larger national and constitutional questions of the day. The move had some effect, it should be noted, because the Mashpees were eventually able to cast off the paternalistic overseer system and incorporate as a Massachusetts township. It is instructive, in this regard, to see that the issue of nullification impacted Indian politics throughout the entire nation, and not just in the South, during the 1830s.

FURTHER READING: Carlson, David J. *Sovereign Selves: American Indian Autobiography and the Law.* Urbana and Chicago: University of Illinois Press, 2006; Satz, Ronald. *American Indian Policy in the Jacksonian Era.* Norman: University of Oklahoma Press, 2002.

DAVID J. CARLSON

Ogden Land Company

The dispossession of the Seneca Indians of western New York was intricately connected to the interests of private land speculators in the region. The Senecas struggled to hold on to several different reservations in the vicinity of Buffalo at a time when both state and national interests sought to develop a territory whose importance had grown with the completion of the Erie Canal. By the late 19th century, however, only a few reservations remained. The Senecas had been able to retain a small fraction of their former lands and worked hard to resist the push for removal from state and federal officials.

During a 50-year period from the 1790s to the 1840s, the U.S. government negotiated a series of treaties dealing with the lands of the Seneca Indians in western New York. One of the first was signed in 1794, when the United States negotiated an agreement with all of the Six Nations of the Iroquois Confederacy. In that treaty, designated lands in western New York were set aside "to be the property of the Seneca nation; and the United States will never claim the same, nor disturb the Seneca nation, nor any of the Six Nations, or of their Indian friends residing thereon and united with them, in the free use and enjoyment thereof: but it shall remain theirs, until they choose to sell the same to the people of the United States, who have the right to purchase." This 1794 agreement also described the specific boundaries of the Seneca lands. The first cession of Seneca lands occurred in an 1802 treaty, but that was only the beginning.

The pressure on Seneca lands in western New York in the first several decades of the 19th century grew out of local, state, and national developments. The passage of the **Indian Removal Act** in 1830 illustrated that the dispossession and relocation of American Indians living east of the Mississippi River reflected a national sentiment. But the case of the Seneca Indians was wrapped up in regional concerns that were just as important.

The end of the War of 1812 set off substantial movements of American citizens to the territories west of the Appalachian Mountains. Tens of thousands of men and women moved to the Old Northwest. In New York, western expansion was driven in large part by the construction of the Erie Canal. Construction began in 1817, but it was not until October 1825 that former New York governor DeWitt Clinton was able to celebrate the grand opening by traveling the length of the canal. At journey's end, Clinton poured a barrel of Lake Erie water into the Atlantic Ocean.

The construction and completion of the canal initiated a demographic explosion in the western counties of New York. It also led to a tremendous amount of real estate speculation among those who wanted to profit from the canal's existence. The Erie Canal stretched over 300 miles, beginning in Albany and ending in Buffalo on the shores of Lake Erie. This made the land around Buffalo extremely valuable.

One of the organizations that intended to profit from the canal's arrival in Buffalo was named the Ogden Land Company. Its namesake was David A. Ogden, who founded the company in 1810 before the construction of the Erie Canal had gained official approval. In previous years, Ogden had served as the primary attorney for a similar organization known as the Holland Land Company. Ogden and other leading members of this land company set their sights on the Seneca territory around Buffalo well before the canal was completed. Through the efforts of David A. Ogden, the company gained the preemptive right to purchase the nearly 200,000 acres encompassed by the Cattaraugus, Buffalo Creek, Allegany, Caneadea, and Tuscarora reservations. For most of the 1810s and 1820s, therefore, they advocated the removal or concentration of Seneca Indians from western New York. They, along with most New York citizens, believed it was necessary to build up Buffalo as part of the larger development of western New York.

From 1810 to the late 1830s, the Ogden Land Company petitioned state and federal officials for the removal of the Indians. David Ogden in particular argued that the Senecas were more degraded than other Indians and had done nothing to improve the land on which they lived. He and his partners asserted that American citizens could do much more with the land if given the opportunity. David A. Ogden's successors, Thomas L. Ogden and Joseph Fellows, continued those efforts.

Even as the Ogden Land Company pushed for the removal of the Senecas, individual Indian leaders like Red Jacket pushed back. Red Jacket became one of the most outspoken opponents of land cessions in the 1820s among the Senecas. But his opposition also made him a target, and it soon became clear that he could not stop Thomas L. Ogden and Joseph Fellows. From the mid-1820s to the early 1840s, the new leaders of the Ogden Land Company successfully gained tens of thousands of acres of Seneca land.

The first victory for land speculators came with an agreement signed in 1826. This was not an official treaty but was conducted with oversight by American officials. In this agreement with the Ogden Land Company, the Seneca Indians consented to cede their land in the Genesee Valley and to reduce the size of several reservations around Buffalo. It represented an exchange of nearly 90,000 acres from the Senecas to the Ogden Land Company. Red Jacket and other prominent Seneca leaders protested the validity of this agreement without success. Overall, the completion of the Erie Canal and the 1826 agreement sparked substantial white settlement in the area and increased the pressure on Seneca lands.

The treaty of 1838 finished part of what the 1826 agreement had started. Under this treaty, the Senecas ceded all of their land in New York except for one small reservation in exchange for part of nearly 2 million acres west of the Missouri border. The federal government would arrange and provide support for the removal of those Senecas who chose to move west. The Ogden Land Company gained all of the land the Senecas ceded in that treaty.

Representatives of a number of different New York Indian tribes signed the 1838 **Treaty of Buffalo Creek**. Cayugas, Tuscaroras, Oneidas, and others joined the Senecas in this arrangement of cession and removal. But the treaty did not lead to the removal of many of the Senecas and other Indians from the region. Instead, it led to substantial protests from both Indians and non-Indians. The objections focused on the fraud and coercion that may have led the Indians to sign the treaty. In response to the protests, the federal government signed two different treaties in 1842 and 1857. The 1842 treaty arranged for the Ogden Land Company to permit the Senecas to remain on the land encompassed by the Allegany and Cattaraugus reservations. The treaty of 1857 focused on the interests of the **Tonawanda Senecas**, who had not signed the 1838 agreement. Under this agreement, the Tonawandas gave up any claim to lands west of the Mississippi River in exchange for the right to purchase the lands of the Tonawanda reservation from the Ogden Land Company.

By the end of the 1850s, therefore, a population of approximately 2,500 Senecas lived on just over 65,000 acres in western New York. The Senecas on the Allegany and Cattaraugus reservation lived under a new government formed in 1848. The Tonawandas lived on their reservation under the traditional government connected to the Iroquois Confederacy. But the Senecas had lost over 100,000 acres of land in just a few decades, and some of their people had moved west of the Mississippi or north across the Canadian border. Meanwhile, the city of Buffalo had grown to nearly 75,000 people as the non-Indian population of the region increased rapidly.

FURTHER READING: Hauptman, Laurence. *Conspiracy of Interests: Iroquois Dispossession and the Rise of New York State*. Syracuse: Syracuse University Press, 1999; Joint Committee on Indian Affairs of the Four Yearly Meetings of Baltimore, Genesee, New York, and Philadelphia (Society of Friends: Hicksite). *The Case of the Seneca Indians in the State of New York: Illustrated by Facts (1840)*. Philadelphia: Merrihew and Thompson, Reprint Whitefish, MT: Kessinger Publishing, 2008; Kappler, Charles, comp. and ed. *Indian Affairs: Laws and Treaties*. Vol. 2. Washington, DC: U.S. Government Printing Office, 1904; Sturtevant, William C. "Seneca-Cayuga." In *Handbook of the North American Indians*. Vol. 15: *The Northeast*. Ed. Bruce G. Trigger. Washington, DC: Smithsonian Institution, 1978, pp. 537–543; Tooker, Elisabeth. "Iroquois since

1820." In *Handbook of the North American Indians*. Vol. 15: *The Northeast*. Ed. Bruce G. Trigger. Washington, DC: Smithsonian Institution, 1978, pp. 449–465.

JOHN P. BOWES

Oneidas

The Oneida Nation was part of the Iroquois Confederacy around Lake Oneida in present-day central New York State. During the Revolutionary War the Oneidas and the Tuscaroras sided with the Americans, but this did not stop the United States from clearing Oneida land of its people as white settlers moved into the area. State of New York officials, too, signed documents that purported to "lease" Oneida lands, whereas they were really bills of sale. As the Oneida land diminished, the United States signed a treaty in 1794 with the tribe that included further land sessions but guaranteed the Oneidas that no further cessions would take place. However, this stipulation was ignored by state officials, who found leaders among the Iroquois, including the Oneidas, who would sign land cession treaties; New York State and the Iroquois entered into such treaties in 1794, 1805, 1807, and 1809. By the War of 1812, the Oneidas had lost almost all of their land, and the tribe had opened land for the occupancy of eastern tribes escaping white pressure, the Stockbridge-Munsees and the **Brothertons.** The Oneidas debated whether it would be better to remove to the West than to remain the prey of white land speculators.

By the end of the War of 1812, Eleazar Williams, an Episcopal Mohawk preacher who knew the Oneida language, came to proselytize among the Christian party, at the time a very dispirited group, and the Pagan party, so called because of their adherence to the traditional Iroquois religion. Williams was able to convert some of the "pagans" and to reinvigorate some of the Christians. However, he was unable to unite them as a cohesive group.

Williams and Jedidiah Morse concluded that the Oneidas would best be served by selling their New York lands and moving to the lands west of Lake Michigan, at the time relatively free of white settlers. This plan had the concurrence of the federal government, which offered to help with the negotiations. Accordingly, Williams led a delegation to Green Bay in 1821 and negotiated with the **Menominees** and **Ho-Chunks,** then known as Winnebagos, for lands that the Oneidas, the Stockbridge-Munsees, and the Brothertons could settle. Two treaties, signed in 1821 and 1822, turned over nearly 8 million acres in the Fox River Valley and Lake Winnebago areas to the New York tribes. As the first of the emigrants began to filter into Wisconsin, a dispute arose, in which the Menominees and Ho-Chunks claimed that their intent was not to sell the land but to share it, a common practice among Indians of the western Great Lakes. As the Oneida First Christian party arrived, followed by the Methodist Orchard party, the argument heated up. Aware of the difficulties before them, some of the Oneidas diverted to southern Ontario, an easy detour because the New York Indians traveled by boats through the Great Lakes. The federal government finally had to mediate the dispute, and in 1831 and 1832, in a series of three treaties, the Oneidas were allowed to stay, although on reduced acreage, while the Stockbridge-Munsees were relocated north to land adjacent to Menominee lands (*see* **Stockbridge-Munsee Removal**).

In 1834, the federal government opened Wisconsin Territory to white settlement, and territorial officials such as Governor Henry Dodge were avid advocates for white arrivals. Dodge was instrumental in removing Indians from the territory, and in 1845 he approached the Oneidas, demanding that they remove west of the Mississippi. Some of the Oneidas were willing to go if favorable terms could be reached, but Orchard party leader Jacob Cornelius and others refused to even enter into negotiations. By this time, the Oneidas were farming successfully, living in frame houses, and providing their people with schools and churches. The next assault on the tribe came in the 1850s when logging companies sought Oneida land, offering to buy out individual farmers. The tribes resisted this voluntary allotment program, knowing that it meant the demise of the Nation. They were able to hold out until 1890, when the federal government allotted the land in severalty; by the 1920s, only a few hundred acres remained in the hands of Oneida tribal members. The remainder of the 65,400 acres was owned by whites. In 1936, under the Indian Reorganization Act, the Oneidas reinstituted their tribal government. The following year, they began to buy back land.

FURTHER READING: Ellis, Albert G. "The Advent of the New York Indians into Wisconsin." *Collections of the State Historical Society of Wisconsin* 2 (1855): 415–449; Loew, Patty. *Indian Nations of Wisconsin.* Madison: Wisconsin State Historical Society Press, 2001; Oneida Nation. At www.oneidanation.org/; "Oneida Treaties and Treaty Rights." At www.mpm.edu/wirp/ICW-106.html.

JAMES W. PARINS

Opothleyohola (c. 1798–1863)

Opothleyohola, a Creek from Tuckabatchee town, became the most powerful headman in the Creek Nation during their removal period (1827–1838) (*see* **Muscogee (Creek) Removal**). He was at the forefront of Creek attempts to remain on their ancestral land in the East in the face of white encroachment and government interference in Creek affairs. Opothleyohola first served nationally as the speaker for Big Warrior, the principal chief of the Upper Creeks. After Big Warrior's death in 1825, Opothleyohola served as "prime minister or Chief Councillor of the Nation."

In 1825, acting as the speaker for the Upper Creeks, Opothleyohola traveled to Indian Springs, Georgia, to warn William McIntosh against ceding all Creek land in Georgia and portions of land in Alabama to the federal government. McIntosh disregarded these warnings and signed the Treaty of Indian Springs, for which he was later executed. In addition, the treaty was a removal document that set aside land in present-day Oklahoma in exchange for the ceded land. Opothleyohola and a delegation of Creek headmen traveled to Washington and were successful in overturning the Treaty of Indian

Springs. The Creeks agreed to a revised treaty in 1826 that restored their Alabama lands; however, under heavy pressure from the Americans, the Creeks were unable to recoup their land in Georgia. Opothleyohola was staunchly opposed to voluntary removal, and he rejected government overtures to emigrate his people west.

The pressure to voluntarily emigrate became more intense as white squatters settled illegally on Creek land. The problem became so widespread that Opothleyohola and other headmen traveled to Washington in 1832 to negotiate a treaty that gave the Creeks legal title to their land. The government did not enforce the articles of the treaty to the Creeks' satisfaction, however. Compounding the problem were widespread frauds by which whites cheated the Creeks out of their land reserves.

Sensing the inevitability of Creek removal and opposed to emigrating to **Indian Territory**, Opothleyohola attempted to secure a deed to a tract of land in Texas in 1834. The deal fell through because it was illegal under a treaty signed between the United States and Mexico. In 1835, Opothleyohola began making preparations to emigrate to Indian Territory, and that year he sent a number of his slaves west. But, before Opothleyohola was ready

Engraving of a portrait of Opothleyohola, "Speaker of the Councils," chief of the Upper Creeks, by 19th-century American painter Charles Bird King, from *The Indian Tribes of North America*. (McKenney, Thomas L. and James Hall. *The Indian Tribes of North America*, 1836–1844)

to move west himself, the Second Creek War broke out in east-central Alabama in 1836. Opothleyohola, **Tustenuggee Emathla** (Jim Boy), and others commanded warriors who helped the U.S. Army bring an end to hostilities. The war provided an excuse for Andrew **Jackson** to forcibly remove all Creeks to the West.

Opothleyohola was assigned to detachment one, which consisted of 2,318 Creeks, mostly from Tuckabatchee. The party left Tallassee on August 31, 1836, and traveled through Wetumpka and Tuscaloosa to Memphis, where they arrived on October 9, before they boarded the steamboat *Farmer* to Rock Roe. Opothleyohola and the rest of detachment one traveled overland through the Grand Prairie and Cross Roads and out to Cadron, where the road joined the military road from Little Rock to Fort Smith. Their progress was slow because of bad roads and rain. The party arrived at Fort Gibson in Indian Territory on December 7, 1836. Seventy-eight Creeks from detachment one died along the journey. After arriving, Opothleyohola settled near the Canadian River. Although he maintained his role as one of the principal chiefs in the West, his status was superseded by William McIntosh's brother Roly.

Opothleyohola did not find peace in the West. During the American Civil War, Confederate regiments of McIntosh Creeks drove Opothleyohola and his people as well as loyal Seminoles and blacks to Kansas, partly as retribution for his role in McIntosh's 1825 execution. Opothleyohola died in Kansas sometime around 1863.

FURTHER READING: Green, Michael D. *The Politics of Indian Removal: Creek Government and Society in Crisis.* Lincoln: University of Nebraska Press, 1982; Haveman, Christopher D. "The Removal of the Creek Indians from the Southeast, 1825–1838." PhD diss., Auburn University, 2009; Meserve, John Bartlett. "Chief Opothleyahola." *Chronicles of Oklahoma* 9 (1931):4: 439–451.

CHRISTOPHER D. HAVEMAN

Oshkosh (1795–1858)

Oshkosh was chief of the Menominees (*see* **Menominee Removal**) in the years in which the New York tribes came to Wisconsin and afterward, when the U.S. government was trying to remove the Menominees west of the Mississippi under the terms of the **Indian Removal Act**. In the 1820s, groups from various Indian nations living in New York State planned to move to the western side of Lake Michigan, including the **Oneidas,** Stockbridge-Munsees (*see* **Stockbridge-Munsee Removal**), and **Brothertons.** The lands in Wisconsin that these groups considered for settlement were those around Green Bay and the Fox River Valley. At the time, these lands were occupied by the Menominees as well as the **Ho-Chunks,** or Winnebagos, as they were known.

Oshkosh was the chief negotiator for the Menominees, and as such walked a tight line between protecting the rights of his people against the wishes not only of the New York Indians but also of the U.S. government. Other parties to the negotiations were the Ho-Chunks and French traders and land speculators centered at Green Bay. The upper Great Lakes had only recently passed into American hands from the British, but the main white people in the area were the French, who had come into the area beginning in the 17th century to exploit the fur trade and other resources. Many of these were powerful landowners and traders, the bulwarks of local government, trade, and religion. They hoped to profit from any land cessions made by the two Wisconsin tribes.

Initial negotiations allowed the New York Indians to take control of a tract of land along the Fox River; later, this area was expanded. In the meantime, the French claimed a sizeable portion of land adjacent to the ceded tract, but the claim was disallowed by the federal government. When the eastern Indians began to arrive in Wisconsin, it became clear that they were

Menominee chief Oshkosh, 1795–1858. (Wisconsin Historical Society/WHS Image ID 3954)

taking exclusive control of the lands involved. Oshkosh protested, saying that the Menominees and Ho-Chunks had agreed to the cessions with the understanding that the land was to be shared, a common practice among the Wisconsin tribes. The protest continued, although the New York Indians maintained a steady stream of immigrants.

In 1830, with the passage of the Indian Removal Act, Oshkosh found that any bargaining position his people might have had had vanished. The Ho-Chunks were being removed out of the territory, as were the Sauks and Mesquakies, leaving the Menominees isolated in the eastern part of the state. The federal government began negotiating with Oshkosh for further land cessions, and in 1832, the Menominees ceded 3 million acres, half a million of which were to be used for the benefit of the New York Indians. Payment to the Menominees for this vast tract was to be $146,500 paid over twelve years.

However, as more white settlers poured into Wisconsin Territory, they demanded more land. In 1836, the Menominees gave up the eastern half of their remaining land. In 1848, Wisconsin became a state, and the government of Wisconsin petitioned the federal government to remove the Menominees entirely. By presidential decree, the Nation was ordered to a reservation along the Crow Wing River in Minnesota. Oshkosh and a delegation of Menominees visited the area and returned dissatisfied, largely because of the fighting there between the Ojibwe and Dakota people. Oshkosh announced that his people would remain in Wisconsin. "The poorest land in Wisconsin," he is alleged to have declared, "was better than the Crow Wing."

Oshkosh then visited the president in Washington, D.C., and managed to persuade him to temporarily hold the order for Menominee removal. Pressure continued on the tribe to remove, but Oshkosh and the tribal council delayed. Finally, they were able to negotiate the Treaty of 1854 by which the Menominees reserved 270,000 acres of forested land along the Oconto and Wolf Rivers. Oshkosh died there in 1858. This was the tribe's home until the federal government once more disrupted it with termination of tribal status in 1961. The tribe's federal recognition was restored in 1973.

FURTHER READING: Ellis, Albert G. "The Advent of the New York Indians into Wisconsin." *Collections of the State Historical Society of Wisconsin* 2 (1855): 415–449; Loew, Patti. *Indian Nations of Wisconsin: Histories of Endurance and Renewal.* Madison: Wisconsin State Historical Society, 2001; Ourada, Patricia K. *The Menominee Indians. A History.* Norman: University of Oklahoma Press, 1979.

JAMES W. PARINS

Ottawa Removal

The removal era, begun in force with the 1830 **Indian Removal Act**, affected some of the Ottawas more than others, often depending on geography more than other factors. In the latter half of the 17th century, the people known as the Odawak, or Ottawas, who had lived in the western Great Lakes region for centuries, loosely divided into three groups. The first group, largely unaffected by the American removal policy, lived in the archipelago in Lake Huron and the Georgian Bay, with Manitoulin Island at the center of this polity. The next group remained near the Michilimackinac Straits, which had become the major regional trading center of the western Great Lakes. This group, the Michigan Ottawas, eventually spread southward into northwestern lower Michigan as far south as the Indiana border. A third group traveled to the region near present-day Detroit and Toledo, settling on the Detroit and Maumee Rivers, as well as Walpole Island. This third group is the Ohio Ottawas, the group most affected by the removal period.

The Ohio Ottawas became involved in the geopolitics of England and America during the 18th century. Pontiac, an Ottawa *ogema* (leader, headman, or speaker in Anishinaabemowin) born on the Maumee River, took credit for organizing a major military campaign by dozens of Indian communities against British forts in the Great Lakes and Ohio Valley regions in 1763. This war involved the siege of Detroit and the fall of most British forts in these regions, including the major fort at Michilimackinac. Although Detroit never fell and the British regained all of its lost ground shortly thereafter, the fact that so many disparate Indian groups in two large regions could band together in a coordinated military campaign was a shock to the British and American governments and militaries.

As a likely result of this military and political capability, the British crown promulgated the Proclamation of 1763, which established British crown control over all Indian affairs, excluding the American colonial governments and citizens. The Ohio Ottawas exerted a great deal of influence in the major trading and military center of Detroit, and they became known as formidable fighters as well as powerful traders, part of Pontiac's legacy. But by 1795, after suffering a critical military setback at the Battle of Fallen Timbers (along with several other tribes), the Ohio Ottawas had lost much of this influence and power. They agreed to the Treaty of Greenville that year, which ceded much of Ohio, Indiana, and Illinois to the Americans. In 1807, the Ohio Ottawas also participated in the Treaty of Detroit, ceding control of Detroit to the Americans. For the most part, the Ohio Ottawas sat out the War of 1812, in which many Great Lakes region Indians (including the Michigan Ottawas) took up arms with the British against the Americans.

In 1830, Andrew **Jackson** championed Congress's Indian Removal Act, which established Indian removal west of the Mississippi River as the dominant American Indian affairs policy. The Ohio Ottawas, residing still on the Maumee River, a region the Americans prized for its agricultural potential, became targets for removal. In 1831, they signed their first removal treaty with the United States. Several groups of Ohio Ottawas agreed to travel west to Kansas, at great discomfort and tragedy. When this first group arrived, many immediately returned to the Maumee River in great torment, telling the rest of the Ohio Ottawas that Kansas was a wasteland. To woodlands Indians dependent on the lakes and rivers of their home region, a vast prairie with no lakes, rivers, or trees would have appeared to be a desolate and uninhabitable place.

For the next several years, the remaining Ohio Ottawas avoided forced removal, but in 1837, 1838, and 1839, the U.S. military forced additional removals in a piecemeal fashion. In all, about half of the population fled to Canada, to Manitoulin and Walpole Islands, and about half of those who attempted the trek to Kansas died along the way. Only a few hundred Ottawas populated the Ottawa reservation in Kansas.

Kansas was an unmitigated disaster for the Ottawas. Upon arrival, unscrupulous whites tricked them into spending their remaining capital on a university for Ottawa children. Sadly, this became known as the Ottawa University fraud. Worse, the reservation lands truly were desolate and virtually useless for purposes of agriculture and livestock raising.

By the 1850s, American policy had shifted to confining the disparate Indian groups to smaller and smaller reservations in **Indian Territory**. And in the 1860s, the Kansas Ottawas removed once again, this time to Indian Territory. This group became organized in 1938 under the Oklahoma Indian Welfare Act, later terminated by Congress in the 1950s, and then later restored by Congress in the 1970s. Since that time, the Ottawa Tribe of Oklahoma has not demonstrated significant political or economic might. It remains a very small and very poor tribe.

The Michigan Ottawas and Chippewas divided northern Michigan south of the Mackinac Straits in half, with the Chippewas taking the eastern, Lake Huron side and the Ottawas taking the western, Lake Michigan side. The Ottawas settled the western half at least as far as the Grand River. The groups now known as the Little Traverse Bay Bands of Odawa Indians established the largest and most prominent communities, known as the L'Arbre Croche ("Crooked Tree") villages in the region closest to Mackinac. Further south, the Grand Traverse Bay Ottawas, along with two Chippewa villages, established several communities. A very prominent group of Ottawa agriculturalists resided on the Grand River Valley, where the oft-flooded valley offered fertile lands for crops. Many Ottawa villages dotted the Lake Michigan shoreline as far south as the Indiana border.

Northern Ottawas were seasonal people, residing in larger villages during the summer, which was the prime farming, fishing, and trading season. In the fall, the smaller family units would retreat inland and south to reside in their winter hunting and trapping villages. Some Ottawa families would join their cousins in the Grand River Valley, or even further south into Indiana and Illinois. In the spring, the Ottawas would travel to maple groves and engage in six weeks or so of making sugar. Then, the Ottawas would return to the summer places.

Michigan Ottawas were not as prominent fighters as the Ohio Ottawas. In the 19th century, these Ottawas were well known for their astounding canoes and traveling capabilities. They did participate in the 1763 war attributed to Pontiac, burning the key British fort at Michilimackinac, and many Ottawas fought in the War of 1812 for the British. But the northern Michigan Ottawas, with the exception of the more southern Grand River Ottawas, did not face the acute pressure of American settlement faced by the Ohio Ottawas, and so did not often engage non-Indian militaries.

That does not mean the 1830s policy of Indian removal did not touch them. In 1836, the United States sought to remove the Michigan Ottawas west to Kansas or Iowa, along with the Ohio Ottawas. But the Michigan Ottawa and Chippewa treaty negotiators instead bargained for a permanent homeland, several reservations dotting the upper and lower peninsulas of Michigan. The U.S. Senate unilaterally abrogated that portion of the treaty after the fact. Henry **Schoolcraft**, the Michigan Indian agent and 1836 treaty commissioner for the United States, promised the Anishinaabeks that they would retain usufruct rights over unsettled lands in northern Michigan, thereby persuading the Anishinaabeks to sign on to the Senate's amendments. In the 1830s and 1840s, the United States administered smallpox vaccinations to over 11,000 Michigan Anishinaabeks in accordance with the Indian Vaccination Act of 1832.

In 1855, after decades of uncertainty and continued threats of removal, the Michigan Anishinaabeks negotiated another treaty. This one provided for individual property ownership, after a federal trust period, within the traditional homelands of the Ottawas and Chippewas. And so the Michigan Ottawas attempted to select lands under this treaty, only to be defeated by federal official incompetence and corruption, non-Indian frauds, intimidation, violence, abuse of legal processes, and so on. Few Michigan Ottawas were able to secure lands for any significant period of time. Most Ottawas lived on wage labor and their wits for decades. Even worse, the U.S. Department of Interior misread an innocuous treaty provision and treated the Michigan Ottawas as terminated tribes beginning in the 1870s.

But the Michigan Ottawas had one clear asset: the usufructary rights on lands not yet required for settlement. They might have little or no land for themselves, but less than a third of northern Michigan was ever required for settlement, at least in the way that the Indians would have understood that term.

Eventually, after years of underground living, the Michigan Ottawas and Chippewas began to seriously assert their treaty rights in the 1960s. In numerous federal and state court cases, they were successful in securing rights to commercially harvest fish on Lakes Michigan and Superior. In the 1980s and 1990s, three Michigan Ottawa communities—the Grand Traverse Band of Ottawa and Chippewa Indians, the Little Traverse Bay Bands of Odawa Indians, and the Little River Band of Ottawa Indians—earned federal recognition from the United States.

FURTHER READING: Bauman, Robert F. "Kansas Starvation, Canada, or Starvation." *Michigan History* 36 (1952): 287–299; Cleland, Charles E. *Rites of Conquest: The History and Culture of Michigan's Native Americans*. Ann Arbor: University of Michigan Press, 1992; Gray, Susan E. "Limits and Possibilities: White-Indian Relations in Western Michigan in the Era of Removal." *Michigan Historical Review* 20 (1994): 71–91; McClurken, James M. "The Ottawa." In *People of the Three Fires: The Ottawa, Potawatomi, and Ojibway of Michigan*. Ed. James A. Clifton, George L. Cornell, and James M.

McClurken. Grand Rapids, MI: Grand Rapids Inter-Tribal Council, 1986, pp. 1–38; Neumeyer, Elizabeth. "Michigan Indians Battle against Removal." *Michigan History* 55 (1971): 275–288; Satz, Ronald. "Indian Policy in the Jacksonian Era: The Old Northwest as a Test Case." *Michigan History* 60 (1976): 71–93; "Treaty with the Chippewa, etc., 1833." Indian Affairs: Laws and Treaties. At http://digital.library .okstate.edu/kappler/Vol2/treaties/chi0402.htm; Unrau, William E., and H. Craig Miner. *Dispossession and the Ottawa Indian University Fraud.* Norman: University of Oklahoma Press, 1985.

MATTHEW L. M. FLETCHER

P

Panoahah (dates unknown)

Panoahah was a Kickapoo leader who, at the time of removal, was a member of **Mecina**'s band, which was allied with the Sauk chief **Black Hawk**. After the winter hunt in Illinois in 1831, the U.S. government expected Black Hawk's band to cross the Mississippi and take up residence in Iowa on the lands provided for in the **Sauk and Mesquakie (Fox) removal** treaty (*see* **Black Hawk War**). However, Black Hawk returned to Saukenuk, the traditional village of his Nation at the confluence of the Rock River and the Mississippi, where the women began to plant corn, squash, and beans as they had always done. By this time, white settlers had moved into the vicinity and had begun to complain to the authorities about Indians destroying fences and killing livestock. When the farmers demanded enforcement of the removal treaty, Governor John Reynolds sent the Illinois militia to Saukenuk, and Black Hawk and his followers retreated over the Mississippi. The Kickapoos who had remained in Illinois watched these events with interest, especially members of Mecina's band.

Black Hawk did not remain in Iowa for long. In April 1832, he crossed the Mississippi to take control of the lands around Saukenuk, which by now had been settled by an influx of whites. During that winter, Black Hawk had sent recruiters among the tribes trying to bolster his forces. His men visited even the distant Cherokees, whom Black Hawk knew to be resisting removal. Many of the Kickapoos were eager to rally to his cause, doubtless because of the helplessness they felt at seeing their lands filled with white settlers. This was especially true among the two Kickapoo bands that remained in Illinois, those of **Kennekuk** and Mecina.

Both Kennekuk and Mecina urged their followers to ignore what was going on around the Rock River and to go about their peaceful life. Both men seemed to believe that the white men would leave them alone as long as they lived peacefully with their new neighbors. Panoahah and many of the younger warriors were eager to join Black Hawk, however. They had seen other peaceful tribes forcefully removed and believed that only by strength in numbers could they resist the white expansion. Further, they had seen how the settlers made no distinction between tribes, between those who were "peaceful" and those who were "warlike." Some Kickapoos, too, knew of the "Winnebago Prophet" who advised Black Hawk. While on a recruiting trip as far as Canada, Neapope, one of Black Hawk's lieutenants, had conferred with the Winnebago, who informed him that if Black Hawk reclaimed the Sauk and Mesquakie lands east of the Mississippi, his band would be joined by the Potawatomis, Ojibwes, and Ottawas as well as British troops. With this information and their natural desire to oppose their enemies, Panoahah and his followers left Mecina's band to join Black Hawk. With his band thus decimated, Mecina saw no choice but to join Kennekuk.

Once Panoahah and his warriors joined the Sauk and Mesquakie forces, a rift was opened among the Kickapoos. Instead of strengthening the Kickapoos, as Panoahah intended, his actions contributed to weakening the Nation. Panoahah's band of around 100 warriors along with a small number of Winnebagos accompanied Black Hawk's followers on their historic journey as they were pursued by the militia into Wisconsin and defeated at the confluence of the Bad Axe River and the Mississippi. Panoahah and the other Kickapoos did not make it that far, however. Once Black Hawk's people were forced away from Lake Koshkonong near present-day Madison, Wisconsin, and dispersed into the swamps, great deprivation followed. The Kickapoos saw that the allies whom Black Hawk had been promised were not forthcoming and decided to return to their people. Defeated by hardship, disappointment, and the Illinois militia, they straggled back to Kennekuk's band.

FURTHER READING: Gibson, Arrell M. *The Kickapoos: Lords of the Middle Border*. Norman: University of Oklahoma Press, 1963; Jackson, Donald, ed. *Black Hawk: An Autobiography*. Urbana-Champaign: University of Illinois Press, 1987; Nichols, Roger L. *Black Hawk and the Warrior's Path*. Arlington Heights, IL: Harlan Davidson, Inc., 1992.

JAMES W. PARINS

Parker, Ely S. (1828–1895)

Beginning about 1845, Ely S. Parker served as one of the principal spokespeople in the **Tonawanda Seneca** resistance campaign against removal and the legal battle against the **Ogden Land Company**. While his brother Nicholson **Parker** served as liaison between himself and Seneca leaders, Ely Parker was instrumental in keeping the issue at the forefront of the minds of legislators in Albany and in Washington D.C., where he spent a significant amount of his young life. In 1857, with the help of several non-Native citizens and lawyers, Parker brought the legal battle and the removal crisis to a conclusion. The Tonawanda Senecas were able to remain in a portion of their homeland and purchase a permanent title to the land. In 1861, Parker returned again to Tonawanda to reform the structures of governance there in an effort to

Ely S. Parker (1828–1895), a Seneca, also known as "Hasanoanda," helped wage a public campaign against removal. (National Archives)

combat the aftereffects of the removal crisis, especially the disruption it caused to customary notions of power and authority.

Perhaps the most significant of the emerging generation of Seneca leaders in the early to mid-19th century, Parker pursued educational opportunities at the Baptist Mission school on the Tonawanda reservation and then at the Yates and Cayuga Academies in western New York State. He also descended from a politically powerful family and was a member of the Wolf clan, the same as famed Seneca orator Red Jacket. During one of his trips to Albany, he met Lewis Henry Morgan and later became his close friend and informant on his research for *The League of the Ho-De-No-Sau-Nee, Or Iroquois* (1851). In 1851, in recognition of his leadership during the resistance campaign, the Tonawandas raised Parker to the position of sachem, an uncommon honor for a man as young as he.

In the aftermath of the removal crisis, Parker served as a civil engineer for the U.S. Department of the Treasury, became a brigadier general and Ulysses S. Grant's personal military secretary in the Civil War, and then was appointed to be the first Native American commissioner of Indian affairs.

Parker, though not yet an adolescent when the 1838 **Treaty of Buffalo Creek** took effect, demonstrated an aptitude for the English language that drew the attention of Tonawanda leaders. That he descended from a powerful family and clan also prepared him for a leadership role. As a teenager, Parker served as an interpreter for Tonawanda leaders when they traveled to Albany, but soon the young man began expressing his own opinions and ideas, based on his experiences in non-Native academies. Parker helped create a three-pronged resistance strategy for the Tonawandas that involved physically blocking any attempts the Ogden Land Company made at settlement and appraisement, applying for judicial action to remove trespassers at the state level, and filing appeals to national-level politicians to invalidate officially the treaties through the Senate Committee on Indian Affairs. Although Parker became frustrated and depressed at many points throughout the campaign, usually because of real or perceived factionalism among the Senecas, he also benefited from strong kin and clan relations that helped sustain him through the difficult periods. The Tonawanda Senecas maintain a portion of their homeland to this day, in large part because of the work Parker did in the 1840s and 1850s.

FURTHER READING: Armstrong, William H. *Warrior in Two Camps: Ely S. Parker, Union General and Seneca Chief.* Syracuse, NY: Syracuse University Press, 1978;

Genetin-Pilawa, C. Joseph. "Confining Indians: Power, Authority, and the Colonist Ideologies of Nineteenth-Century Reformers." PhD diss., Michigan State University, 2008; Parker, Arthur C. *The Life of General Ely S. Parker: Last Grand Sachem of the Iroquois and General Grant's Military Secretary.* Buffalo, NY: Buffalo Historical Society, 1919.

C. JOSEPH GENETIN-PILAWA

Parker, Nicholson (c. 1820–1892)

Following the **Treaty of Buffalo Creek** in 1838, Nicholson Parker served as one of the chief strategists and spokespeople for the Tonawanda community in their resistance campaign against removal. He was educated at the Albany Normal School, fluent in English as well as Hodenosaunee, and a Christian convert, though he also followed the teachings of the Seneca Prophet, Handsome Lake. While his younger brother Ely S. **Parker** traveled between Albany and Washington, D.C., to bring the **Tonawanda Seneca** case against removal before the state and federal legislators, Nicholson remained on the reservation and served as a liaison between Ely and the other Tonawanda leaders. His correspondence with the younger Parker reveals much about the community-level consequences of a removal crisis for Indian people, including the disruption of customary notions of power and authority and traditional structures of governance.

Born in or around 1820, Parker spent much of his early life at the Tonawanda reservation. He studied on and off the reservation, excelled as a farmer, and served as one of Lewis Henry Morgan's key Indian informants in the research for *The League of the Ho-De-No-Sau-Nee, Or Iroquois* (1851). Nicholson also worked as an interpreter for Asher Wright, a missionary who worked among the Senecas. Among other things, he translated the Bible into Hodenosaunee and married Wright's niece, a non-Native woman named Martha Hoyt. Parker spent most of his adult life on the Cattaraugus reservation, where he served as an interpreter for the Bureau of Indian Affairs in the aftermath of the legal battle with the **Ogden Land Company**. His grandson, Arthur Caswell Parker, became the New York State archaeologist and published the first biography of Ely S. Parker, *The Life of General Ely S. Parker* (1919).

During the removal crisis, Nicholson, along with his father William Parker, provided his brother Ely with information and insights from Tonawanda as the younger Parker petitioned senators and other lawmakers, often sending daily letters. In 1846, Nicholson was arrested by the Genesee County sheriff for following Ely's advice and planting a field that had been cleared by a non-Native settler employed by the Ogden Land Company. At times in their letters, both the Parker brothers expressed frustration and concern with factionalism at Tonawanda, while at others they demonstrated fear that they would not be able to help their community as much as they would like. It must be remembered that both men were quite young for such responsibilities (late teens and early 20s). Nicholson frequently provided encouraging words to his younger brother, assuaging his fears and reminding him of the support he had among his family and friends. The fears and frustration expressed in these letters demonstrate the difficult position in which many young Indian leaders found themselves during a removal crisis. The strong family bond, however, allowed the Parkers to chart a course that resulted in the Tonawanda Senecas successfully thwarting the Ogden Land Company's removal efforts and maintaining a portion of their homeland.

FURTHER READING: Armstrong, William H. *Warrior in Two Camps: Ely S. Parker, Union General and Seneca Chief.* Syracuse, NY: Syracuse University Press, 1978; Konkle, Maureen. *Writing Indian Nations: Native Intellectuals and the Politics of Historiography, 1827–1863.* Chapel Hill: University of North Carolina Press, 2004; Parker, Arthur C. *The Life of General Ely S. Parker: Last Grand Sachem of the Iroquois and General Grant's Military Secretary.* Buffalo, NY: Buffalo Historical Society, 1919.

C. JOSEPH GENETIN-PILAWA

Peoria-Kaskaskia-Piankeshaw-Wea Removal

The earliest French explorers identified the Algonquian tribes that lived on lands between the Great Lakes and the Mississippi as the Illinois or Illini. The several tribes within the Illinois group were the Cahokias, Kaskaskias, Michigameas, Moingwenas, Peorias, and Tamaroas. As these people came under pressure from tribes moving west from the eastern Great Lakes and the Ohio River Valley, they began to migrate south and west, crossing the Mississippi as early as 1763. In the course of these migrations, the tribes dwindled as they lost many people to disease and famine and to warfare waged against them by the Kickapoos and Mesquakies. By the second decade of the 19th century, four tribes emerged from the Illinois group: the Peorias, Kaskaskias, Piankeshaws, and Weas. The Peorias at this time were closely allied with the Kaskaskias and the Weas with the Piankeshaws.

Once the **Indian Removal Act** was enacted, the survivors of the four tribes were forced to move from their remaining lands in Missouri; the Treaty of Lewisville in 1832 ceded their remaining lands there for two adjoining parcels of land on the Osage River in Kansas. In 1854, the four tribes were united as the Confederated Peoria. The 1854 treaty also provided that the Confederation lands be divided, with 10 sections to be held by the tribes in common, while other lands were allotted to individuals. The "surplus" land was then offered for sale to white settlers. When Kansas became a state in 1861, many of those who had accepted allotments lost their lands to tax sales and other legal maneuvers. After the Civil War, the Confederation was party to the Omnibus Treaty of 1867, which removed them once again, this time from Kansas to **Indian Territory**, where land was purchased from the Quapaws (*see* **Quapaw Removal**). The Confederation was terminated in 1959, but it was reinstated as a federally recognized tribe in 1978.

FURTHER READING: Peoria Tribe of Indians of Oklahoma. At www.peoriatribe .com/history.php; "Treaty with the Kaskaskia, etc, 1832." Indian Affairs: Laws and Treaties. At http://digital.library.okstate.edu/kappler/Vol2/treaties/kas0376.htm;

Wright, Muriel. *A Guide to the Indian Tribes of Oklahoma.* Norman: University of Oklahoma Press, 1951.

JAMES W. PARINS

Piankeshaw Removal

See Peoria-Kaskaskia-Piankeshaw-Wea Removal

Pierce, Maris Bryant (1811–1874)

Maris Bryant Pierce, or Ho-dya-no-dah, "Swift Runner," was a central figure in the Seneca struggle against removal from New York. Born on the Allegany reservation, Pierce was educated at a local Quaker academy and a series of boarding schools in New York and Vermont. In 1836, he enrolled at Dartmouth College and after graduation read law at the Buffalo offices of Tillinhard and Smith. While enrolled at Dartmouth, Pierce assumed the position of a Seneca "young chief"; in this capacity he was involved in the events leading to the signing of the fraudulent removal **Treaty of Buffalo Creek** in 1838. Pierce signed that agreement but immediately repudiated his support for it, becoming a leading voice for the Seneca majority opposed to removal. Pierce first delivered an *Address on the Present Condition and Prospects of the Aboriginal Inhabitants of North America, with Particular Reference to the Seneca Nation* on August 28, 1838. This oration, the most forceful Seneca-authored anti-removal text, was printed twice during the following year. Having been appointed one of the attorneys representing the Senecas of the Tonawanda, Allegany, Cattaraugus, and Buffalo Creek reservations, Pierce also carried out other prominent activities, such as coauthoring a letter to President Martin **Van Buren** in 1838, protesting the Buffalo Creek agreement, and petitioning Secretary of War Joel Poinsett in 1839 to request modification of that treaty.

The U.S Senate ratified the Treaty of Buffalo Creek in 1840, but Pierce continued his public campaign against removal, serving the Seneca leadership as translator and secretary. Partly through his efforts, a supplemental removal agreement was signed on May 20, 1842, enabling the Senecas to keep their lands on the Allegany and Cattaraugus reservations. Pierce removed from Buffalo Creek to Cattaraugus in 1848 and continued to serve the Nation until the so-called Seneca Revolution of 1848, when the "old chiefs" were deposed and replaced by an elective system of government.

Pierce's obviously conflicted position during Seneca removal highlights the complex pressures on Indian mediator figures during the removal era. Aware of the struggles of various southern tribes to develop more forceful legal arguments against removal, Pierce adapted the paternalistic discourse of federal Indian law to obtain concessions from the government, invoking the notion of the United States' "trust" responsibility toward its Indian wards (articulated by John Marshall in the recent Cherokee cases) in his effort to revise the Buffalo Creek agreement. The 1838 *Address*, in particular, engages with conventional European understandings of cultural hierarchy, one of the principles buttressing the removal policy. Pierce's main argument against Seneca removal was that his Nation's collective desire to be "improved" was best served by proximity to Euro-American settlers. Rehearsing the history of the colonial law of discovery and the Senecas' "occupancy" rights to their own lands, he strategically conceded the superiority of the "Enlightened" culture surrounding Seneca lands. Arguing from a position of weakness, then, Pierce carved out a provisional space for resistance. In the political climate of the time, however, such resistance could only be partially successful.

FURTHER READING: Carlson, David J. *Sovereign Selves: American Indian Autobiography and the Law.* Urbana and Chicago: University of Illinois Press, 2006; Littlefield, Daniel F., Jr. "'They Ought to Enjoy the Home of Their Fathers': The Treaty of 1838, Seneca Intellectuals, and Literary Genesis." In *Early Native American Writing: New Critical Essays.* Ed. Helen Jaskoski. New York: Cambridge University Press, 1996, pp. 83–103.

DAVID J. CARLSON

Poarch Band of Creek Indians

Descended from about a dozen friendly Creek mixed bloods who escaped Creek removal (*see* **Muscogee [Creek] Removal**), the Poarch Creeks tie their history to a provision in the Treaty of Fort Jackson of 1814 that set aside mile-square reservations for each Creek chief and warrior who had remained friendly to the United States during the Creek War of 1813–1814. The treaty required that the Creeks and their descendants remain on the land, which reverted to the United States if they left it. In addition to the original reserve selections, in 1836 and 1837, additional Creeks were allowed to select reservations under the terms of the treaty. Poarch Creek progenitors managed to remain on the lands in several communities in what are now Baldwin and Escambia Counties, Alabama, despite the fraud and **land speculation** that followed implementation of the **Treaty of Washington** in 1832, the Creek War of 1836, and the forced Creek removal that followed the war.

In 1845, an estimated 160 Creeks and their slaves were still in Alabama and Georgia. That year, Cochamy (later known as Ward Coachman), son of **Tustenuggee Emathla** (Jim Boy), who had remained in Alabama, removed to the West. Three years later, he made a return trip to Alabama and managed to take 65 Creeks to the West. He found that a number of Creeks were being held as slaves by whites in Coosa and Autauga Counties. He tried to obtain their release and removal, but he was threatened by their "masters." He believed at the time that there were perhaps a hundred Creeks remaining in Alabama. There were, no doubt, many more. Another 44 removed in 1849, and others apparently removed in 1850.

Little is known about the history and numbers of those who became known as the Poarch band between removal and 1900. Contemporary Poarch Creeks descend from a few families, most prominent of whom were named McGhee and Monac. By the turn of the 20th century, identifiable communities, including Poarch, existed north of Atmore, Alabama. Continuous occupation of the McGhee reservation allowed the title to remain in U.S. trust into the 20th century.

In 1924, the United States gave title of the reservation to the McGhee descendants. Most of the land passed from Creek hands. In the 1920s, 1930s, and 1940s, the Poarch Creeks worked in the timber industry and as sharecroppers, suffering poverty and social discrimination. They had little access to education, only what they could provide at their own expense. A school run by the Episcopal Church was established in 1939. By then, the Creeks were acculturated, English speaking, and basically Christian.

In 1947, their community took a new direction. They successfully sued for public-supported schools, and a public school was built in the community in 1950. For political action, the Creek communities organized into the Perdido Band of Friendly Creek Indians of Alabama and Northwest Florida, later changing their name to the Creek Nation East of the Mississippi. They intervened in a suit filed before the Indian Claims Commission by the Oklahoma Creeks for land lost in Alabama. In 1962, the Commission awarded nearly $4 million in the claim. The funds were appropriated in 1967 and distributed in 1972, the Poarch Creeks sharing equally with the Oklahoma Creeks. Much of this work was spearheaded by Calvin McGhee, who had been elected permanent chairman of the Creeks in 1951 and provided strong leadership until his death. Continued successful prosecution of their claims led to federal recognition of the band in 1984. The Poarch Creek Reserve is in the Poarch community north of Atmore, and the band consists of more than 2,000 members today.

FURTHER READING: Paredes, J. Anthony. "Back from Disappearance: The Alabama Creek Indian Community." In *Southeastern Indians since the Removal Era*. Ed. Walter L. Williams. Athens: University of Georgia Press, 1979, pp. 123–141; Paredes, J. Anthony. "Creek in the East since Removal." In *Handbook of North American Indians*. Vol. 14: *Southeast*. Series ed. William C. Sturtevant, vol. ed. Raymond D. Fogelson. Washington, DC: Smithsonian Institution, 2004, pp. 404–406; Poarch Creek Indians. At www.poarchcreekindians-nsn.gov/xhtml/index.htm; *Poarch Creek News*, 1999–2010.

DANIEL F. LITTLEFIELD, JR.

Potawatomi Removal

In the centuries before the removal era, the Potawatomis (or *Bodewadmik*, the Keepers of the Fire) lived in the areas around the southwestern and southeastern shores of Lake Michigan and the accompanying river valleys. As the time of the removal era approached, the leading Potawatomi villages clustered around the St. Joseph and Tippecanoe River Valleys in southwestern Michigan and northern Indiana. After passage of the **Indian Removal Act**, the United States forced the removal of most Potawatomis to lands west of the Mississippi, but a small number of Potawatomi communities persuaded federal officers to allow them to remain.

There are at least 11 Potawatomi nations in the United States and Canada today. The Pokagon Band of Potawatomi Indians of Michigan and Indiana, the Huron Nottawaseppi Band of Potawatomi Indians of Michigan, and the Match-E-Be-Nash-She-Wish Band of Potawatomi Indians of Michigan are the three federally recognized Indian tribes that successfully avoided removal to the West during the removal era. The Michigan Potawatomis form one-third of the Three Fires Confederacy with the Michigan Ottawa and Chippewa Indians. The Prairie Band Potawatomi Nation of Kansas and the Citizen Potawatomi Nation are federally recognized Potawatomi communities that the United States removed to the west of the Mississippi River. The Hannahville Indian Community of the upper peninsula of Michigan and the Forest County Potawatomi Community of Wisconsin are other federally recognized tribes that the United States removed to the West, but they returned to the Great Lakes region to join with other disparate Potawatomis. The remaining four Potawatomi nations are located in Canada, and many of their citizens are descendants of American Potawatomis who fled removal by settling in Canada with relatives.

The Potawatomis had been signatories to several land cession treaties before the removal era. Of note, they had been major players in the 1795 Treaty of Greenville in which dozens of tribal communities ceded large swaths of land north of the Ohio Valley. Many Potawatomis participated on the side of the British during the War of 1812, often at the urging of the Shawnee Prophet Tenskwatawa and his half-brother, Tecumseh.

As the removal era approached in the 1820s, the Potawatomis had loosely divided into the "prairie" and "woodland" (or "wood") Indians. The prairie Potawatomis lived in the more southern Tippecanoe River Valley and could be characterized by their refusal to "civilize" under American pressure. The wood Indians generally lived in the more northern areas near the St. Joseph River Valley and had made efforts to "civilize." During the early 19th century, American efforts to "civilize" American Indians meant numerous changes to the Indians' way of life: the conversion of Indians to Catholicism or Protestantism, the adoption of a more organized agrarian and trade-oriented economy, and an increased recognition of Anglo-style private property structures. The prairie Potawatomis had resisted the efforts to engage in these civilization projects, whereas the wood Potawatomis had cleared land, built stick houses, converted to Christian religions, and begun to live like the Americans. This set the stage for the partial removal of the Potawatomis.

The biggest stumbling block to the removal era was successful "civilization" by American Indians. American policy favoring civilization assumed, in part, that Indians would not or could not become civilized under the terms asserted by the Americans. However, some tribal communities did exactly what the Americans pressured them to do. From the perspective of the wood Potawatomi leadership (or *wkamek*), the United States had no call to remove a "civilized" Potawatomi community. They had conformed to the American way and did not pose a threat or problem, unlike the prairie Potawatomi communities, who continued to rely more on hunting for sustenance and refused to convert to a Christian religion. Ironically, this situation likely was more perception than reality, as large Potawatomi "gardens" in the southern Great Lakes provided massive sources of food to Potawatomis, neighboring tribal communities, and non-Indians throughout the region.

This dichotomy came to a head in 1826 when the United States began negotiations to plan and construct the Michigan Road, a federal road that would connect Logansport in north-central Indiana to southwestern Michigan. The road would cleave the Potawatomi communities. The wood Potawatomi *wkamek* generally saw the Michigan Road as an opportunity to cement their status as civilized Indians, retaining their autonomy as Indian communities while increasing their ability to participate in trade with the Americans and provide access to supplies generally unavailable in their communities.

The wood Potawatomi *wkamek* negotiated successfully with federal officials, in particular Secretary of War Lewis **Cass,** who sought the complete cession of all remaining Potawatomi lands and their removal, and persuaded the United States to construct the Michigan Road in a way that would link the northern Potawatomi villages. When Indiana and Michigan state government officials attempted to control the construction of the road in complete violation of the terms negotiated by the Potawatomi *wkamek*, federal officials, especially local Indian agent Thomas McKenney, preserved Potawatomi interests even after the 1830 Indian Removal Act. The village of Potawatomi *wkama* Leopold Pokagon became a crossroads of sort, connecting the Michigan Road to the Chicago Road running east-west and the Fort Wayne Road. In 1829, the Catholic Church constructed the first contemporary chapel at Pokagon's village, further cementing his community's claims to civilization.

In 1833, the United States called all of the Potawatomi communities to Chicago for a final removal treaty. The prairie Indians of the Tippecanoe River Valley reluctantly agreed to cede all of their remaining claims to land and remove west. The wood Indians strenuously objected to removal and were partially successful. Leopold Pokagon, it is told, went into a tent with the American treaty commissioner to negotiate the removal of his villages and came out of the tent armed with treaty annuities and a treaty right to remain in place. Other wood Potawatomi communities had less success, such as the one led by the leader named Menominee, who, along with other chiefs, was placed in a wood cage by American military personnel before they captured his entire community and forced them west in 1838.

Menominee's people were preceded by a party that left Indiana in the summer of 1837. The party, with George H. Profitt as conductor, left the enrolling camp on Crooked Creek near Monticello on August 23, 1837. Their journey took them through Monticello and Lafayette to Danville, Illinois. There they turned south to Georgetown and from there went west-southwest to Vandalia and west to Alton. Finding the ferry out of commission, they went south to St. Louis, where they crossed the Mississippi River and then crossed the Missouri River at St. Charles. From there they went west through Warrenton, Danville, Fulton, and on to Independence, Missouri, and into the western territory, arriving at their destination on the Osage River on October 23.

In August and September, the party endured heavy rains, bad roads, and excessive heat, which at times forced them to stop for a period in the middle of the day. It took them over a month to cross Missouri, where swollen streams and lack of ferries or bridges held them up for days at a time.

Health of the party was generally good, despite the steady diet of beef and flour or bacon and flour, rations of which were issued to the people at intervals along the way. There were illnesses, but the party reached the West having suffered only one death.

The most devastating removal for the Potawatomis occurred in the summer and fall of 1838. Artist George Winter, who was with the Potawatomis at the time of their departure, called the roundup "a deceptive (in a moral point of view) and cunning cruel plan." John Tipton called a meeting of the chiefs and headmen at Twin Lakes near Plymouth, ostensibly as a friendship gesture, but, in an act similar to the tactics used by Gen. Thomas S. **Jesup** with the Seminoles, he took them prisoner and held them hostage while squads of militia scoured the countryside, forcing the Potawatomis into a holding camp. With militia guarding the chiefs, the party departed on September 4, 1838, with the prison wagon carrying the chiefs at the head of the column, followed by baggage wagons and then people following on horses and afoot.

Their journey from September 4 to November 4 took them from Twin Lakes to Rochester, Logansport, Lafayette, and Williamsport, Indiana; Danville, Sidney, Springfield, Jacksonville, and Quincy, Illinois; Palmyra, Huntsville, Carrollton, Lexington, and Independence, Missouri; and to their final destination at Potawatomi Creek in eastern Kansas, then known as the "western territory."

The militia guard remained with the party as far as Danville, Illinois, where they were dismissed and the guard of 16 army dragoons continued with them. Part of their duty was to guard the camp to prevent whiskey peddlers from entering. Also at Danville, Tipton was relieved of his duty, and William Polke became the conductor who continued with them during the remainder of their journey. At Danville, too, on September 16, Father Benjamin Marie Petit joined the train. By then, illness had placed its mark on the people. The baggage wagons were being used to carry not only baggage but also women and children too weak to walk. The children, particularly, were debilitated by the heat and were described as listless and depressed. Father Petit vouched for the chiefs, and from Danville on, they were no longer treated as prisoners of war but could move about the camps.

When they departed Danville, the train was headed by a dragoon carrying a U.S. flag, followed by a military officer. Then came the baggage wagon, the prison wagon still being used by the chiefs, then one or two chiefs on horseback. Behind them was a line of 250 to 300 horses carrying men, women, and children, traveling in single file. Flanking both sides of the column were dragoons, who hastened stragglers on. The baggage wagons, carrying baggage and the debilitated, brought up the rear. The wagons were topped by canvas ostensibly to protect the sick from the excessive heat, but it most likely exacerbated their condition.

Illness had set in early in the journey, the people becoming weak and fatigued by fever, diarrhea, scrofula, and the excessive heat. At the worst point, about 300 were ill. On several occasions, the sick had to be left behind with others to take care of them until they were well enough to catch up. It was not until the advent of cooler weather in October that their general health began to improve. Still, deaths were frequent. Most were buried Christian fashion, leaving a trail of little crosses over three states.

Throughout September and early October, the people suffered from heat and dust as they struggled over the landscape. Water was scarce. By the time they approached Springfield, Illinois, sickness and traveling conditions had taken their toll. Polke asked them to clean up and dress up before they went through the town "to ensure a good appearance," and he bribed them with a promise of tobacco to do so. At Jacksonville, people turned out in large crowds to see them. They were a spectacle, Polke said, that was "as great a rarity as a travelling Caravan of wild animals."

The last leg of their journey was less grueling than their earlier trek. Their health improved as the weather turned cool. However, at times they faced cold weather, snow, and rain. In October, Polke issued shoes to the destitute because the weather was too cold for them to march barefoot. Also, the conductors began to loosen their grip on the people. Their diet was primarily beef and flour and, at times, potatoes, issued at regular intervals. The men were given the freedom to hunt and supplement their diet with game, which they greatly preferred. Also, they were granted permission to stop and observe the Sabbath.

Others joined the party while they were on the road. Agents had enrolled 714 at the outset, but Polke counted 756 people at the end of the journey. Sixty-eight escaped along the trail, and 39 died on their 62-day trek. These numbers stand in stark contrast to the single death in the 1837 removal. They earned for the trek the name the Potawatomis gave it in later years—the Trail of Death.

On September 29, 1838, the American military at the order of Lewis Cass began the forced march of more than 800 Potawatomi Indians from their gathering point at Twin Lakes, Indiana, through Springfield, Illinois, and on to western Iowa and northwestern Missouri, where the United States had established interim reservations. Dozens of young children died along the way, with fewer than 700 people surviving the Trail of Death. Further devastating removals of these Indians to Kansas and Oklahoma followed.

In 1841, American military personnel at the urging of Michigan officials informed Pokagon that they would commence the removal of the Pokagon band to the west. He contacted Associate Michigan Supreme Court Justice Epaphroditus Ransom, who issued a legal opinion that the 1833 treaty guaranteed the Pokagon band protection from removal to the West. Pokagon walked on later that year.

On July 28, 1851, the United States, acting through private contractors instead of the military, initiated the removal of over 600 Potawatomi Indians from Dodge County, Wisconsin. During the trek to Kansas, a cholera outbreak struck the Potawatomis, killing several. Perhaps as many as 300 Potawatomis from the area did not join the march, remaining in Wisconsin or fleeing to Canada.

FURTHER READING: Cleland, Charles E. *Rites of Conquest: The History and Culture of Michigan's Native Americans.* Ann Arbor: University of Michigan Press, 1992; Clifton, James A. *The Prairie People: Continuity and Change in Potawatomi Indian Culture, 1665–1965.* Lawrence: The Regents Press of Kansas, 1977; Clifton, James A. *The Pokagons, 1683–1983: Catholic Potawatomi Indians of the St. Joseph River Valley.* Lanham, MD: University Press of America, 1984; Douglas, Jesse C. "Removal Journal Part I." *HowNiKan* 9 (June 1987): 5, 7, 15; Douglas, Jesse C. "Removal Journal Part II." *HowNiKan* 9 (July 1987): 14–15; Edmunds, R. David. *The Potawatomis: Keepers of the Fire.* Norman: University of Oklahoma Press, 1978; Low, John N. *Keepers of the Fire: The Pokagon Potawatomi Nation.* 2006. At www.pokagon.com/presentation/SMCppt_20080112.pdf; Neumeyer, Elizabeth. "Michigan Indians Battle against Removal." *Michigan History* 55 (1971): 275–288; Pepper, A. C. "Removal Journal—The Trail of Death." *HowNiKan* 9 (August 1987): 6–8; Secunda, Ben. "The Road to Ruin? 'Civilization' and the Origins of a 'Michigan Road Band' of Potawatomi." *Michigan Historical Review* 34 (2008): 118–149; "Treaty with the Potawatomi, 1836." Indian Affairs: Laws and Treaties. At http://digital.library.okstate.edu/kappler/Vol2/treaties/pot0450.htm (Turkey Creek Prairie); "Treaty with the Potawatomi, 1836." Indian Affairs: Laws and Treaties. At http://digital.library.okstate.edu/kappler/Vol2/treaties/pot0457.htm (Tippecanoe); "Treaty with the Potawatomi, 1836." Indian Affairs: Laws and Treaties. At http://digital.library.okstate.edu/kappler/Vol2/treaties/pot0459.htm; "Treaty with the Potawatomi, 1836." Indian Affairs: Laws and Treaties. At http://digital.library.okstate.edu/kappler/Vol2/treaties/pot0462.htm; "Treaty with the Potawatomi, 1836." Indian Affairs: Laws and Treaties. At http://digital.library.okstate.edu/kappler/Vol2/treaties/pot0470.htm; "Treaty with the Potawatomi, 1836." Indian Affairs: Laws and Treaties. At http://digital.library.okstate.edu/kappler/Vol2/treaties/pot0471.htm; "Treaty with the Potawatomi, 1837." Indian Affairs: Laws and Treaties. At http://digital.library.okstate.edu/kappler/Vol2/treaties/pot0488.htm; Trennert, Robert A. "The Business of Indian Removal: Deporting the Potawatomi from Wisconsin, 1851." *Wisconsin Magazine of History* 63 (1979): 36–50.

MATTHEW L. M. FLETCHER

Q

Quapaw Removal

At the time of the Louisiana Purchase in 1803, the Quapaws occupied an area largely south of the Arkansas River in present-day Arkansas. Their area soon became inundated with white settlers who coveted the fertile farmland as well as the streams, woods, and wetlands with their abundant wildlife. Subsequently, the tribe signed a treaty in 1818 accepting a reservation of 1 million acres between the Arkansas and Ouachita Rivers. By 1824, however, pressure from white settlers was so great that the Quapaws were forced to cede their lands in Arkansas for a reservation among the Caddos in northwestern Louisiana in addition to goods and a $2,000 annuity for 11 years. However, severe flooding along the Red River made it impossible for the tribe to carry on its traditional means of subsistence through farming, hunting, and fishing. So one Quapaw band under **Sarasin** returned to Arkansas, where they farmed wherever they could and hired themselves out as laborers, living as squatters on the land they had previously owned. Nonetheless, they began to build a community in Arkansas, using the annuity money to buy farm implements and to send Quapaw boys to schools.

By 1830, the rest of the Quapaws had returned to Arkansas under their leader **Heckaton**. The federal government saw the tribe's position as untenable, as they had no legal land base, so officials searched for a solution. They suggested that the Quapaws remove once again and live among the Cherokees or the Osages, as they were friendly with the former and linguistically linked to the latter. The Quapaws rejected this suggestion, fearing a loss of national identity, and continued to lobby to remain in Arkansas. By 1832, the situation was such that tribal members had been pushed off the land they had squatted on and had resorted to camping out in the woods and swamps. Recognizing that their tribe was disintegrating, the Quapaws signed another treaty in 1833 that granted them 150 sections of land in the northeastern corner of **Indian Territory**, near where other tribes had been removed as well. The tribe remains in this area around the town of Quapaw, Oklahoma, where it maintains an active and viable presence.

FURTHER READING: Baird, W. David. *The Quapaws: A History of the Downstream People.* Norman: University of Oklahoma Press, 1980; Encyclopedia of Arkansas History and Culture. 2009. At http://encyclopediaofarkansas.net; Key, Joseph Patrick. "Outcasts upon the World: The Quapaws and the Louisiana Purchase." In *A Whole Country in Commotion: The Louisiana Purchase and the American Southwest.* Ed. Patrick Williams, S. Charles Bolton, and Jeannie M. Whayne. Fayetteville: University of Arkansas Press, 2005; The Quapaw Tribe of Oklahoma. 2009. At www.quapawtribe.com/site/view/12817_TribalHistory.pml; "Treaty with the Quapaw, 1833." Indian Affairs: Laws and Treaties. At http://digital.library.okstate.edu/kappler/Vol2/treaties/qua0395.htm.

JAMES W. PARINS

Quinney, John W. (1797–1855)

Born in New York, John W. Quinney was a Stockbridge-Munsee leader who was involved in most of the removals that his people went through in the 19th century (*see* **Stockbridge-Munsee Removal**). He was a delegate in the group of Stockbridge-Munsees, **Brothertons,** and **Oneidas** that traveled to Wisconsin in 1821 to secure land from the Menominees along the Fox River (*see* **Menominee Removal**). Quinney also had helped to negotiate the monetary settlement for his tribe when they ceded their land in New York and moved to Indiana. The Stockbridge-Munsees' sojourn in that state was short-lived, because the government was encouraging whites to settle on lands previously set aside for the Indians. Quinney helped to organize the Stockbridge-Munsee removal between 1822 and 1829 to Wisconsin, where they first settled on the Fox River near Kaukauna, but they subsequently moved to a site near Lake Winnebago. Although Quinney was the author of the Stockbridge-Munsee constitution of 1837, which replaced the sachems or traditional leaders with elected officials, he was considered a sachem for the rest of his life. The constitution was also an attempt to thwart federal removal policies as they related to the tribe. The document was embraced by some of the group but was opposed by others. When the government passed an act in 1843 making the Stockbridge-Munsees U.S. citizens, Quinney worked to have the act repealed; he saw that with citizenship came allotment in severalty, or "apportionment" as it was called then, and early acquaintance with that process had demonstrated that many Indians lost their lands through tax auctions and other less legal means.

Portrait of John W. Quinney. (Wisconsin Historical Society/WHS Image 49)

In 1838, the federal government's removal policy impacted the tribe directly when they were informed that they must remove to west of the Mississippi to accommodate the white settlers flooding into the new Wisconsin Territory. Instead, Quinney negotiated with Congress and was able to secure compensation for the lost Wisconsin land, which was then used to purchase land from the Menominees, who made room for them on their reservation northwest of Green Bay. Today, the tribe occupies two townships in Shawano Country, Wisconsin.

FURTHER READING: Davidson, J. N. *Muh-he-ka-ne-ok: History of the Stockbridge-Munsee Nation.* Milwaukee: S. Chapman, 1893; Loew, Patti. *Indian Nations of Wisconsin.* Madison: Wisconsin Historical Society Press, 2001.

JAMES W. PARINS

R

Richardville, Jean Baptiste (1761–1841)

Miami metis Jean Baptiste Richardville led the Miamis in the Fort Wayne region of Indiana through the removal era (*see* **Miami Removal**). He was the principal chief of the Miamis from 1813, when his uncle Little Turtle died, until his own death in 1841. Son of a French trader and a highly placed Miami woman, he received some formal education at a school in Ontario and learned the fur trade business from his mother Tacumwah's second husband, another French trader. His uncle, Chief Little Turtle, rounded out his education by teaching him to be a warrior and a chief. Richardville favored accommodation with Americans. With Little Turtle at his side, he signed the Treaty of Greenville in 1795 and treaties in 1802 and 1809 that extinguished Miami title to lands in southern Indiana.

Physically, Richardville looked more like a Frenchman than a Miami, but he was accepted as a chief by his people because of his mother's lineage, his generosity, and his shrewd business practices. The Indiana Miamis relied on him to scrutinize and translate treaties, annuity receipts, land sales, and other important transactions with Americans. He became wealthy through his many economic ventures, operating trading posts and ferries at the portages between the Wabash and Maumee rivers. When Indiana became a state in 1816, he was already reputed to be the richest man in the state.

When the fur trade declined, Richardville made money at his trading posts by providing the Miamis with food and other goods in exchange for payment in annuities. He readily sold goods to tribal members on credit and then collected their annuities when they arrived, a common trading practice. Continued land cessions, which added to the tribe's annuities, helped to enrich him further. Because he was charitable to poor Miamis, he continued to enjoy popularity among his people, and his political influence increased, as did his personal fortune. He hosted horse races and feasts and was famed for his great hospitality.

John Hays, the Indian agent between 1820 and 1823, was jealous of the control Richardville wielded over the annuity payments and tried to reduce Richardville's political influence. Richardville also encountered opposition from other competing merchants who wanted a larger share of the Miamis' annuities. But the Miamis feared the influence of non-Indian merchants even more than Richardville's monopoly of their business, perhaps perceiving that the federal government wanted to use their indebtedness to obtain their remaining lands. In 1829, Indian agent John Tipton moved the annuity payments away from Richardville's trading posts. Richardville asked his people not to accept the annuities as a way to protest Tipton's action, but they ignored his request. Richardville prevailed, however. After Governor James Noble of Indiana warned Tipton that they did not want to alienate the chief, whose influence would be needed to secure further Miami land sales, Tipton distributed the annuities the next year at a place of Richardville's choosing.

Like earlier land cessions, the Treaty of St. Mary's (1818) and the Treaty of 1838 provided sections of lands to Richardville, his sons, and his friends, and additional payment in farm implements and livestock. With the Treaty of 1840, Richardville agreed to move the tribal government west of the Mississippi, where annuities would henceforth be paid. Richardville died less than a year later. After many attempts to avoid forced exile, in October of 1846, approximately 500 Miamis boarded canal boats to Kansas. Richardville's successor and son-in-law, Chief Francis LaFontaine, and the other chiefs who signed the removal treaty remained behind on private lands. The lands that Richardville set aside became islands of refuge for Miamis who refused to remove to Kansas or who removed and were dissatisfied and then returned to Indiana. More Miamis live in Indiana today than in Oklahoma, where the Kansas Miamis were forced to remove a second time in 1873.

FURTHER READING: Anson, Bert. *The Miami Indians.* Norman: University of Oklahoma Press, 1970; Chaput, Donald. "The Family of Drouet de Richerdville: Merchants, Soldiers, and Chiefs of Indiana." *Indiana Magazine of History* 74 (1978): 103–116; Edmunds, R. David. *Enduring Nations: Native Americans in the Midwest.* Urbana: University of Illinois Press, 2008; Rafert, Stewart. *The Miami Indians of Indiana: A Persistent People, 1654–1994.* Indianapolis: Indiana Historical Society, 1996.

MELISSA A. RINEHART

Ridge, John (c. 1803–1839)

John Ridge had his family and his tribe's aspirations pinned to him from early on. His father, Major **Ridge**, had achieved prominent stature in the Cherokee Nation as both a warrior and a wise counselor, and he brought up his son to follow in his footsteps. John suffered with an ailing hip that caused him to limp from an early age, so he was never expected to become a warrior. However, his intellect was recognized by his teachers, and his mind was nurtured and cultivated for service to his people. After attending schools near his home, he was sent along with several other Cherokee boys to the Cornwall Mission School in Connecticut, an institution founded by

John Ridge was one of the Cherokees who supported removal in negotiation of the Treaty of New Echota. (Library of Congress)

the Congregationalists for boys from various indigenous backgrounds. Upon his return to the Cherokee Nation, he was regarded as a leader and as such was engaged in his people's resistance to removal pressure.

In the Creek difficulties with Georgia (*see* **Georgia and Indian Removal**) in the mid-1820s, the Cherokees urged the Creeks to resist the land cessions that some of the Creeks under William McIntosh were willing to make. When President John Quincy Adams sent Gen. Edmund P. Gaines to the Georgia-Alabama area to keep order after the assassination of McIntosh, John Ridge and his father Major Ridge represented the interests of the main body of Creeks. When the Creek delegation went to Washington to sign the treaty brokered by Gaines, they wished to include John Ridge and David Vann as delegates. Gaines denied permission because most federal officials were of the opinion that the Cherokees were encouraging the Creeks to resist removal. However, Gaines allowed the pair to attend as "secretaries," even though their real role was as legal advisors to Creek leader **Opothleyohola**. In November 1825, Opothleyohola and the Ridges' negotiations with the government resulted in the 1826 Treaty of Washington. Under the terms of the treaty, the Creeks vacated most of their land in Georgia in return for a monetary settlement instead of an exchange of land. As part of the settlement, as John Ridge advised, Ridge and Vann were to receive $15,000 in fees, with another $10,000 going to Major Ridge for his part in negotiating the abrogation of the McIntosh treaty. Although the amount of these fees was later reduced, they caused an outcry in Congress. Opothleyohola insisted that they be paid because the Council of the Upper Town Creeks had invited the Cherokees as counselors. However, many people in the Cherokee Nation were incensed by the fees Ridge was attracting and the publicity he was garnering. Ridge's alleged short temper and his dismissal of opposing views were other reasons for his growing unpopularity among some segments of the Cherokees.

After the second **Treaty of Washington** (1832), a strip of land in Georgia was still held by the Creeks. Thomas L. McKinney was sent by the federal government to negotiate the turnover of this land to Georgia, and the Creeks were once again represented by John Ridge. Among McKinney's first actions was to attack Ridge, repudiating him as the spokesman for a tribe he did not belong to and accusing him of conspiring to take over the Creek treasury. By 1828, Ridge had stopped acting as an agent for the Creeks and turned his talents to Cherokee affairs. By this time, Georgia, having ridded itself of Creeks, began to concentrate its efforts on removing Cherokees.

As a delegate of the Cherokees, Ridge conferred with allies in Congress and other whites who opposed removal. He argued the Cherokee line, using the same points his father had used in his Turkey Town speech to rally his tribesmen: the Cherokees were a civilized people now, having followed the policies of Washington, Jefferson, Monroe, and Madison. As such, there was no need to remove them to the West. These were the same points that Elias **Boudinot** was hammering home as editor of the *Cherokee Phoenix.*

In 1832, Ridge and Boudinot, a cousin and classmate at Cornwall, were part of a delegation to Washington that presented to the government a list of grievances against Georgia citizens for depredations against the Cherokees. This list was rejected out of hand by Secretary of War Lewis **Cass**, and the Cherokees were told that if conditions were bad, the Nation should move west of the Mississippi. Boudinot and Ridge then embarked on a speaking tour to raise money for the cash-strapped *Cherokee Phoenix* and to seek support in several eastern cities and among members of Congress who were known to have opposed Jackson's removal policy. But the advice they were given by friends as well as pro-removal officials was to make the best of a bad situation and remove to lands set aside west of Arkansas. Ridge and Boudinot reviewed their position and reassessed it in the light of several recent factors: Andrew **Jackson**'s election as President in 1828 and his adamant determination to remove the tribes west of the Mississippi; the discovery of gold in the Cherokee Nation, which encouraged an influx of intruders; legislation by Georgia lawmakers that brought the Cherokees under the state's jurisdiction; and the imprisonment of white missionaries who had refused to leave the Nation after being ordered to do so by Georgia officials. In early 1833, Ridge met with Andrew Jackson and made a personal plea for relief against the depredations of the Georgians. The president rebuffed him entirely and repeated Cass's statement that the Cherokees would get relief from the Georgians only after they vacated the state and removed to the West. From this time on, Ridge was convinced that the Cherokees were espousing a lost cause in their resistance to removal. The former beliefs of the young Cherokee were shaken. This change in attitude was sensed by federal officials, to the point that at least one congressman wrote for the local press saying that a Cherokee treaty was imminent. Ridge felt compelled to publish an article of his own in the *National Intelligencer* refuting the idea and reasserting Cherokee solidarity against removal. But privately, his mind was changing.

In April 1833, Cass offered the Cherokee delegations the basis for a removal treaty, including the following terms: land in the West close to where the Old Settler Cherokees had removed when they left Arkansas, permission to retain their government, a congressional delegate, future territorial status, protection against white intruders, the choice of travel mode for the removal journey, and government subsistence for a year after removal. Cass further promised annuities and support for schools and public buildings. These terms were the most generous offered so far, as the delegates were well aware. Upon the heels of Cass's carrot, a negative incentive followed in the next month when John Ridge received a letter from David Greene of the American Board of Commissioners for Foreign Missions, the sponsor of missionaries, Samuel A. **Worcester**, Daniel S. **Butrick**, Elizur Butler, and others. Greene informed Ridge that all of his allies in the East now realized the futility of the Cherokee position and urged the Cherokees to take the best offer they could get and leave their land in the state of Georgia.

If protection from the Georgians could not be found in Washington, it did not exist. Reluctantly, Ridge returned to the Cherokee Nation and laid out his conclusions to his father, Elias Boudinot, Andrew Ross, and others. They came to the same conclusion that Ridge had reached. Accordingly, they began to try to convince the Cherokee people and leadership of the futility of a hard stand against removal from their ancestral lands. In 1832, John **Ross** had called a special council to take up the issues surrounding resistance to removal. It was convened at Red Clay, Tennessee, to avoid interference by the Georgia Guard, although the Ridges had objected that it should be held at the Cherokee capitol. Upon John Ridge's return from the East in 1833, he read a letter sent to him by Elbert Herring, commissioner of Indian affairs, who stated that federal assistance against intruders and lottery winners seizing Cherokee farms was not forthcoming to the Indians in Georgia. Ridge also took this opportunity to speak positively about the prospects of removal.

The response to Ridge and Boudinot's arguments was largely negative, and the split between Ross followers, now called the National Party, and those advocating removal, called the Treaty Party, opened widely. Physical assaults between the groups were reported, and bitterness grew. Treaty adherents were regarded as traitors by many Ross followers, and Boudinot was removed as editor of the *Phoenix*.

However, Ridge, Boudinot, Andrew Ross, and others let it be known in Washington that at least some of the Cherokees were willing to enter into a removal treaty. As a result, the government appointed the Rev. John F. **Schermerhorn** to negotiate such a treaty, and he arrived in the Nation in 1835. In December, the **Treaty of New Echota** was signed by Schermerhorn and the Treaty Party against the wishes of the majority of the tribe. The treaty provided for the exchange of Cherokee lands in the East for 13.8 million acres west of Arkansas as well as a payment of $4.5 million and an annuity to support public schools in the nation. Among the 20 or so signers was Major Ridge, whose comment upon marking his X on the document was "I have signed my death warrant." He was right.

While Treaty Party people and others began to pack up and leave for the West after the removal treaty was ratified, John Ross followed a delaying policy, trying to buy time before the removal date stipulated by the treaty. He used this time to negotiate with the federal government, rejecting one offer that would have given the Nation a larger amount of settlement money. When the removal date arrived, many of the Cherokees who remained in Georgia— by far the majority of the people—were unprepared for the uprooting that was to come. As a result, the Nation suffered grievously in the internment camps in which they were herded before their embarkation for the West.

John Ridge and his family departed from the Eastern Cherokee Nation before the main body of the Nation did so. They traveled the northern route, crossing the Mississippi opposite Cape Girardeau, Missouri, and riding across the southern sections of that state until they entered northwestern Arkansas (*see* **Arkansas and Indian Removal**) and then reached **Indian Territory**. At Honey Creek, they found Major Ridge and his wife at the general store they had started there, and John and his slaves set to work to build their home. Ridge took a journey through the new Cherokee Nation, noting the best places for homesteads and ranches and beginning to plan for a prosperous future he believed his Nation would enjoy. Ridge and other Treaty Party members met with and became allied with the Old Settlers, those Cherokees who had lived in Arkansas under the treaties of 1818 and 1819 and who had removed to Indian Territory with the treaty of 1828.

However, after the main body of Cherokees arrived in 1839, John Ross immediately imposed his dominion over the Cherokees who were already there, and tensions between the groups began to rise. Ross called a council for June 3 at Takatoka, near Tahlequah, to establish his authority as principal chief. The Old Settlers in attendance were amicable, but tension rose when the Ridges, Boudinot, and other Treaty Party members appeared. After a day, Ross dismissed the Old Settlers and Treaty Party and continued the council with members of his own party. On June 22, John Ridge was dragged from his bed by several men and, in front of his family, stabbed repeatedly until he was dead. On the same day, Major Ridge was waylaid and shot on a road, and Elias Boudinot was stabbed and his skull was split with an axe as he worked to build his house at Park Hill. Boudinot's brother, Stand Watie, was able to escape the attempt on his life.

FURTHER READING: McLoughlin, William. *Cherokee Renascence, 1794–1833.* Princeton, NJ: Princeton University Press, 1987; Parins, James W. *John Rollin Ridge: His Life and Works.* Lincoln: University of Nebraska Press, 1991; Wilkins, Thurman. *Cherokee Tragedy: The Story of the Ridge Family and the Formation of a People.* New York: Macmillan, 1970.

JAMES W. PARINS

Ridge, Major (1771–1839)

The Ridge, later known as Major Ridge, was born at Hiwasee, a Cherokee settlement in what is now Tennessee. His mother was half Cherokee and half white, the daughter of a Scots frontiersman. She was of the Deer clan and married a Cherokee named Oganstota or Dutsi. Ridge's upbringing was that of a traditional Cherokee youth; he and his brother, David Watie or Oo-watie, were taught how to hunt with blowpipes and bows and arrows even as they learned the customs and lore of their people. Major Ridge married Susanna Wickett, whose Indian name was Sehoya, around 1792. By this time, Ridge had distinguished himself in battle to the extent that he was granted a voice in the tribal council. From that time, he was considered a leader. Later, he would distinguish himself in the Red Stick War, in which he earned the title "Major."

During the winter of 1826–1827, the two principal Cherokee leaders, Pathkiller and Charles Hicks, died. Taking their places were John **Ross**, who

Engraving of a portrait of Major Ridge, a Cherokee chief, by 19th-century American painter Charles Bird King, from *The Indian Tribes of North America*. (McKenney, Thomas L. and James Hall. *The Indian Tribes of North America*, 1836–1844)

was elected president of the National Committee, and Major Ridge, elected speaker of the council. In their first year of office, President John Quincy Adams sent three generals to the Cherokees to negotiate a removal treaty, but Ross and Ridge had other plans; they, along with other leaders of the nation, were busy drafting a constitution that, they hoped, would help convince federal officials that the Cherokees were a civilized people entitled to hold their present country and not be subjected to removal. The Georgia legislature was infuriated by the Cherokee constitution; in 1827, it declared that the Cherokees were temporary tenants of the land they lived on and that the legislature was empowered to take the land at any time by force or otherwise. Over the next five years, the legislature continued to pass laws that restricted the Cherokees, established the Georgia Guard to enforce these policies (*see* **State Militias and Removal**), and encouraged the Pony Club, a band of mounted criminals who terrorized the Cherokees living near the Georgia frontier, and other intruders into the Nation (*see* **Georgia and Indian Removal**).

In the first election under the new constitution in 1828, John Ross was elected principal chief, George Lowrey second chief, and Major Ridge counselor. When Secretary of War John H. **Eaton** pressed for removal in the new presidential administration of Andrew **Jackson** in 1829, John Ross went to Washington while he sent Major Ridge throughout the Cherokee Nation to arouse the people against removal. On this tour, Ridge gave his famous Turkey Town speech, in which he declared that the Cherokees had become civilized, following the wishes of Washington, Jefferson, Madison, and Monroe. He further argued that if the lands promised in the West were so wonderful, why hadn't whites settled them?

Ridge and his wife believed in an "English" education for their children and other Cherokee children. They supported the work of missionary schools and sent their children there to study. Ridge's son, John **Ridge**, was a promising scholar and studied at the more advanced mission school for indigenous children at Cornwall, Connecticut. After John married a white girl from the town, he returned to the Cherokee Nation and became, along with his cousin Elias **Boudinot**, a leading young man of the tribe. Boudinot and John Ridge were heavily involved in the Cherokee campaign to convince influential white people in eastern cities that the Cherokees were "civilized" and therefore should not be subject to the removal policies of the federal government. John Ridge accompanied Boudinot in 1832 on a speaking tour of the East to raise support for the *Phoenix*, but more importantly, Ridge and Boudinot worked to convince their white audiences that the Cherokees were a civilized people. When the decision came down from the Supreme Court in the *Worcester v. Georgia* case, they saw reason for optimism.

However, in 1833, when John Ridge led a delegation to Washington to find relief from the atrocities on Cherokees being carried out by Georgians and to determine what the government's plans were in relation to the *Worcester* decision, they were met by Secretary of War Lewis **Cass**, who reiterated Jackson's demands that they remove to the West. Ridge returned to the Nation and convinced Major Ridge, Elias Boudinot, Andrew Ross, and others that the best course of action was to make the best bargain they could with the government, remove to the West, and build a new Cherokee Nation in **Indian Territory**. This group of men became known as the "Treaty Party" when they signed the **Treaty of New Echota**, which ceded Cherokee lands in the Southeast for a tract west of Arkansas and monetary considerations. Major Ridge, upon adding his mark to the treaty document, commented that he had just signed his death warrant.

In 1837, Major Ridge left for the West, settling at Honey Creek near the Missouri line in northeastern Indian Territory, leaving behind a vast orchard of some 1,500 fruit and nut trees, a ferry, a farm, and interest in a general store. Shortly after his arrival in the West, Ridge opened a store in which he planned to extend credit to the Cherokees yet to come to the territory. However, after the main body of Cherokees had removed to Indian Territory, Boudinot, John Ridge, and Major Ridge were assassinated by followers of John Ross in retribution for their signing the removal treaty. Ironically, the killings were carried out under the terms of the Cherokee Blood Law, a resolution introduced by Major Ridge that called for the execution of anyone who ceded any tribal land in Georgia to the whites. The families of the slain men subsequently fled to Arkansas, fearing further reprisal from followers of John Ross.

FURTHER READING: McLoughlin, William. *Cherokee Renascence, 1794–1833.* Princeton, NJ: Princeton University Press, 1987; Parins, James W. *John Rollin Ridge, His Life and Works.* Lincoln: University of Nebraska Press, 1991; Wilkins, Thurman. *Cherokee Tragedy: The Story of the Ridge Family and the Decimation of a People.* New York: Macmillan, 1970.

JAMES W. PARINS

Ross, John (1790–1866)

John Ross was of Scottish and Cherokee ancestry and only one-eighth Cherokee. However, he served as principal chief of the Cherokee Nation for nearly forty years. Primarily because of his role in opposing removal, 20th-century historians of the Cherokees depicted him as almost larger than life and cast him as the would-be savior of the Cherokee people. Yet his leadership during **Cherokee removal** had other aspects as well.

When he was elected chief in 1828, Ross already had over a decade of service in various political positions. He had served as delegate to Washington, clerk to chiefs, member of the Cherokee National Committee, and delegate to the Cherokee Constitutional Convention. By the time of his

John Ross, the greatest leader of the Cherokee Nation during the 19th century, led the legal battle against Cherokee removal. (Library of Congress)

election, voluntary Cherokee removal had been going on for more than a decade, and American public opinion was mounting in favor of removing all Cherokees from inside the boundaries of Georgia (*see* **Georgia and Indian Removal**). Soon after his election, Georgia extended its laws over the Cherokee lands. That year, as well, Andrew **Jackson** was elected president with a full commitment to Indian removal as Indian policy.

Early in his tenure as principal chief, Ross confronted two major issues: maintaining the integrity of the boundaries of the Cherokee Nation and resisting mounting pressure for Cherokee removal. Extension of Georgia's laws over the Nation gave license to gold hunters and other intruders to move onto Cherokee lands. Ross put his faith in the U.S. court system to give the Cherokees some relief. Under his leadership, the Cherokees challenged Georgia's usurpation of Cherokee lands before the Supreme Court in *Cherokee Nation v. Georgia* in 1831, which failed to resolve the conflict over jurisdiction between Georgia and the Cherokee Nation. In 1832, Ross led the Cherokee legal fight against Georgia's claim to jurisdiction. Although the Supreme Court would affirm Cherokee Nation sovereignty that year in *Worcester v. Georgia*, President Andrew Jackson refused to enforce the ruling.

Following Jackson's decision, Cherokee resolve began to falter. The so-called Treaty Party emerged, led by Major **Ridge**, his son John **Ridge**, and Elias **Boudinot**. Boudinot had been the able editor of the *Cherokee Phoenix*, the Cherokee national newspaper that had been a propaganda outlet for anti-removal arguments. Boudinot had been a staunch anti-removal editor until after the *Worcester* case, when he and others began to believe that the die was cast and removal was inevitable. Ross removed him as editor, and relations between the removal proponents and Ross disintegrated.

Despite Ross and his allies' protests, memorials, and delegations to Washington, in December 1835 John F. **Schermerhorn** negotiated the **Treaty of New Echota** with the Treaty Party, providing for the cession of Cherokee lands in the East and Cherokee removal to the West. Though that party represented a minority of Cherokees, the government considered the treaty binding upon the entire Nation.

Because the treaty gave the Cherokees three years to remove, Ross and his allies continued as regular delegates to Washington, trying to reverse the implementation of the treaty. Because of Ross's continuous urging, Cherokees had faith that they might somehow escape removal, and few prepared to move. When the deadline passed, more than 14,000 remained in the Nation, as well as a large number of Creeks who had taken refuge there in the early 1830s to escape Creek removal (*see* **Muscogee [Creek] Removal**).

Ross and his delegation were in Washington when forces under the command of Gen. Winfield **Scott** began to round up Cherokees and force them into holding camps in preparation for departure for the West. Sickness and death were common in the camps in the late spring and summer of 1838. Ross finally realized that he must salvage what he could for the people and struck a bargain with federal officials to allow the Cherokees to conduct their own removal.

Those Cherokees who had been rounded up traveled west overland in twelve groups, or contingents, during the fall and winter of 1838–1839. The Cherokee leadership appointed the Cherokee contingent leaders, determined the routes the overland contingents would take, and procured the rations for people and their animals along the routes, which became labeled in the 20th century as the **Trail of Tears**.

Early-20th-century historians cast Ross as a hero because of his stand against removal, but evidence points to other, less ideal, aspects of his character. He was a consummate politician in the best and worst sense of the word. A businessman before he became chief, he was an entrepreneur, never reluctant to use the power of his office for his personal financial gain. By the time of removal, he was wealthy by the standards of the day. Like most of the Cherokee leaders at the time, he was a slaveholder whose ownership of a large number of slaves made him part of a privileged class. Slaveholding Cherokees and their families were allowed to remain in their homes when other Cherokees were rounded up and sent to the holding camps for removal. Not only did Ross escape the rigors of the camps, but he and his family also made large sums of money off removal. Contracts for providing rations and subsistence for removal parties and their animals went to his brother Lewis, who was assisted by his nephew William Shorey Coodey. If the Cherokees suffered because of lack of food or other supplies or because of bad road conditions, the Cherokee leaders must bear much of the blame because they chose the routes and were in charge of the removal.

Ross and his family also escaped the rigors of the removal trail. Conducted by his nephew John Drew, Ross's party traveled down the Tennessee River aboard flatboats to Tuscumbia, Alabama, where Ross bought the steamboat *Victoria*. From there, the group traveled to the **Indian Territory** by way of the Tennessee, Mississippi, and Arkansas rivers to within only a few miles of their destination.

Once in the West, Ross was ruthless in reasserting his authority. A political coalition had emerged between the Old Settlers, or Western Cherokees, and the Treaty Party Cherokees. Ross and his followers disposed of the Treaty Party leaders by assassination, overwhelmed the Old Settler Party leadership by the power of numbers, wrote a constitution that favored their own political and economic well-being, and took possession of the most lucrative economic enterprises of the Nation. The spree of revenge killings and violence engendered by the removal and Ross's assertion of his power in the West lasted until a treaty aimed at reconciliation was signed in 1846.

FURTHER READING: Anderson, William L., ed. *Cherokee Removal Before and After.* Athens: University of Georgia Press, 1991; Littlefield, Daniel F., Jr. *The John Drew Detachment.* Resources on Indian Removal No. 2. Little Rock: Sequoyah National Research Center, 2006; Moulton, Gary E. *John Ross, Cherokee Chief.* Athens: University of Georgia Press, 1978; Moulton, Gary E., ed. *The Papers of Chief John Ross.* Norman: University of Oklahoma Press, 1984; Wardell, Morris L. *A Political History of the Cherokee Nation, 1838–1907.* Norman: University of Oklahoma Press, 1938.

DANIEL F. LITTLEFIELD, JR.

S

Saginaw Chippewa Removal

The Saginaw Chippewa Indian Tribe originated in the several Chippewa, or Ojibwe, bands of mid- and southeastern Michigan, clustered around Saginaw Bay on Lake Huron. Many Chippewas and their close Ottawa relatives had established villages in the region by the latter half of the 18th century, if not earlier. The Saginaw Chippewa communities are closely related to, and largely intermarried with, other Michigan Anishinaabek communities, especially the Ottawas and Potawatomis of the Grand River Valley. Collectively, the Chippewas, Ottawas, and Potawatomis of Michigan form the Three Fires Confederacy.

In 1819, the Saginaw Chippewa communities entered into a treaty with the United States that ceded much of the land in the Saginaw Bay watershed to the federal government, while retaining significant reservations in present-day Isabella County and near Swan Creek and Black River nearer Lake Huron and Lake St. Clair. The Isabella reservation in particular rested on the cusp of what recent scholars have identified as the northernmost boundary of the area where the growing season is sufficiently long for large-scale agriculture. For this reason, during the Indian removal period of the 1830s and 1840s, American settlers did not move into lands to the north of this boundary in large numbers, helping to reduce the pressure on the Saginaw Chippewa communities.

The Swan Creek and Black River Indians entered into a major treaty with the United States in 1836, the same year that the Michigan Ottawas and Chippewas of northern lower Michigan and the eastern upper peninsula ceded about one-third of the lands that now constitute the state of Michigan. These two groups simply sold their reservation lands to the United States, at a time when **land speculation** and prices were on a dramatic upswing, reserving much smaller parcels for themselves. Although they expected large cash payments from the sales of their reservations, they were thwarted by the Panic of 1837, in which the Michigan land speculation market completely collapsed. Ironically, the 1837–1839 national economic depression following the 1837 collapse all but halted the flow of eastern settlers moving into Michigan, removing for some years the main impetus for the federal government to remove the Michigan Indians, including the Saginaw Chippewas.

In 1837, the Saginaw Chippewas, now including many of their Swan Creek and Black River relatives, entered into a similar treaty in which they ceded all of their lands in mid-Michigan. From 1837 on, the Saginaw Chippewas became virtually homeless. It is important to note that the 1836 and 1837 treaties provided for the Chippewas to select lands in Missouri, close to the same region that the federal government hoped to remove the more northern Michigan Anishinaabek. Like the other Anishinaabek communities, the Chippewas who traveled to Missouri and also to Kansas to inspect the lands returned to Michigan harshly critical of what they had seen. Those dry, treeless prairie lands bore no resemblance to the lands that the Anishinaabek needed for hunting, fishing, sugar production, berry cultivation, and agriculture. Moreover, they were not the lands in which the ancestors of the Anishinaabek were buried. Several large groups of Saginaw Chippewas emigrated to Canada rather than remove west to these lands.

The national economic collapse in the late 1830s, along with the reduction in American settler pressure, as well as the Chippewas' refusal to remove west of the Mississippi River, effectively staved off the removal of the Saginaw Chippewas. Only a small fraction of the Chippewa population moved west, with larger numbers fleeing to Canada. The rest of the community remained in mid-Michigan, living near Christian missionaries and contributing mightily to the local economy. An additional factor preventing the removal of the Saginaw Chippewa Indians was their powerful presence in the Saginaw Bay fur trade. The American fur traders of the region viewed the Saginaw Chippewas as indispensable to the operation of the trade, and they also had become dependent on the Indians' economic clout. Finally, a smallpox epidemic devastated the Saginaw Chippewa communities in late 1837, further reducing the possibility of removing them.

And so during the 1840s and into the 1850s, the Saginaw Chippewa Indian communities continued to live in the mid-Michigan area, renting, leasing, and buying land from Americans, utterly unwilling to remove to the West. Although some Americans bristled at the Indians in their midst and urged their removal in accordance with the 1837 treaty, the federal government took no major action to force the removal of the Saginaw Chippewas.

In 1855, the Saginaw Chippewa Indian Tribe entered into yet another treaty with the United States. The cash promised from the sales of their reservations at Saginaw Bay and elsewhere in eastern and mid-Michigan never materialized, and the Chippewas came to the table with the expectation that they would receive a permanent home in mid-Michigan. The 1855 treaty provided for the allotment of the former lands held by the Saginaw, Swan Creek, and Black River Chippewa communities in exchange, once again, for the cession of their claims to the lands of mid- and southeastern Michigan. The treaty provided for lands within Isabella County to be selected by Indian families, formally ending the threat of removal. And in an 1864 treaty, the Saginaw Chippewa and the United States agreed to create a permanent reservation base in Isabella County.

FURTHER READING: Cleland, Charles E. *Rites of Conquest: The History and Culture of Michigan's Native Americans.* Ann Arbor: University of Michigan Press, 1992; Neumeyer, Elizabeth. "Michigan Indians Battle against Removal." *Michigan History* 55 (1971): 275–288; Satz, Ronald. "Indian Policy in the Jacksonian Era: The Old Northwest as a Test Case." *Michigan History* 60 (1976): 71–93; Stout, David B. "Ethnohistorical Report on the Saginaw Chippewa." In *American Indian Ethnohistory: Chippewa Indians V.* New York: Garland Publishing, 1974, pp. 87–132; Tanner, Helen Hornbeck. "The Chippewa of Eastern Lower Michigan." In *American Indian Ethnohistory: Chippewa Indians V.* New York: Garland Publishing, 1974, pp. 347–377; "Treaty with the Chippewa, 1837." Indian Affairs: Laws and Treaties. At http://digital.library .okstate.edu/kappler/Vol2/treaties/chi0482.htm.

MATTHEW L. M. FLETCHER

Sanford, John W. A. (1798–1870)

John W. A. Sanford exemplifies the Jacksonian Democrats who were on the ground in Indian country as treaties generated under the **Indian Removal Act** of 1830 were carried out. Like the man with a cattle prod, pushing cattle into the chute at a slaughterhouse, he and his kind worked at making Indians' lives so miserable that they resigned themselves to removal, which presented new opportunities for such men to make money in the process. Their actions effectively negated any humanitarian argument the government might have made regarding the justification for removal. Sanford first made a name for himself as commander of the Georgia Guard, arresting Cherokees and whites under Georgia law. Then he moved to Columbus, a town that had sprung up on the border with Alabama in 1828 after the McIntosh Creeks had been exiled from the state. Opportunist that he was, he was lured there no doubt by the frenzy of **land speculation** that gripped the Alabama Creek country immediately after the **Treaty of Washington** in 1832. Once that frenzy had died, he engaged in removing Creeks, and once the Creeks had departed, he sank into a quiet political life and disappeared from Indian affairs.

Sanford first made his name as commander of the Georgia Guard. This group of forty Georgians was created by the Georgia legislature in 1831 for the specific task of guarding the recently discovered gold fields from miners, either Cherokee or white. Not part of the militia, the Guard was not answerable to any authority. Charged generally with enforcing the laws of Georgia in the Cherokee country, it was the Guard that arrested the missionaries Samuel Worcester and Elizur Butler, an action that resulted in the important case of *Worcester v. Georgia.*

When the missionaries complained of being harshly clapped into irons by Sanford's men, Governor George Gilmer came to Sanford's defense.

Gilmer argued that Sanford was not responsible for, nor could he punish, the actions of his men, who were no doubt angered by the insolence of the missionaries; the missionaries therefore deserved whatever treatment they received. Gilmer assured Sanford that he was free to do what was necessary to carry out the law. Thus unbridled, the Guard as a unit and individually became an anathema to the Cherokee people.

Another of Sanford's charges was to rid the Cherokee country of the Pony Club, a band of mounted criminals who terrorized the Cherokees living near the Georgia frontier, robbing, harassing, and sometimes killing them. Not only did Sanford fail to rout them from the Cherokee lands, but most of them ultimately received permits to live there.

After his stint with the Georgia Guard, Sanford moved to Columbus, Georgia, which had sprung up on land newly opened by the exodus of the McIntosh Creeks forced out of Georgia by the Treaty of Indian Springs. There, he was president of the Farmer's Bank of Chattahoochee, which became insolvent in the spring of 1834, apparently because it was tied to the land speculation that was rampant at the time in Alabama.

When sale of Creek allotments began in the winter of 1833–1834 to mollify land speculators and intruders in the Creek lands, Sanford was one of the agents appointed to approve sales contracts. Fraud in sales quickly became widespread. Sanford, who worked Russell and Barbour Counties, reported the fraud to the War Department, which held up the contracts. However, War Department officials and Sanford came to agreement, with the sanction of President Andrew **Jackson**, that Sanford should tone down his reports of fraud, that neither he nor they could prevent fraud, and that it was better to look the other way than to jeopardize land sales and removal of the Creeks.

Sanford organized the Sanford Emigrating Company, made up primarily of land speculators, at Columbus. In the winter of 1834, his company conducted the first major removal of more than 600 Lower Creeks, who traveled overland from Fort Mitchell to Tuscaloosa and Columbus, Mississippi, and then to Memphis. From there most traveled to **Indian Territory** by steamboat, while some went overland by way of Little Rock. The military observer was Capt. John Page, who attended the group to ensure that the Sanford Company met its contract. The company's member and representative was William J. Beattie, a Vermonter and land speculator who had found Creek removal an opportunity to enrich himself and was willing to practice extortion to get what he wanted from the Indians. Only 469 Creeks survived the journey, arriving on March 28, 1835.

By that time, Sanford had begun his political career. He was elected to the 24th Congress as a Jacksonian Democrat but served only from March until July of 1835, resigning to conduct his business of removing Indians.

Sanford's underling Beattie conducted the next major party of more than 500 Fish Pond, Kealedji, and Hilibi Creeks, organized near Wetumpka in early December 1835. This group went north by way of Montevallo, Elyton, Moulton, and Tuscumbia, Alabama. From there they traveled by a steamboat towing two keelboats and reached Indian Territory in late January 1836.

Sanford at times appeared outraged by the actions of the land speculators, but he was either pretending or developed an "If you can't beat them,
join them" attitude. His emigration company was made up of a group of
Columbus-based speculators. When the government finally began a half-
hearted investigation of speculation fraud, Sanford was given the task of taking testimony from the Creeks. Although some Lower Creeks under **Eneah
Micco** wanted to testify, land speculators made them afraid that they would
be seized and sent west if they traveled to Columbus. Sanford refused to
travel to Alabama to see them, even though the Creeks asked him. Later,
Sanford's testimony in the matter of fraud generally supported the speculators. His actions without question added to the frustrations of Eneah Micco's people, who in the spring began hostilities known as the Creek War.

When the war broke out in May 1836, Sanford whipped up the flames,
alleging that Columbus was in immediate danger of being attacked. Sanford
apparently placed himself at the head of a militia group with the rank of
major general. When the war ended and the Lower Creeks under Eneah
Micco, **Eneah Emathla**, and Jim **Henry** were captured that summer, Sanford's company conducted their removal.

The party of some 2,300 Eufaulas, Chiahas, Hichitis, Kasihtas, and Yuchis
were sent to the West in August. The men and boys were shackled together
and marched to Montgomery with the women and children following in
wagons. From Montgomery, they traveled on steamboats by way of Mobile
and New Orleans to Rock Roe, Arkansas. From there, their journey took
them overland to Indian Territory.

The next contingent of Creeks to leave the East was directed by the Alabama
Emigrating Company, Sanford's company under new management. Members
of James C. Watson Company, one of the most active speculation companies,
who had been part of the Sanford Emigrating Company, were also members
of the Alabama Emigrating Company. Watson, president of the Insurance
Bank of Columbus, was also a slave trader of note, whose claims against the
Seminoles helped generate opposition to Seminole removal. The Alabama
Emigrating Company had little regard for the Creeks in their charge.

The Kasihta and Coweta contingent that left Tallassee in September 1836
bore the brunt of the company's disregard. The estimated 2,000 people who
traveled overland to Memphis had to endure forced marches of up to
20 miles a day, despite repeated requests by their leader, **Tuckabatche
Hadjo**, for days of rest. They departed camp whether the people were ready
or not, leaving stragglers scattered along the roads. Lt. John T. Sprague
accompanied the group to make certain that the company met its contrac-
tual obligations. At Memphis, he threatened to nullify their contract and
take charge of the removal himself if Creeks did not receive better treatment. His threat apparently worked, for they received better treatment during their journey through Arkansas.

How active Sanford was in the company's activities at this time is uncertain. He returned to politics and was elected state senator in 1837. He served
as Georgia's secretary of state from 1841 through 1843. By then his

opportunistic schemes appear to have ended. He was like many opportun-
ists who preyed upon Indians. Once removal ended, so did the opportunities for them to ply their usual trades.

FURTHER READING: *Cherokee Phoenix.* March 5, June 4, August 20, and October
7, 1831; Foreman, Grant. *Indian Removal: The Emigration of the Five Civilized Tribes of
Indians.* Norman: University of Oklahoma Press, 1989; Young, Mary E. *Redskins,
Ruffleshirts and Rednecks: Indian Allotments in Alabama and Mississippi, 1830–1860.*
Norman: University of Oklahoma Press, 1961.

DANIEL F. LITTLEFIELD, JR.

Sarasin (d. c. 1832)

After the 1824 treaty in which the Quapaws ceded their lands in Arkansas,
11 French-Quapaw mixed bloods were allowed to keep 80 acres each near
Arkansas Post while the rest of the tribe were removed to the Red River
country. Sarasin (also Saracen or Sarrisin) was one of these; however, the
Quapaw leader went with his people to the new lands (*see* **Quapaw
Removal**). When it became apparent that the area in which they were
attempting to live was untenable, Sarasin led a large contingent of Quapaws
back to Arkansas.

Sarasin had gained fame among the white settlers when he allegedly rescued two children who had been captured by the Chickasaws and carried
the children to their white parents. This reputation did not hurt the Quapaw cause when they returned to their homeland and found themselves to a
large extent at the mercy of the white population. His stature was further
enhanced in Arkansas when Governor James Miller named him a tribal
chief, in spite of the fact that, traditionally, these roles were filled with full
bloods. However, Sarasin began to work to reestablish his people in southern Arkansas, petitioning President John Quincy Adams in 1827 not only
for land but also for the annuity payments that had been paid to **Heckaton**
in the Red River country. The government's response was to contact Governor George Izard requesting that he convince the Quapaws to return to
Caddo country. Izard did not want to do that, however, and left it to Secretary of War James Barbour to send a letter to Sarasin saying that if the tribe
did not want to return to its assigned lands, it should join the Cherokees.
For his part, Izard sent the tribe supplies to take care of their immediate
needs, and he suggested that they join the Osages.

In 1830, while Sarasin was trying to negotiate for land in Arkansas, his
group was joined by the rest of the tribe as Heckaton led them out of the
Caddo country. Now most of the tribe was assembled on the Arkansas River,
vowing never to split again. However, this was not to be. The tribe once more
negotiated with the government, and in 1833, Sarasin, Heckaton, Tonni-
jinka, and Hakeketteda met with John F. **Schermerhorn** at New Gascony in
Arkansas, where Schermerhorn praised the new land that he wanted to
assign to the Quapaws, **Indian Territory**. Sarasin insisted that the Quapaws
inspect the new land before removing there, and he accompanied the

exploratory party to northeastern Indian Territory. Upon his return to Arkansas, Sarasin died; he is buried at Pine Bluff in the city cemetery.

FURTHER READING: Baird, W. David. *The Quapaw Indians: A History of the Downstream People.* Norman: University of Oklahoma Press, 1980; Nieberding, Velma Seamster. *The Quapaws.* Wyandotte, OK: Gregarth Publishing Company, 1999; Quapaw Tribe of Oklahoma. 2009. At www.quapawtribe.com/site/view/12817_Tribal History.pml; "Sarasin." The Encyclopedia of Arkansas History and Culture. 2009. At www.encyclopediaofarkansas.net/encyclopedia/.

JAMES W. PARINS

Sauganash

See Caldwell, Billy

Sauk and Mesquakie (Fox) Removal

The Sauk and Mesquakie tribes relocated and were removed to lands west of the Mississippi River over the course of several decades in the mid-19th century. Although the **Black Hawk War** of 1832 played an important role in that history, that conflict represents one element of the larger history of dispossession and removal that began with a treaty signed in 1804. Because of treaties, land cessions, and American western expansion, by the 1880s, communities of Sauk and Mesquakie Indians could be found from Iowa to the **Indian Territory**.

The origin of Sauk and Mesquakie removal lies in a treaty signed in St. Louis in 1804 when the American government made its first inroads into the upper Mississippi River Valley. During the mid- to late 18th century, the Great Lakes region underwent tremendous changes due to ongoing warfare first between the French and the British and then between the British and the American colonists. At the conclusion of the American Revolution, the Sauks and Mesquakies still held strong ties to the British. However, they also looked to the new American nation and its citizens as a potential source for trade goods.

A source of trouble in this new relationship came from American treatment of the Indians in and around St. Louis. After the Louisiana Purchase in 1803, President Thomas Jefferson and his administration had to develop relations with Indian tribes on both sides of the Mississippi River. It was not easy. The Sauks in particular believed that the Americans unfairly favored the western communities of Osage Indians, who had been enemies of the Sauks for years. This rivalry between the Sauks and Osages was evident in their competition over hunting grounds on the western side of the Mississippi River. And when American officials attempted to halt Sauk and Mesquakie raids on the Osage villages, settlements of American citizens became new targets. Such was the case in 1804, when a small raiding party of Sauk Indians killed three Americans at a settlement north of St. Louis.

In the aftermath of this attack, two things happened. First, five minor Sauk village chiefs traveled to St. Louis to negotiate for peace. Second, the governor of Indiana Territory, William Henry Harrison, decided to take advantage of the circumstances and pushed the Indian delegation to sign a treaty that ceded land. Although they did not have the authority to do so, the five men signed an accord that surrendered all of the Sauk territory located east of the Mississippi River. In these negotiations and in the final treaty, Harrison referred to the "Sac and Fox tribes," therefore grouping together two Indian communities who had close ties but no official communal political organization.

Despite protests within both Sauk and Mesquakie villages that the five Indian signatories did not have the authority to surrender the named territory, the Treaty of 1804 remained valid according to the American government. Further conflict was avoided because the treaty allowed the Sauks and Mesquakies to remain on their land for the time being. However, the land cession included in that agreement served as the foundation for all future removals of Sauk and Mesquakie communities in the decades that followed.

The war between the British and Americans that lasted from June 1812 to December 1814 had a distinct impact on the Sauk communities east of the Mississippi River. Many Sauks maintained relationships with the British traders at Fort Malden and Amherstburg in the first decade of the 19th century, and therefore they had a decision to make when the war began. For a portion of the Sauk community, the war provided an opportunity to respond to the increasing expansion of American settlements into the Great Lakes region. Those Indians who had particularly benefited from British generosity in trade goods chose to fight against the Americans. **Black Hawk** was one of the most prominent Sauk warriors who allied with the British over the next two years.

But even as Black Hawk and dozens of other men joined the British, a contingent of Sauks hoped to maintain their neutrality by moving away from the violence. After a series of councils with William **Clark**, the territorial governor of Missouri Territory, these Sauks relocated in the fall of 1813. All told, approximately 1,500 Sauk, Mesquakie, Piankeshaw, and Iowa Indians traveled by canoe up the Missouri River to a spot west of the Mississippi River.

This separation during the War of 1812 led to the negotiation of several distinct treaties in the years following the conflict. The Missouri Sauks signed two treaties, each of which recognized the truce that ended the war and also confirmed the terms of the Treaty of 1804. In addition, the Missouri Sauks agreed to remain separate from those who had remained east of the Mississippi and allied with the British. The Sauks who remained in their villages on the Rock River in northern Illinois signed a peace treaty in 1816. But they did not believe they had suffered a defeat, and American officials referred to Black Hawk and those who followed him as the British Band.

American settlement in the western Great Lakes region increased dramatically in the decade after the end of the War of 1812. Illinois became a state in 1818, and the non-Indian population more than tripled from 1820 to 1830. But the Sauk and Mesquakie homes in the northwestern part of the state had more to fear from the miners who flocked to the rich lead deposits in the upper Mississippi Valley. Tensions between miners and Indians in the Fever River region in particular helped cause the Ho-Chunk (Winnebago) Uprising in 1827. In the years that followed, American officials tried to relocate the Sauks and Mesquakies from their homes east of the Mississippi in the hopes of avoiding another war.

The Indian agents in the region received some cooperation in the person of **Keokuk**, a Sauk warrior whose status as a civil leader had risen in the decade after the War of 1812. Keokuk was intent on protecting Sauk and Mesquakie land west of the Mississippi and believed that it was necessary to surrender the eastern lands in the process. This belief made him a very appealing leader in the eyes of American officials, and they worked to increase his influence and authority. As of the fall of 1829, Keokuk and his followers were residing in villages on the Iowa River west of the Mississippi River.

In contrast, Black Hawk and the Sauk and Mesquakie members of the so-called British Band refused to support the terms of the Treaty of 1804 and intended to maintain a residence at Saukenuk, the center of Sauk lands in the Rock River region. By the early 1830s, however, American officials were determined to enforce the removal of the Sauks and Mesquakies. Therefore, when Black Hawk and approximately 800 men, women, and children crossed the Mississippi River and headed to Saukenuk in the summer of 1832, many Illinois residents considered their movement hostile. A series of misunderstandings and heightened tensions sparked what is known as the Black Hawk War. More of a pursuit than a war, this conflict ended on August 2 when an American military force of more than 1,300 men caught up to the British band on the Bad Axe River and killed at least 300 Sauk and Mesquakie men, women, and children.

In the aftermath of the Black Hawk War, American treaty commissioners forced the Sauks and Mesquakies to confirm a final cession of all their lands along the Mississippi River. They wanted to avoid further bloodshed by separating these Indians from the white Americans who continued to populate Illinois and the Wisconsin Territory. Within a decade, however, U.S. treaty commissioners visited the Sauks and Mesquakies to discuss their presence in the new state of Iowa. A treaty signed in 1842 arranged for the cession of all Indian land claims in Iowa and the relocation of approximately 2,300 Sauks and Mesquakies to present-day Kansas.

Over the next four decades, the community of Sauks and Mesquakies encountered another wave of American expansion and moved in several directions. More than 100 Mesquakies returned to Iowa in the 1850s and lived on a small parcel of land they obtained through purchase. A majority of the Sauks and the remaining Mesquakies removed one more time to present-day northeastern Oklahoma. The descendants of the Missouri Sauks who separated in the War of 1812 continue to live on a reservation that spans the Nebraska and Kansas borders.

The Sauk and Mesquakie removal is most often associated with the Black Hawk War of 1832 and its illustration of the last militant Indian resistance in the Old Northwest. However, the westward movements of the Sauk and Mesquakies encompassed the first three decades of the 19th century and demonstrated the growing push for Indian removal that culminated rather than began with the **Indian Removal Act**.

FURTHER READING: "The Black Hawk War." Wisconsin History. At www.wisconsin history.org/turningpoints/tp-012/; Bowes, John P. *Black Hawk and the War of 1832*. New York: Chelsea House Publishers, 2007; Hagan, William T. *The Sac and Fox Indians*. Norman: University of Oklahoma Press, 1958; Jackson, Donald, ed. *Black Hawk: An Autobiography*. Urbana-Champaign: University of Illinois Press, 1987; Nichols, Roger L. *Black Hawk and the Warrior's Path*. Arlington Heights, IL: Harlan Davidson, 1992; Trask, Kerry A. *Black Hawk: The Battle for the Heart of America*. New York: Henry Holt and Company, 2006; "Treaty with the Sauk and Foxes, 1832." Indian Affairs: Laws and Treaties. At http://digital.library.okstate.edu/kappler/Vol2/treaties/sau0349.htm.

JOHN P. BOWES

Schermerhorn, John F. (1786–1851)

John F. Schermerhorn, a New Yorker educated at Union College, was a minister first in the Congregational and then in the pro-removal Dutch Reformed Church. He was a strong supporter of Andrew **Jackson** and his removal policy and, as an agent of the government, practiced whatever tactics were necessary to generate a removal treaty.

When the U.S. House established a commission in July 1832 to visit **Indian Territory**, Schermerhorn was appointed to serve with Montfort Stokes, the chairman, and Henry L. **Ellsworth**. Their task was to recommend a plan of government for the region. Secretary Lewis **Cass** instructed them to treat with the tribes who had relocated, stressing the government's guarantee of a permanent home and protection from intruders, the promotion of "civilization," and the consolidation of tribes that were similar in customs and manners.

In late 1832, Schermerhorn and Ellsworth negotiated articles of agreement, adjusting the common landholdings of the United Nation of Senecas and Shawnees, who had removed to the northeastern corner of the Indian Territory from near Lewistown, Ohio, under a treaty in 1831. In February 1833, he, Ellsworth, and Stokes signed agreements with the Western Cherokees clarifying their boundaries and making other provisions in anticipation of Eastern **Cherokee removal**, as well as with the McIntosh Creeks, preparing the way for Creek removal and a union in the West of the Creeks and Seminoles (*see* **Muscogee [Creek] Removal**).

The next month they negotiated a disastrous treaty with a Seminole delegation that was visiting Fort Gibson. This treaty, which provided for **Seminole removal**, was made on questionable authority. In 1832, James Gadsden had gone to Florida to negotiate a removal treaty with the Seminoles. He insisted that the Seminoles remove west and unite with the Creeks. When they refused, he threatened to pay their annuity to the Creeks, from whom they would have to collect it. The Seminoles gave in and signed the Treaty of Payne's Landing. However, removal was contingent on the report from a delegation to the West that the land was satisfactory. It was this delegation that Schermerhorn, Stokes, and Ellsworth maneuvered into signing the treaty at Fort Gibson, although the delegation had no authority to negotiate an agreement. The document they signed provided for the removal of the Seminoles and their union with the Creeks. Although the Seminoles protested the validity of the treaty, the United States claimed it was valid and ordered the Seminoles to prepare for removal. In this manner, Schermerhorn helped lay the groundwork for the **Second Seminole War**. The treaty of Fort Gibson was Schermerhorn's first application of the government's divide-and-conquer tactic that was often used in treaty making.

Before he left the West, on May 13, 1833, Schermerhorn negotiated a final removal treaty with the Quapaws, who relinquished the Caddo lands on the Red River given them by their Treaty of 1824 (*see* **Quapaw Removal**). The treaty provided for their resettlement in the northeastern corner of the Indian Territory next to the Senecas and Shawnees.

Schermerhorn's second major application of underhanded tactics was the **Treaty of New Echota**, which he and William **Carroll** concluded on December 29, 1835. This infamous document, like the Seminole Treaty of Fort Gibson, was signed by only a small faction of Cherokees but was applied to the entire tribe. Schermerhorn's duplicitous tactics became well known to the public. Carroll somehow escaped the criticism, for the treaty became known as "Schermerhorn's Treaty." Andrew Jackson, of course, defended the treaty.

Unlike the Seminoles, who resisted removal by arms, the Cherokees chose to put their faith in the American political system; although this approach delayed removal, ultimately the Cherokees were forced west by the army, making Schermerhorn a hated figure in Cherokee history.

FURTHER READING: Foreman, Grant. *Indian Removal: The Emigration of the Five Civilized Tribes of Indians.* Norman: University of Oklahoma Press, 1972; Satz, Ronald. *American Indian Policy in the Jacksonian Era.* Lincoln: University of Nebraska Press, 1975; U.S. Congress. House. *Regulating the Indian Department.* 23rd Cong., 1st sess., 1834. H. Rept. 474.

DANIEL F. LITTLEFIELD, JR.

Schoolcraft, Henry Rowe (1793–1864)

Henry Rowe Schoolcraft was a geologist, explorer, and writer whose interests ultimately focused on Indian culture. As a young man, he became knowledgeable about the trans-Mississippi West when he led explorations to mining regions in Missouri, Arkansas, the upper Mississippi, and Lake Superior between 1817 and 1820. In a later exploration, he sought to discover the source of the Mississippi River.

In 1822, Schoolcraft became involved in Indian affairs when he was named agent to the tribes of Lake Superior. He further enhanced his ties to Indian society when he married a quarter-blood Ojibwe woman the following year. From 1836 through 1841, he served as superintendent of Indian affairs for Michigan and as such oversaw the removal of a number of groups. On May 6, 1836, he negotiated a removal treaty with the Swan Creek and Black

River bands of Chippewas in Michigan and on May 28 with the Ottawas and Chippewas of Mashigo, Grand River, Michilimackinac, Sault Ste Marie, L'Arbre Croche, and Grand Traverse, in which the tribes ceded approximately the northern third of lower Michigan and the eastern half of upper Michigan. Removal to the West depended on the tribes' location of lands to buy from other tribes or suitable lands provided by the United States.

When the **Whig Party** took power in 1841, Schoolcraft lost his position in Indian affairs and moved to the East. In his later years, he wrote prolifically about his travels, Indian traditions, and his years of work among the Indians. Perhaps his best-known work is his six-volume *Historical and Statistical Information Respecting the History, Condition, and Prospects of the Indian Tribes of the United States* (1851–1857).

FURTHER READING: Hough, Walter. "Schoolcraft, Henry Rowe." *Dictionary of American Biography*. Ed. Dumas Malone. Vol. 16. New York: Charles Scribner's Sons, 1935, pp. 456–457; Schoolcraft, Henry Rowe. *Personal Memoirs of a Residence of Thirty Years with the Indian Tribes on the American Frontiers*. Philadelphia: Lippincott, Grambo and Co., 1851.

DANIEL F. LITTLEFIELD, JR.

Scott, Winfield (1786–1866)

Gen. Winfield Scott, a Virginian and veteran of the War of 1812, was a ranking officer when the **Indian Removal Act** was passed. A vain and ambitious man known as "Old Fuss and Feathers," he played a role in the affairs of four tribal groups during the removal period.

In 1832, after the Battle of Stillman's Run in the **Black Hawk War**, President Andrew **Jackson** sent Scott to Illinois to take command of the forces against **Black Hawk**. The fighting was over by the time he arrived; his duties involved dealing with the aftermath of the war and reaching treaty agreements with the Sauks and Foxes and other tribes that brought an end to the conflict and reinforced earlier removal agreements with the Sauks and Mesquakies (Foxes) and Ho-Chunks (Winnebagos) (*see* **Sauk and Mesquakie [Fox] Removal**; **Ho-Chunk Removal**).

In 1836, Scott commanded American forces in Florida during the **Second Seminole War**, which had begun as a dispute between pro-removal and anti-removal Seminoles. The army's job was to subdue the Seminoles and force **Seminole removal** to the West. However, eluded by the

Winfield Scott was the founder of America's professional army. He served in the War of 1812 and the Black Hawk War, and commanded the troops who gathered the Cherokees for removal. (Library of Congress)

Seminoles, Scott was unable to engage them in any significant battle. Frustrated, he blamed the quality of forces under his command. His public disparagement of the Florida militiamen under his command earned him the enmity of Floridians.

Scott's service in Florida ended when he was dispatched to Georgia in May 1836 to lead forces in quelling the Creeks under **Eneah Emathla** (or Neamathla), who had begun raiding whites because of injustices against them by white intruders and land speculators and because of their growing poverty and hunger as a result of crop failures due to drought. Scott planned a strategy for containing the Creeks, but his subordinate Gen. Thomas S. **Jesup** acted outside Scott's orders, captured Eneah Emathla and some 300 Creeks, and sent them and their families immediately to the West as the first contingent in the forced **Muscogee (Creek) removal**.

In May 1838, Scott was dispatched to the Cherokee Nation to enforce **Cherokee removal**. When he arrived, he found that the regular soldiers he had requested had not reached the Cherokee Nation. He issued a proclamation to the Cherokee people on May 8, telling them to report to collection camps for removal. Because May 23 was his deadline and the Cherokees did not respond, he sent state militiamen under his authority to round up the Cherokees. The Cherokees were forced from their homes and sent to holding camps to await being sent to departure points. Scott had hoped for humane treatment of the Cherokee people, but the militiamen burned homesteads, looted property, and committed other atrocities.

The Cherokee leadership under John **Ross** sought and received permission for the Cherokee Nation to take charge of removing its own people. The removal did not begin until October. Throughout the hot summer of 1838, the Cherokees suffered in the holding camps called "forts" that Scott and his forces had established. Much of the disease and high mortality rates often attributed to the hardships of the removal trail in reality occurred in the camps before departure.

Winfield Scott also played an indirect role in Chickasaw postremoval affairs. He became general-in-chief of the army in 1841 and used his position to help Secretary of War John Spencer, Treasury Department officials, and President John Tyler to suppress a report written by Maj. Ethan Allen Hitchcock, revealing fraud in the management of rations supplied the Creeks, the Cherokees, and especially the Chickasaws upon their arrival in the West. The report exposed close associates of Andrew Jackson and other high-ranking officials, who escaped all legal consequences for their acts.

In the postremoval period, Scott went on to distinguish himself in the Mexican War and was President Abraham Lincoln's first commander during the Civil War, during which he developed the Anaconda strategy that was used in defeating the South.

FURTHER READING: Eisenhower, John S. D. *Agent of Destiny: The Life and Times of General Winfield Scott.* Norman: University of Oklahoma Press, 1999; Elliott, Charles Winslow. *Winfield Scott: The Soldier and the Man.* New York: Macmillan, 1937; Mahon,

John K. *History of the Second Seminole War, 1835–1842.* Gainesville: University Press of Florida, 1967; Scott, Winfield. *Memoirs of Lieut-General Scott, LL.D., written by himself.* New York: Sheldon, 1864.

DANIEL F. LITTLEFIELD, JR.

Second Seminole War (1835–1842)

Negotiations between the Seminoles and U.S. government representatives were completed in 1835 for the removal of the Indians to lands west of the Mississippi. January 1, 1836, was set for the Seminoles to report to Tampa to be shipped west. Gen. D. L. Clinch, who as a colonel had attacked the Seminoles at Fort Apalachicola 20 years earlier in the First Seminole War, mustered a body of 200 troops to force the removal if it was not undertaken voluntarily. A few days prior to the appointed date for compliance, the Seminoles attacked Fort King and on the same day intercepted Maj. Francis L. Dade's force moving from Fort Brooke in Tampa to Fort King, near present-day Dade City. These engagements serve as testimony to the rising prominence of Osceola as a leader within the Seminole people. He had personal grievances with one of the casualties at Fort King, a government-appointed agent to the Seminoles, for having contributed to the abduction of his wife and for placing him under arrest at a previous meeting.

By the end of February, an agreement seemed likely. A conference was held at which the government proposed that the Seminoles relocate south of the Withlacoochee River in central Florida and cease raids and hostilities. In return, the troops would not follow them. Agreement was reached on these terms, but then Gen. Clinch, apparently unaware of the agreement, arrived and assailed the Seminole party at the conference. The Seminoles fled, convinced that they had been betrayed yet again.

In April 1836, a party of 407 Seminoles under Holata Emathla, a pro-removal chief who had helped precipitate the outbreak of war, left Tampa Bay en route to Little Rock for further removal. Of that party, 87, including Holata Emathla, would die. Despite this development, hostilities continued, culminating with the surrender of **Miconopy**, the recognized chief of the Seminoles, in 1837. Deputies of Miconopy treated with Gen. Thomas S. **Jesup**, agreeing to the removal of their party under the condition that they could take their slaves with them to the West, thus protecting the slaves from being sent or sold to white slave owners. Jesup agreed, and on March 18, Miconopy surrendered himself to be used as a hostage to ensure compliance with the treaty. With Miconopy came Jumper, **Hulbutta Tustenuggee** (Alligator), and **Abraham**. Missing from Miconopy's party was Osceola. In time, those represented by the parties to the agreement assembled near Tampa Bay and were staged for removal. Pressure began to mount on Jesup to give over the **African-descended people** among the Indians (whom the whites regarded as runaway slaves) and return them to their "owners." Jesup eventually capitulated, even though this was an obvious violation of the agreement's conditions. Subsequently, Miconopy, Jumper, and others took their people and left the vicinity. The ongoing effort to round up other Seminoles continued in the aftermath of this failed agreement, with the Muscogee (Creek) warriors being supplemented by other Indian tribes, including the Shawnees, Delawares, and Choctaws. Ongoing negotiation led to Miconopy, Alligator, and Jumper again bringing their people in for removal. Through violation of a flag of truce and treaty protocol orchestrated under Jesup's command, Wildcat (**Coacoochee**) and then Osceola were captured. Many soldiers, army officers, and citizens of the time were very much disappointed and chagrined by the dishonorable means by which Osceola was captured and the way he was subsequently treated.

As the military campaign continued, the Seminoles moved further south into areas for which army tactics were ill designed. Defeats and hollow victories against what was an essentially nebulous foe added to the army's already low morale and lack of confidence in leadership. From above, Jesup was burdened by a damaged reputation and a loss of political will for further prosecution of what many considered an unwinnable war. These factors led the superior officers within Jesup's command to advocate striking a truce with the Seminoles, leaving them all of southern Florida. Jesup approached the secretary of war, who would only allow a temporary truce but insisted on continuing the push for removal. In 1838, Jesup was recalled from the command of the army in Florida. His own estimates were that in the approximate year previous to his recall from command, 1,978 Seminoles were captured and staged for removal, of which 23 escaped.

Gen. Zachary Taylor replaced Jesup in command. Taylor's primary effort appeared to be not so much prosecuting a war against the Seminoles as facilitating the shipment of immigrants to the West. In April 1839, Taylor was replaced by Gen. Alexander Macomb, who was assigned specifically to negotiate a peace. In May, a peace was negotiated, the agreement of which was similar to what Jesup had suggested. The agreement met with wide approval from policymakers and citizens outside of Florida. But the citizens of Florida wanted nothing less than annihilation or removal and pressed on with provocative actions and hostilities. Because of their actions, the agreement was not allowed to succeed.

In late 1842, Col. E. A. Hitchcock was charged with reopening the war that, by his estimation, "had been closed so often heretofore." Through evenhanded dealing and patience, he gained the respect of the Seminole leaders and eventually succeeded where others had failed in brokering a peace that terminated involuntary removal, although intimidation and other influence continued to be used toward the goal of total removal. The citizens of Florida still wished for removal, and incentives were offered for voluntary removal in 1849, 1851, and 1856. The brief **Third Seminole War** (1855–1858) resulted in almost 300 émigrés to the West. Seminole tradition suggests that several other small family groups of Seminoles left Florida after the Civil War ended in 1865.

In 1881, again the federal government took up the policy of removal and sent Clay McCauley to Florida to investigate the Seminole presence there.

As a result of McCauley's report, the notion of removal was overturned and the Congress, in 1884, began appropriating annual sums for disbursement to the Seminoles in Florida, thereby establishing a relationship with the Seminoles remaining in Florida that was similar to that reached with those who had been relocated to what would become Oklahoma.

FURTHER READING: Covington, James. W. *The Seminoles of Florida.* Gainesville: University Press of Florida, 1993; Foreman, Grant. *Indian Removal.* Norman: University of Oklahoma Press, 1989; Mahon, John K. *History of the Second Seminole War, 1835–1842.* Gainesville: University Press of Florida, 1967; Wright, J. Leitch, Jr. *Creeks and Seminoles.* Lincoln: University of Nebraska Press, 1986.

FRED E. KNOWLES, JR.

Seminole Removal

The federal policy of removal of American Indians in Florida was aimed at the Seminoles in the aftermath of the Seminole Wars (*see* **Second Seminole War**, **Third Seminole War**) and in response to southern expansion. The relationship between the Seminoles and the U.S. government was, and remains, a complex and convoluted thing. After the removal process, significant numbers of Seminoles remained in Florida even after years of concentrated efforts to move the population to the West. The First Seminole War ended in 1818, and the next year Florida was purchased from Spain.

Some have argued that the Seminole identity was born in response to European and white American incursion. Many scholars believe that the Seminoles descended from the Muscogees (Creeks), including absorbed peoples who moved south into Florida as life in Georgia and Alabama became untenable in the face of white expansion. These separatists filled a void in the indigenous population that was left by the interactions of the Spanish with previous inhabitants. The Seminoles began to become identified as a people separate and distinct from their Muscogee (Creek) brethren in about 1775 (*see* **Muscogee [Creek] Removal**). In dealing with the Indian question, the federal government used the national definitions that best suited its motives. If configuring the Seminoles and Muscogee (Creeks) as one entity allowed a stronger position for the government, then the parties were defined collectively. If separating the two was deemed useful, severance was used.

The issue of African slavery was a primary sticking point in the development of policy toward the Seminole Nation. In 1790, in a treaty with the Muscogees (Creeks) that attempted to placate white Georgia citizens in their claims of depredations at the hands of the Muscogees (Creeks), the federal government held the Muscogee Nation accountable for slaves who ran away and settled with the Seminoles. This was not an insignificant number of slaves, and the point would prove to be of primary importance in undercutting cohesion between the Muscogee and Seminole peoples. The issue of slavery would also serve as an underlying reason for the Seminole Wars.

The First Seminole War (1816–1818) began with Col. D. L. Clinch joining forces with the Muscogee (Creek) chief McIntosh and engaging the

Seminoles at Fort Apalachicola, in Spanish Florida. The fort was said to have harbored escaped slaves, and McIntosh's stated mission was to locate runaway slaves and return them to their "lawful" owners. This engagement signaled formal governmental approval and a militarization of what were previously civilian "slave raids" into north Florida. It is important to understand that the First Seminole War and Muscogee (Creek) involvement were greatly influenced by the Red Stick War (1813–1814) within the Muscogee Nation. It is through that conflict that McIntosh came to prominence and the conditions of the relationship between the Lower Creeks and the federal government were forged.

The purchase of Florida from Spain in 1819 erased any legal misgivings regarding incursion into the territory of a sovereign European power. It would now be more convenient to deal with the problem of runaway slaves and placate other complaints of perceived deprivations. In addition to the recovery of lost slaves, which often involved the return of the descendants of runaway slaves to the descendants of the owners of the original runaway slaves, efforts began in earnest to move the Seminoles southward.

The Treaty of Moultrie Creek (1823) called for the removal of the Seminoles from north to central Florida, from the areas of the Apalachicola and Suwannee rivers south, below Tampa Bay. It also required the return of runaway slaves. Many chiefs refused to turn over the sought-after "runaways" and refused to move, as the land in central Florida was considerably poorer than the cultivated land that they were being required to leave. Slaves continued to escape servitude in Georgia and seek haven in Florida. Obviously and predictably, slave raids recurred, although now apparently without military mandate or assistance. In the aftermath of the Treaty of Moultrie Creek, the subject of removal to places west of the Mississippi River was broached. The Seminoles were immediately suspicious, and some, especially the freed and assimilated blacks, feared enslavement by the Muscogees (Creeks) upon their own removal. The wedge between the two nations had been driven deeply and was used to best advantage by the federal government. The focus of federal policy shifted from removal southward to removal westward.

The **Indian Removal Act** provided for the removal of all American Indians from locations east of the Mississippi River to locations west of the river. The old nemesis of the Muscogees (Creeks) and Seminoles, Andrew **Jackson**, was then president, an office to which he had been elected in part because of his espousal of a removal policy. Pursuant to the new law, in 1832, Col. James Gadsden began negotiation with the Seminoles for removal west. Gadsden found the Seminoles in desperate conditions. A drought had decimated their crops, and Gadsden reported that the Seminoles were "naked and starving." Whether this was true or not, those who met with Gadsden seemed amenable to removal only if the federal government would provide for a party of Seminoles to go to the proposed site to inspect the new land. The Seminoles were told that they would be required to reaffiliate with the Muscogees (Creeks) and that annuity payments for them would be made to the Muscogees to then be distributed to them. Fears of subservience to the

Creeks arose, but an uneasy accord was formalized by the Treaty of Payne's Landing in 1832. The exploratory delegates found the western site suitable, and at Fort Gibson, **Indian Territory**, they signed a document to that effect. The government held that the delegates spoke for the entire Seminole leadership and that their approval satisfied the requirements of the Treaty of Payne's Landing, subsequently binding the Seminoles to remove. The Seminoles back in Florida disagreed, holding that the delegation was advisory and was not charged with the authority to act on a larger mandate. This disagreement was a primary cause of the Second Seminole War.

January 1, 1836, was set for the Seminoles to report to Tampa to be shipped west. Gen. Clinch, who as a colonel had attacked the Seminoles at Fort Apalachicola 20 years earlier, mustered a body of 200 troops to force the removal if it was not undertaken voluntarily. A few days prior to the appointed date for compliance, the Seminoles attacked Fort King and on the same day intercepted Maj. Francis L. Dade's force moving from Fort Brooke in Tampa to Fort King, near present-day Dade City. These engagements serve as testimony to the rising prominence of Osceola as a leader within the Seminole people.

By the end of February, an agreement seemed likely. A conference was held at which the government proposed that the Seminoles relocate south of the Withlacoochee River, in central Florida, and to cease raids and hostilities. In return, the troops would not follow them. Agreement was reached on these terms, but then Gen. Clinch, apparently unaware of the agreement, arrived and assailed the Seminole party at the conference. The Seminoles fled, convinced that they had been betrayed yet again.

From then until 1842, hostilities continued between those who refused to be removed and government troops in what became known as the Second Seminole War. In 1842, the United States unilaterally decreed an end to the fighting and resorted to other tactics to encourage voluntary removal: sending delegations of Seminoles from the Indian Territory to negotiate and paying monetary incentives to leaders and agents to encourage removal.

Seminole removal, which continued throughout and after the Second Seminole War, differed from all other removals because the Florida Indians, with a few exceptions, made their entire journey from Florida to Indian Territory by water. They traveled by steamboat or schooner, primarily from Tampa Bay. Sailing ships were towed by steamboats from the mouth of the Mississippi to New Orleans, where the Seminoles' stopover was at Jackson Barracks. There, they boarded steamboats and, quite frequently, flatboats or keelboats towed by the side-wheelers up the Mississippi and Arkansas rivers to a landing near Fort Gibson. From there, the trip was overland into the western part of the Creek Nation. At times, low water levels on the Arkansas River forced parties to disembark and travel overland during the remainder of their journey. These were usually the most difficult parts of the journey for both the Indians and their conductors. The former were not prepared for overland travel, and the conductors at times had difficulty making on-the-spot arrangements.

Seminole removal began in April of 1836, when a party of 408 Seminoles under Holata Emathla left Tampa Bay en route to the West. They traveled by schooner to New Orleans and then up the Mississippi in a steamboat towing a keelboat. Because of low water, they were forced to disembark at McLean's Landing between Dardanelle and Fort Smith, Arkansas, and continue their journey overland. Of the party, 87, including Holata Emathla, died. Because they were the only band that had chosen not to resist removal in the Second Seminole War, they were estranged from the other Seminoles and settled among the Creeks.

Subsequent removals were a result of the hostilities that continued between those who refused to be moved and government troops. Removal parties were assembled as leaders and their bands were captured or surrendered. The government attempted to keep bands and families together, sometimes delaying embarkation until families could be sorted out.

In 1838, six major parties went west. In May and June, the bands of **Miconopy**, Emathla (Philip), and Jumper, numbering 878 Seminoles and 257 "negro Indians," traveled on one boat. Some 453, including about 150 Spanish Indians, were on board a second. The third carried 674. In addi-

Engraving of a portrait of Miconopy, nominal chief of the Seminoles, by 19th-century American painter Charles Bird King, from *The Indian Tribes of North America.* (McKenney, Thomas L. and James Hall. *The Indian Tribes of North America,* 1836–1844)

tion, 33 "negroes" who belonged to the last group were detained in New Orleans because of a slave claim dating back for several years in Florida. Two of the three steamboats carrying these parties also carried 10 American soldiers each as guards, the only known instance in which the army sent troops with the Seminoles. Fifty-four died, including Jumper, who died in New Orleans, and Emathla. In May 1838, Coe Holata's band also removed, and Talmas Neah's party of 349 removed in June, as did the 33 "negro Indians" who had been detained in New Orleans. The latter were delayed by low water and a lack of shallow-draft steamboats at Little Rock. They finally joined a steamboat load of removing Cherokees but were again stopped by low water at Lewisburg. There, the Seminole party hired two wagons and continued overland. In July, a group of 67 led by **Hulbutta Tustenuggee** (Alligator) removed and at Clarkesville, Arkansas, picked up the 33 "negro Indians." The Indians were grounded again below Fort Coffee and completed their journey overland. Finally, a group of Apalachicolas and Dog Island Muscogees, numbering 250, also ran aground above Little Rock and had to complete their journey overland.

In 1839, as the Florida war activity waned, only two groups went west. In March, 205 members of **Coe Hadjo**'s band removed. Coe Hadjo had been seized with Osceola in one of Gen. Thomas S. **Jesup**'s infamous violations of the flag of truce and was imprisoned at St. Augustine. In late 1838, he had been permitted to take a delegation of Cherokees led by John **Ross**, who hoped to mediate a peace, to meet with Miconopy and other leaders. Much to the Cherokees' chagrin, they were held as hostages to try to force others to surrender. Coe Hadjo's removal party numbered 204, primarily women and children, but also including 48 slaves and 13 free blacks. Among the blacks were **Abraham**, Cudjo, and Tony Barnett, who had served as interpreters and scouts for the U.S. Army. The second removal party of 1839 was a group of St. Augustine prisoners, who in November left St. Augustine by schooner for New Orleans, where they boarded a steamboat for the remainder of their journey.

Because the army was having little luck in forcing or persuading more Seminoles to remove, in the fall of 1840 the government sent a delegation of Seminoles who had removed to Indian Territory back to Florida. Led by Capt. John Page, the delegation of Holatachee, Nocose Yohola, and 12 other Seminoles with Toney and Primus, their black interpreters, arrived at Tampa Bay in early November. Page was given authority to negotiate and also to offer Seminoles monetary incentives to remove.

It was without question the monetary incentives and not persuasion that made 1841 another significant year in Seminole removal. The first group, who removed in March, consisted of 221 Tallahassees and others, who were joined in New Orleans by an additional 205 Indians, 6 "Indian negroes," and a black. Included in the combined party were the Tallahassee band of Echo Emathla, 24 Spanish Indian women and children, the 5-member household of a free black named Dennis, and slaves. This party joined Miconopy's people on the Deep Fork in the western Creek Nation. A second group of 206, not identified with any particular leader or band, removed in June 1841, but they were carefully protected to prevent slave hunters from attempting to take some of them captive. Perhaps the most important group to remove in 1841 was a party of about 200 who left Florida in October, primarily the band of Hospitakee, who had been persuaded by **Coacoochee** (Wildcat) to surrender. Coacoochee and part of his band were also among the group. Next to Osceola, he had been the most charismatic leader of the war of resistance. In the fall of 1841, another delegation, headed by Alligator, returned to Florida to try to persuade others to remove.

Partly as a result of the delegation's work, two significant removals occurred in 1842. The first involved a party of nearly 300, consisting of Coacoochee's band and others, who removed in April, including Coacoochee's family, his aunt and her family, and a sister of Alligator. Coacoochee's band settled next to Alligator's in the Cherokee Nation not far from Fort Gibson, refusing to go on to the Creek Nation. The second group to remove in 1842 consisted of bands belonging to **Halleck Tustenuggee** and John **Cavallo**, or Gopher John, both well-known leaders in the Second Seminole War. Their steamboat was grounded a few miles below Little Rock, forcing them to hire wagons to complete their journey overland to the Creek Nation by way of the Choctaw Agency.

Only one removal occurred in 1843. It consisted of Octiarche and his band and Thlocco Tustenuggee (Tiger Tail) and 26 followers for a total of

99, Pascofa's band, and Passochee's band of 62. These parties arrived at different times at New Orleans, where Thlocco Tustenuggee died. From Jackson Barracks, the combined parties traveled to their final destination, oddly enough aboard a steamboat owned by "Rich" Joe Vann, a prominent Cherokee from Webbers Falls, Cherokee Nation.

After this removal, a number of years passed before another took place. In 1844, the United States began to develop a new policy in Seminole removal. Because of the decrease in the number of removals, the War Department contemplated turning removal over to military officers in Florida rather than maintaining a removal agent there. Although such lines of authority became policy in 1845, no other removal occurred until 1849, when 85 Indians, primarily from Capichuchi's and Cotcha Fixico's bands, left in March. A small party removed in late 1850. In 1851, the government sent Luther Blake to Florida to attempt to bribe or otherwise persuade other Seminoles to remove. Blake worked hard because he was to receive a bounty for every Seminole he brought in, but after a year, he had persuaded only 36 to remove. Another delegation was sent from the Indian Territory in 1854, but these delegates persuaded only seven to return to the West with them.

No more removals occurred until 1858. By 1855, the Indians remaining in Florida had retreated for the most part into the Everglades, primarily north of Lake Okeechobee. **Hulbutta Micco**, better known to Americans as Billy Bowlegs, was recognized as the leader of the Miccosukees, although he may not have had full authority. That year, a crew of American surveyors wantonly destroyed his banana plantation, setting off what became known as the Third Seminole War. In 1858, another delegation of 40 Seminoles from Indian Territory, led by John Jumper, returned to Florida and, by offering Bowlegs money, persuaded him to remove. In May, he and his band of 125 Miccosukees traveled to the West. Late that year, he returned to Florida and convinced 75 others to go west in early 1859.

Hulbutta Micco's return to Indian Territory brought Seminole removal unofficially to an end. It is estimated that some 2,968 Seminoles were removed from 1836 to March 1841, when the United States had unilaterally called off the war, and 934 from April 1841 to April 1842, a total of 3,903. Adding the earlier parties, an estimated 4,200 Seminoles were sent to the West.

Seminole removal was remarkable in several ways. First, it was the only tribal removal that involved an extended war of resistance. Second, it was the first removal in which the government made it policy to offer bounties for each person who removed. Third, it is unknown how many perished in the long war of attrition, but during the journey west, the Seminoles had the lowest mortality rates of any of the southeastern tribes except the Chickasaws. That fact was due, in part, to the inoculation of the Seminoles against smallpox before they reached Indian Territory. Fourth, Seminole removal was the longest removal, spanning 23 years. The United States finally and officially ceased efforts to remove those who remained in Florida in 1881.

FURTHER READING: Covington, James W. *The Seminoles of Florida*. Gainesville: University Press of Florida, 1993; Foreman, Grant. *Indian Removal*. Norman: University of Oklahoma Press, 1989; Paige, Amanda L., et al. The North Little Rock Site on the Trail of Tears National Historic Trail: Historical Contexts Report. 2003. At http://anpa.ualr.edu/trail_of_tears/indian_removal_project/site_reports/ north_little_rock/northlittlerock_report.htm; "Treaty with the Seminole, 1832." Indian Affairs: Laws and Treaties. At http://digital.library.okstate.edu/kappler/ Vol2/treaties/sem0344.htm; "Treaty with the Seminole, 1833." Indian Affairs: Laws and Treaties. At http://digital.library.okstate.edu/kappler/Vol2/treaties/ sem0394.htm; Wright, J. Leitch, Jr. *Creeks and Seminoles*. Lincoln: University of Nebraska Press, 1986.

FRED E. KNOWLES, JR.

Seminole Tribe of Florida

The two federally recognized Indian tribes of Florida today are the products of more than a century of resistance to removal. With the last major removal under **Hulbutta Micco** (Billy Bowlegs) following the **Third Seminole War**, an estimated 300 Miccosukees and Creek Seminoles remained in Florida.

For more than two decades after the war, the Seminoles remained primarily in the Everglades and Big Cypress Swamp in southern Florida, engaging very little with the whites. In fact, they possessed a nagging fear that the government would continue its attempts to move them to the West, so they avoided contact when possible. In 1881, the United States once more briefly considered undertaking removal, but in 1884, Congress began appropriating funds primarily for the purchase of homesteads for them. Nevertheless, some Seminoles carried their fear of removal well into the 20th century. They developed a trading economy with the whites that lasted from the 1880s into the 20th century, and the building of drainage canals and a highway through the Everglades in the early decades resulted in a tourist trade.

From the early 1890s though the 1930s, reservations were established by the state of Florida and the United States. Though boundaries changed, there emerged three reservations: Brighton, primarily Creek Seminoles; Big Cypress, primarily Miccosukees; and Hollywood, mixed Creek Seminoles and Miccosukees. The three groups maintained separate social and political practices.

The Seminoles had shown little interest in organizing as a tribe under the Indian Reorganization Act of 1934. However, New Deal projects and World War II, as well as more rapid assimilation through education, impacted on social attitudes. Thus, interest in reorganization was kindled by the government's termination policy of the early 1950s, and in 1957, the Seminoles organized as the Seminole Tribe of Florida.

By that time, however, widening differences between the Creek Seminoles and Miccosukees became more evident in their lifestyles and economic philosophies. In the late 1950s, the Miccosukees broke away and organized as the Miccosukee Tribe of Indians, now called the Miccosukee Seminole Nation. For both peoples, however, removal looms large in tribal history. Today, the Seminoles of Florida refer to themselves and the Miccosukees as the descendants of "the last few Indian resisters" to removal and call themselves "the only tribe in America who never signed a peace treaty."

FURTHER READING: Covington, James W. *The Seminoles of Florida*. Gainesville: University Press of Florida, 1993; Kersey, Harry A., Jr. "Those Left Behind: The Seminole Indians of Florida." In *Southeastern Indians since the Removal Era*. Ed. Walter L. Williams. Athens: University of Georgia Press, 1979, pp. 174–190; Seminole Tribe of Florida. 2010. At www.semtribe.com; Sturtevant, William C., and Jessica R. Cattelino. "Florida Seminole and Miccosukee." In *Handbook of North American Indians*. Vol. 14: *Southeast*. Gen. ed. William C. Sturtevant, vol. ed. Raymond D. Fogelson. Washington, DC: Smithsonian Institution, 2004, pp. 429–449.

DANIEL F. LITTLEFIELD, JR.

Seneca Removal

The Senecas are one of the Five Nations of the Iroquois Confederation that have their roots in present-day upper New York State near the Genesee River and Lake Canandaigua. Some of the Senecas moved from New York to Ohio at the beginning of the Revolutionary War, settling along the Sandusky River. When that conflict ended, a band of the Cayugas moved to the area, where they were granted a reservation. The Iroquois, with the exception of the Oneidas, had sided with Britain in the war, so many feared reprisals from the victorious Americans. To complicate matters further, the defeated British had ceded land claims for their Indian allies as well their own in the peace negotiations. Subsequently, some of the Iroquois moved from New York to Canada, but others negotiated with the Americans for reservations on their former lands. Other Iroquois bands found themselves without lands in the eyes of the Americans and so were forced west, where they joined the Cayugas in Ohio. These included Mingoes, Conestogas, Eries, Mohawks, Oneidas, Tuscaroras, and Onondagas as well as the Shawnees of Ohio, who were also feeling pressure from the whites, and the Senecas of Sandusky, as they were known. Another group of Senecas had affiliated with a band of Shawnees and, known as the Mixed Band of Senecas and Shawnees, had a tract of land in Logan County, Ohio (*see* **Shawnee Removal from Ohio**).

After the **Indian Removal Act**, the Senecas of Sandusky entered a treaty at Washington with the U.S. commissioner from Ohio, James B. **Gardiner**, on February 28, 1831. The agreement was signed by Comstick, Small Cloud Spicer, Seneca Steel, Hard Hickory, and Capt. Good Hunter and ceded 40,000 acres in Ohio in exchange for lands in **Indian Territory**. The Senecas prepared well for the journey, packing up household goods, agricultural implements and tools, and seeds. They left their village on the Sandusky in the late autumn and traveled to Dayton, undergoing unceasing rain and cold weather. The Senecas were taken by canal boat to Cincinnati, where they were to embark on the steamboat *Benjamin Franklin* to travel to St. Louis. However, many of the people feared explosions and fires on the riverboats, so they elected to travel on horseback. For both those traveling overland and those on the steamboat, it took eight months to travel the rest of the way to the northeastern corner of Indian Territory because they were delayed by bad weather, floods, and sickness. When the *Franklin* arrived in St. Louis, the conductor, Henry C. Brish, attempted to make the Senecas comfortable as they waited for their wagons for the overland journey. In early December 1831, they left St. Louis for Indian Territory, traveling by wagon, on foot, and on horseback. When they reached about 55 miles from St. Louis, they could go no further, being beset by the extreme cold and an outbreak of measles. They camped for the winter near Troy, Missouri.

In the meantime, the group that left Ohio on horseback reported that their conductor had deserted them, leaving the people without money or sustenance, near Muncie, Indiana. Their leaders, Small Cloud Spicer and Seneca John, sent a letter to President Andrew **Jackson** as well as to Brish seeking help. Brish left his people camped at Troy, went to Muncie, and led that party overland to Troy. There he found the encampment filled with sick and dying Indians. The combined party set out again, on muddy roads and through high water. On the way, the people suffered and some died, but Brish pushed them on. On July 4, 1832, the Senecas reached their new lands in northeastern Indian Territory.

The Mixed Band of Senecas and Shawnees, meanwhile, negotiated a treaty with the federal government that was concluded in July 1832, by which they ceded their Ohio lands for 60,000 acres in Indian Territory. The Mixed Band was scheduled for removal along with some Shawnees from Wapakoneta and Hog Creek as well as Ottawas from four small reservations in northwestern Ohio. Refusing to travel by steamboat, the Indians engaged in a running argument with the federal government, which favored water transport because it was faster and cheaper than overland travel. The argument delayed their departure until September 1832. Members of the Seneca-Shawnee contingent traveled on horseback, their possessions carried in oxen-drawn wagons. They were followed by the Wapakoneta Shawnees and the Ottawas. Along the way, the Indians were accosted by whiskey sellers and other whites eager to cheat them out of money and rations. Even the disbursing agent and his relatives extorted money from the meager funds allotted for the removal. The weather was bad, with rain, snow, cold, and high winds, thus slowing progress. At one point, the contingent ran out of rations and hunted animals to eat. On December 13, 1832, the Mixed Band of Senecas and Shawnees arrived in the new land.

Upon arrival, they were amazed to find out that the land promised them lay entirely inside the Cherokee Nation. The federal government consequently treated with the Sandusky Senecas and the Seneca-Shawnees to settle the issue. Under the terms of the treaty signed at Buffalo Creek on December 29, 1832, the two groups were combined as the "United Nation of Senecas and Shawnees," and they were to hold lands east of the Neosho, north of the Cherokee line, and west of the Missouri state line. The Mixed Band was to occupy the northern half of the tract, and the southern portion went to the Senecas of the Sandusky.

When the Civil War broke out, the Senecas and Shawnees signed a treaty with the Confederacy, thus bringing down the enmity of federal troops when they invaded Indian Territory in spring and summer of 1862. Two-thirds of the people fled to Kansas, where they took refuge with the Ottawas until the war ended; they returned to their war-torn lands bereft of livestock and other goods. In 1867, the federal government imposed its Omnibus Treaty, which provided for the sale of part of the Senecas and Shawnees' lands to other tribes being removed from the North. Another major provision was to separate the Senecas and the Shawnees; the Senecas of Sandusky and the Mixed Band Senecas were united as the Senecas, and the Shawnees became known as the Eastern Shawnees.

FURTHER READING: Foreman, Grant. *The Last Trek of the Indians.* New York: Russell and Russell, 1972; "Treaty with the Seneca, 1831." Indian Affairs: Laws and Treaties. At http://digital.library.okstate.edu/kappler/Vol2/treaties/sen0325.htm; Wright, Muriel H. *A Guide to the Indian Tribes of Oklahoma.* Norman: University of Oklahoma Press, 1977.

JAMES W. PARINS

Shawnee Removal from Ohio

The Shawnees who were removed from Ohio were a fraction of the Shawnee people who once inhabited the eastern portion of North America. Many believe that Shawnee roots date to prehistoric times in the Ohio Valley, but throughout their history they were a migrating people. Avoiding the conflicting Native American and Euro-American cultures drove them across most of eastern North America. In the mid-18th century, the Shawnees returned to the Ohio Valley, but small segments remained in the East and Southeast. On the Ohio, their struggle to retain their culture and land reached its height. Factions split off to avoid white encroachment, others moved further west to continue the struggle, and some remained in the Ohio country. By 1820, the Ohio Shawnees were concentrated in western Ohio on three reserves created by the Treaty of the Foot of the Rapids in September 1817.

After the War of 1812, less than 1,000 Shawnees in Ohio resided on three reservations: approximately 100 on the Hog Creek Reserve, 600 at the Wapakoneta Reserve, and 200 on the Lewistown Reserve. Among the remaining Shawnees, there was a desire for removal prior to 1830. Tenskatawa (the Prophet) and Quatawapea (Col. Lewis) were leading proponents of voluntary removal, and in the decade before 1830, over 1,000 Shawnee migrated west.

On March 29, 1831, James B. **Gardiner**, who had successfully arranged a removal treaty with the Senecas of the Sandusky River, was appointed special agent and commissioner to negotiate removal with the remaining tribes in Ohio. Gardiner was directed by Secretary of War John H. **Eaton** to explain to the remaining Indians the federal government's position.

He was to promise the exchange of Indian land in Ohio for an equal amount of land west of the Mississippi River and to make clear in the agreement that the government would deduct from the sale of land the following: 70 cents per acre, the cost of surveying and selling the land, and the cost of all buildings erected by the government on the new land. The government would hold the balance of the money from the sale, and a 5 percent annuity would be ensured for 30 years unless Congress acted differently.

Before Gardiner's appointment, the Seneca leaders who had already agreed to leave Ohio and Henry Brish, their subagent, had arranged a general meeting of the Ohio people for late April. The Shawnees expressed no desire to have another meeting. Regardless, Gardiner held the meeting to present the conditions of the removal treaty and told the Shawnee he would return for their answer.

In mid-July 1831, Gardiner met with the Shawnees and Senecas of Lewistown, and the treaty was signed on July 29, 1831. The people gave up their land in Ohio for 60,000 acres in the West next to the Senecas of the Sandusky. The general conditions of the **Indian Removal Act** were included as well as a guarantee of the continuation of annuities agreed to in former treaties and the erection of a sawmill and blacksmith shop on the new land.

Gardiner then proceeded to the Wapakoneta and Hog Creek Shawnees. As with the Lewistown group, there was division among the people. Gardiner urged removal for the good of the Shawnees. Hinting that they might be subject to Ohio laws soon, he also suggested that the only way to rid themselves of their debts to the whites and continue the Shawnee ways was to remove to the West. The Shawnees stated that if Gardiner would honor what he promised and add to his offer the payment of all their debts, they would sign the treaty. Gardiner agreed to place an article in the treaty binding the government to pay the debts that the chief of the Shawnees approved as valid. The treaty was signed on August 8, 1831.

The Shawnees of Wapakoneta, with the advice of Quaker missionary Henry Walker, gained the support of Congressman Joseph Vance of Ohio in a hearing regarding Gardiner's negotiations. Questions evolved around the government paying off their debts, the location of the western land, and Gardiner's actions during the negotiations. The Senate hearings approved the treaty as presented and ratified it in April 1832. Appropriations of the funds for removal were made in June 1832.

Assuming that the move west would start in the spring of 1832, many Shawnees sold their chattel during the fall and winter. There was no need to plant spring crops because they would be gone by harvest. In late spring, however, it became evident that the Shawnees would not depart when anticipated. Conditions mounted, creating turmoil among the people. The method of travel created a delay; the Shawnees wanted to go by land, but President Andrew **Jackson** wanted them removed by water. Finally, in August, Jackson consented to the land route.

Meanwhile, arguments occurred between Gardiner and the commissary general of subsistence over authority and personnel. Shoeing the Indian horses, vaccinating the Indians, and dealing with lack of food delayed removal throughout July and August. The government's supply of blankets, rifles, and Russian sheeting for tents did not arrive until the end of August, adding to the delay. The Shawnee annuity payment due in the spring was made in early fall. The need for money for food created a major concern among the Indians. Hunting parties were sent out regularly, but lack of game accentuated the problem. This situation was made worse by the constant presence of whiskey traders taking full advantage of the confusion. The final days of the Shawnees on their Ohio land were spent shoeing horses, making tents, saying farewell to friends. and caring for the remains of their family and friends by performing the proper ceremonies and rituals.

During this period, a group of Shawnees from the Hog Creek Reserve refused to participate in any of the removal procedures. They proclaimed they would not travel with the main body of Wapakoneta Shawnees because they were drunkards and too violent to travel with. These 84 Shawnees represented a dozen families. They remained on their land until the summer of 1833.

Gardiner's plan for emigration was to divide the Indians into three detachments: the Senecas and Shawnees of Lewistown, the Shawnees of Wapakoneta and Hog Creek, and the Ottawa people. Since the final destination of the Senecas and Shawnees was considerably south of that of the Wapakoneta and Hog Creek Shawnees, the plan was to separate the detachment in central Illinois. But Gardiner's plan to keep them apart on the journey at intervals of about 10 to 20 miles was never achieved.

Gardiner's inability to control the pace of the detachments and the growing struggle between Gardiner and Lt. J. F. Lane created a failure to access supplies. Lane was disbursing agent for the emigration, but his many disagreements with Gardiner caused the Shawnees great difficulties. A lack of available federal funds after leaving Indianapolis forced Gardiner to borrow from the Shawnees to provide for the people and their horses. This act undermined the Shawnees' confidence in Gardiner. Gardiner was unable to control the Indians and the white people who constantly intruded into the camps as curiosity seekers and whiskey traders. In addition, rain and snow resulted in illness and death en route.

Finally, Col. J. J. Abert was sent to expedite the removal and settle the issue between Gardiner and Lane. Gardiner was relieved of his duty in October, and Lane was assigned to the Seneca-Shawnee detachment. Both detachments arrived at their destinations in December 1832. The roll of the Lewistown group was 220, and that of the Wapakoneta group 334. Both were put under the care of Shawnee groups who had emigrated previously.

The Lewistown people refused to settle on the treaty lands. In January 1833, they signed a treaty giving them 60,000 acres north of the Senecas of the Sandusky River and formed the "United Nation of the Seneca and Shawnees." The Wapakoneta and Hog Creek people spent the winter with the Shawnees of Missouri. The following spring, they moved to their new lands.

Eighty-two Shawnees from Hog Creek who refused to travel with the main body left for the West in the summer of 1833. Led by Joseph Parks, a mixed-blood interpreter who had been living with them, they arrived in the West on September 15, 1833, joining the rest of the emigrants.

FURTHER READING: Buchman, Randall. *A Sorrowful Journey.* Defiance, OH: Defiance College Press, 2008; Colloway, Colin. *The Shawnee and the War for America.* New York: Penguin Books, 2007; Harvey, Henry. *History of the Shawnee Indians.* Cincinnati: n.p., 1855; Klopfenstein, Carl. "The Removal of the Ohio Indians." PhD diss., Western Reserve University, 1948; "Treaty with the Seneca, etc., 1831." Indian Affairs: Laws and Treaties. At http://digital.library.okstate.edu/kappler/Vol2/treaties/sen0327.htm.

RANDALL L. BUCHMAN

Sprague, John T. (1810–1878)

John T. Sprague, a Massachusetts native, first served in the military at Detroit when Lewis **Cass** was governor of Michigan. When Cass became secretary of war in 1831, Sprague became a member of his staff and served until 1834, when he was commissioned a lieutenant in the military; he served until his retirement in 1870.

During the removal period, Sprague was detached to assist in the

John T. Sprague, a colonel in the U.S. Army and the military governor of Florida during Reconstruction, was in charge of a number of parties of Indians during their removal to the West. (ABC-CLIO)

Creek removal from Alabama (*see* **Muscogee [Creek] Removal**). Although the Creeks were removed by civilian contractors, the United States sent a military officer with each group to make certain that the contractors fulfilled their obligations to the Indians. Sprague accompanied a contingent of about 2,000 Cussetas and Cowetas who departed Tallassee on September 5, 1836, and arrived at Fort Gibson, **Indian Territory**, on December 7. The Creeks were subjected to marches of up to 20 miles a day and were forced to leave those who were too slow on the road without assistance.

At Memphis, Sprague became a champion of the Cussetas and Cowetas. He threatened to take authority from the Alabama Emigrating Company and direct the removal himself if the contractor did not give better treatment to the people. At Little Rock and beyond, Sprague defended **Tuckabatche Hadjo**, one of the main leaders of the group, from threats by the state's governor that he would call out the state militia to force the party to move more rapidly.

In 1839, Sprague became an aide to Alexander Macomb, general of the army, who was one in a line of military men who had attempted to end the **Second Seminole War** and complete **Seminole removal**. In 1840, he became an aide to Col. William Jenkins Worth, commander in Florida. Sprague understood the Florida Indians' desire to retain their homeland, and in 1848, based on his years of experience in Florida, he wrote a sound history, *The Origin, Progress, and Conclusion of the Florida War*, the only history of the war until 1967.

FURTHER READING: Mahon, John K. *The Second Seminole War, 1835–1842.* Gainesville: University Press of Florida, 1967; Paige, Amanda L., et al. The North Little Rock Site on the Trail of Tears National Historic Trail: Historical Contexts Report. 2004. At http://anpa.ualr.edu/trail_of_tears/Indian_removal_project/site_reports/north_little_rock/northlittlerock_report.htm; Pingenot, Ben E. "Sprague, John Titcomb." *The Handbook of Texas Online.* 2008. At www.tshaonline.org/handbook/online/articles/SS/fsp30_print.html; Sprague, John T. *The Origin, Progress, and Conclusion of the Florida War.* New York: D. Appleton, 1848.

DANIEL F. LITTLEFIELD, JR.

State Militias and Removal

Among the many popular misconceptions about Indian removal is the belief that Indians were herded west at the point of a bayonet by U.S. Army regulars. Army regulars were called out when warfare broke out, and army, navy, and marine officers reporting along the chain of command to the secretary of war managed the logistics of removal and served as conductors of removing parties, observers of civilian contracts, and disbursing agents during the removal process. Many of the cruel and unjust acts attending removal, often attributed to army personnel, were in reality the work of militiamen, whom army officers had little respect for but sometimes had to rely on because of the limited numbers of regular troops.

Artist George Winters, who witnessed the Indiana militia's roundup of the Potawatomis for their Trail of Death in 1838, described the militia this way: "Some were of the highest respectability in the state, and others, in appearance at least, vagabonds and pillagers of the lowest order." It was an accurate depiction of militia units involved in removal in all parts of the country. Like the lynch mobs of the late 19th and early 20th centuries, whose purpose was to murder a helpless victim, the local militia unit was a place where the upper crust and the dregs of society could unite in a common cause: to round up, harass, or kill Indians. At the head of the militia was usually a prominent businessman, politician, or veteran of the War of 1812 or an earlier Indian war who was prone to give himself a military rank of colonel or higher. The men under him were undisciplined, many often had a personal motive behind their rally to service, and many were cowards who ran at their first encounter with the Indians in war. Unfortunately, because the regular army was very low in numbers during the removal period, these were the kinds of men who were called out to fight the Indians, round them up for removal, or prod them along on various segments of the removal trails. At times, they were also used by state leaders who wanted to demonstrate the state's stand on the removal issue.

The **Black Hawk War** was fought primarily by Illinois militia. When **Black Hawk** and his followers tried to reoccupy their old village in 1832, Edmund P. Gaines, general of the western division of the army, sent Gen. Henry Atkinson to the scene. Because he had only 200 regulars at his command, he called on Governor John Reynolds, who raised 1,700 militiamen. Under Gen. Samuel Whiteside and the governor himself, a force of 1,500 went in pursuit of Black Hawk's people. Reynolds sent 275 militiamen under Maj. Isaiah Stillman ahead of the main force. Stillman encountered Black Hawk on the Rock River. Black Hawk was apparently ready to surrender at that point, but the militiamen, who were reportedly drunk, fired on his emissaries, killing two. Black Hawk and his warriors charged, the militiamen turned and ran, and Black Hawk and his people escaped.

Dubbed the Battle of Stillman's Run, the episode was an embarrassment to the army. President Andrew **Jackson** sent Gen. Winfield **Scott**, who called up regulars and departed with them from New York. By the time they reached Chicago in early July, 53 of his 220 men had died of cholera and a large number of others were ill. By the time he got into the field, the war was over. Black Hawk had been caught by Atkinson's 350 regulars and 950 Illinois militiamen at the Bad Axe River, where they slaughtered men, women, and children alike.

When the Creek War of 1836 broke out, the army found itself lacking the troops to quell the Creeks. Thus, Gen. Thomas S. **Jesup** called for volunteers for stationing in Alabama and Florida. Alabama and Georgia militia units were

active in pursuit of the Lower Creeks. In a combined attack, they drove the Creeks under Jim Henry from Roanoke, which they had captured, looted, and partially burned. Though short-lived, the war remained a long-lasting excuse for the local militia groups to harass Creeks for months to come. An Indian "scare" was good for local economies because there was money to be made in powder and lead and camp equipment. Local citizens used events whenever possible to encourage enough excitement that the state would ask the militia to raise a vigilante group and call it "militia." Even some Alabama and other newspapers questioned how widespread the Creek War was and believed that land speculators may have fanned the flames of war.

When the **Second Seminole War** began in late 1835, Florida territorial governor John H. **Eaton**, Jackson's first secretary of war, called for a fighting force of regulars. If the War Department used militia units, the war would drag on

Portrait of General Thomas Sidney Jesup.
(Florida Photographic Collection)

for years. The Jackson administration rejected the notion because Jackson and others would have to drain the eastern seaboard of troops to supply a sufficient number to fight the Seminoles. Thus, Gen. Thomas S. Jesup called on volunteers, and by January 1836, nearly 1,000 men had enlisted for service in Florida. By the end of 1837, there were 4,636 regulars and 4,078 volunteers from Tennessee, Louisiana, South Carolina, Georgia, Alabama, Florida, and Missouri. The various state units had the same composition as the Illinois and Indiana units, a "respectable" or ambitious member of the state power structure at the top and rabble at the bottom. The Tennessee militia, for example, was headed by Robert Armstrong, the apple of Andrew Jackson's eye.

Militia units were present at most serious skirmishes and battles of the Second Seminole War and, later, the **Third Seminole War**. Regular army officers found the Florida militiamen particularly despicable. They no doubt agreed, however, with the sentiments of Representative David Levy of Florida, who, when the army proposed to reduce its size in 1842 by dismissing the militia, argued that only the militia could protect Floridians from the Seminoles, whom he called "demons" who had no human heart. "If they cannot be emigrated," Levy said, "they should be exterminated." Militia engagement in the Third Seminole War involved primarily Florida units.

By far the worst treatment the Indians received occurred at the hands of militiamen during the roundups preparatory to removal. In the wake of the Creek War of 1836, hundreds of Creek warriors under **Tustenuggee Emathla** (Jim Boy) signed an agreement with Gen. Thomas S. Jesup to go to Florida to assist in the war against the Seminoles. Jesup promised the warriors that their families could remain in their homes until the warriors could return and prepare them for removal to the West. However, when their return from Florida was delayed, squads of militia from Russell County, Alabama, and Franklin County, Georgia, attacked the families, killing old men, shooting women and children, burning houses, stealing goods and slaves, driving off livestock, and taking men and boys captive and marching them to Tuskegee for removal to the West. The threat of forced removal without their families caused the Creeks agree to remove, and some 4,000 were assembled. In another incident, when Gen. John Tipton called a council of the Potawatomi chiefs and headmen at Twin Lakes, Indiana, in the summer of 1838, he took them captive and held them hostage while the Indiana militia rounded up their people. He then sent squads of militia to various camps and villages to capture men, women, and children and to burn their villages. An old woman, the mother of Chief Black Wolf, was one of those who, from fear, hid out in the woods, injured, unable to walk, and without food for nearly a week, when she was rescued by an Indian and taken to South Bend.

Similar scenes were repeated in Georgia, Alabama, and Tennessee when the Cherokees were gathered for removal in the same spring and summer as the Potawatomis (*see* **Cherokee Removal**). The year before, Gen. John Ellis Wool and his troops had been dispatched to the area to disarm the Cherokees and to suppress any opposition to the **Treaty of New Echota**. Like many

U.S. military officers, he had expressed sympathy for the Cherokees. What swayed Wool was the large number of whites who flooded into the Cherokee lands solely for the purpose of taking Cherokee property, particularly in Alabama (the Cherokees had already been stripped in Georgia). The governor of Alabama, angered at Wool's attempts to protect the Cherokees, charged him with usurping the power of the state and called for an investigation. An inquiry was held, but Wool was exonerated.

The Martin **Van Buren** administration needed a less sympathetic hand in preparing the Cherokees for removal and assigned Gen. Winfield Scott to the task in April 1838. The plan was to remove the Cherokees by water. Scott divided the Cherokee lands in Alabama, Georgia, Tennessee, and North Carolina into three districts and planned to set up holding camps from which the Cherokees would be sent to departure points on the Tennessee River. The army had promised 3,000 regulars, but none had arrived before Scott reached the Cherokee agency in Tennessee, so the task of maintaining the 23 collection camps fell to 4,000 state militiamen. The treaty set May 23 as the date for removal. The militia in Georgia began to round up Cherokees on May 26, and Tennessee and Alabama militias went to work 10 days later. Scott told the men to carry out their work in a humane way, ordering that horses should be used for those who were unable to march. Gen. Wool had said that the white men were like vultures, who were "watching, ready to pounce upon their prey and strip them of everything they have." Unfortunately, many of the men who were rousting Cherokees from their homes were the very men Wool had described. The militiamen were followed by other rabble, who looted and burned the abandoned homes and drove livestock away. Some of the militia squads were described as driving the Cherokees along to the collection stations like cattle, yelling and calling like drovers. At departure points, militia forced Cherokees aboard boats at the point of a gun. By mid-June 1838, most of the regulars had arrived and began to manage the collection stations, which were then called "forts."

Instances of militia units escorting Indian removal parties to the West are rare. In the spring of 1838, a party of Cherokees conducted by Capt. G. S. Drane revolted at Bellefont, Alabama, and a number escaped because they had heard that Chief John **Ross** had received permission from the government for the Cherokee Nation to conduct its own removal, which had been delayed until the fall. Drane called out a squad of local militiamen, who accompanied the group as guards to Waterloo, Alabama, where the Cherokees were put aboard a steamboat bound for the West. In the summer of that year, Indiana militiamen escorted the Potawatomis that departed from Twin Lakes out of the state, leaving the remainder of their journey on the Trail of Death to army dragoons. Once the Indians were safely on their journey west, the militia usually went no further.

Along the routes to the West, removal officers and state officials sometimes called out militia to hasten the Indians on their way. For example, removal officers called on the governor of Arkansas at Little Rock to call up the state militia to help them take a number of slaves away from a removal party of Seminoles so that they might be returned to the man who claimed them in Florida. In another instance, the Pope County, Arkansas, militia rode to the camp of Creek chief **Tuckabatche Hadjo** to move him from his camp, where he had been lingering too long.

Public officials often used their state militias to back up their stand regarding Indian removal. Perhaps the best example is Georgia. During the mid- to late 1820s, Georgia determined to drive the Creeks from within the limits of the state in accordance with the Georgia Compact of 1802. Following the treaties at Indian Springs with the infamous William McIntosh, Georgia tested the determination of the U.S. government to challenge the state's usurpation of federal authority over Indian affairs. During the late years of the Adams administration, the governor of the state threatened to challenge the U.S. Army with his militia and to invade the Creek country in Alabama if necessary. Adams recognized in one instance that a military confrontation would likely result in civil war and let Georgia have its way. Learning that the state could defy the federal government and get away with it, Georgia then turned its attention to the Cherokees with the intent to drive them out of Georgia as well.

Part of the public misperception of the role of state militias in Indian removal has evolved from the narrative of John Burnett, a member of the Tennessee militia who as an old man wrote his reminiscences of the Cherokee removal, describing how he and his unit accompanied the John Ross party on the removal trail. Elaborate in his detail, at one point he tells how Mrs. Ross gave her blanket to a sick child, took sick herself, died, and was buried on the trail. Burnett wrote the narrative to tell his children about his life. For whatever reason, he fabricated the story, which historians for years took as fact. John Ross and his family removed aboard a steamboat that Ross owned. Quatie Ross was ill before they left the East, and she died aboard the boat a short time before it reached Little Rock, where she was buried in the city's cemetery. Burnett presents himself as sympathetic to the Cherokees and the militiamen as kind to the Cherokees on the trail, feelings and actions that characterized a few regular military officers but were generally lacking in militiamen of the day.

FURTHER READING: Eisenhower, John S. D. *Agent of Destiny: The Life and Times of General Winfield Scott.* Norman: University of Oklahoma Press, 1997; Foreman, Grant. *Indian Removal: Emigration of the Five Civilized Tribes of Indians.* Norman: University of Oklahoma Press, 1989; Green, Michael D. *The Politics of Indian Removal: Creek Government and Society in Crisis.* Lincoln: University of Nebraska Press, 1982; Mahon, John K. *History of the Second Seminole War, 1835–1842.* Gainesville: University Press of Florida, 1967.

DANIEL F. LITTLEFIELD, JR.

Stockbridge-Munsee Removal

The Stockbridge-Munsees are Algonkian-speaking peoples descended from the Mohicans and Munsee Delawares who were displaced from their homelands on the eastern seaboard. Feeling the pressure from white settlers during the 1780s, they moved from western Massachusetts, where they were known as the Stockbridge Indians, and formed a Christian community near the Oneidas in New York. Their leader at this time was Hendrick Aupaumut, a sachem who believed that his people would do better to accept Euro-American culture than to resist it. Nonetheless, he counseled his people to avoid proximity to American settlements. Aupaumut and his people fought on the American side during the War of 1812, rejecting the teachings of Tecumseh and the Prophet, who fought for the British.

By 1817, the **Ogden Land Company** planned to remove three New York tribes to the Northwest Territory, including the **Oneidas**, Stockbridges, and Munsees. Governor of Michigan Territory Lewis **Cass** agreed and promised government backing to the venture to remove the Indians to west of Lake Michigan. In 1818–1819, many of the Stockbridges under leaders John W. **Quinney** and John **Metoxin** removed to Indiana to join their relatives, the Munsee Delawares. The land on which they settled, though, was being claimed by the Miamis, and Aupaumut discovered that the government planned to remove the tribe again to Missouri and sell the Indiana land to white settlers. Some of the group did indeed remove to the West, where they joined the Swan Creek and Black River bands of Ojibwes on a reservation in Kansas. After the Civil War, white settlers demanded their removal, and they eventually settled down in **Indian Territory**, where the Cherokees made room for them.

The Stockbridges who remained in or returned to New York began to look for another place to settle. In 1821, the sachems led a delegation to Wisconsin, along with the Oneidas and **Brothertons,** to treat with the Menominees and the Winnebagos for the purchase of lands around Green Bay, the Fox River, and Lake Winnebago. A reserve of 860,000 acres was purchased as a result, and in the following year, a 6.72-million-acre tract was added. The Stockbridges began to move to Wisconsin and were shortly joined by the Munsees. Meanwhile, the Menominees and Winnebagos objected to the 1821 and 1822 treaties, and a dispute broke out with the two Wisconsin tribes on one side and the Oneidas and Stockbridge-Munsees on the other. The Menominees and Winnebagos argued that, under the 1821–1822 treaties, they had agreed not to sell the land but to share it with the newcomers. This had been common practice among the western Great Lakes nations since time immemorial. The Wisconsin tribes further argued that the terms of the treaties were not made clear to them when accurate translations were available after the signings. After the federal government mediated among the tribes, three treaties were signed in 1831 and 1832. Under the treaties' terms, the Stockbridge-Munsees gave up their settlement near Kaukauna on the Fox River for $25,000 and moved to new lands east of Lake Winnebago.

But peace did not reign among the Indians in their new territory. In 1837, John W. Quinney wrote a constitution for the Stockbridge-Munsees that replaced the sachems with elected officials. The constitution was also an attempt to thwart federal removal policies as they related to the tribe. The document was embraced by some of the group but was opposed by others. In 1838, the federal government's removal policy impacted the tribe directly when they were informed that they must remove to west of the Mississippi to accommodate the white settlers flooding into the new Wisconsin Territory. Some tribal members left for Missouri, believing that to stay in Wisconsin would make them lose their tribal identity, but many of these returned after finding conditions difficult.

In 1843, the federal government passed a law making all the Stockbridge-Munsees citizens. Some in the tribe embraced the idea and became known as the Citizen Party. Others, led by Quinney, worked to get this act repealed; they became known as the Indian Party. After citizenship, the land held in common on the shores of Lake Winnebago was allotted to individual tribal members. Over time, most of this land was lost through sales to white settlers or, often, at public auction when the Indians were unable to pay local taxes. The sheriff's auction became a common means of taking land from the Indians in Wisconsin and turning it over to whites. Today, the Mohican Nation, Stockbridge-Munsee band has a reservation adjacent to the Menominee Reservation.

FURTHER READING: Ellis, Albert G. "The Advent of the New York Indians into Wisconsin." *Collections of the State Historical Society of Wisconsin* 2 (1855): 415–449; Loew, Patti. *Indian Nations of Wisconsin.* Madison: Wisconsin State Historical Society Press, 2001; Stockbridge-Munsee Community, Band of Mohican Indians. 2010. At www.mohican.com/; "Treaty with the Menominee, 1856." Indian Affairs: Laws and Treaties. At http://digital.library.okstate.edu/kappler/Vol2/treaties/men0755.htm; "Treaty with the Stockbridge and Munsee, 1839." Indian Affairs: Laws and Treaties. At http://digital.library.okstate.edu/kappler/Vol2/treaties/sto0529.htm.

JAMES W. PARINS

Strong, Nathaniel Thayer (1810–1872)

Nathaniel Thayer Strong was an educated, Christian, pro-removal advocate from the Cattaraugus reservation who served as the interpreter for the 1838 **Treaty of Buffalo Creek**. He worked as an assistant to James Stryker, the subagent to the New York Indians at Buffalo; operated behind the scenes to facilitate treaty terms that favored the **Ogden Land Company**; and was one of the document's Seneca signers. After the initial Ogden Land Company efforts to remove the Senecas failed, Strong played a key role in the debates surrounding the restructuring of governance at the Allegany and Cattaraugus reservations.

Although little is known about Strong's life, he represented an emerging generation of Seneca leaders in the early to mid-19th century, including Nicholson **Parker**, Maris Bryant **Pierce**, and Ely S. **Parker**, who pursued education in non-Native academies and spoke fluent English as well as Hodenosaunee. The removal crisis destabilized customary notions of power and authority among the Senecas, and these young leaders, because of their language skills and ability to understand and negotiate Euro-American legal and political structures, rose to positions previously held by older community members. This shift in power and authority did not take place smoothly.

Unlike Pierce and the Parker brothers, who opposed the treaty as well as **Seneca removal**, Strong argued that removal to Kansas as outlined in the treaty provided the best opportunities for their future. As debates developed about the validity of the Buffalo Creek treaty, Strong penned a defense of the agreement and of his, as well as the other signers', actions entitled *Appeal to the Christian Community on the Condition and Prospects of the New York Indians* (1841). In it he asserted that the Seneca leaders who opposed removal did so because of personal greed and because of their connection to local, non-Native citizens who sold liquor to the Indians, leased water rights, bought lumber, and held licenses to live on their lands. He argued that all of these individuals stood to profit in many ways from the Indians' continued presence in the state.

Strong's vociferous support for removal, apparent in his *Appeal*, demonstrated the evolving and significant factionalism among the Senecas. In 1848, this factionalism resulted in the "Seneca Revolution" in which the Tonawanda band of the Senecas splintered from the other New York State Senecas, who became known, after a constitutional convention held by Allegany and Cattaraugus groups, as the Seneca Nation of New York. To complicate matters further, during this political controversy, Strong disregarded their previous differences and banded together with his former enemy Maris Bryant Pierce to support the customary Seneca leadership, called the "old chiefs," in their battle against the "New Government Party," as the revolutionaries became known. Strong's complex life and political career provide a stark example of how removal efforts could and did disrupt Indian communities, destabilize structures of power and authority, and open rifts between talented and ambitious potential allies.

FURTHER READING: Carlson, David J. *Sovereign Selves: American Indian Autobiography and the Law.* Urbana: University of Illinois Press, 2006; Littlefield, Daniel F., Jr. "'They Ought to Enjoy the Home of Their Fathers': The Treaty of 1838, Seneca Intellectuals, and Literary Genesis." In *Early Native American Writing: New Critical Essays.* Ed. Helen Jaskoski. New York: Cambridge University Press, 1996, pp. 83–103; Peyer, Bernd C., ed. *American Indian Nonfiction: An Anthology of Writings, 1760s–1930s.* Norman: University of Oklahoma Press, 2007.

C. JOSEPH GENETIN-PILAWA

T

Tennessee and Indian Removal

The history of what is now the state of Tennessee before and during removal offers a microcosmic version of the overall history of the United States during these times. The groups involved in the politics of the area include Cherokees, Creeks, Chickasaws, and Shawnees as well as English, French, and Spanish settlers. The complexity of the situation was exacerbated by the existence of factions within each of these groups. The final complex component was the fight between state and federal power over territorial issues. As the colonies that would be America were dividing over the issue of revolution, many of the Native communities looked to England to protect them from the incursion of settlers. The increasing number of American settlers crossing the mountains through the Cumberland Gap was depleting game and resources. When a group of Cherokee chiefs ceded land to the Transylvania Company's Richard Henderson in 1775, a dissenting group led by Dragging Canoe, Glass, Bloody Fellow, Doublehead, Pumpkin Boy, John Watts, and others consolidated in an area shared with the Creeks and Chickasaws. They founded a group of towns between Chickamauga and Muscle Shoals and began to join the resistance movements of the Creeks to the south and the Shawnees to the north.

With the Hopewell Treaty in 1785, Congress agreed to the Cherokee version of its tribal boundaries and recognized the Cherokees' right to evict whites who had settled within those boundaries. However, the treaty gave the federal government the sole right to determine what was proper within the Cherokee boundaries and claimed that the Cherokees acknowledged their status under the protection of the new U.S. government. The federal government failed to enforce the protection of Cherokee rights against the state government, and the citizens of the State of Franklin (an autonomous U.S. territory that existed 1784–1788, led by John Sevier and James Robertson), were set to eradicate all Cherokees in the territory. These eradication attempts led to the murder of Old Tassle in 1788 and Hanging Maw's wife, along with 15 other Indians gathered for peace talks in 1788. In 1791, Governor William Blount announced at the Council at Holston that the federal government could not guarantee the land decreed in the Hopewell Treaty and asked the Cherokees to cede more land. The chiefs, led by Bloody Fellow, objected. When Blount refused to uphold the Hopewell Treaty, even at the behest of President George Washington, the warfare between the tribes and the settlers escalated.

From the time of Dragging Canoe's organization of the Chickamauga towns until the time of the removal, the animosity between Indians and settlers remained constant. Although there were factions within the Cherokee groups, mostly Upper Towns, that attempted peace with the settlers and the state, the Lower Towns joined with the Creeks to fight the incursion of settlers into the region. In many cases, the state of Tennessee did not discriminate between peaceful towns and towns with which it was at war when it attacked the Indian communities in retaliation. In 1794, with the defeat of Bloody Fellow and John Watts by Col. James Ore, Tennessee proclaimed the war with the Cherokees to be over.

The year 1794 opened an era in which both the state and federal governments attempted to "civilize" the Cherokees. However, the resistance of the Lower Towns and the continued incursion of the settlers led to renewed violence. In addition, whereas Indians were prosecuted for murders and crimes against settlers, the reverse was not the case. The federal government's attempts to force the state to prosecute and punish settler crimes against Indians failed, both because the juries would not convict and because Indians were not allowed to give testimony. After 1803, the federal government attempted to stem Indian retaliation by paying the families of those murdered. When further payment for other crimes was required, the federal government incurred a substantial loss.

A renewal of violence occurred between 1806 and 1810 when the state of Tennessee attempted to take the mining rights on Cherokee land along the Tennessee River, an action that led to the 1807 execution of Doublehead because of his willingness to cooperate with the Tennessee land seekers. From 1810 to the fourth official attempt at removal in 1838–1839, the Cherokees struggled to keep their boundaries and unify their chiefs. The chiefs became divided on the issue of removal, some wanting to take the money offered and move west. Lack of food and poverty, along with the pressure to assimilate into "civilized" society, began to entice some to the idea of removal. By 1820, a large population of Cherokees occupied the lands of the Cherokee Nation West in Arkansas Territory. Attempts to force emigration to the West by coercion failed in 1828 when the Arkansas Cherokees were removed west to what would become **Indian Territory**. However, with the election of Andrew **Jackson**, the fate of the Indians east of the Mississippi was sealed. Instead of favoring federal authority over that of the states, and in contradiction of the Supreme Court's ruling in *Worcester v. Georgia* (1832), Jackson supported the state of Georgia in its claim to all the land within its borders. With federal government support for Georgia's claims, the states of North and South Carolina then declared all land within their boundaries to be under state control. Tennessee followed, declared title to all land, and began selling parcels before the forced removal of the Indian occupants.

Chief John **Ross** had resisted removal with the hope that the Supreme Court would support the treaties. When the Supreme Court found in favor of the Cherokees, designating the Cherokee Nation a "domestic nation," Ross attempted to use these words to establish that the Cherokees were not "wards of the government." He failed to forestall removal when the pro-removal Cherokees signed the **Treaty of New Echota** in 1835. Regardless of the fact that these Cherokees were both few in number and did not have the support of the people required by the Cherokee constitution, Jackson used it as a binding agreement for all Cherokees. Approximately 2,000 of the 15,000 Cherokees emigrated following the treaty, but the vast majority made no preparations to go. When the Cherokees were forced to remove in 1838–1839, it is estimated that 1,000 to 2,000 Cherokees escaped to the mountains. Those who remained in the mountains and their descendants became known as the **Eastern Cherokees**.

Tennessee played an important role in the logistics of removal. When forced removal began in the spring of 1838, Ross's Landing at present-day Chattanooga and the Cherokee Agency on the Hiwassee River were the sites of large concentration camps in which the Cherokees were held during the summer of 1838 while awaiting removal. The agency was the place from which agents, army officers, and others coordinated **Cherokee removal**. Ross's Landing served as a major launching place for departing groups traveling by both water and land. Finally, the office of the disbursing agent for Indian removal east of the Mississippi was in Memphis and played a key role in coordinating transportation of supplies and subsistence rations for removal parties of not only Cherokees but also Creeks, Choctaws, and Chickasaws.

Tennesseans, perhaps more than any others except Arkansans, profited economically from Indian removal. Every overland contingent of Cherokees crossed a major part of the state, most traveling to Nashville and then northwest into Kentucky, and one group traveling from Ross's Landing to Memphis. The established roads they took passed through well-settled areas. Farmers supplied rations for the people and feed for animals. Merchants supplied dry goods, utensils, and other products. Keepers of tollgates (some hastily constructed just for the Cherokees) made easy money.

Finally, Tennessee supplied perhaps the largest number of key people who carried out Indian removal in the South. Andrew Jackson filled key posts with his loyal followers: John H. **Eaton**, secretary of war and negotiator of treaties; Carey A. Harris, commissioner of Indian affairs; John **Coffee**, treaty maker; William **Carroll**, conegotiator of the Treaty of New Echota and overseer of Chickasaw land sales; William **Armstrong**, western superintendent for Indian affairs; and many others of lesser note, but all of a single mind—to rid the Southeast of its Indian population.

FURTHER READING: Cotterill, R. S. *The Southern Indians: The Story of the Civilized Tribes before Removal.* Norman: University of Oklahoma Press, 1954; Foreman, Grant. *The Five Civilized Tribes: Cherokee, Chickasaw, Chocktaw, Creek, Seminole.* Norman: University of Oklahoma Press, 1934; McLoughlin, William G. *Cherokee Renascence in the New Republic.* Princeton, NJ: Princeton University Press, 1986; Mooney, James. *History, Myths, and Sacred Formulas of the Cherokees.* Asheville, NC: Historical Images, 1992; United States Department of the Interior, National Park Service, Denver Service Center. *Trail of Tears National Historic Trail: Alabama, Arkansas, Georgia, Illinois, Kentucky, Missouri, North Carolina, Oklahoma, Tennessee. Comprehensive Management and Use Plan.* Denver: U.S. Department of the Interior, National Park Service, 1992.

LAVONNA LOVERN

Third Seminole War (1855–1858)

In announcing the end of the **Second Seminole War** on February 14, 1842, Col. W. J. Worth stated that those Florida Indians who did not want to remove could occupy lands assigned to them on a "temporary" basis south of the Peace River. The following summer Billy Bowlegs (**Hulbutta Micco**), Fus Hajo, and Nokosi Emathla went to Fort Brooke at Tampa Bay, where an end to hostilities was announced on August 14. The estimated 300 remaining Seminoles, Miccosukees, Creeks, and Tallahassees had retreated into the Big Cypress Swamp in the late 1830s, where they ran into conflicts with not only whites but also Spanish Indians. Led by Sam Jones, they had retreated into the Everglades, settling on the north side of Lake Okeechobee. There, after 1842, they enjoyed a few years of relative quiet, farming and raising livestock. By the end of the decade, however, white encroachment led to sporadic clashes. By that time, too, Billy Bowlegs had risen in authority as Sam Jones declined so that Americans considered Bowlegs leader of all of the remaining Indians, whom they referred to as Seminoles. Despite his attempts to stay out of the whites' way and to prevent his people from raiding them, continued white encroachment led to the outbreak of the Third Seminole War.

Bowlegs was opposed to removal and worked to defeat it. In 1849, he promised the army that he would keep his people in line and would cooperate in stopping any Indian depredations against the whites. Later that year, he delivered to authorities at Tampa Bay three men and the hand of another who had raided a farm, killing some whites. He vowed that if any of his people crossed their boundary and raided whites thereafter, he would take his people to the seashore himself and wait for a boat to take them to the West.

But Bowlegs's best intentions could not stop the tide of events. Although whites considered him chief of all the Indians, he may not have had authority to control them all. Sam Jones, though old, was spiritual leader of the Miccosukees, and Chipco led the Creeks. And there were also members of all groups who operated independently; it was these independent groups that Bowlegs turned in for punishment in 1849. In 1850, after a white man was killed, Bowlegs again brought in three guilty men, who later hanged themselves in jail. White-Indian conflict increased after 1850 when the Swamp Lands Act turned reclamation of swampland over to the states.

This act precipitated an event that instigated the outbreak of war. War Department surveyors began surveying the Everglades. In late 1855, some surveyors were approaching Bowlegs's settlement when they came upon his banana plantation, which they destroyed without provocation, apparently because of their dislike for Bowlegs. On December 20, Bowlegs and his warriors retaliated, killing or wounding a number of the surveying crew. Next, they attacked a scouting party sent out from Fort Myers. So began the Third Seminole War.

Because there were only an estimated 100 warriors, during the ensuing months the Indians could use only hit-and-run tactics, stealing slaves and taking or destroying other property. In January 1856, they attacked a wood-cutting party and a settlement near Miami. In March, they raided Sarasota Bay. In May, they attacked the homestead of Robert Bradley and three days later a wagon train on its way from Fort Brooke to Fort Fraser. The governor of Florida mobilized the state's militia. The combined American force consisted of nearly 1,500 troops, including federal and state, who stood against Bowlegs's small force.

What might be considered the only battle of the war occurred in June 1856. Warriors under Oscen Tustenuggee attacked the Willoughby Tillis farmstead about three miles from Fort Meade. Militia units from there and Fort Fraser went out, resulting in Seminole and white deaths, among them Oscen Tustenuggee. The Indians forced the Floridians to retreat, and they returned to their settlements. Oscen Tustenuggee had been active in many of the raids, and after his death, large-scale raiding ceased, perhaps because Billy Bowlegs was the undisputed leader of the Indians who remained.

From 1849 until the start of the Third Seminole War, the United States reverted to tactics it had used to encourage removal during the Second Seminole War: bribery and delegations of Seminoles from the West. In 1849, Gen. David Twiggs had offered Billy Bowlegs over $215,000 to remove, but Bowlegs refused. In early 1854, he was again offered a bribe to remove but again declined. Some of his followers, however, agreed to go west. In early 1850, 85 came in and were sent west; with them went the three that Bowlegs had turned in to authorities in 1849. In 1852, the government appointed Luther Blake, who was little more than a bounty hunter, as agent. He was paid $800 for each warrior and $450 for each woman or child that he could remove. However, he was successful in sending only 36 west in 1854, and he was dismissed.

The government used delegations headed by respected Seminole leaders from **Indian Territory** to try to persuade those in Florida to remove. One was headed by **Halleck Tustenuggee** in 1849 and 1850. The next year, another was headed by John Jumper, who had replaced **Miconopy** as chief of the Seminoles, with **Abraham** as interpreter. Jumper and five others took Bowlegs on an extended tour of Washington and New York in an attempt to convince him that removal was inevitable. Although Bowlegs was opposed to it, he signed an agreement to go west in the spring of 1852, but his people refused. In 1854, another delegation traveled from the West but again failed in an attempt to bribe Bowlegs to remove.

Persistence brought results. In 1858, a delegation of 40 Seminoles and Creeks with John Jumper at their head arrived from the Indian Territory. The government offered Bowlegs a bonus of $6,500 to remove, $1,000 for each of his subchiefs, and lesser amounts for warriors, women, and children. Bowlegs surrendered and agreed to bring his people in for removal, thus ending the Third Seminole War.

It was probably not the bonus alone that caused Bowlegs to agree to remove. No doubt the Seminole and Creek delegates were persuasive. Also, his followers had dwindled to the point that resistance became futile. An additional fact, and probably an important one, was that in 1856 a Seminole Nation had been established independent of the Creek Nation in Indian Territory. Whatever the reason, in May 1858, Bowlegs brought in 171 people for removal. They arrived in Fort Smith, Arkansas, later that month and traveled overland from there to Little River in the Seminole Nation. On this leg of their journey, sickness struck them, and several died. That same year, the United States abandoned the forts it had established in Florida during its 23 years of efforts to remove the Seminoles.

Near the end of 1858, Bowlegs went back to Florida and convinced 75 others to remove. They left Florida on February 15, 1859. After that, the government chose not to pursue Seminole removal any further. The estimated 100 people who remained provided the founding families for the present-day **Seminole Tribe of Florida** and the **Miccosukee Seminole Nation**. The United States briefly considered removal of these people again in the early 1880s but finally gave up the idea.

FURTHER READING: Covington, James W. "An Episode in the Third Seminole War." *Florida Historical Quarterly* 45 (July 1966–April 1967): 45–59; Covington, James W. "Billy Bowlegs, Sam Jones, and the Crisis of 1849." *Florida Historical Quarterly* 68, no. 3 (1990): 299–311; Porter, Kenneth W. "Billy Bowlegs (Holata Micco) in the Seminole Wars (Part I)." *Florida Historical Quarterly* 45, no. 3 (1967): 219–242.

DANIEL F. LITTLEFIELD, JR.

Tishomingo (c. 1740–c. 1839)

Tishomingo was one of the surviving hereditary head chiefs of the Chickasaw Nation at the time of removal. In the early 19th century, the Chickasaws had delegated authority to George and Levi **Colbert** to act as chief at different times, but they retained the hereditary form of government with minko and chief, with the chief serving as speaker of the council. The Chickasaw government had undergone other changes as well. Near the end of the second decade of the century, for example, the Nation was divided into four districts, primarily to facilitate the payment of annuities. Tishomingo served as one of the district chiefs until **Chickasaw removal**. When the Chickasaws signed the **Treaty of Pontotoc** in 1832, they paid homage not only to

Tishomingo but also to the traditional form of government by providing a pension to the venerable chief for his service to the Nation.

Although they signed the removal treaty, Tishomingo and other leaders were dissatisfied with it. Their objections were various, but paramount among them was the treaty's misrepresentation of the Chickasaw concept of household and the government's determination to hold Chickasaw funds in trust rather than give control of them to the Nation. Tishomingo was part of a delegation that started to Washington to adjust the treaty, but at the last minute he could not continue, perhaps because of age.

At the time, Tishomingo was also involved in a landmark case that tested the legality of the extension of Mississippi civil and criminal laws over the Indians of the state and the state's act of outlawing their government. Passage of the laws was demoralizing to the Chickasaws, who ultimately realized that they could not live peaceably with the Americans. Their beliefs were verified when the aged chief fell victim to the state court system in what became an interesting chapter in the history of **Mississippi and Indian removal**. Pistalatubbee and Tishomingo had repeatedly complained to the Chickasaw subagent, John Allen, about intruders settling on Chickasaw land, ranging their livestock in the Chickasaw domain, and peddling goods. The old chief, fulfilling his role as a traditional head chief or as district chief as in earlier days, seized and sold half of the goods of two peddlers who were illegal intruders in the Chickasaw Nation, as was Chickasaw practice. He delivered the other half to Allen. The peddlers brought charges in a Mississippi district court against Tishomingo and Allen for criminal trespass. In September 1832, the two defendants were jailed at Athens, Mississippi, and went to trial that November. Tishomingo and Allen based their defense in treaty stipulations forbidding illegal trade in the Indian nations. The jury found them guilty and fined them. The judge ruled that Tishomingo had no authority to act and that there could not have been a treaty violation because Tishomingo had seized the goods before any were sold. Tishomingo appealed. *Mingo & Allen v. Goodman* was heard in Jackson, Mississippi, in early 1837, when the High Court of Errors and Appeals affirmed the decision of the lower court. By the time the final judgment was rendered, the Chickasaws had negotiated for a permanent home in the West with the Choctaws, and preparations were under way for their removal.

When and how Tishomingo removed is just as uncertain as his postremoval history. Some claim that he died at about 102 years of age near Little Rock, Arkansas, in 1838 while he was on the removal trail. However, most evidence suggests that he completed the journey to the West. It appears that a party of Chickasaws who migrated overland to Fort Coffee, **Indian Territory**, had experienced an outbreak of smallpox just as they crossed the Arkansas River at Dardanelle, Arkansas. When they arrived at Fort Coffee, they carried the disease to those already encamped there, including Tishomingo, who had camped with his family about two miles from the post. He was supposedly one of the first fatalities. Wherever or however he died, Tishomingo's demise marked the end of hereditary government among the

Chickasaws. **Ishtehotopa**, the minko, the surviving major figure in the traditional hereditary government, lived at least until 1848.

FURTHER READING: Anonymous. "On the Cover: War Chief Is Honored." *Chickasaw Times* 7 (April–June 1978): 2, 7–8; Cushman, H. B. *History of the Choctaw, Chickasaw and Natchez Indians.* Ed. Angie Debo. Norman: University of Oklahoma Press, 1999; Henderson, Richey. *Pontotoc County Men of Note.* Pontotoc, MS: Pontotoc Progress Print, 1940.

DANIEL F. LITTLEFIELD, JR.

Tonawanda Senecas

The Tonawanda Senecas are one of the principal groups of New York State Senecas and live on the Tonawanda Reservation, named after a nearby creek. They successfully thwarted removal efforts by the **Ogden Land Company** in the period of the 1838 **Treaty of Buffalo Creek** and the Tonawanda Treaty of 1857. In the aftermath of the removal crisis, they established themselves as the Tonawanda Band of Senecas, distinct from the Seneca Nation of New York at the Allegany and Cattaraugus reservations.

By the end of the 18th century, the Iroquois of eastern New York State had suffered dispossession to a large extent, first by American colonists, then by state and federal officials. Although the Iroquois in western New York State maintained much of their customary homeland, this homeland existed within a complicated set of Euro-American legal arrangements. The Tonawanda Senecas fell within New York's political and geographic boundaries, but, if they chose to sell their lands, Massachusetts would profit financially. This preemptive right changed hands several times during the subsequent decades, ultimately ending up with David Ogden and the Ogden Land Company in 1810.

The Ogden Land Company attempted, throughout the 1820s, 1830s, and 1840s, to remove all of the western New York Senecas to turn the highest profit possible on their **land speculation**. In many ways they succeeded. In 1826, despite the previous and continuing efforts of Red Jacket, Cornplanter, Handsome Lake, Governor Blacksnake, and other prominent Seneca leaders to hold on to all of their remaining lands in New York, the Ogden Company negotiated a land cession treaty in 1826 in which the Senecas ceded all of their remaining lands in the Genesee Valley and agreed to a reduction of the Tonawanda, Cattaraugus, and Buffalo Creek reservations.

In the 1838 Treaty of Buffalo Creek, land company officials used alcohol, bribery, forgery, threats, misinformation, and contempt for customary Seneca governmental practices to dispossess the Indians of all their remaining New York lands except the unoccupied, one-square-mile Oil Spring reservation, as well as their rights to Wisconsin lands purchased for them by the United States. In return, the Ogden Company paid them $202,000 and the federal government provided a large reservation on lands west of Missouri, to be settled by all of the Iroquois nations. Almost immediately,

Quakers in New York, Baltimore, and Philadelphia filed charges of fraud against the Ogden Land Company. Seneca groups claimed that most Iroquois did not support the treaty and that only a minority actually signed it.

In 1842, after four years of intense protest, federal, state, and Ogden Company representatives once again met with the Senecas at Buffalo Creek. This time they drafted a compromise treaty that returned the Allegany and Cattaraugus reservations to the Indians but did not return either Buffalo Creek or Tonawanda. As they had with the previous treaty, the Tonawanda Senecas refused to sign the 1842 compromise agreement. At critical moments during the negotiations, prominent Tonawanda leaders spoke out against the proceedings and those Senecas who signed the document. In so doing, they separated themselves from the communities at Allegany and Cattaraugus, a political move that proved significant later in the 1840s and throughout the 1850s.

Following the 1842 treaty, Tonawanda residents Ely S. **Parker** and Nicholson **Parker**, serving first as interpreters for older community members, led a resistance campaign against removal and a legal battle against the Ogden Land Company at the state and federal levels. Aided by several non-Native citizens and lawyers, the Parkers helped create a three-pronged resistance strategy for the Tonawandas that involved physically blocking any attempts the Ogden Land Company made at settlement and appraisement, applying for judicial action to remove trespassers at the state level, and filing appeals to national-level politicians to officially invalidate the treaties through the Senate Committee on Indian Affairs. Throughout this period, Nicholson and Ely maintained a lengthy correspondence, and their letters reveal the profound ways the removal crisis affected the Tonawanda community. Among other things, it disrupted customary notions of power and authority and destabilized structures of governance on the reservation. Although he was at times frustrated and concerned about factionalism and a general lack of support from Tonawanda community members, Ely Parker divided his time between the halls of government in Albany and Washington, D.C., and the councils at Tonawanda. In 1857, after a decades-long battle, the Tonawanda Senecas thwarted removal and purchased a permanent title to a portion of their homeland from the Ogden Land Company. The land remains in their hands today.

FURTHER READING: Armstrong, William H. *Warrior in Two Camps: Ely S. Parker, Union General and Seneca Chief.* Syracuse, NY: Syracuse University Press, 1978; Conable, Mary H. "A Steady Enemy: The Ogden Land Company and the Seneca Indians." PhD diss., University of Rochester, 1994; Hauptman, Laurence. *Conspiracy of Interests: Iroquois Dispossession and the Rise of New York State.* Syracuse, NY: Syracuse University Press, 1999; "Treaty with the Seneca, Tonawanda Band, 1857." Indian Affairs: Laws and Treaties. At http://digital.library.okstate.edu/kappler/Vol2/treaties/sen0767.htm; Wallace, Anthony F. C. *The Death and Rebirth of the Seneca.* New York: Vintage Books, 1969.

C. JOSEPH GENETIN-PILAWA

Trail of Tears

The phrase "Trail of Tears" originally referred primarily to the overland routes taken by the Choctaws, Muscogees (Creeks), Seminoles, Chickasaws, and Cherokees during their removal to the West (*see* **Choctaw Removal, Muscogee [Creek] Removal, Seminole Removal, Chickasaw Removal, Cherokee Removal**). During the past century, however, the term has become a popular metaphor for the tribes' removal experiences. Because of the Cherokees' great popularity among historians, Cherokee removal has received much more publicity than other Indian removals, so that now the general public uses the expression to refer primarily to the Cherokee removal experience, often at the expense of the other tribes' history.

Historians agree that the origin of the term is uncertain. Cherokees claim that it is theirs. However, late 19th- and early 20th-century Cherokee tribal historians who wrote about removal, such as White Horse (Henry C. Reece), DeWitt Clinton Duncan, and John Oskison, did not use the term. Choctaws also claim the term. They say that during their 1831 removal, a newspaperman at Little Rock, Arkansas, interviewed one of their chiefs, who said that the Choctaws' removal to that point had been "a trail of tears and death." They also say that the term was picked up and popularized by the eastern press. However, those events have not been verified to date in newspapers contemporary with Choctaw removal. The Choctaws who remained in Mississippi had a song in their repertoire describing their feelings as they saw their fellow tribespeople leave to cross the Mississippi. The song said, basically, "They saw the trail to the Big River, and they cried." By the first decade of the 20th century, non-Indian Oklahoma historians had begun to use "trail of tears" to refer to the roads that had led *all* of the tribes into the **Indian Territory**.

Whatever its origins, the expression was popularized during the first quarter of the 20th century. It was a time when Indians were thought to be vanishing from the American scene and could, therefore, safely be romanticized, even idealized, by emerging American youth organizations such as the Woodcraft Indians and Boy Scouts of America, both founded in the first decade of the century. Romanticizing Indian removal was primarily the work of Cherokee women college students, who popularized the expression in historical studies, oratory, and poetry. Rachel Caroline Eaton made "Trail of Tears" the title of a chapter of her 1914 thesis at the University of Chicago. Anne Ross, dressed in Plains tribe fashion and calling herself Princess Galilolle, toured the country in 1916 talking about the "Trail of Tears." And Ruth Muskrat (later Bronson of Indian activism fame) published a poem in 1922 titled "The Trail of Tears." Choctaw writers Winnie Lewis Gravit and James Culberson also used the term in the 1920s. By the 1930s, "Trail of Tears" had become a metaphor for removal and had become embedded in the language of historical literature about the subject.

During the last half of the 20th century, artists—primarily Cherokees—enhanced the metaphor by creating images of removal that often little resembled the reality: people trudging through deep snow when, in reality, heavy snow was (and is) a rarity in the South; soldiers riding as escort, when army escort attended only a few removing parties of Seminoles aboard steamboats; and people trudging through a trackless wilderness, whereas removal parties followed well-established routes. Perhaps the most fallacious image is that a majority of the people are walking. Choctaws walked more miles of their trail than any other people among the southern tribes. In reality, every available mode of transportation was used in removing Indians to the West: horse, cart, wagon, steamboat, keelboat, flatboat, canal boat, railway, and sailing ship. Members of the southern nations traveled more miles by water than by any other means. Nevertheless, the artistic license of these renderings in no way mitigates the terrible experience that removal was or the overriding question about removal: Why were people forced to leave their homelands?

In recent years, Cherokees have politicized the expression "Trail of Tears." Their appeals to Congress resulted in legislation in 1987 establishing the Trail of Tears National Historic Trail to commemorate Cherokee removal. The act alienated the other southern tribes, whose removals were also devastating. They had removed or begun their removals before the Cherokees, and some had endured hardships much more severe than those suffered by the Cherokees. Despite research to the contrary—and much of it done by Cherokee scholars—the Cherokee Nation continues to espouse the romanticized images of the Trail of Tears by its sponsorship of filmmakers and its Web site, which publishes inaccurate information, such as the number of Cherokee casualties on the Trail and John Burnett's alleged eyewitness account, which is well known to be spurious. Elsewhere, new findings about the removal process have fair prospects of reforming the way the public thinks about the Trail of Tears.

FURTHER READING: Eaton, Rachel Caroline. *John Ross and the Cherokee Indians.* Menasha, WI: George Banta Publishing Company, 1914; Green, Len. "Trail of Tears from Mississippi Walked by Our Choctaw Ancestors." *Bishinik* (March 1995): 4–5; Owens, Pamela Jean. "Trail of Tears." In *American Indian Religious Traditions: An Encyclopedia.* Ed. Suzanne J. Crawford and Dennis F. Kelley. London: ABC-CLIO, Oxford University Press, 2005, p. 1106; Thoburn, Joseph B., and Isaac M. Holcomb. *A History of Oklahoma.* San Francisco: Doubleday & Company, 1908; United States Department of the Interior, National Park Service, Denver Service Center. *Trail of Tears National Historic Trail: Alabama, Arkansas, Georgia, Illinois, Kentucky, Missouri, North Carolina, Oklahoma, Tennessee: Comprehensive Management and Use Plan.* Denver: U.S. Department of the Interior, National Park Service, 1992.

DANIEL F. LITTLEFIELD, JR.

Treaty of Buffalo Creek (1838)

Considered one of the worst frauds in American Indian history, the Treaty of Buffalo Creek of 1838 affected all of the Iroquois in New York, especially the Senecas in the western part of the state. In the treaty negotiations, three **Ogden Land Company** officials—James W. Stryker, Ransom H.

Gillet, and John F. **Schermerhorn**—used alcohol, bribery, forgery, threats, misinformation, and a contempt for customary Seneca governmental practices to dispossess the Indians of all their remaining New York lands (the Allegany, Cattaraugus, Buffalo Creek, and Tonawanda reservations as well as various smaller holdings) except the unoccupied, one-square-mile Oil Spring reservation, as well as their rights to Wisconsin lands purchased for them by the United States. In return, the Ogden Land Company paid them $202,000, and the federal government provided a large reservation on lands west of Missouri, to be settled by all of the Iroquois nations. The treaty led to the removal of a large proportion of Iroquois from the state.

At the end of the American Revolution, western New York was contested territory. By 1790, many of the eastern nations of the Iroquois Confederacy, particularly the Oneidas and Onondagas, had sold their land to the state, but the Senecas still retained considerable tracts in the west. Simultaneously, both Massachusetts and New York also claimed this land, the former through the charter of the Massachusetts Bay Company, and the latter through a royal grant to the Duke of York. When these two states met in Hartford, Connecticut, in 1786, Massachusetts transferred its claim to political rights within the disputed ground to New York in exchange for the preemptive rights to the soil. Thus, the Seneca homeland fell within New York's political and geographic boundaries. If the Senecas chose to sell their lands, however, Massachusetts would profit financially. This preemptive right changed hands several times during the subsequent decades, ultimately ending with David Ogden and the Ogden Land Company in 1810.

Following the completion of the Erie Canal and later building upon the removal efforts of the Andrew **Jackson** administration, the Ogden Land Company attempted to profit from its **land speculation** and the non-Native population growth in the region around Buffalo Creek. Although Red Jacket, Cornplanter, Handsome Lake, Governor Blacksnake, and other prominent Seneca leaders rejected many offers to sell their remaining lands in New York, individualistic interests, factionalism, confusion, and occasional fatalism instigated by Ogden and the state commissioners resulted in an important land cession treaty in 1826. In it, the Senecas ceded all of their remaining lands in the Genesee Valley and agreed to a reduction of the Tonawanda, Cattaraugus, and Buffalo Creek reservations. The election of Andrew Jackson and his vice president, New Yorker Martin **Van Buren**, emboldened the Ogden Land Company, and throughout the 1830s it continued to pressure the New York Senecas by moving non-Native settlers closer to reservation lands and developing the region around the Buffalo Creek.

The 1838 Treaty of Buffalo Creek resulted in instantaneous controversy. Quakers in New York, Baltimore, and Philadelphia filed charges of fraud against the Ogden Land Company. Seneca groups claimed that most Iroquois did not support the treaty and that only a minority actually signed it. In 1842, after four years of intense protest, federal, state, and Ogden Company representatives once again met with the Senecas at Buffalo Creek. This time they drafted a compromise treaty that returned the Allegany and Cattaraugus reservations to the Indians but did not return either Buffalo Creek or Tona-wanda. As they had with the previous treaty, the Tonawanda Senecas refused to sign the 1842 compromise agreement. At critical moments during the negotiations, prominent Tonawanda leaders spoke out against the proceedings and those who signed the document. In so doing, they separated themselves from the communities at Allegany and Cattaraugus.

The Buffalo Creek Treaty was significant for federal Indian policy and Iroquois history in many ways. As in other removals, many tribal people died en route or after arriving in the West. Furthermore, the removal crisis itself disrupted customary notions of power and authority and destabilized structures of Seneca governance, so much so that a political revolution took place at Allegany and Cattaraugus in 1848. At this point, the Tonawanda Senecas, who had previously worked to separate themselves from the other New York Indians, formally became a separate political entity. In 1857, under the leadership of Ely S. **Parker** and several non-Native citizens and lawyers, the Tonawanda Senecas purchased a portion of their homeland from the Ogden Land Company, thus ending the removal crisis and decades-long legal battle.

FURTHER READING: Armstrong, William H. *Warrior in Two Camps: Ely S. Parker, Union General and Seneca Chief.* Syracuse, NY: Syracuse University Press, 1978; Conable, Mary H. "A Steady Enemy: The Ogden Land Company and the Seneca Indians." PhD diss., University of Rochester, 1994; Genetin-Pilawa, C. Joseph. "Confining Indians: Power, Authority, and the Colonist Ideologies of Nineteenth-Century Reformers." PhD diss., Michigan State University, 2008; Hauptman, Laurence. *Conspiracy of Interests: Iroquois Dispossession and the Rise of New York State.* Syracuse, NY: Syracuse University Press, 1999; "Treaty with the New York Indians, 1838." Indian Affairs: Laws and Treaties. At http://digital.library.okstate.edu/kappler/Vol2/treaties/new0502.htm.

C. JOSEPH GENETIN-PILAWA

Treaty of Dancing Rabbit Creek (1830)

Between the election of Andrew **Jackson** in 1828 and his inauguration in early 1829, the Mississippi state legislature, like legislatures in Alabama and Georgia, extended state jurisdiction over the Indian tribes within the state's boundaries. With Jackson's support, Congress passed the **Indian Removal Act** in May 1830. Immediately, the Jackson administration turned its attention to the large tribes in the South. The Choctaws and Chickasaws were the first priority for three reasons: Jackson had better relations with those tribes than with any others, his fear of foreign invasion made him intent on securing full control of the lower Mississippi Valley, and he wanted to blunt the **nullification** movement afoot in the states to take control of Indian affairs. Out of talks that began in the late summer of 1830 came the Treaty of Dancing Rabbit Creek with the Choctaws, the first removal treaty to be ratified under the Indian Removal Act.

The United States invited the Choctaws and Chickasaws to go to Franklin, Tennessee, in the summer of 1830 to talk about removal. Only the Chickasaws went. The Choctaws refused to send a delegation to negotiate outside the

Choctaw Nation. Jackson sent what he considered his ablest team to negotiate: John H. **Eaton**, his close friend and secretary of war, and John **Coffee**, his close friend and relative by marriage. Jackson himself attended and stressed the inevitability of removal to the tribes. The Americans were successful in getting the Chickasaws to sign the Treaty of Franklin, which failed to be ratified. Then, in September, Eaton and Coffee went to the Choctaw Nation at the invitation of Greenwood **LeFlore**, who, through political machinations, had got himself named chief of the entire Choctaw Nation.

The result was the Treaty of Dancing Rabbit Creek. The treaty provided for the cession of Choctaw lands in Mississippi in exchange for lands west of the Territory of Arkansas between the Arkansas and Red rivers. It guaranteed the Choctaws self-government, protection by the United States, removal of intruders from Choctaw land, and punishment of American offenders who committed crimes on Choctaw land. It also provided a section of land for each head of household who decided to remain in Mississippi and become subject to the state's laws. To the three district chiefs—LeFlore, Nitakechi, and **Mushulatubbee**—the treaty provided four sections of land and handsome annuities and guaranteed them annual salaries for their service. The treaty provided for **Choctaw removal** by wagon or steamboat and for rations for 12 months after the Choctaws arrived in the West, as well as blankets, rifles, farming utensils, and other items. It also provided for the government sale of the Choctaws' cattle, promising to pay them in the West or to replace the cattle, whichever they chose. The treaty provided for a survey of Choctaw land and the allotment or reservation of lands for Choctaw households, with special dispensations to former chiefs, other officials of the Nation, and old warriors who had fought for the American side in earlier wars. The land could be sold when the Choctaws removed. The United States promised to keep Americans off of Choctaw lands until that time.

Failures of the United States to keep its side of the agreement are too numerous to list, but a few examples are worth noting. Most Choctaws did not receive just compensation for their lost livestock, guaranteeing that they arrived destitute in the West. The government also refused to remove intruders who poured into the Choctaw country as soon as the treaty was signed. Crimes such as theft and whiskey sales became common. Moreover, the allotment system was an open invitation to **land speculation**. At first local merchants and then capitalist syndicates used Choctaws to help locate allotments for other Choctaws, ensuring that the best lands were acquired for speculation. Almost chaotic conditions prevailed at times.

The Jackson administration used the Treaty of Dancing Rabbit Creek to intervene in, and disrupt, Choctaw social and political structures. The Choctaw people responded negatively to the treaty. They tossed LeFlore, Nitakechi, and Mushulatubbee out of office, electing George Harkins, Joel Nail, and Peter Pitchlynn to replace them. However, Eaton refused to recognize any chiefs except those who had signed the treaty.

This intervention directly affected the settlement patterns of Choctaws in the West. Those loyal to LeFlore, Nitakechi, and Mushulatubbee went to the

Arkansas watershed, and those loyal to the anti-removal elected chiefs and others went to the Red River.

Choctaw removal under the Treaty of Dancing Rabbit Creek exemplified a number of the most terrible stories of Indian removal: poor provisions, deprivation of property, harsh weather, disease and death, and difficult traveling conditions. Choctaws walked more miles during their removal than the people of any other tribe. Their descendants, with good reason, often refer to the experience as the Long Walk.

FURTHER READING: DeRosier, Arthur H., Jr. *The Removal of the Choctaw Indians.* Knoxville: University of Tennessee Press, 1970; Satz, Ronald N. *American Indian Policy in the Jacksonian Era.* Lincoln: University of Nebraska Press, 1975; "Treaty with the Choctaw, 1830." Indian Affairs: Laws and Treaties. At http://digital.library .okstate.edu/kappler/Vol2/treaties/cho0310.htm; Young, Mary E. *Redskins, Ruffleshirts and Rednecks: Indian Allotments in Alabama and Mississippi.* Norman: University of Oklahoma Press, 1961.

DANIEL F. LITTLEFIELD, JR.

Treaty of New Echota (1835)

The Treaty of New Echota was signed on December 29, 1835, in New Echota, Georgia, the capital of the Cherokee Nation. The Cherokees were split about removal. Some believed that removal was inevitable and thought it was in their interest to cooperate and negotiate for favorable terms. Known as the "Treaty Party," their leaders included Major **Ridge**; his son John **Ridge**; Elias **Boudinot**, the former editor of the *Cherokee Phoenix* newspaper; and his brother Stand Watie. Most Cherokees were opposed to leaving their land and homes. They were the "Anti-Treaty Party" or National Party and were led by principal chief John **Ross**.

The U.S. commissioners sent to treat with the Cherokees were the Rev. John F. **Schermerhorn** and Gen. William **Carroll**. The commissioners called a meeting of the general council for December 21 and stated that they were prepared to make a treaty with whoever assembled there, but that those who did not attend would be considered to have given their assent to whatever was done at the meeting. The Anti-Treaty Party decided not to attend the general council. When the Anti-Treaty Party refused to meet, the commissioners signed a removal treaty with the Treaty Party.

In the terms of the treaty, the Cherokees ceded all of their lands east of the Mississippi River and released all claims against the United States for $5 million. The treaty detailed the boundaries of the land west of the Mississippi to be held by the Cherokees, 7 million acres, and promised a "perpetual outlet west." The United States had the right to establish post and military roads and forts within the Cherokee land. The United States promised that the lands ceded to the Cherokee Nation "shall, in no future time without their consent, be included within the territorial limits or jurisdiction of any State or Territory." Provisions were made for money and vehicles for removal, and for subsistence for the first year after removal. Cherokee

Nation members who did not want to remove and were willing to live under the laws of the state of Georgia could receive their share of the annuities set up for the tribal members. The treaty required that removal be done within two years of the ratification of the treaty.

The treaty was contested by the majority of Cherokees, but Congress approved it by a one-vote margin, and it was signed into law by President Andrew **Jackson** in May 1836. The Anti-Treaty Cherokees worked to get the treaty overturned. Religious and philanthropic groups wrote Congress and the president to revoke the treaty, and more than 15,000 Cherokees signed a petition to Congress challenging the validity of the treaty. In it, John Ross wrote as follows:

> We are overwhelmed! Our hearts are sickened, our utterance is paralized [sic], when we reflect on the condition in which we are placed, by the audacious practices of unprincipled men, who have managed their stratagems with so much dexterity as to impose on the Government of the United States, in the face of our earnest, solemn, and reiterated protestations.
>
> The instrument in question is not the act of our Nation; we are not parties to its covenants; it has not received the sanction of our people. The makers of it sustain no office nor appointment in our Nation, under the designation of Chiefs, Head men, or any other title, by which they hold, or could acquire, authority to assume the reins of Government, and to make bargain and sale of our rights, our possessions, and our common country.

But the U.S. government did not change its position. After the deadline for removal passed, state militias and federal troops were sent to the Cherokee Nation to round up the Cherokee people and prepare them for removal. After the main body of Cherokees reached the West in 1839, the Cherokee leaders Elias Boudinot, John Ridge, and Major Ridge, who had signed the treaty, were assassinated.

FURTHER READING: Hoig, Stanley W. *The Cherokees and Their Chiefs: In the Wake of Empire.* Fayetteville: University of Arkansas Press, 1998; Moulton, Gary E., ed. *The Papers of Chief John Ross.* Vol. 1, 1807–1839. Norman: University of Oklahoma Press, 1985; Prucha, Francis Paul. *American Indian Treaties: The History of a Political Anomaly.* Berkeley: University of California Press, 1994; Prucha, Francis Paul. *The Great Father.* Lincoln: University of Nebraska Press, 1984; "Treaty with the Cherokee, 1835." Indian Affairs: Laws and Treaties. At http://digital.library.okstate.edu/kappler/Vol2/treaties/che0439.htm.

JILL E. MARTIN

Treaty of Pontotoc (1832)

As soon as the **Indian Removal Act** passed, Andrew **Jackson** focused his attention on the Choctaws and Chickasaws for two reasons. First, he harbored a long-standing fear of invasion by foreign powers, and he wanted the lower Mississippi Valley safely in the hands of white Americans. Second, he had a "fondness" for those tribes, having dealt with them through a number of years. Because a basic argument of anti-removal politicians and others was that the United States should honor its treaties with the tribes, he set out to negotiate removal treaties to legitimize removal, and he believed he would have a better chance of success with the Mississippi tribes than with others. Thus he called them to Franklin, Tennessee, in August 1830. The Choctaws refused to go, but the Chickasaws negotiated the Treaty of Franklin, which called for their removal, with the stipulation that they must find a suitable land in the West before the treaty could be valid. After attempts to find such a land failed, the Treaty of Franklin became void.

General John Coffee (1772–1833). (Hulton Archive/Getty Images)

Having failed with the Treaty of Franklin, Jackson ordered new treaty negotiations with the Chickasaws. Once more, as at Franklin, his negotiators were Secretary of War John H. **Eaton** and John **Coffee**, both his close friends and Coffee a relative by marriage. Eaton and Coffee knew what Jackson wanted. Eaton was prevented from attending, and Coffee was left to develop his own tactics in dealing with Levi **Colbert**, recognized as the chief. Colbert was ill, but he was on the treaty grounds. Coffee found it hard going, for the Chickasaws strongly resisted most of his proposals.

With John Terrell, an Alabamian, as a go-between, their discussions went back and forth for days. On the one side were Coffee and those whom Coffee called the "half-breeds" and Colbert called the "half-people," who wanted to salvage the Treaty of Franklin. On the other were Colbert and the Chickasaw leaders. Interest groups, including whites and Chickasaw mixed bloods, tried to influence both sides. Coffee presented an outline for an agreement. He proposed that the lands reserved to individuals before removal be sold by the government, but the Chickasaws wanted control of sales. Coffee proposed that the proceeds from sales be invested by the United States, but the Chickasaws wanted control of their funds. The plan had no guard against speculation, which the Chickasaws wanted, and it provided reservations for the negotiators and others, to which the Chickasaws objected.

Coffee used various tactics to bring the Chickasaws around. He threatened, saying Jackson wanted reservations set aside as rewards for Chickasaw negotiators. Colbert responded that most Chickasaws were against reservations. Coffee wanted to revive parts of the Treaty of Franklin, but Colbert could see no value in talking about the dead. Coffee withheld payment of the annuity, which was supposed to be paid at the time, to try to starve the Chickasaws into submission. Exasperated, Coffee threatened to write a treaty containing his own ideas, and if the Chickasaws refused to sign it, he would go home. Coffee returned to the treaty grounds with what became the Treaty of Pontotoc, which provided for more than 40,000 acres in reservation gifts. When the Chickasaws objected, Coffee tried to meet with the Chickasaws without Colbert. Failing there, Coffee tried to bribe Colbert, or at the least, compromise him by including a reservation of 9,920 acres for him. The question of reservations drove a wedge between the old leaders and the "half-people," who supported Coffee. Coffee threatened to treat with only the latter. When Colbert responded that they had no power, Coffee angrily ordered Terrell and the other whites who had been advising Colbert to leave the treaty camp.

The Chickasaws found themselves at a disadvantage. Coffee had deprived them of the people they trusted to advise them, although their trust of Terrell was misplaced. Coffee drafted another treaty and demanded that the Chickasaw leaders sign it. They distrusted the language of some provisions. Colbert was so ill that he was confined to his camp. The Chickasaw leaders brought the treaty to him, and they deliberated for two days but could not understand it and refused to sign. Food was running low, and some of the leaders had left. Coffee called those remaining together, dismissed their objections, and berated them as ignorant, duplicitous, and mean, accusing them of denigrating his official character and trampling on his private feelings. If they did not sign, he threatened, he would leave, and the government would refuse to treat with them again, leaving them to the Mississippi state laws. In Colbert's absence, some of the leaders signed.

Then Coffee turned to trickery. The day after the first leaders signed, he brought another paper for them to sign, telling them that Colbert and others had read and approved it, thus tricking them into signing. The following day, Coffee brought a supplement, which he read and said that it cured all of the ills of the first document. Colbert later claimed that he had read neither document. On the night before Coffee left, Colbert asked for copies of the papers that had been signed, but Coffee denied his request.

In the Treaty of Pontotoc, the Chickasaws ceded all of their lands east of the Mississippi but with stipulations ostensibly aimed at safeguarding individual Chickasaw wealth and property until removal. The treaty called for a survey of the land and provided allotments according to the number of people in a household. The allotments guaranteed the Chickasaws secure homes until they removed, at which time they could sell the land. The money received from the sale of surplus land would become a national fund held in trust by the federal government to pay for expenses of land surveys, land sales, removal, and subsistence of the people for one year following removal. Chickasaws were guaranteed compensation for the improvements on their homesteads that they abandoned when they removed. To guard against **land speculation**, there were provisions for public sales of land and prohibitions against fractionizing allotments and sales to combinations of buyers. Unfortunately, when land sales later began, the Chickasaws found that these attempts to prevent land speculation were futile. The supplement, dated

October 22, prohibited leases of allotments, set sale prices, lowered the age to 17 for single men to qualify for allotments, and provided allotments for orphan girls and widows.

Objections to the treaty soon followed. Levi Colbert's name appears on the treaty and supplement, although he claimed not to have signed either. Coffee blamed white men and mixed bloods who wanted reservations, including John D. Terrell, whom Coffee had ejected from the treaty council ground. Terrell was a planter from Alabama and was in league with Alabama land speculators. Although Colbert had considered him a friend to the Chickasaws, he was in reality an emissary from Andrew Jackson who had been sent to promote pro-removal sentiment among the Choctaws and Chickasaws. Terrell accompanied a group of disgruntled Chickasaws to Washington in 1832–1833 to protest the treaty. At Washington, Coffee defended his actions at Pontotoc, and Secretary John H. Eaton supported him. The treaty was proclaimed on March 1, 1833.

In March 1834, the Chickasaws appointed Levi Colbert, Isaac Alberson, Henry Love, Martin Colbert, and Benjamin Love as a delegation to Washington to attempt to amend the Pontotoc treaty. Levi Colbert became too ill to travel and gave his brother George authority to act for him. The delegation in May amended the Treaty of Pontotoc regarding reservations and land sales. The delegates revised the size of allotments according to the number in each household and provided extra land for those who were slaveholders. Orphans were granted a half section. Money generated through sales of surplus land would go into a general tribal fund to be invested in stocks and against which the government would charge the expenses of land survey and sales and removal. Titles to individual allotments were to be given in fee simple, and when the land was sold, the money would go to the individual. The supplemental agreement established the Chickasaw Commission, whose task was to oversee the sale of each allotment and determine the competency of the holders to manage their own affairs and thus receive their payments. Each land sale would require the signature of at least two of the commissioners. The Treaty of Pontotoc had been remarkable among Chickasaw cession treaties because it had not provided large gifts to the negotiators. The supplemental treaty of 1834 corrected that aberration to some extent by granting reservations to individuals, but the gifts were modest compared to some given in the past.

Ratification of the Treaty of Pontotoc and the supplemental agreement did not result in immediate removal. Survey of the land did not begin until 1835, and official sales and deed transfers began in 1836. However, full implementation of the treaty turned on the Chickasaws' finding a suitable land in the West. They had sent a number of exploring parties west since the Treaty of Franklin in 1830, but to no avail. Finally, a delegation in early 1837 reached an agreement with the Choctaws at Doaksville in the Choctaw Nation west, providing for the settlement of the Chickasaws in a separate district in the western part of the Choctaw Nation. **Chickasaw removal** did not begin until July 1837.

FURTHER READING: Gibson, Arrell M. *The Chickasaws.* Norman: University of Oklahoma Press, 1971; Paige, Amanda L., et al. *Chickasaw Removal.* Ada, OK: Chickasaw Press, 2010; "Treaty with the Chickasaw, 1832." Indian Affairs: Laws and Treaties. At http://digital.library.okstate.edu/kappler/Vol2/treaties/chi0356.htm.

DANIEL F. LITTLEFIELD, JR.

Treaty of Washington (1832)

The Treaty of Washington, signed by the Muscogees (Creeks) and the federal government on March 24, 1832, ceded all Creek land east of the Mississippi River (*see* **Muscogee (Creek) Removal**). The treaty relinquished the Creeks' sovereign claim to their land in exchange for legal title to individual land reserves. It also ended government recognition of the Creek Nation in the East.

The treaty signing was the culmination of a number of events in the Creek Nation. Many Lower Creeks were on the edge of starvation as a result of losing their Georgia lands in the 1826 Treaty of Washington. Moreover, between 1827 and 1829, the state of Alabama extended legal jurisdiction over the Creek Nation (*see* **Alabama and Indian Removal**). When Andrew **Jackson** came to office in 1829, he supported the state's policy and urged the Creeks to either submit to Alabama law or voluntarily emigrate west. Many whites, partly influenced by the extension law, flooded onto Creek land to settle. Many of these intruders established farms, mills, and shops, and the most brazen took forceful possession of Creek homes, fields, and livestock. When the town of Irwinton was established on the Chattahoochee River on land that contained the Creek town of Eufaula, the whites wasted little time in driving the Eufaulas away and burning their town to the ground. Compounding the Creeks' problems, a severe drought in 1830 and 1831 resulted in a smaller harvest than usual. Some Creeks also suffered from the effects of alcohol, which they had bought from white traders. Then, in 1831, an outbreak of smallpox killed untold numbers of Creeks. Fearing that they had no other option, a delegation of Creek headmen, led by **Opothleyohola**, traveled to Washington in March 1832 with the consent of the National Council to sell their lands.

Among its provisions, the Treaty of Washington granted all Creek heads of families half-sections of 320 acres and chiefs full sections of 640 acres. The Creeks could sell their reserves (under the supervision of the federal government for the first five years) or remain on their land in perpetuity. The treaty allocated money to pay Creek annuities, debts, and judgments against Creek headmen and to compensate the Creeks for lost ferries, bridges, and causeways. Most important to the Creeks, the federal government agreed to remove all white intruders from Creek land. The treaty was not a removal document, although Andrew Jackson hoped that heads of families would sell their land to white citizens and emigrate west.

In accordance with the treaty, a census was taken of the Creek Nation between 1832 and 1833. Afterward, locating agents visited each Creek town and assigned reserves in the presence of the town chiefs. Reserves were clustered according to town to best preserve Creek traditions and customs. Creek headmen and those with improvements were located first. Creeks without improvements were situated around members of their town who had improvements and as near to the town's council house as possible, but not closer to the council house than those with improvements.

Despite its promise, from the Creeks' perspective the Treaty of Washington failed to accomplish almost all of the goals it set out to achieve. White traders and land companies rushed into the former Creek Nation with whiskey and food to trade on credit in exchange for title to land reserves. Many Creeks signed away their land while intoxicated. There was widespread use of impersonation, whereby whites bribed other Creeks to claim ownership of a reserve that was not theirs. Once the reserve was certified by a government agent, the land was turned over to the speculator. In other cases, the Creeks' land was valued at up to one-fifth its value. Many Creeks, devastated by debt, chased by creditors, and cheated of their land reserve, committed suicide.

Although the government appointed agents to investigate the land frauds committed on the Creeks, whites tried to interfere in the investigations. Many Creeks feared they would never find justice. It was for this reason that a small band of Lower Creeks lashed out at white encroachment in the spring of 1836. The Second Creek War, as it came to be called, was partly a reaction to the failure of the 1832 Treaty of Washington and the frauds perpetrated on the Creeks. Those who started the uprising were primarily from the towns most affected by the frauds. As a result of the war, Andrew Jackson ordered all the Creeks to move to the West.

FURTHER READING: Green, Michael D. *The Politics of Indian Removal: Creek Government and Society in Crisis.* Lincoln: University of Nebraska Press, 1982; Haveman, Christopher D. "The Removal of the Creek Indians from the Southeast, 1825–1838." PhD diss., Auburn University, 2009; "Treaty with the Creeks, 1832." Indian Affairs: Laws and Treaties. At http://digital.library.okstate.edu/kappler/Vol2/treaties/cre0341.htm; Young, Mary E. *Redskins, Ruffleshirts and Rednecks: Indian Allotments in Alabama and Mississippi, 1830–1860.* Norman: University of Oklahoma Press, 1961.

CHRISTOPHER D. HAVEMAN

Tuckabatche Hadjo (dates unknown)

Tuckabatche Hadjo was regarded as a chief of Kasihta (Cusseta) and Coweta towns. After passage of the **Indian Removal Act**, he was a member of a delegation of Lower Creeks sent by the chief of the Lower Towns, **Eneah Micco**, to present the Lower Creeks' concerns to the government. The delegation focused on two major issues: opposition to removal and extension of Alabama laws over the Creeks. The laws operated unequally, they claimed, and whites sold the Creeks whiskey and stole their property. The delegates warned Secretary of War John H. **Eaton** of the possibility of bloodshed because of incursions into Muscogee territory from Alabama and Georgia white residents, but Eaton responded that the government was powerless to interfere with state law. The delegates tried to talk personally to Andrew **Jackson** but were only able to leave a written message for the president. Tuckabatche Hadjo later accompanied a contingent of Muscogees to Texas in a failed attempt to purchase a tract of land from the Mexican government. Still later, he and warriors under his command assisted Gen. Thomas S. **Jesup** in bringing the Creek War of 1836 to an end and was one of the leaders who entered an agreement with Gen. Jesup to send Creek warriors to assist the U.S. forces against the Indians in Florida. However, the Creek War had resulted in orders for the forced removal of all the Creeks (*see* **Muscogee [Creek] Removal**).

In September 1836, Tuckabatche Hadjo led a contingent of 1,984 Creeks from Kasihta and Coweta towns on their way to the West. Lt. John T. **Sprague** was sent to observe the contractors, the Alabama Emigrating Company. Tuckabatche Hadjo had tried to persuade Sprague to allow the people to wait until they could gather their crops and sell their livestock, but he was refused. The party left Tallassee on September 5, reached Memphis in October, and encamped there for most of the month. On that leg of the journey, the Creeks had been forced to march, and many stragglers had been left behind despite Tuckabatche Hadjo's repeated requests for days of rest. To Sprague's credit, at Memphis he threatened to relieve the contractors of their duty if they did not give the Creeks better treatment. There, Tuckabatche Hadjo agreed to split his contingent into two groups, one traveling overland through the Mississippi Swamp by way of the Military Road and the other traveling to **Indian Territory** aboard the *John Nelson*. As the party progressed through Arkansas, Tuckabatche Hadjo often argued with Sprague, usually about the chief's refusal to move on when the removal party left. Sprague felt that Tuckabatche Hadjo had been unduly reluctant at times to move on, and his refusal to move from the Arkansas River opposite Little Rock brought threats from the governor of the state to call out the militia. Sprague claimed that the chief wanted to remain at the site to be close to a supply of whiskey, but Sprague's harsh estimation of Tuckabatche Hadjo's reasons for staying was most likely inaccurate, for wherever the Muscogees or any other removal groups camped, whiskey peddlers followed them, always providing a ready supply. Sprague also called Tuckebatche Hadjo's decision to remain behind an act of a leader without authority. This was probably a misreading, because the chief's reluctance to move was consistent with his actions on the trail from Tallassee to Memphis: he wanted more days of rest more frequently than the contractors were willing to grant so that he could wait for the stragglers of his group to catch up.

Tuckabatche Hadjo repeated this behavior at the ration supply depot near Kirkbride Potts's home at present-day Pottsville, Arkansas, where he caught up with the main body of his people after having remained for a number of days near Little Rock. When Sprague's party left Potts's place, the chief remained. Three more removal parties passed, and still he remained. As time passed, he was joined by stragglers who reached the Potts encampment. In January 1837, the *Arkansas Gazette* reported that, in late December, Potts had ordered the chief and his followers to leave but that they refused, "saying they were west of the Mississippi, and it was not in the power of any one to compel them to go on. They said threats of the whites might alarm little boys—but they were men!" The commander of the Pope County militia mustered 100 men and marched on the camp only to find that the Muscogees had moved on the night before. Tuckabatche Hadjo's actions at Potts's camp were consistent with his actions east of Memphis and at Little Rock. The chief voluntarily joined Lt. Edward **Deas**'s contingent when it reached Potts's place. That was the last major Muscogee contingent to move through the state, and it had picked up all of the stragglers from Rock Roe westward. Among them were probably some of Tuckabatche Hadjo's original party, without whom he was unwilling to go on to Indian Territory. His actions bear the mark of a man who lived up to his rank and his responsibilities as a leader, unwilling to leave his people scattered along the roads of Arkansas.

FURTHER READING: Foreman, Grant. *Indian Removal: The Emigration of the Five Civilized Tribes of Indians.* Norman: University of Oklahoma Press, 1989; Paige, Amanda L., et al. The North Little Rock Site on the Trail of Tears National Historic Trail: Historical Contexts Report. At http://anpa.ualr.edu/trail_of_tears/indian_removal _project/site_reports/north_little_rock/northlittlerock_report/htm.

AMANDA L. PAIGE

Tustenuggee Emathla (c. 1793–?)

Tustenuggee Emathla, or Jim Boy, a mixed African-Creek, had been in charge of Creek warriors who fought against the Red Stick Creeks at Burnt Corn Creek in July 1813. Later, he claimed to have been present, but not a warrior, at the attack on Fort Mims in August and at the Battle of Cahawba, but he claimed to have had no further role in the Red Stick War. Little is known about his life between the war and the removal period.

In the wake of the **Treaty of Washington** in 1832, Tustenuggee Emathla, like **Opothleyohola**, came to believe that removal was inevitable. However, Opothleyohola did not like the western land assigned to the Creeks. In late 1834, the Upper Creeks sought to buy a tract of land in Texas from the Mexican government. In the winter of 1834–1835, Tustenuggee Emathla was a member of a group headed by Opothleyohola who went to Nacodoches, from which they toured lands on the Sabine and Trinity rivers. They liked the land, and in early 1835 they made a contract with the Galveston Bay and Texas Land Company, but Texans and others objected, and the contract fell through.

In the spring of 1836, a large number of Lower Creeks found their situation intolerable as **land speculation** in Creek allotments led to fraud, dispossession

Engraving of a portrait of Tustenuggee Emathla, a Creek chief, by 19th-century American painter Charles Bird King, from *The Indian Tribes of North America.* (McKenney, Thomas L. and James Hall. *The Indian Tribes of North America,* 1836–1844)

of the Creeks, and widespread intrusion of whites into Creek lands. They struck out in what was known as the Creek War of 1836. Tustenuggee Emathla was at the head of a large group of warriors who went to the aid of Gen. Thomas S. **Jesup**, who had been sent to quell the uprising. His service helped bring a close to the conflict, directly following which the government undertook the forced removal of the entire Creek population.

While the major part of the forced Creek removal went on (*see* **Muscogee [Creek] Removal**), Tustenuggee Emathla led 450 Creek warriors, including two of his sons who had enlisted to help the U.S. Army fight the Seminoles, who were also resisting removal in what was called the **Second Seminole War**. In addition to a number of skirmishes, they fought in the Battle of Wahoo Swamp and were in the heaviest fighting for several days.

The warriors served in Florida according to an agreement with Jesup signed by Tustenuggee Emathla and other Creek leaders. The warriors were promised that they could return home in early 1837. As a condition of their service, the government promised that their families could remain in their homes unmolested until the warriors returned and could prepare to remove west. Jesup, however, kept the Creek warriors in Florida for months beyond their scheduled return. Meanwhile, whites became determined to be rid of all the Creeks. Squads of Alabamians—those from Russell County were particularly vicious—began raiding and burning their homes, killing, raping, stealing property, and chasing women and children into the swamps. White mobs attacked Jim Boy's town, among others, and began rounding up men with the intent of sending them to camps at Tuskegee. Local U.S. Army officials gave the Creek men the choice of being separated from their families or gathering up everyone for immediate removal. Militia squads hunted down those who were hiding out, killing a number.

By early March 1837, nearly 4,000 of the friendly Creeks were in camps near Montgomery. From there, they were sent to Mobile Point to await transportation to New Orleans. Deprived of property and personal effects, they were in dire straits. Sickness was widespread, and many Creeks died. Capt. John Page, who was in charge of their removal, consulted the leaders of the towns represented in the camps, and together they decided to move the holding camps to Pass Christian, Mississippi. Unfortunately, the sickness and deaths continued. It was to these conditions that Tustenuggee Emathla and the other Creek warriors returned to their families after their service in Florida.

Removal from Pass Christian did not begin until October 1837. Tustenuggee Emathla arrived at New Orleans on October 16. There, the Creeks boarded nine steamboats to take them to Arkansas. Among the boats was the *Monmouth*, an aging craft that carried more than 600 people. On the upward journey, the boat collided with the *Trenton*, which broke it in half, resulting in the greatest loss of life in any single event during the Indian removal era: 311 people. Tustenuggee Emathla had gone on an earlier boat, but one of his wives and nine of his children were on board the *Monmouth*. Four of his children drowned. One of his daughters recalled having been told the story of the wreck of the *Monmouth* and having been taught a song sung by one of the survivors: "I have no more land, I am driven away from home, driven up the red waters, let us all go, let us all die together and somewhere upon the banks we will be there." Whether Tustenuggee Emathla's second wife survived removal is uncertain. One of his sons, Cochamy, later chief of the Creek Nation known as Ward Coachman, remained in Alabama until 1845.

The wreck of the *Monmouth* had implications for other removals. **Chickasaw removal** was under way at the time. Late in October, Chickasaws began arriving in Memphis, where they were to board steamboats that would take them to **Indian Territory**. When reports of the *Monmouth* reached Memphis, hundreds of Chickasaws refused to board the boats and decided, instead, to brave the dreaded Mississippi Swamp on the west side of the river and travel overland, much to the consternation of U.S. government officials.

In addition to the loss of a number of his family members, removal resulted in great material loss to Tustenuggee Emathla. Besides the property that his family members were forced to abandon in Alabama, one of his slaves, whom he used as interpreter and guide, was killed in Florida, and he did not receive the blacks that warriors under his command had captured in Florida and claimed as plunder according to their agreement with Jesup.

Details of Tustenuggee Emathla's life in the West are sketchy. In 1845, he helped Lower Creek chief Roley McIntosh mobilize warriors to protect the western lands of the Creek Nation from raiding parties of Pawnees. After the Civil War Battle of Honey Springs in the Creek Nation in July 1863, he moved his family, along with other Confederate sympathizers, to Texas to wait out the war. After that he dropped from public view. By then, he would have been about 70 years old.

FURTHER READING: Foreman, Grant. *Indian Removal: The Emigration of the Five Civilized Tribes of Indians.* Norman: University of Oklahoma Press, 1989; McKenney, Thomas L., and James Hall. *The History of the Indian Tribes of North America, with Biographical Sketches and Anecdotes of the Principal Chiefs, Embellished with One Hundred Portraits from the Indian Gallery in the Department of War, at Washington.* Philadelphia: E. C. Biddle, 1836–1844.

DANIEL F. LITTLEFIELD, JR.

V

Van Buren, Martin (1782–1862)

Martin Van Buren succeeded Andrew **Jackson** as president of the United States in 1837. Nicknamed "the Little Magician" for his astute and effective use of the political machines of New York and his manipulation of the spoils system, his political reputation suffered during his presidency because of the Panics of 1837 and 1839, and he was defeated for reelection in 1840. His new nickname was "Martin Van Ruin."

Van Buren was, as much as Andrew Jackson, responsible for the development of the American political party system. Whereas Jackson's personality was essential in the forging of the Democratic Party, Van Buren was the strategist and quasi-official spokesman who made the party a political force. His work for Jackson's election in 1828 created the system of state chairmen and local organizers that marks the modern national political parties in the United States. His reward was the State Department in Jackson's first term, the vice presidency in Jackson's second, and being anointed as Jackson's successor when Jackson retired to the Hermitage.

However, Jackson's retirement was hardly the end of Jackson's influence. Van Buren's term of office is sometimes referred to as "Jackson's third term," and in Indian affairs, it is a fair name. Van Buren's personal style of governing made it far more difficult for him to wield power than the aggressive Jackson, but in matters related to Indian affairs, Jackson's tenets held. The process of removal was continued, with treaties negotiated and emigrant parties sent west.

Van Buren retained Jackson's commissioner of Indian affairs, Tennessean and Jackson intimate, Carey Harris. This proved to be a mistake, however, as Harris became involved in **land speculation** and manipulating removal subsistence contracts. Jackson learned of Harris's activities and warned Van Buren against him in mid-1838. Harris's defense of his activities was deemed "not sufficient" by the president, and Harris resigned in October 1838.

Van Buren next appointed T. Hartley Crawford, an ardent Jackson supporter, as commissioner. Crawford had supported the **Indian Removal Act** when in the House representing Pennsylvania in 1830, and had investigated fraud in purchases of Creek lands for Jackson in 1836. His report had strongly condemned speculation in Indian lands, and that, together with his personal friendship with Jackson, made his appointment an easy one for Van Buren. He would prove successful in the position and would serve the next three presidents, Whigs William Henry Harrison and John Tyler as well as Democrat James K. Polk.

Politicization of the Indian field service, the network of agents and subagents necessary to carry out the mechanics of removal, made scores of small federal offices available for political supporters of the administration. And although Van Buren had earned "the Little Magician" nickname through his use of the spoils system, there existed many agents of talent and compassion, and the Van Buren administration made considerable effort to develop better methods of supervision than had existed during Harris's commissionership.

As President Andrew Jackson's campaign manager, political confidant, secretary of state, vice president, and, finally, handpicked successor, Martin Van Buren played a major role in national politics and the establishment of Jacksonian democracy as a significant political force. (Library of Congress)

In 1838, Congress began once more debating the creation of an organized **Indian Territory** that would, among other provisions, allow Indians a representative in Congress. The Van Buren administration opposed the Indian Territory bill, preferring to continue using the system of agents to influence tribal governments. Additionally, southerners, an essential element of Van Buren's Democratic Party, opposed the bill on sectional grounds, claiming that an Indian Territory would prevent the expansion of slavery to the West and would remove all the North's Indians to areas bordering the South. The murder of the Cherokee leaders of the so-called Treaty Party in 1839 led the administration to reaffirm its opposition to an organized territory. Van Buren, friendly with the Treaty Party members for their cooperation in negotiating **Cherokee removal**, demanded that the Cherokees surrender the guilty parties to U.S. authorities. The Cherokees declined, pointing out that the United States had no authority over Indian-on-Indian crimes. Secretary of War Joel Poinsett then dispatched a military contingent to the Cherokee lands in the West and cut off their annuity payments, strategies that would not have been open to the administration had there been an organized territory.

To demonstrate Van Buren's support for the Indians in the West, despite opposing their representation in Congress and in the spirit of Jackson's belief that American Indians were doomed to extinction unless they became acculturated, Crawford developed an educational plan for Indians, including both local schools and larger boarding schools. This served the additional purpose of attempting to lessen the impact of nongovernment missionaries among the Indians, giving, it was hoped, the federal government another lever with which to influence Indian behavior. The plan stressed manual labor training and the education of girls. Van Buren strongly supported the plan and urged Congress to create a long-range funding mechanism. Late in his administration, a school was started at the abandoned Fort Coffee on the Arkansas River, and an elaborate Indian education system would be later created under **Whig Party** administrations, using the model developed by Crawford.

"Jackson's third term" was hardly a success, and the Panics 1837 and 1839 greatly reducing the funds available to the federal government for the internal improvements that Van Buren had hoped to continue, but he was able to carry on with Jackson's removal plans, leaving removal as a proven success for his Whig successors to continue, despite their philosophical opposition.

FURTHER READING: Howe, Daniel Walker. *What God Hath Wrought: The Transformation of America, 1815–1848.* New York: Oxford University Press, 2007; Satz, Ronald N. *American Indian Policy in the Jacksonian Era.* Lincoln: University of Nebraska Press, 1975; Van Buren, Martin. *The Autobiography of Martin Van Buren.* Washington, DC: U.S. Government Printing Office, 1920.

TONY R. ROSE

W

Wea Removal

See Peoria-Kaskaskia-Piankeshaw-Wea Removal

Whig Party

The presidential election of 1824 did not give any of the four national candidates—Andrew **Jackson**, John Quincy Adams, Henry Clay, or William Crawford—a majority of the electoral votes. Thus, the election was decided in the House of Representatives, where Clay threw his support to Adams and ensured his victory. The election of 1824 was the last presidential election that was not shaped by party politics. The Adams-Clay alliance coalesced into what was at first called the National Republican Party and later the Whig Party.

Jackson's opponents in Congress quickly drew together: Anti-Masons, nullifiers, and supporters of the United States Bank found common cause in their rejection of Jackson. Adams declared in 1829 that the new parties being organized would find Indian issues their dividing point. By 1834, a formal Whig Party had organized in opposition to Jackson's Democratic Party.

The Whig Party elevated national political discourse from issues of personality to questions of national policy through the creation and distribution of a party political platform in 1840. But much of the development of that platform stemmed from simple opposition to Andrew Jackson. Although a review of political rhetoric leads to some distinction of Whig and Democrat positions on matters of humanitarianism and reform (religious values, the legislation of morality, and slavery), the matter of Indian policy appears to come down to one of anti-Jacksonism. An analysis of the congressional vote on the **Indian Removal Act** of 1830 shows that party considerations weighed heavier than sectionalism, the factor that would influence much of antebellum legislation. Since the removal act was Jackson's policy, the nascent Whigs were in opposition. John Bell and Hugh Lawson White, both of Tennessee, introduced the removal bill in the House of Representatives when they were Jackson supporters, but when they moved to the Whig Party in 1835, they both switched from voting pro-removal to voting pro-Indian. Henry Clay, who fiercely opposed Jackson and the removal act, had remarked to John Quincy Adams in 1825 that "although he would never use or countenance inhumanity towards them, he did not think [the Indians], as a race, worth preserving." Throughout the removal period, Democrats voted consistently in favor of removal and were anti-Indian; the Whigs voted consistently against the Democrats. Many Whig leaders used opposition to removal as the test of a true party supporter.

Other reasons for opposition to removal existed, of course. Theodore Frelinghuysen of New Jersey, who led the Senate opposition to the removal act and who ran as the Whig vice-presidential candidate in 1844, was a temperance advocate and very active in his church governance. His opposition to removal was eloquently expressed in terms of simple humanitarianism, but one must look at his opposition to removal and his church activities with a cynical eye. At the time of the removal debate, Frelinghuysen was a member of the American Board of Commissioners of Foreign Missions, an organization through which passed many of the funds dedicated by the federal government for "civilizing" the Indians. The removal of the Indians to the West would imperil the continued flow of those funds.

It would be expected that when the Whigs took control of both the executive and legislative branches in 1840, Indian policy would change. However, the death of William Henry Harrison one month after taking office put Virginian John Tyler in the White House. Tyler broke with his party over banking and tariff legislation, and, by the summer of 1841, he was officially read out of the Whig Party by the congressional leadership. Maneuvering between the White House and Congress resulted in a great many policies left to drift, and Indian policy was one of them.

An exception was in the appointment of Ethan Allen Hitchcock in early 1841 by Secretary of War John Bell to investigate the possibility of fraud in Indian country under the just-ended Martin **Van Buren** administration. By the time Hitchcock returned to Washington in April 1842, the Tyler cabinet had resigned, and his report was not greeted with enthusiasm by the new president. Tyler claimed executive privilege and refused to send the report to the Whig Congress, in part because the records of wrongdoing that Hitchcock had collected implicated men whom Tyler was courting in his bid to create a political base from which to run for reelection in 1844. Tyler ultimately capitulated and transmitted the report to the House in early 1843.

Tyler's administration negotiated a treaty with the Sioux in the fall of 1841 that included an enormous land cession and provisions for the creation of a northern Indian territory. The treaty was a significant departure from previous removal treaties in the efforts made to provide for the comforts of the Sioux, but the combination of Whigs and Democrats in the Senate refused to ratify it.

In 1842, the War Department informed Tyler that although there were still some Indians living east of the Mississippi, "there is no more land east of the Mississippi, remaining unceded, to be desired by us." It was not altogether true when one considers the Indians of New York, but, when combined with the army's unilateral conclusion of the **Second Seminole War** that same year, Tyler was comfortable in turning away from the decade-old issue. Jackson's goal was accomplished, and Indian affairs became matters of management, rather than removal, for incoming Democratic and Whig administrations.

FURTHER READING: Howe, Daniel Walker. *What God Hath Wrought: The Transformation of America, 1815–1848.* New York: Oxford University Press, 2007; Parsons, Lynn Hudson. "'A Perpetual Harrow upon My Feelings': John Quincy Adams and the American Indian." *New England Quarterly* 46, no. 3 (1973): 339–379; Rolater, Fred S. "The American Indian and the Origin of the Second American Party System." *Wisconsin Magazine of History* 76, no. 3 (1993): 180–203; Satz, Ronald N. *American Indian Policy in the Jacksonian Era.* Lincoln: University of Nebraska Press, 1975.

TONY R. ROSE

Wildcat

See Coacoochee

Winnebago Removal

See Ho-Chunk Removal

Wirt, William (1772–1834)

William Wirt was a prominent lawyer who served as U.S. attorney general from 1817 to 1829 and later ran for president under the Anti-Mason label in 1832. He strengthened the position of attorney general during his tenure. Among other things, Wirt initiated the practice of preserving his official opinions so that they could be used as precedents. Early in his career, he was an advocate of states' rights, but he later supported constitutional nationalist policies. This philosophy led to his defense of the Cherokee Nation. In 1829 and 1830, the state of Georgia enacted a series of laws that, among other things, abolished Cherokee law within its boundaries, thus negating the tribe as a political or legal entity. The tribal leaders objected and asked President Andrew **Jackson** to take action to countermand the Georgia laws. When Jackson refused, the Cherokees,

U.S. Attorney General William Wirt (1817–1829). (Chaiba Media)

represented by Wirt, filed a writ with the U.S. Supreme Court, asserting that they were a sovereign nation whose treaties with the federal government made them immune from the vagaries of such actions as those taken by Georgia. Wirt argued that the Cherokee Nation had the same standing as a foreign nation with which the United States had a treaty.

In *Cherokee Nation v. Georgia*, while disagreeing with Wirt's contention that the Cherokees enjoyed the privileges of a foreign nation, Chief Justice John Marshall did clarify the situation. Writing for the majority in the case, Marshall declared the Cherokee Nation and other Indian nations to be "domestic dependent nations." This term remains an important one in deciding cases involving sovereignty issues among the various branches of American government and Indian nations.

FURTHER READING: Berutti, Ronald A. "The Cherokee Case: The Fight to Save the Supreme Court and the Cherokee Indians." *American Indian Law Review* 17 (1992): 291–308; *Cherokee Nation v. Georgia*. 30 U.S. (5 Pet.) 1 (1831). Kennedy, John P. *Memoirs of the Life of William Wirt: Attorney-General of the United States*. 1849. Reprint, Buffalo, NY: W. S. Hein, 1973.

JAMES W. PARINS

Women during Removal

The national public debate on Indian removal brought attention to Georgia's intent to rid the state of the Cherokees as the final fulfillment of the government's promises under the Georgia Compact of 1802. The plight of the Cherokees caught the attention of American women, who, led by Catharine Beecher in 1829, engaged in a vigorous anti-removal campaign. Groundwork for this campaign, it has been argued, rested in anti-removal protests by Cherokee women in 1817 through 1819, particularly the efforts of older women and Margaret Scott, who strongly influenced Lydia Sigourney, active in the movement a decade later. These early protests against removal had less effect on the development of removal legislation and the physical removal of peoples than they would have later on the anti-slavery movement. Although their efforts failed to prevent passage of removal legislation, they developed organizational and protest strategies that later proved effective in the debate over slavery.

Because American officials dealt almost exclusively with men during the removal period, evidence of women's participation in the shaping of removal treaties and other documents is scant, and their participation in the physical removal of their people has been treated anecdotally. An understanding of women's actual roles in this period will remain casual until systematic studies of Indian women's participation in resistance to removal, preparation for it, and participation in it have been completed.

In many ways, women had more to lose in removal than men did. The older Cherokee women who petitioned the national council in 1817 compared the ceding of land and removal to men killing their mothers. Although there is little documentation, some evidence points to women playing significant roles in resistance to removal. Cherokee women apparently verbally abused the Georgia Guard because in 1831 rumors circulated in the Cherokee Nation that the Guard had orders to whip women who insulted them. Later that year, the women of Salequoyee and Pine Log sent a written statement to the national council, calling the plan to remove the Cherokees to appease Georgia "oppressive, cruel, and unjust" and urging the council to resist. Evidence indicates that **Black Hawk** was in some haste to reoccupy his old village in 1832 before the season waned so that the women could plant their crops. When the Illinois militia caught the retreating band at the Bad Axe River, they slaughtered the women and children along with the warriors in what has gone down in history as the **Black Hawk War**. Reports in 1836 claimed that Lower Creek women who escaped the Alabama militia and the U.S. Army in the Creek War fought alongside the men. There were also reports that, while the women were running from their pursuers, they engaged in infanticide, a practice permitted in the old Creek society to keep infants out of reach of the military.

In the social disruption of tribal communities during preparations for removal, women were often vulnerable. When he began rounding up Cherokees in 1838, Gen. Winfield **Scott** ordered the state militiamen under his command to give assistance to infants, old people, the insane, and women, but evidence indicates that they disregarded his orders. Women were dragged from their houses and driven before the militia like animals. Accustomed to the comforts of home, they were unaccustomed to, and ill prepared for, life in the holding camps to which they were herded. In the camps, soldiers at times assaulted women and turned some into prostitutes, who were cast out by their families. Promises of protection made by other military officers also failed. Gen. Thomas S. **Jesup** enlisted more than 700 Creek warriors in 1836 to go to Florida to fight the Seminoles, promising them that, while they were gone, their families would be exempt from the forced removal of the Creeks and would be safe in their homes until the men could return and prepare for removal. But in 1837, squads of white men, particularly from Russell County, Alabama, looted and burned their homes, stole slaves and children, assaulted women and girls, and killed old men. The militia rounded up Creek families without giving them time to gather their property and marched them to departing points. They languished in camps at Mobile Point, Alabama, and Pass Christian, Mississippi, for months before they finally were sent to the West.

Hardships of daily life on the removal trail fell heavily on women. Although the attending physician for one Cherokee removal party had the latest in obstetric equipment, pregnant women of most tribes received no special treatment during removal. Women cared for their children under the difficult circumstances of trail and camp life. Transforming the rations of beef or pork and corn, cornmeal, or flour into meals for their family was an everyday responsibility, even during steamboat removals. Boats at times stopped at night so that the people could build cooking fires on land; others had temporary hearths built on the decks. Eyewitness accounts frequently depict women engaged in domestic duties of cooking and sewing well after dark.

Such drudgery was not the lot of all Indian women. Eyewitness accounts also describe slave women among the southeastern tribes performing domestic duties along the removal route. Some Cherokee women served as interpreters, hospital matrons, and nurses during removal.

The losses sustained by women during removal were great. For example, women and children accounted for the highest number of deaths from diseases and accidents during the journeys west. Many of the casualties were the matriarchs of the tribes, such as the mother of Potawatomi chief We-wissa, as well as women who held special positions of honor in the tribes, such as the "Queen" of the Chickasaws, wife of minko **Ishtehotopa**. A large number of the 311 Creek victims of the wreck of the steamboat *Monmouth* were women and children. Hundreds of other women witnessed the deaths of their children, in whom the future of their clans and their nations or tribes resided. The impact of such losses on the social and political life of Indian communities is impossible to determine.

Women attempted to protect their children during their journey. At Memphis in 1832, for example, in the midst of a cholera epidemic, Choctaw women refused to allow their children to board the steamboats for fear of contracting the disease, presuming correctly that passengers on the boats were spreading it. The women chose to cross the dreaded Mississippi Swamp and travel overland rather than risk taking the boats. Their revolt forced the government to make hasty arrangements for overland travel for the removal parties, whose removal had been planned to take place completely by water.

Women's material losses varied. Most Seminole women, who before the removal era had been the principal property owners, had little to lose by the time they left Florida. Constant movement as a result the Treaty of Moultrie Creek in 1823 and the **Second Seminole War** that began in 1835 had led to attrition of their property, particularly in livestock. When they surrendered or were captured, they were sent to prison or to holding camps in preparation for removal and, in the process, were relieved of what little remained of their personal property. Because their slaves had been able to travel with them before their removal, a number of Seminole women managed to retain their slaves through the removal process, despite claims by whites for many of them. Some Creek women, too, managed to reach the West with their slave property. However, most Creek women reached the West in complete poverty. The **land speculation** and harassment by white intruders that had beset Creek society after the **Treaty of Washington** in 1832 made women, the principal property owners, vulnerable to whites, who stole their slaves and livestock, plundered their homes, and at times assaulted them. In the forced removal that followed the Creek War of 1836, they were rousted out of their homes and sent to holding camps in preparation for departure with little opportunity to dispose of their property, which they were not allowed to take with them. Potawatomi women in Indiana faced a similar situation in the summer of 1838, when their chiefs were taken captive by deception and squads of militia were sent out to round the people up in preparation for their hasty departure for the West. Choctaw women had to dispose of their property, usually at prices far below their value, and many were destitute when they reached the West.

On the eve of removal some Cherokee women, such as Elizabeth Pack and Sally Bark, numbered among the successful farmers and businesspeople of the Cherokee Nation. Pack owned a large farmstead with a wood frame house, farm buildings, and slave houses. Her slaves worked her vast orchards of hundreds of apple, peach, and other fruit trees. Cherokees like Pack, who had large numbers of slaves, were among the elite class who did not have to endure the crowded holding camps in preparation for removal but were allowed to remain at home. Bark was a businesswoman who was part owner of ferries and turnpikes. Property valuation and claims records indicate that Cherokee women in general held extensive personal property in the form of houses, horses, cattle, hogs, orchards, and crops of corn and wheat. Removal, however, reduced most to poverty by forcing the abandonment of their property to the Americans.

In stark contrast to Cherokee and other tribal women, Chickasaw women fared much better during removal. Chickasaw treaty negotiators during the removal period attempted to provide for the women of their Nation. The Treaty of Franklin of 1830, which was not ratified, provided for allotments preceding removal, granting widows with families and single individuals, including women, a quarter section of land in fee simple. The **Treaty of Pontotoc** in 1832 provided for allotments according to the number of people in households. These allotments ostensibly guaranteed the Chickasaws secure homes until they removed, at which time they would sell the land. Individual Chickasaws protected their personal property by a stipulation guaranteeing compensation for the improvements on their homesteads that they abandoned when they removed, and the money received at the sale of allotments was retained by the allotment owner. Although U.S. officials considered men to be the heads of households, it was the women who ultimately benefited most from the sale of allotments, for Chickasaw women were well known for protecting their property and caring for their children. Articles of agreement that amended the Treaty of Pontotoc in 1834 corrected some provisions of the earlier treaty regarding reservations, or parcels of land, for individuals. Orphan girls of 17 years old whose families did not provide for them and widows in similar condition were given reservations. Margaret Colbert Allen, wife of the subagent, and Mintahoyea, a widow of Levi **Colbert**, received special gifts of reservations under the agreement.

Implementation of the provisions of the agreement of 1834 establishing heads of household for the purpose of allotment threatened to dispossess many Chickasaw women. Government officials generally held that when a Chickasaw had two or more wives at the time of ratification of the Pontotoc treaty, the wives and their respective children were enrolled as one household with the husband at the head. The Chickasaw leaders protested that that was not the Chickasaw interpretation of "head of household." Their intent was to secure the rights of every Chickasaw family, without exception. The leaders argued that the Chickasaw should be allowed to determine what constituted a Chickasaw family according to Chickasaw customs and practices.

The rule that a man and all his wives and children constituted one family had dire economic implications for many Chickasaws. Under the American system, if a man died, his wife and children inherited his property. But what if there were more than one wife? Some Chickasaws had several wives who generally kept separate homes, usually distant from one another. Rarely, and only if they were sisters, did the wives live in the same house. The children claimed no relationship to their father's children by other wives but considered them, as the chiefs said, as strangers. In these various homes, a Chickasaw man often had more than 10 children. The example offered by the chiefs was the late Levi Colbert, who had several wives and about 20 children.

To the Chickasaw leaders, the several wives and their children did not constitute a single Chickasaw family. Matrimonial bonds between men and women were "slight," they said, "contracted without formality," and "dissolved at the pleasure of either party." Descent was always traced through the maternal line. The father was under no obligation to support his children, whose care and nurturing were exclusively the mother's duty. Upon her death, the father assumed no responsibility for the children; their care became the responsibility of the mother's female relatives. When the father died, whether he had one wife or more, the children did not inherit his property; instead, it went to his oldest collateral relatives, who often took it and left the wife and children with none of his property. It was an ancient and universal Chickasaw law, the leaders said, that the wife had a separate estate in all her property, whether she inherited it or acquired it, and she was at liberty to dispose of it in any way she chose.

The Mississippi courts recognized Chickasaw women's rights of property in the well-publicized Betsy Allen case. When Mrs. Allen died, her estate of personal property was extensive: horses, cattle, fowl, household furniture, dry goods, kitchenware, loom, tools, and slaves. In that case, the Mississippi court ruled that her husband's claim to her property was not valid.

Unlike the women of other tribes, who were destitute, Chickasaw women reached the West with much of their property. Some used the money they received for their allotments to buy household goods, even furniture, which they took with them. Whereas individuals of other tribes were limited to 30 pounds of private property, the Chickasaws, because they paid for their own removal, averaged 450 pounds each. In the West, Chickasaw women were considered wealthy, so much so that Chickasaw men became afraid that the Chickasaws would lose their national identity because so many Choctaw men sought wives among the Chickasaws because of their wealth.

Of course, Chickasaw women's experience regarding property was an exception to the general experience of most tribal women during the removal era. Although retaining their property was a feat in itself, given the circumstances, it could in no way mitigate the experience of removal they shared with other tribal people: oppression by white intrusion, destruction of tribal government, the decline of traditional social and economic practices, departure from traditional homelands, the rigors of removal trails, and the hardships of starting anew in an alien environment. *See also* **Indian Women's Roles and Removal**.

FURTHER READING: Hershberger, Mary. "Mobilizing Women, Anticipating Abolition: The Struggle against Indian Removal in the 1830s." *Journal of American History* 86, no. 1 (1999): 15–40; Miles, Tiya. "'Circular Reasoning': Recentering Cherokee Women in the Antiremoval Campaigns." *American Quarterly* 61, no. 2 (2009): 221–243; Paige, Amanda L. *Chickasaw Removal.* Ada, OK: Chickasaw Press, 2010; Perdue, Theda. "Cherokee Women and the Trail of Tears." *Journal of Women's History* 1, no. 1 (1989): 14–30; Perdue, Theda, and Michael D. Green. *The Cherokee Removal: A Brief History with Documents.* Boston: Bedford Books of St. Martin's Press, 1995; Pesantubbee, Michelene E. "Beyond Domesticity: Choctaw Women Negotiating the Tension between Choctaw Culture and Protestantism." *Journal of the American Academy of Religion* 67, no. 2 (1999): 387–409; Portnoy, Alisse. *Their Right to Speak: Women's Activism in the Indian and Slave Debates.* Cambridge, MA: Harvard University Press, 2005.

DANIEL F. LITTLEFIELD, JR.

Women's Roles and Removal

Understanding the role of women in Indian societies remains a challenge because of the lack of attention given to women by academics in the fields of history, sociology, and anthropology. The assumption that a European cultural model of patriarchy, relegating women to a socially inferior position, existed in Indian societies led to many misinterpretations of Indian women that are still seen in textbooks and the media.

The majority of tribes east of the Mississippi were matrilineal, meaning that the hereditary clan structure was passed through the female line. Furthermore, although the communities were matrilineal, they were also egalitarian. This egalitarianism allowed for a division of labor along gender lines but a social structure that required equity of power between men and women. In this way, the community maintained a balance between the genders based on equal respect for the jobs done, all of which were understood as necessary for survival.

Examples of powerful women are observed throughout the eastern tribes. Within the Iroquois Confederacy, the tribes often designated a woman as the head of each lineage who was chosen for her wisdom and diplomacy. The council of women for each tribe was then responsible for choosing male leaders as well as for organizing economic tasks such as growing and distributing food. In the event of the death of a male leader or a problematic male leader, the women advised as to replacement or removal. Settlers reported similar female council structures or powerful women throughout the eastern territories, referring to "queens" or "princesses" and commenting on their "ladies in waiting." Reports of these powerful women extended from Massachusetts to Virginia and down into Georgia. The designation of "queen" seems to have come from the fact that women were the holders of property and in charge of the planting and the distribution of food products. In many Indian societies, women held part or all of the property, and that property was kept in her lineage when she passed, handed from mother to daughter or son. If she had no children, property usually passed to her siblings.

Like the northeastern tribes, the southeastern tribes also had a matrilineal structure that gave the mother's clan responsibility for childrearing. Although the father of the child could be involved with childrearing, the decision-making process remained with the "blood relative," that is, the female bloodline, including her male relatives. Both men and women were allowed to divorce, but the property, with the exception of specific items, remained with the women. Polygamy was common in these areas, allowing for both men and women to have multiple partners as long as they maintained them equitably. Moreover, the men would not go to war without the advice and, more importantly, the consent of the women's councils.

Because of the ability to give life, the title of "Mother" was a designation of power, not one of sentimentality. The power of the "Mother" position can be seen in such titles as "Clan Mother," "Beloved Woman," and "Mother Earth." Because of the power associated with the position of mother and the female's spiritual and economic control, Indian women were respected and protected. The level of respect accounts for the low levels of violence toward females in the tribes and the extreme sanctions when violence occurred. Throughout the eastern tribes, violence against women was met with sanctions ranging from castration to death. In many accounts, the offender was required to "go over the hill": that is, given a chance to end his own life. If he did not, he was assisted. In many of these situations, it was the women's council that would carry out an execution.

Women's roles had begun to change well before removal as a result of such influences as Protestant missionary teachings, intermarriage with white men, the assumption of agricultural duties by men, the shrinking of tribal land bases, and the decline of communal farming impacted on women's roles. The removal process contributed to a continued and significant disruption of the egalitarian social structure. Since the American government refused to involve women in treaty negotiations and refused to recognize the economic power and property control of Indian women, negotiations were not done according to Indian cultural procedure. The refusal to give women a voice in the decision-making process created a situation that was alien to the tribes. Even when tribes attempted to put forward women's voices, as in the case of Nancy Ward in 1785 at Hopewell, they were ignored. In accordance with Western practices of coverture, the American political and social structure did not generally allow women to own property, and heredity was passed through the male line. This meant that when American laws were enforced on Indian tribes, property and power distribution were taken out of the hands of Indian women and placed completely in the hands of men, thus disrupting tribal structures. The government's failure to recognize the role of women in Indian society also created problems during the preparation of tribes for removal. Because treaty stipulations regarding per capita payments, heads of households, and family structures were paternalistic, the lists of households on rosters, which placed men at the head, left a false image of family structures.

The erosion of women's power and the American government designation of Indian women as an inferior gender created a power disruption in the tribes that allowed for an increase in violence against Indian women as well as an increase in poverty levels of Indian women and their children. In postremoval times, these trends continued and can be directly linked to the removal efforts. *See also* **Women during Removal**.

FURTHER READING: Anderson, Terry L., ed. *Property Rights and Indian Economies.* Lanham, MD: Rowman & Littlefield Publishers, 1992; Deer, Sarah, et al., eds. *Sharing Our Stories of Survival: Native Women Surviving Violence.* Lanham, MD: Altamira Press, 2008; Deloria, Vine, Jr., and Clifford M. Lytle. *American Indians, American Justice.* Austin: University of Texas Press, 1983; Mooney, James. *History, Myths, and Sacred Formulas of the Cherokees.* Ashville, NC: Historical Images, 1992; Smith, Andrea. *Conquest: Sexual Violence and American Indian Genocide.* Cambridge, MA: South End Press, 2005; Swanton, John R. *The Indians of the Southeastern United States.* Washington, DC: Smithsonian Institution Press, 1979.

LAVONNA LOVERN

Worcester, Samuel A. (1798–1859)

Samuel Austin Worcester, one in a long line of clergymen, was born on January 19, 1798, in Worcester, Massachusetts, the son of Elizabeth Hopkins and Leonard Worcester, who had begun his adult life as a printer but later became a minister. After college, the younger Worcester enrolled in a seminary, where he continued his work with languages as well as studied theology. When he was ordained on August 25, 1825, the newly married Worcester with his wife Ann set out for the Cherokee Nation as a missionary for the American Board of Commissioners for Foreign Missions (ABCFM), a Congregationalist organization. Once he arrived, he was to remain with the Cherokees for the rest of his life as missionary and teacher; like Evan **Jones**, he was a figure in the political history of the tribe as well, including removal.

As a Christian proselytizer and pastor, Worcester was intensely interested in using the Cherokee language as a means for reaching new and prospective converts. Accordingly, he tried to learn Cherokee, enlisting the help of several young men of the tribe. Elias **Boudinot** assisted him in this, and the two worked to bring a printing press to the Cherokee Nation. Boudinot was interested in publishing a newspaper that would carry the Cherokees' message to the cities of the eastern seaboard, communicating the idea that the nation was a civilized one and as such should not be subjected to removal from its ancestral lands. Once the *Cherokee Phoenix* appeared in 1828 in Philadelphia, New York, Boston, and Washington, both its physical reality and the words on its pages, printed in both Cherokee and English, proclaimed this to be true. Worcester used the press as well to turn out religious documents in the Cherokee syllabary, including translations of the Bible and other tracts. Worcester's association with Boudinot earned him the reputation of a man determined to vigorously support the Cherokees' stand against removal.

In general, individual missionaries followed their boards' stances on the question of removal. The ABCFM was against removal in general because the majority of its members belonged to the **Whig Party**, and as such opposed the Democrat Andrew **Jackson**. More to the point, the board opposed removal because it was counter to the civilization policy that had been followed since at least James Monroe's presidency and that underpinned the missionary movement to the Indians. Once the **Indian Removal Act** was passed, this fact was driven home by two actions by Jackson. First was an executive order that ended payments to missionaries under the Education Fund, a major source of funding. Second, Jackson altered the method of payment for funds due to the tribes; instead of paying the tribal entities, which then might divert some of the funds to missionaries, Jackson's new policy was to make direct per capita payments to individuals. Thus, the removal effort was both a theoretical and a practical threat to missions to the Indians. In 1830, the ABCFM tried to garner public support against removal by organizing rallies in eastern cities to oppose Jackson and his policy.

Worcester agreed with the ABCFM's anti-removal position and took steps himself to oppose Jackson. In 1830, he welcomed a gathering of missionaries to his home in New Echota, including 12 pastors from four denominations. Evan Jones and Daniel S. **Butrick** were among the group who wrote and signed a manifesto, citing eight arguments against the policy. This strong statement was published in the *Cherokee Phoenix*, which by now had a substantial readership in the eastern cities, as well as in the *Missionary Herald*, a widely read publication in Protestant circles.

Worcester was a principal in an important Supreme Court case, ***Worcester v. Georgia***, which pitted Cherokee sovereignty against the jurisdiction of the state of Georgia. In 1829 and 1830, Georgia passed laws that assigned Cherokee lands to Georgia counties, declared all Cherokee laws extinct, and replaced them with Georgia law. In addition, the state enacted a law that required all white persons living within the confines of the Cherokee Nation to apply to the state for a license to do so. Failure to comply was punishable by a prison term of four years at hard labor. When Worcester and missionary Elizur Butler refused to apply for a license, they were arrested, sentenced under Georgia law, and sent to the state penitentiary. A writ of error was filed with the U.S. Supreme Court, which had ruled against the state earlier in ***Cherokee Nation v. Georgia***. In that case, John Marshall's Court had avoided the constitutional question by ruling that the Court had no jurisdiction and that the Cherokee Nation was not a foreign nation under the language of the Constitution. However, in *Worcester v. Georgia,* the Court ruled that the Georgia law in question was null and void.

Georgia did not release the missionaries, however, relying on the fact that Andrew Jackson agreed with the state and not the Court. Jackson, they knew, was concerned about the **nullification** issue and feared that Georgia would use this decision to insist on the primacy of state law over federal law.

Searching for a compromise, Jackson suggested to Georgia's governor that he pardon Worcester and Butler, thus avoiding the basic question but removing the immediate source of the difficulty. The governor agreed, and the missionaries, after a dismal year in prison, accepted. Both Jackson and the state government of Georgia were confident of their success in the long run, however, because by this time, Congress had passed the Indian Removal Act. The long history of the Cherokee Nation in the southeastern United States was coming to an end.

In the days leading up to removal after the **Treaty of New Echota**, Worcester's reputation suffered as a result of his close association with Boudinot. However, he remained with the Nation and removed early with the Treaty Party followers to **Indian Territory**, setting up his mission in Park Hill, just outside Tahlequah, the Cherokee capital. The Congregationalists' standing in the Cherokee Nation was damaged further by the appointment of Boudinot as a lay missionary in the West. Boudinot was assassinated near the mission in 1839. At Park Hill, Worcester continued the translation and publishing work he had started in the eastern Nation and died there in 1859.

FURTHER READING: Bass, Athea. *Cherokee Messenger.* Norman: University of Oklahoma Press, 1936; McLoughlin, William C. *The Cherokees and Christianity, 1794–1870: Essays on Acculturation and Cultural Persistence.* Athens: University of Georgia Press, 1994; McLoughlin, William C. *Cherokees and Missionaries, 1789–1839.* New Haven, CT: Yale University Press, 1984.

JAMES W. PARINS

Worcester v. Georgia (1832)

In the 1802 Compact between Georgia and the United States, Georgia had ceded its western lands, and the United States had agreed to extinguish Indian title in lands within the boundaries of Georgia. The extinguishment had not happened, so Georgia passed laws in 1829 and 1830 that divided the Cherokee land among the surrounding Georgia counties; declared that all Cherokee laws, judgments, and governing decisions were null and void; and extended Georgia law over the Cherokee territory. The Georgia legislature did this knowing that President Andrew **Jackson** believed that Indians should either be removed west of the Mississippi River or be subject to state law. The Georgia laws also required that white persons living within the Cherokee Nation without a license from the governor of Georgia were guilty of a high misdemeanor and would be punished by confinement and hard labor at the state penitentiary for a term not less than four years. Georgia was trying to evict the missionaries who encouraged the Indians against removal.

Samuel **Worcester** was a Vermont citizen who was a missionary with the American Board of Commissioners for Foreign Missions. He was living in New Echota, the capital of the Cherokee Nation, with the permission of the United States and the Cherokees. Worcester was arrested, charged in the local Georgia county court, and found guilty of being on Cherokee land without a license. He argued that he had received permission from the president and from the Cherokees, and that Georgia could not pass such laws, as they were all in violation of treaties between the Cherokees and the United States. However, he was sentenced to four years of hard labor.

Worcester was offered a pardon, but he wanted to test the legality of the laws. A writ of error was issued by the U.S. Supreme Court for the case to appear before it. Unlike in *Cherokee Nation v. Georgia*, here it was clear that the Supreme Court had jurisdiction, and Cherokees were eager to have the Court address the merits of this case because four justices in *Cherokee Nation v. Georgia* had found that the Cherokees maintained tribal sovereignty. Georgia did not appear in court to represent its position, and it was unclear whether Georgia would follow the Court's decision.

The Supreme Court, under Chief Justice John Marshall, framed the issue as whether the Georgia laws were consistent with, or repugnant to, the Constitution, laws, and treaties of the United States. Marshall reviewed the entire history of European discovery and of interactions between Indians, European nations, and the United States. After examining the provisions of the various treaties that the Cherokees had signed with the United States, he found that the Cherokees had not given up their right to self-governance by accepting the protection of a stronger nation. Only the federal government could change the terms of the agreements with the Cherokees. He stated the following:

> The Cherokee nation, then, is a distinct community occupying its own territory, with boundaries accurately described, in which the laws of Georgia can have no force, and which the citizens of Georgia have no right to enter, but with the assent of the Cherokees themselves, or in conformity with treaties, and with the acts of congress. The whole intercourse between the United States and this nation, is, by our constitution and laws, vested in the government of the United States.

The Court accepted the Cherokees' argument. It found that the Georgia laws were void, and therefore the judgment against Worcester was annulled. This case recognized the sovereignty of the Cherokee nation and the primacy of the federal government in dealing with Indians.

The Court issued a special mandate ordering the release of Worcester, but it needed a further order to be enforced, as Georgia refused to comply voluntarily. The Judiciary Act of 1789, which governed court procedure, was deficient. The Court had adjourned, but there was no provision made for the enforcement of the mandate. Nothing could be done until the Court reconvened the following January.

President Jackson urged the Georgia governor to pardon Worcester in order to resolve the issue without federal intervention. This time, Worcester accepted the pardon. Although Jackson believed the Indians would have to remove, he was concerned about maintaining the supremacy of the Constitution, and also concerned about evolving states' rights and **nullification** movements, which could expand if the federal government had to enforce the order against Georgia.

The common tale is that Jackson allegedly said, "John Marshall has made his decision, now let him enforce it." There is no actual proof of this statement. The Cherokees won the case and were recognized as having sovereignty. But it did not stop them from being removed.

FURTHER READING: Berutti, Ronald A. "The Cherokee Case: The Fight to Save the Supreme Court and the Cherokee Indians." *American Indian Law Review* 17 (1992): 291–308; Garrison, Tim Alan. *The Legal Ideology of Removal: The Southern Judiciary and the Sovereignty of Native American Nations.* Athens: University of Georgia Press, 2002; Norgren, Jill. "Lawyers and the Legal Business of the Cherokee Republic in Courts of the United States, 1829–1835." *Law and History Review* 10 (1992): 253–314; Swindler, William F. "Politics as Law: The Cherokee Cases." *American Indian Law Review* 3 (1975): 7–20; *Worcester v. Georgia.* 31 U.S. (6 Pet.) 515 (1832).

JILL E. MARTIN

Wyandot Removal

One of the last Native communities to remove from the state of Ohio, the Wyandots living in Crawford County relocated to their new home at the confluence of the Kansas and Missouri rivers in the summer of 1843. Approximately 670 men, women, and children made the journey under the auspices of a treaty signed in 1842 at their council house in Upper Sandusky. This treaty and the subsequent removal occurred after years of attempts by Wyandot leaders to resist the pressure from local, state, and federal officials to leave Ohio.

In the two decades before they signed the treaty at Upper Sandusky, the Wyandots were under pressure from a number of external forces that called for their relocation west of the Mississippi River. The federal government encouraged treaty commissioners to promote removal in the region, and from the late 1810s to the early 1830s, most of the Delawares had relocated west and the Shawnees living in the villages of Lewistown, Hog Creek, and Wapakoneta had signed treaties and joined their relatives in the western territories. State and local officials also wanted the Wyandots to cede their lands and remove.

After scouting parties in 1831 and 1834 rejected land allocated for them in the West, a final western exploration in 1839 illustrated the divisions within the Wyandot community over removal. Three members of that expedition now favored a move west, but the other three resisted. This vote was also a reflection of the growing division within the community based on religion. The first Methodist missionary to the Wyandots had arrived in 1816, and by the late 1830s, several hundred Indians had become converts. By the early 1840s, most of those Christian converts supported staying in Ohio, while the majority of the so-called Pagan Party favored removal.

In the 1830s, Wyandot leaders had signed two different land cession treaties with the United States. The first of these, signed in 1832, ceded all

16,000 acres of the Big Spring reservation in Crawford County. The second treaty, signed in 1836, ceded a five-mile tract of land from the eastern end of their reservation in Upper Sandusky. Neither treaty indicated a desire to move west, although the 1832 pact did note that the Big Spring band of Wyandots might relocate to Canada or to the Wyandot villages along the Huron River in southern Michigan.

But the federal government increased the pressure on the Wyandots in the early 1840s. Negotiations between the Indians and government officials illustrated a growing frustration with the effects of white encroachment and settlement in their region. The most dramatic incident had occurred in early December 1840, when three white men killed their principal chief Summundowat and two others, only to have the charges dismissed.

The final removal treaty was concluded on March 17, 1842. It ceded all Wyandot lands in Ohio and southern Michigan in exchange for 148,000 acres west of the Mississippi River. In addition, the Wyandots would receive a perpetual annuity of $17,500 and would receive money for their property left behind once they removed west.

Preparations for removal began shortly after the treaty was ratified, but it was not until the late spring and early summer of 1843 that the Wyandots were ready to leave. Wyandots from the Huron River in Michigan arrived in Upper Sandusky in early March to join the emigrant parties headed west. From April through June 1843, the Wyandots prepared for removal by selling property they could not take with them and packing the goods they could carry. A small group of Wyandots, including George I. Clark and Silas Armstrong, traveled ahead of the main emigration to prepare for their arrival in the town of Westport, located along the Missouri River on the western border of Missouri.

The emigrant train left Upper Sandusky on July 12, 1843. Their itinerary first took them on wagons to Cincinnati, a journey that lasted only seven days. On July 21, the Wyandots boarded two different steamboats, the *Nodoway* and the *Republic*, and began their descent down the Ohio River to St. Louis. The trip to St. Louis was accomplished in short order, and the Wyandots soon boarded two different boats to make the final journey from St. Louis to Westport. Less than three weeks after leaving Sandusky, the Wyandots had traveled more than 1,000 miles and arrived in the western territories.

Although the removal occurred without a tremendous amount of difficulty, the Wyandots confronted substantial obstacles when it came to establishing their new homes. Despite the terms laid out in the 1842 treaty, the federal government was unable to provide the Wyandots with the land promised in that accord. Moreover, the Wyandots initially were unable to secure any land through negotiations with the neighboring Delawares and Shawnees. As a result, from the late summer through the fall of 1843, they made a temporary home on the east bank of the Kansas River. The new climate and the unsettled nature of their living conditions contributed to the dislocation of removal, creating a deadly set of circumstances. In the first several months at their temporary quarters, approximately 100 Wyandots died. One measles epidemic in particular took the lives of many young children.

Not until mid-December did the Wyandots finally reach an agreement with the Delawares to secure a land for their people. The terms included 39 sections of land encompassing nearly 25,000 acres for the price of $46,080. The Wyandots would pay most of this amount over the next 10 years. In 1848, the U.S. government officially acknowledged this independent agreement between the Delaware and Wyandot leaders.

Those Wyandots who survived the first few months of hardship and the winter that followed succeeded in building a stable new home for their community. They cleared land for farming purposes and built structures to house a blacksmith shop, a schoolhouse, and a Methodist church. Some of the wealthier men, like William Walker and his brothers Matthew and Joel, became businessmen and real estate investors in the state of Missouri just across the Kansas River. Just over a decade after their removal, however, the Wyandots would once again face American expansion with the passage of the Kansas-Nebraska Act in 1854. In 1855, Wyandot leaders signed a treaty that provided for both allotment and citizenship for members of their Nation. Although many struggled to hold on to their lands in what became the town of Kansas City, Kansas, most Wyandots once again relocated in the late 1860s and early 1870s to **Indian Territory**.

FURTHER READING: Bowes, John P. *Exiles and Pioneers: Eastern Indians in the Trans-Mississippi West.* New York: Cambridge University Press, 2007; Klopfenstein, Carl G. "The Removal of the Wyandots from Ohio." *Ohio Historical Quarterly* 66 (1957): 119–136; Norwood, Frederick. "Strangers in a Strange Land: Removal of the Wyandot Indians." *Methodist History* 13 (1975): 45–60; Smith, Dwight L. "An Unsuccessful Negotiation for Removal of the Wyandot Indians from Ohio, 1834." *Ohio Archaeological and Historical Quarterly* 58 (1949): 305–331; "Treaty with the Wyandot, 1832." Indian Affairs: Laws and Treaties. At http://digital.library.okstate.edu/kappler/Vol2/treaties/wya0339.htm.

JOHN P. BOWES

ANNOTATED BIBLIOGRAPHY

Secondary Sources

Akers, Donna L. "Removing the Heart of the Choctaw People: Indian Removal from a Native Perspective." *American Indian Culture and Research Journal* 23, no. 3 (1999): 63–76. Akers examines Choctaw removal from a Choctaw perspective.

Anderson, Gary Clayton. "The Removal of the Mdewakaton Dakota in 1837: A Case for Jacksonian Paternalism." *South Dakota History* 10, no. 4 (1980): 310–333. This article details the events leading up to and following the 1837 Mdewakaton Dakota removal.

Anson, Bert. "Chief Francis Lafontaine and the Miami Emigration from Indiana." *Indiana Magazine of History* 60, no. 3 (1964): 241–268.

Anson, Bert. "Variations of the Indian Conflict: The Effects of the Emigrant Indian Removal Policy, 1830–1854." *Missouri Historical Review* 59, no. 1 (1964): 64–89. Anson gives an overview of Indian removal policy and its effects on the removed Indians.

Berry, Kate, and Melissa A. Rinehart. "A Legacy of Forced Migration: The Removal of the Miami Tribe in 1846." *International Journal of Population Geography* 9, no. 2 (2003): 93–112. Looks at the immediate and long-term effects of removal on the Miamis.

Berthrong, Donald J. "John Beach and the Removal of the Sauk and Fox from Iowa." *Iowa Journal of History* 54 (1956): 313–354. Berthrong focuses on politics and white pressure for the removal of the Sauks and Foxes from Iowa after 1840.

Blais, M. Jeanne. "The Imposing Alliance: Jackson, Georgia, and Indian Removal, 1825–1832." *Indian Historian* 8 (Winter 1975): 47–53. The alliance between President Jackson and Governor Lumpkin aided removal of Georgia's Indians.

Bollwerk, Elizabeth. "Controlling Acculturation: A Potawatomi Strategy for Avoiding Removal." *Midcontinental Journal of Archaeology* 31, no. 1 (2006): 117–141. Well-written article examining the Potawatomi bands' differing resistance to removal; uses archaeological evidence at three removal-era sites.

Bolton, S. Charles. "Jeffersonian Indian Removal and the Emergence of Arkansas Territory." *Arkansas Historical Quarterly* 62, no. 3 (2003): 253–271. Well-written article on Jeffersonian removal policy and how it shaped Arkansas Territory.

Bragaw, Stephen G. "Thomas Jefferson and the American Indian Nations: Native American Sovereignty and the Marshall Court." *Journal of Supreme Court History* 31, no. 2 (2006): 155–180. Bragaw's article is a well-written history of Jeffersonian removal's influence on Jacksonian removal policy and the Marshall Court.

Burke, Joseph C. "The Cherokee Cases: A Study in Law, Politics, and Morality." *Stanford Law Review* 21, no. 3 (1969): 500–531. A study of decision making in *Cherokee Nation v. Georgia* and *Worcester v. Georgia*, in which the judges considered politics and morality as well as law in their landmark rulings.

Carson, James T. "State Rights and Indian Removal in Mississippi, 1817–1835." *Journal of Mississippi History* 57, no. 1 (1995): 25–41. Chronicles the growth of the states' rights movement among Mississippi politicians and its effects on the Choctaws and Chickasaws.

Cave, Alfred A. "Abuse of Power: Andrew Jackson and the Indian Removal Act of 1830." *Historian* 65, no. 6 (2003): 1330–1353. Examines the Indian Removal Act and how Jackson abused presidential power in carrying out the act.

Clark, Carter Blue. "'Drove Off like Dogs'—Creek Removal." In *Indians of the Lower South: Past and Present*. Ed. John K. Mahon. Pensacola, FL: Gulf Coast History and Humanities Conference, 1975, pp. 118–124. A brief account of the inhumane treatment of the Creeks as a result of Jacksonian removal policy.

Clifton, James A. "The Post-Removal Aftermath." In *The Historic Indian in Ohio*. Ed. Randall Buchman. Columbus: Ohio Historical Society, 1976, pp. 38–46. A good examination of Ohio Indians in the postremoval period.

Cooke, Sarah E., et al. *Indians and a Changing Frontier: The Art of George Winter*. Indianapolis: Indiana Historical Society, 1993. George Winter, painter, was an eyewitness to removal of northern tribes in the 1830s.

Corn, James F. "Conscience or Duty: General John E. Wool's Dilemma with Cherokee Removal." *Journal of Cherokee Studies* 3 (Winter 1978): 35–39. Gen. John E. Wool's humane treatment of the Cherokees angered superiors and local whites, leading to a court of inquiry hearing.

Covington, James W. "Billy Bowlegs, Sam Jones, and the Crisis of 1849." *Florida Historical Quarterly* 58, no. 3 (1990): 299–311. The author uses the delivery of prisoners to the United States for punishment to argue that it was Sam Jones, not Bowlegs, who was the leading authority among the Florida Indians.

Covington, James W. "An Episode in the Third Seminole War." *Florida Historical Quarterly* 45, no. 1 (1966): 45–59. Analyzes the role of the Florida militia in the Third Seminole War.

Covington, James W. *The Seminoles of Florida*. Gainesville: University Press of Florida, 1993. The best comprehensive study of the Florida Indians during the pre-removal, removal, and postremoval eras.

Cutter, Donald C. "President Andrew Jackson and the West." *Journal of the West* 31, no. 3 (1992): 38–43. An overview of President Jackson and his western policy, including American Indians and removal.

DeRosier, Arthur H., Jr. "The Choctaw Removal of 1831: A Civilian Effort." *Journal of the West* 6, no. 2 (1967): 237–247. The focus is on challenging the commonly held view that Choctaw civilian agents treated Indians inhumanely.

DeRosier, Arthur H., Jr. "Myths and Realities in Indian Westward Removal: The Choctaw Example." In *Four Centuries of Southern Indians*. Ed. Charles M. Hudson. Athens: University of Georgia Press, 1975, pp. 83–100. Challenges traditional views of Choctaw removal, correcting the myths presented in school textbooks by detailing the reality of Choctaw removal.

DeRosier, Arthur H., Jr. *The Removal of the Choctaw Indians*. Knoxville: University of Tennessee Press, 1970. The most detailed and comprehensive history of Choctaw removal.

Duffield, Lathel F. "Cherokee Emigration: Reconstructing Reality." *Chronicles of Oklahoma* 80, no. 3 (2002): 314–347. Analyzes historical treatments that romanticize removal and challenges scholars to go back to the original documents to create a new interpretation of events.

Edmunds, R. David. "Potawatomis in the Platte Country: An Indian Removal Incomplete." *Missouri Historical Review* 68, no. 4 (1974): 375–392. Lack of communication and planning turned the settlement of the Potawatomis in Missouri into a temporary settlement.

Edmunds, R. David. "The Prairie Potawatomi Removal of 1833." *Indiana Magazine of History* 68, no. 3 (1972): 240–253. Prairie Potawatomi removal from Indiana to west of the Mississippi was hampered by a lack of planning.

Edwards, John Carver. "'Oh God the Horror of That Night Will Never Be Forgot': Ann Margaret McCall and the Creek War of 1836." *Manuscripts* 28 (Spring 1976): 140–145.

Eisenhower, John S. D. *Agent of Destiny: The Life and Times of General Winfield Scott*. Norman: University of Oklahoma Press, 1997. An excellent study of Scott's life, providing good insights into his involvement in removal of the Sauks and Foxes, Seminoles, and Cherokees.

Ellenberg, George B. "An Uncivil War of Words: Indian Removal and the Press." *Atlanta History: A Journal of Georgia and the South* 33, no. 1 (1989): 48–59. Illustrates how four newspapers covered removal differently, based on location, with southern papers supporting Jacksonian removal policy.

Ellisor, John T. "'Like So Many Wolves': Creek Removal in the Cherokee Country, 1835–1838." *Journal of East Tennessee History* 71 (1999): 1–24. Presents the aftermath of the Treaty of Cusseta, which led to Creeks fleeing into Cherokee territory, from which they were removed into the West.

Evans, E. Raymond. "Fort Marr Blockhouse: The Last Evidence of America's First Concentration Camps." *Journal of Cherokee Studies* 2 (Spring 1977): 256–263. Presents history of the Fort Marr blockhouse, used to confine Cherokees prior to removal west.

Fabin, W. W. "Indians of the Tri-State Area, the Potawatomis, the Removal." *Northwest Ohio Quarterly* 40, no. 2 (1968): 68–84. Focuses on later Potawatomi removals after the 1836 treaty, a process that lasted for years.

Finger, John R. "The Saga of Tsali: Legend versus Reality." *North Carolina Historical Review* 56, no. 1 (1979): 1–18. A well-researched article that challenges the legend of Tsali using historical evidence to point out inaccuracies.

Foreman, Grant. *Indian Removal: The Emigration of the Five Civilized Tribes of Indians*. Norman: University of Oklahoma Press, 1989. A detailed but dated study of the removal of the large southeastern tribes, but still the most comprehensive study of the removal of the Creeks, Seminoles, and Cherokees.

Foreman, Grant. *Last Trek of the Indians.* New York: Russell & Russell, 1972. Deals primarily with tribes of the Midwest and Northwest.

Fritz, Henry E. "Humanitarian Rhetoric and Andrew Jackson's Indian Removal Policy." *Chronicles of Oklahoma* 79, no. 1 (2001): 62–91. Examines Andrew Jackson's rhetoric and its relation to his Indian removal policy.

Garrison, Tim Alan. "Beyond 'Worcester': The Alabama Supreme Court and the Sovereignty of the Creek Nation." *Journal of the Early Republic* 19, no. 3 (1999): 423–450. As *Worcester* remained unenforced, Alabama expansionists used the state supreme court to force Indian removal in their state.

Gibson, Arrell Morgan, ed. *America's Exiles: Indian Colonization in Oklahoma.* Oklahoma City: Oklahoma Historical Society, 1976. Reprint of *Chronicles of Oklahoma* 54 (Spring 1976), presenting an overview of Indian removal into Oklahoma, emphasizing the Five Civilized Tribes' experiences.

Gibson, Arrell Morgan. "The Great Plains as a Colonization Zone for Eastern Indians." In *Ethnicity on the Great Plains.* Ed. Frederick C. Leubke. Lincoln: University of Nebraska Press, 1980, pp. 19–37. Analyzes removal of eastern Indians to the Great Plains and the conflicts that arose with whites who wanted their new lands.

Goodyear, Frank H., III. "'Nature's Most Beautiful Models': George Catlin's Choctaw Ball-Play Paintings and the Politics of Indian Removal." *International Journal of the History of Sport* 23, no. 2 (2006): 138–153. Examines Catlin's paintings of Choctaw ball play in the context of Indian removal and how it marginalized Choctaw suffering as a result of Indian removal.

Gray, Susan E. "Limits and Possibilities: White-Indian Relations in Western Michigan in the Era of Removal." *Michigan Historical Review* 20, no. 2 (1994): 71–91. Analyzes the relationship between whites and Potawatomis in Michigan during the removal period.

Green, Michael D. *The Politics of Indian Removal: Creek Government and Society in Crisis.* Lincoln: University of Nebraska Press, 1985. An excellent study of Creek and national politics before the Creek forced removal, necessary for those seeking an understanding of Georgia's successful efforts to remove the last of the Creeks from within its borders.

Grinde, Donald. "Cherokee Removal and American Politics." *Indian Historian* 8 (Summer 1978): 32–42, 56. Brief explanation of the politics and policies influencing Cherokee removal.

Hauptman, Laurence M., and Gordon L. McLester, eds. *The Oneida Indian Journey: From New York to Wisconsin, 1784–1860.* Madison: University of Wisconsin Press, 1999. An excellent collection of essays on Oneida removals by good scholars and Oneida historians.

Hershberger, Mary. "Mobilizing Women, Anticipating Abolition: The Struggle against Indian Removal in the 1830s." *Journal of American History* 86, no. 1 (1999): 15–40. Analyzes the organized opposition to Indian removal by a national women's petition drive in 1829 and its effect on the debate on the Indian Removal Act.

Horseman, Reginald. *The Origin of Indian Removal.* East Lansing: Michigan State University Press, 1970. Provides background on the development of removal as national Indian policy.

Huber, Donald L. "White, Red, and Black: The Wyandot Mission at Upper Sandusky." *Timeline* 13, no. 3 (1996): 2–17. A history of the Wyandot Mission, including the role it played in removal.

Indiana Historical Society. *The Journals and Indian Paintings of George Winter 1837–1839.* Indianapolis: Indiana Historical Society, 1948. Selected paintings and journals kept by George Winter, including those related to removal.

Jahoda, Gloria. *The Trail of Tears.* New York: Holt, Rinehart and Winston, 1975. A popularized treatment of the application of removal policy to tribes east of the Mississippi River.

Kelleher, Michael. "The Removal of the Southeastern Indians: Historians Respond to the 1960s and the Trail of Tears." *Chronicles of Oklahoma* 78, no. 3 (2000): 346–353. Political and cultural changes in the 1960s influenced historians to renew research into Indian issues, including removal.

Keller, Christian B. "Philanthropy Betrayed: Thomas Jefferson, the Louisiana Purchase, and the Origins of Federal Indian Removal Policy." *Proceedings of the American Philosophical Society* 144, no. 1 (2000): 39–66. Traces the development and ultimate failure of Thomas Jefferson's philanthropic removal policy.

Keller, Robert H., Jr. "The Chippewa Treaties of 1826 and 1836." *American Indian Journal* 9, no. 3 (1986): 27–32. Discusses the Chippewa Treaties of 1826 and 1836, including historical background on the treaties and the efforts to resist removal.

Kern, Kevin. "It Is by Industry or Extinction That the Problem of Their Destiny Must Be Solved: The Wyandots and Removal to Kansas." *Northwest Ohio History* 75, no. 2 (2004): 160–168. Argues that the Wyandots suffered less than other tribes in their removal; however, their successful assimilation into white society led to the tribe's dissolution.

Kersey, Harry A., Jr. "The Cherokee, Creek, and Seminole Responses to Removal: A Comparison." In *Indians of the Lower South: Past and Present.* Ed. John K. Mahon. Pensacola, FL: Gulf Coast History and Humanities Conference, 1975, pp. 112–117. A brief survey that looks comparatively at Cherokee legal tactics, Creek national despair, and Seminole armed resistance as responses to Indian removal.

Klopfenstein, Carl G. "The Removal of the Indians from Ohio." In *The Historic Indian in Ohio.* Ed. Randall Buchman. Columbus: Ohio Historical Society, 1976, pp. 28–38. Provides a history of Ohio Indian land cessions and treaties leading up to removal as well as the removal of the Ohio Indians to the West.

Klopfenstein, Carl G. "The Removal of the Wyandots from Ohio." *Ohio Historical Quarterly* 66, no. 2 (1957): 119–136. Demonstrates how the Wyandots resisted removal west but finally removed in 1845.

Klopfenstein, Carl G. "Westward Ho: Removal of the Ohio Shawnees, 1832–1833." *Bulletin of the Historical and Philosophical Society of Ohio* 15, no. 1 (1957): 3–31. Excellent history of Shawnee removal from their unification in Ohio to their final removal west as a result of the 1830 Indian Removal Act.

Lankford, George E. "Trouble at Dancing Rabbit Creek: Missionaries and Choctaw Removal." *Journal of Presbyterian History* 62 (1968): 51–66. Treats U.S. expulsion of two missionaries to the Choctaws during the 1830 treaty negotiations setting into motion Choctaw removal west.

Lass, William E. "The Removal from Minnesota of the Sioux and Winnebago Indians." *Minnesota History* 38, no. 8 (1963): 353–364. Chronicles the removal of the Sioux and Winnebagos from Minnesota, including accounts by accompanying missionaries.

Littlefield, Daniel F., Jr. *The John Drew Detachment.* Resources on Indian Removal No. 2. Little Rock: Sequoyah Research Center, 2006. Historical account of John Ross's removal to the West in 1838–1839.

Littlefield, Daniel F., Jr. *Removal Muster Rolls, Rosters, and Lists.* Resources on Indian Removal No. 1. Little Rock: Sequoyah Research Center, 2006. A bibliography of rolls, rosters, and lists of Choctaws, Muscogees (Creeks), Chickasaws, Seminoles, and Cherokees who removed or were sent to the West.

Loos, John L. "William Clark: Indian Agent." *Kansas Quarterly* 3, no. 4 (1971): 29–38. An account of the life of Indian agent William Clark, who helped carry out the Indian Removal Act of 1830.

Mahan, Bruce. "Moving the Winnebago." *The Palimpsest* 3, no. 2 (1922): 33–52. Discusses the relocation of Iowa Winnebagos west of the Mississippi and the difficulties they faced.

Mahon, John K. *History of the Second Seminole War, 1835–1842.* Gainesville: University Press of Florida, 1967. The most detailed and authoritative study of the Second Seminole War.

Manzo, Joseph T. "Emigrant Indian Objections to Kansas Residence." *Kansas History* 4, no. 4 (1981): 246–254. Demonstrates how emigrating Indians had concerns regarding the new lands in Kansas they were removing to, including the inhospitable environment and new neighboring tribes.

McClurken, James M. "Ottawa Adaptive Strategies to Indian Removal." *Michigan Historical Review* 12, no. 1 (1986): 29–55. Demonstrates how the Jackson and Van Buren administrations tried to press Ottawa removal and how the Ottawas were able to resist removal by becoming landowners and an important part of the local economy.

McLoughlin, William G. "Georgia's Role in Instigating Compulsory Indian Removal." *Georgia Historical Quarterly* 70, no. 4 (1986): 605–632. Places removal in the context of Georgia's view of removal as a states' rights issue and its determination to control all land within its boundaries.

McLoughlin, William G. "The Murder Trial of the Reverend Evan Jones, Baptist Missionary to the Cherokee in North Carolina, 1833." *North Carolina Historical Review* 62, no. 2 (1985): 157–178. Chronicles how anti-removal missionary Evan Jones faced murder charges brought up by whites who wanted Cherokee lands in Georgia.

McLoughlin, William G. "Thomas Jefferson and the Beginnings of Cherokee Nationalism, 1806 to 1809." *William & Mary Quarterly* 32, no. 4 (1975): 547–580. Demonstrates how a threatened Indian removal led to the growth of Cherokee nationalism in the early 19th century.

Meyers, Jason. "No Idle Past: Uses of History in the 1830 Indian Removal Debates." *Historian* 63, no. 1 (2000): 53–65. Demonstrates how both sides of the Indian removal issue used history in debates over removal.

Miles, Tiya. "'Circular Reasoning': Recentering Cherokee Women in the Anti-removal Campaigns." *American Quarterly* 61, no. 2 (2009): 221–243. Recounts Cherokee women's active involvement in the anti-removal debate over a decade before Anglo women's political involvement.

Morris, Michael. "Georgia and the Conversation over Indian Removal." *Georgia Historical Quarterly* 91, no. 4 (2007): 403–423. Examines how Georgia officials helped shape the debate over Indian removal.

Neumeyer, Elizabeth. "Michigan Indians Battle against Removal." *Michigan History* 55, no. 4 (1971): 275–288. Demonstrates how only a small percentage of

Michigan Indians were removed because of the success Michigan Indians had in resisting removal.

Norgren, Jill L., and Petra T. Shattuck. "Limits of Legal Action: The Cherokee Cases." *American Indian Culture and Research Journal* 2, no. 2 (1978): 14–25. Examines the limitations of legal action to protect Indian sovereignty by using the 19th-century Cherokees as an example.

Norwood, Frederick A. "Strangers in a Strange Land: Removal of the Wyandot Indians." *Methodist History* 13, no. 3 (1975): 45–60. A history of the 1843 Wyandot removal from Ohio to the West and the role Methodists played in the removal.

Owens, Robert M. "Jean Baptiste Ducoigne, the Kaskaskias, and the Limits of Thomas Jefferson's Friendship." *Journal of Illinois History* 5, no. 2 (2002): 109–136. Demonstrates how the relationship between the Kaskaskia tribe and the federal government changed from Thomas Jefferson to Andrew Jackson.

Parsons, Lynn Hudson. "'A Perpetual Harrow upon My Feelings': John Quincy Adams and the American Indian." *New England Quarterly* 46, no. 3 (1973): 339–379. Analyzes John Quincy Adams's views on Indian policy, including removal, as it evolved over time.

Paulson, Howard W. "Federal Indian Policy and the Dakota Indians: 1800–1840." *South Dakota History* 3, no. 2 (1973): 285–309. Demonstrates how federal policy toward the Dakota Indians pushed them further westward in the early half of the 19th century.

Perdue, Theda. "Cherokee Women and the Trail of Tears." *Journal of Women's History* 1, no. 1 (1989): 14–30. Analyzes the role of Cherokee women in removal: their attitudes toward the policy, how it affected them, their experiences along the trail, and how they rebuilt their lives in the West.

Perdue, Theda. "The Conflict Within: The Cherokee Power Structure and Removal." *Georgia Historical Quarterly* 73, no. 3 (1989): 465–491. Analyzes the effects of political factionalism on Cherokee removal.

Perdue, Theda, and Michael D. Green. *The Cherokee Removal: A Brief History with Documents.* Boston: Bedford Books of St. Martin's Press, 1995. An excellent introductory study for students of Cherokee removal.

Porter, Kenneth W. "Billy Bowlegs (Holata Micco) in the Seminole Wars (Part I)." *Florida Historical Quarterly* 45, no. 3 (1967): 219–242. A detailed account of Bowlegs's role in events leading to the Third Seminole War and the last Seminole removal.

Porter, Kenneth W. *The Black Seminoles: History of a Freedom-Seeking People.* Rev. and ed. Alcione M. Amos and Thomas P. Senter. Gainesville: University Press of Florida, 1996. This posthumous study of African-descended people among the Seminoles is the most comprehensive to date.

Porter, Kenneth W. *The Negro on the American Frontier.* New York: Arno Press and the New York Times, 1971. A dated but still useful study of African-descended people and American Indians, with primary focus on the tribes of the Southeast.

Portnoy, Alisse. "'Female Petitioners Can Lawfully Be Heard': Negotiating Female Decorum, United States Politics, and Political Agency, 1829–1831." *Journal of the Early Republic* 23, no. 4 (2003): 573–610. Demonstrates how Catharine Beecher organized a national campaign of white women to petition against Indian removal.

Portnoy, Alisse. *Their Right to Speak: Women's Activism in the Indian and Slave Debates.* Cambridge, MA: Harvard University Press, 2005. Examines the role women played in debates over both Indian removal and abolitionism.

Prucha, Francis Paul. "Indian Removal and the Great American Desert." *Indiana Magazine of History* 59, no. 4 (1963): 299–322. Presents a pro-government view of the early debates regarding Indian removal to the Great American Desert.

Prucha, Francis Paul. "Protest by Petition: Jeremiah Evarts and the Cherokee Indians." *Proceedings of the Massachusetts Historical Society* 97 (1985): 42–58. Analyzes Evarts's role in the anti-removal political debates.

Remini, Robert V. *Andrew Jackson and His Indian Wars.* New York: Viking, 2001. An account of Jackson's Indian policy that is more apologetic of Jackson's role than most.

Satz, Ronald N. *American Indian Policy in the Jacksonian Era.* Lincoln: University of Nebraska Press, 1975. A balanced analysis of Andrew Jackson's Indian removal policy.

Satz, Ronald N. "Indian Policy in the Jacksonian Era: The Old Northwest as a Test Case." *Michigan History* 60, no. 1 (1975): 71–93. An examination of removal policy as it applied to the tribes of the Old Northwest.

Scherer, Mark R. "'Now Let Him Enforce It': Exploring the Myth of Andrew Jackson's Response to *Worcester v. Georgia* (1832)." *Chronicles of Oklahoma* 74, no. 1 (1996): 16–29. Examines the popular misconception regarding Jackson's words and argues that there were not only political but also legal reasons for his inaction regarding the Supreme Court's ruling.

Secunda, W. Ben. "To Cede or See? Risk and Identity among the Woodland Potawatomi during the Removal Period." *Midcontinental Journal of Archaeology* 31, no. 1 (2006): 57–88. Secunda examines removal-period Potawatomis and their split into bands, showing how some bands evaded removal whereas others did not.

Shriver, Phillip R. "Know Them No More Forever: The Miami Removal of 1846." *Timeline* 10, no. 6 (1993): 30–41. Excellent overview of Miami removal and how a small minority stayed in Ohio while the majority of the tribe removed west.

Smith, F. Todd. "After the Treaty of 1835: The United States and the Kadohadacho Indians." *Louisiana History* 30, no. 2 (1989): 157–172. Examines the Caddo removal treaty of 1835 and the aftereffects.

Stein, Gary C. "Indian Removal as Seen by European Travelers in America." *Chronicles of Oklahoma* 51, no. 4 (1974): 399–410. Discusses how Europeans traveling in the United States routinely criticized Indian removal and the American public's lack of criticism.

Stowe, Christopher S. "One Could Not but Feel Melancholy: Ohio Remembers the Wyandot." *Northwest Ohio History* 75, no. 2 (2004): 149–159. Recalls the 1843 Wyandot tribe's removal from Ohio, including Ohio newspaper coverage of the removal.

Strickland, William M. "The Rhetoric of Removal and the Trail of Tears: Cherokee Speaking against Jackson's Indian Removal Policy." *Southern Speech Communications Journal* 47, no. 3 (1982): 292–309. Illustrates how Cherokees spoke out against President Jackson's removal policy.

Stuart, Benjamin F. "Transportation of Pottawattomies: The Deportation of Menominee and His Tribe of the Pottawattomie Indians." *Indiana Magazine of History* 18, no. 3 (1922): 255–265. A sentimental account of the removal of Chief Menominee's band of Potawatomis.

Swindler, William F. "Politics as Law: The Cherokee Cases." *American Indian Law Review* 3, no. 1 (1975): 7–20. Examines the Marshall Court's handling of cases involving the Cherokee Nation and removal.

Syndergaard, Rex. "The Final Move of the Choctaws, 1825–1830." *Chronicles of Oklahoma* 52, no. 2 (1974): 207–219. Examines the policies behind the last removal of the Choctaws to the West.

Trennert, Robert A. "The Business of Indian Removal: Deporting the Potawatomi from Wisconsin, 1851." *Wisconsin Magazine of History* 63, no. 1 (1979): 36–50. Demonstrates how the Ewing family, contractors for Wisconsin Potawatomi removal, profited greatly in removal at the expense of the welfare of the Potawatomi.

Valone, Stephen J. "William Seward, Whig Politics, and the Compromised Indian Removal Policy in New York State, 1838–1843." *New York State History* 82, no. 2 (2001): 106–134.

Vipperman, Carl J. "'Forcibly if We Must': The Georgia Case for Cherokee Removal, 1802–1832." *Journal of Cherokee Studies* 3 (Spring 1978): 103–110. A study of the relationship between Georgia's arguments for claiming Cherokee lands in its borders and the earlier Yazoo Land Act.

Williams, David. "Gold Fever, the Cherokee Nation and the Closing of Georgia's 'Frontier.'" *Proceedings and Papers of the Georgia Association of Historians* 11, no. 2 (1990): 24–29. Analyzes a major event in Georgia's drive to rid the state of its Indian population.

Young, Mary. "The Exercise of Sovereignty in Cherokee Georgia." *Journal of the Early Republic* 10, no. 1 (1990): 43–63. An interesting analysis of the role of Georgians who opposed the prevailing sentiment for forcible eviction of the Cherokees and confiscation of their property.

Young, Mary. "Indian Removal and the Attack on Tribal Autonomy: The Cherokee Case." In *Indians of the Lower South: Past and Present.* Ed. John K. Mahon. Pensacola, FL: Gulf Coast History and Humanities Conference, 1975, pp. 125–142. A thoroughly documented analysis of the role of the federal government as well as Georgia in the destruction of the Cherokee Nation.

Young, Mary. "Indian Removal and Land Allotment: The Civilized Tribes and Jacksonian Justice." *American Historical Review* 64, no. 1 (1958): 31–45.

Young, Mary E. *Redskins, Ruffleshirts and Rednecks: Indian Allotments in Alabama and Mississippi, 1830–1860.* Norman: University of Oklahoma Press, 1961. The most authoritative study of fraud in Indian land sales in the Southeast.

Published Primary Sources

Journals

Foreman, Grant. "Journey of a Party of Cherokee Emigrants." *Mississippi Valley Historical Review* 18, no. 2 (1931): 232–245. Reprints the journal of occurrences kept by Dr. Clark Lillybridge during the removal of a contingent of Treaty Party Cherokees in 1837.

Indiana Historical Society. "Removal of Indians from Ohio: Dunihue Correspondence of 1832." *Indiana Magazine of History* 35, no. 4 (1939): 408–426. Reprints correspondence of the Dunihue family relating to removal of Indians from Lewistown, Ohio.

Litton, Gaston. "Journal of a Party of Emigrating Creek Indians, 1835–1836." *Journal of Southern History* 7, no. 2 (1941): 225–242. Edited transcription of the journal of occurrences kept by Dr. Clark Lillybridge during the removal of a party of Treaty Party Cherokees.

Oklahoma Chapter, Trail of Tears Association. *Cherokee Removal: The Journal of Reverend Daniel S. Butrick, May 19, 1838–April 1, 1839.* Park Hill: Oklahoma Chapter, Trail of Tears Association, 1998. An excellent source on conditions in the Cherokee preremoval holding camps; indispensable for the study of the Taylor contingent of removing Cherokees.

Polke, William. "Journal of an Emigrating Party of Pottawattomie Indians, 1838." *Indiana Magazine of History* 21, no. 4 (1925): 315–336. Reprints the journal kept by officials attending the Potawatomis on their 1838 trek from Twin Lakes, Indiana, to the Osage River in the western territory.

Polke, William. "Removal Journal Part I." *HowNiKan* 9, no. 6 (1987): 5, 7, 15. Reprints the journal kept during removal of Potawatomis from Twin Lakes, Indiana, to Kansas in 1838 on their infamous Trail of Death.

Polke, William. "Journal of Removal—Part II." *HowNiKan* 9, no. 7 (1987): 14–15. Reprints the journal kept during removal of Potawatomis from Twin Lakes, Indiana, to Kansas in 1838 on their infamous Trail of Death.

Proffit, George H. "Removal Journal—The Trail of Death." *HowNiKan* 9, no. 8 (1987): 6–8. Reprints the journal of emigration kept by Proffit during the removal of Potawatomis from near Monticello, Indiana, to Kansas in 1837.

Smith, Dwight L., ed. "The Attempted Potawatomie Removal of 1839." *Indian Magazine of History* 45, no. 1 (1949): 51–80. Reprints correspondence of William Polke regarding Potawatomi removal from Indiana.

Smith, Dwight L., ed. "Continuation of the Journal of an Emigrating Party of Potawatomie Indians, 1838 and Gen William Polke Manuscripts." *Indiana Magazine of History* 44, no. 4 (1948): 393–408. Journal chronicles events related to the Potawatomis after their arrival in Kansas, 1838.

Smith, Dwight L., ed. "Jacob Hull's Detachment of the Potawatomie Emigration of 1838." *Indiana Magazine of History* 45, no. 3 (1949): 285–288. Journal of occurrences of Potawatomis removing from Logansport, Indiana, to the Osage River in the western territory.

Winter, George. "George Winter Meets the Potawatomi." *HowNiKan* 8, no. 7 (1986): 6–7. Excerpts from Winter's journal during his summer 1837 visit to the Potawatomis of Indiana.

Winter, George. "George Winter's Journal, Part II." *HowNiKan* 8, no. 8 (1987): 6–7. Excerpts from Winter's journal during his summer 1837 visit to the Potawatomis in Indiana.

Letters and Other Writings

Boudinot, Elias. *Cherokee Editor: The Writings of Elias Boudinot.* Ed. Theda Perdue. Knoxville: University of Tennessee Press, 1983. Necessary for an understanding of Boudinot's role in the Cherokee removal.

King, Duane H., and E. Raymond Evans, eds. "The Trail of Tears: Primary Documents of the Cherokee Removal." *Journal of Cherokee Studies* 3 (Summer 1978): 131–185. A somewhat dated but still useful attempt to create a sourcebook on Cherokee removal.

Payne, John Howard. "The Cherokee Cause." *Journal of Cherokee Studies* 1 (Summer 1976): 17–22. Reprints the 1835 letter by John Howard Payne defending the Cherokee Indians against removal.

Ross, John. *The Papers of Chief John Ross.* 7 vols. Ed. Gary E. Moulton. Norman: University of Oklahoma Press, 1984. Contains Ross's letters and other documents covering the period 1807–1866; indispensable to any study of Cherokee removal.

Rozema, Vicki. *Voices from the Trail of Tears.* Winston-Salem, NC: John F. Blair, 2003. A collection of documents related to Cherokee removal.

Sturgis, Amy H. *The Trail of Tears and Indian Removal.* Westport, CT: Greenwood Press, 2007. A recent study and source book on Cherokee removal.

Whalen, Brett E., comp. "A Vermonter on the Trail of Tears, 1830–1837." *Vermont History* 66, nos. 1–2 (1998): 31–38.

Congressional Serial Set

Choctaw Indians, contracts for removal. H. Doc. 107. 27th Cong., 2nd sess. Serial 465. Proposals for subsistence for the Choctaws removing in 1840s.

Claims against the Pottawatomie Indians. Letter from the Secretary of War, transmitting the information called for by the resolution of the House of Representatives of the 11th ultimo, relating to the settlement of claims of citizens of the United States against the Pottawatomie Indians. H. Doc.143. 27th Cong., 2nd sess. Serial 403. Documents and letters regarding Potawatomi removal.

Correspondence on the Emigration of Indians, 1831–1833. S. Doc. 512 [5 vols.]. 23rd Cong., 1st sess. Serial 244–248. Correspondence related to all tribes who removed during the first few years after the Indian Removal Act.

Frauds upon Indians—Right of the President to withhold papers. H. Rept. 271. Serial 421. Information collected by Lt. Colonel Hitchcock during his investigation into removal subsistence fraud.

Letter from the Secretary of War, transmitting copies of the proceedings of a court of inquiry, convened at Frederick-town, in relation to the operations against the Seminole and Creek Indians, &c. H. Doc. 78 (25–2). Serial 323. Documents and evidence used in the court of inquiry against Generals Scott and Gaines.

Letter from the Secretary of War transmitting documents in relation to hostilities of Creek Indians. H. Doc. 276. 24th Cong., 1st sess. Serial 292. Correspondence and reports related to the so-called Creek War of 1836 and Creek removal; includes letters written by disbursing officers.

Message from the President of the United States, transmitting Information in relation to Alleged Frauds on the Creek Indians in the Sale of their Reservations. H. Doc. 452. 25th Cong., 2nd sess. Serial 331. Contains documents and testimony regarding fraud committed against the Creeks during the sale of reservation lands in the East.

American State Papers

Causes of hostilities of Creek and Seminole Indians in Florida, and instructions to and correspondence with agents and other persons contracted for their removal to the West. *American State Papers: Military Affairs* 690. 24th Cong., 1st sess. Documents and correspondence regarding the removal of the Creeks and Seminoles.

Causes of Hostilities of Creek and Seminole Indians in Florida; instructions to Brevet Major General Thomas S. Jesup and other officers of army for their removal to the West, and correspondence with governors of States and agents. *American State Papers: Military Affairs* 691. 24th Cong., 1st sess. Documents and correspondence regarding the subsistence of the Creeks and Seminoles removing west.

Military orders and operations against Seminole Indians in Florida and their removal west of Mississippi River. *American States Papers: Military Affairs* 638. 24th Cong., 1st sess. Military reports regarding the Second Seminole War and removal of the Seminoles.

Unpublished Primary Sources

National Archives Microfilm Publications

"Census of Creek Indians Taken by Parsons and Abbott, 1832." Microcopy T275, RG75. 1 roll. Census arranged by town, listing heads of households entitled to allotments in Alabama, enumerating males, females, and slaves in each household.

"Census Roll of Cherokee Indians East of the Mississippi and Index to the Roll, 1835." Microcopy 496. 1 roll. A census of the Cherokees prior to the Treaty of New Echota, providing for their removal, listing heads of families, numbers in households, occupations, and other information.

"Cherokee Land 1823." Microcopy T135. 1 roll. Map of Cherokee land, segregated from Claim 8568, RG 217, Entry 525.

"Correspondence of the Eastern Division Relating to Cherokee Removal, April 1838–December 1838." Microcopy M1475, RG393. 2 rolls. Contains documents related to Gen. Winfield Scott's command during the forced removal of the Cherokees.

"Documents Relating to the Negotiation of Ratified and Unratified Treaties with Various Indian Tribes, 1801–1869." Microcopy T494, RG11. 10 rolls. Often contains useful information about treaty negotiations not available in other resources, providing insights into how well the negotiators conducted themselves.

"Letters Received by the Office of Indian Affairs, 1824–1881." Microcopy M234, RG75. 962 rolls. Arranged by agency or jurisdiction and then by year, includes ordinary agency correspondence as well as segregated files relating to removal of the tribes under the agency.

"Letters Sent by the Office of Indian Affairs, 1824–1881." Microcopy M21, RG75. 166 rolls. Outgoing correspondence complements incoming correspondence in Letters Received (Microcopy M234), especially rolls 1–65 for the removal period 1824–1860.

"Records of the Cherokee Indian Agency in Tennessee, 1801–1935." Microcopy M208, RG75. 14 rolls. Contains correspondence and other records covering the period of early removals to the Treaty of New Echota.

"Records of the Michigan Superintendency of Indian Affairs, 1814–1852." Microcopy M1, RG75. 71 rolls. Correspondence and other records related to a number of tribes in the Old Northwest during the removal period.

"Records of the Southern Superintendency of Indian Affairs, 1832–1870." Microcopy M640, RG75. 22 rolls. Contains correspondence of the Western Superintendency (agency's name 1832–1851) regarding Choctaws, Creeks, Cherokees, Senecas, mixed bands of Senecas and Shawnees, and, later, Quapaws, Seminoles, and Chickasaws.

"Records of the Wisconsin Superintendency of Indian Affairs, 1836–1848, and Green Bay Subagency, 1850." Microcopy M95, RG75. 4 rolls. Contains correspondence, transcriptions of Indian talks, and other types of documents.

"Report Books of the Office of Indian Affairs, 1838–1885." Microcopy M348, RG75. 53 rolls. Includes copies of communications sent from the office to members of the cabinet regarding Indian affairs, covering various aspects of issues, including removal, especially rolls 1–11 for the period 1838–1860.

"Special Files of the Office of Indian Affairs, 1807–1904." Microcopy M574, RG75. 85 rolls. Documents relating to claims and other issues arising from removal of Cherokee, Chippewa, Creek, Delaware, Kickapoo, Ottawa, Sauk and Fox, Miami, Ottawa, Potawatomi, Seminole, Seneca, Winnebago, and other tribes.

National Archives Loose Documents

Records of the Accounting Officers of the Department of the Treasury, RG 217. Records of the Office of the Second Auditor, Entry 524: "Claims Settled under the Chickasaw Treaty, 1833–71." Correspondence, receipts, commutation vouchers, and other records justifying disbursements by the Office of Indian Affairs related to Chickasaw removal.

Records of the Accounting Officers of the Department of the Treasury, RG 217. Records of the Office of the Second Auditor, Entry 525: "Indian Affairs, Settled Accounts and Claims, 1794–1894." Correspondence, receipts, journals, and other records submitted by agents, removal conductors, and disbursing agents to justify disbursements during the removal process; indispensable in documenting day-to-day events.

Records Relating to Indian Removal, RG 75. Records of the Bureau of Indian Affairs. Preliminary Inventory 163, Entries 198–300. A massive collection of loose documents including Records of the Commissary General of Subsistence (Entries 198–216), which contains record categories of Cherokee, Chicago Agency, Choctaw, Creek, Florida, Kickapoo, Ohio, Ottawa, Potawatomi, Quapaw, St. Louis Superintendency, Seminole, Western Superintendency, and Winnebago; Cherokee Removal Records (Entries 217–251); Chickasaw Removal Records (Entries 252–257); Choctaw Removal Records (Entries 258–284); Creek Removal Records (Entries 285–300); and Other Removal Records (Entry 301), containing records of Apalachicola, Seminole, Kickapoo, New York, Ottawa, Potawatomi, Quapaw, and Wyandot removals.

INDEX

Abercrombie, Charles, 2:205, 2:209, 2:211

Abert, J. J., 2:191; letter to Lewis Cass, 2:194–196

aboriginals, 2:52, 2:113, 2:126

Abraham, 1:1–3, 1:4–5, 1:54, 1:78, 1:100–101

acculturation, 1:26, 1:28, 1:65, 1:116, 1:118, 1:271

acquisition of property, 1:65, 1:84, 1:113, 1:145, 2:7, 2:9, 2:38, 2:40, 2:44, 2:113, 2:127–128

Adair, Walter S., 2:82

Adams, John Quincy, 1:36, 1:86–87, 1:102, 1:227, 1:259–261

Aehaia, Epenetus, 2:247

African-descended people, 1:1–2, 1:35, 1:52–54, 1:58, 1:91, 1:101, 1:114, 1:115, 1:284, 2:168–175; and removal, 1:3–6

agriculture, 1:38, 1:139, 1:143, 1:164–165, 1:195, 2:20, 2:22, 2:40–41, 2:49, 2:52, 2:65, 2:129

Alabama, 1:32–33, 1:38–44, 1:59–60, 1:70–75, 1:84–87, 1:96, 1:102–104, 1:109–110, 1:112–114, 1:125–127, 1:146–149, 1:174–175, 1:197–200, 1:224–227, 1:249–252, 2:18–19, 2:23, 2:30, 2:52, 2:59, 2:68, 2:82–83, 2:85, 2:169, 2:172, 2:175, 2:203–204, 2:219, 2:238–239, 2:255, 2:261–262; and Indian removal, 1:6–10

Alabama Creeks, 1:86, 1:197

Alabama Emigrating Company, 1:59, 1:148, 1:199, 1:222, 1:252

Albany, 1:157, 1:169–171, 1:239

Allegany reservation, 1:157–58, 1:173, 1:229, 1:238, 1:239, 1:242–243

Allen, John, 1:237, 1:268

Allen, Thomas, 2:45

Alligator. See Hulbutta Tustenuggee

allowances, personal, 2:138–139

American Board of Commissioners for Foreign Missions (ABCFM), 1:67, 1:269–270

American settlements, 1:22–23, 1:39, 1:60, 1:62, 1:107, 1:165, 1:202, 1:228

Anderson, Richard, 2:171

Anglo-Americans, 2:67–68, 2:70

Anishinaabeks, 1:166, 1:196

Anosta, Atalah, 2:83

anti-removal sentiment, 1:24, 1:27, 1:105, 1:112, 1:116, 1:127–128, 1:173, 1:192, 1:206, 1:245, 1:247, 1:264, 1:270, 2:75–86, 2:245

Anti-Treaty Cherokees, 1:246

Anti-Treaty Party, 1:245

Apalachicolas, 1:70, 1:76–77, 1:208, 1:211–213; removal, 1:11–12

Arbuckle, Matthew, 2:218

Arkansans, 1:15, 1:40, 1:47, 1:94, 1:233

Arkansas, 1:35, 2:18, 2:48–49, 2:65, 2:67, 2:83, 2:89, 2:169–175, 2:179, 2:183, 2:196–197, 2:203, 2:212–217, 2:222–223, 2:229; and Indian removal, 1:13–16

Arkansas River, 1:2, 1:13–14, 1:78, 1:94, 1:146—147, 1:252, 1:258, 2:239–243
Armstrong, Francis, 1:48
Armstrong, Robert, 1:17
Armstrong, William, 1:16–19
army disbursing agents, journals of, 2:196–203, 2:219–224
Articles of Agreement and Cession, 2:1–4
Articles of Convention and Agreement, 1:44
Ash-kum, 2:273, 2:276
Atkinson, Henry, 1:20, 1:23

Bailey, David, 2:177
Baptists, 1:115, 1:132
Barbour, James, 1:86, 1:200, 2:7
Barnett, Tony, 1:4, 1:54, 1:214
Bateman, Capt., 2:210–211
Battle of Horseshoe Bend, 1:31
Battle of Lake Okeechobee, 1:35
Battle of New Orleans, 1:31
Battle of Stillman's Run, 1:22, 1:206, 1:224
Baylor, J. R., 1:30
Bayou Mason, 2:180–182
Beattie, William, 1:12
Bell, John (U.S. Secretary of War), 1:16, 1:17, 1:19, 1:103–104, 1:260
Bell, John A. (Cherokee chief), 1:42, 1:60
Benge, John, 1:10, 1:42, 1:43, 2:86
Big Raft, 1:94–95
Big Town, 1:11, 1:12
Big Warrior, 1:160
Black Hawk, 1:20–21
Black Hawk's band, 1:22
Black Hawk War, 1:20, 1:21–24, 1:34; 1:98, 1:121, 1:122, 1:134, 1:203, 1:224, 1:263
Black Seminole, 1:2, 1:35
Bloody Fellow, 1:231–232
Blount, John, 1:11–12
Blount, William, 1:232
Boudinot, Elias, 1:19, 1:24–26, 1:28, 1:187–192, 1:245, 1:269–271, 2:50, 2:52–53, 2:75, 2:84, 2:86, 2:91, 2:97, 2:99, 2:101, 2:258–259; editorial by, January 28, 1829, 2:50–52; editorial by, June 17, 1829, 2:52–53; editorial by, June 19, 1830, 2:53–55
Bourbon County, 2:2
Bowlegs, Billy. See Hulbutta Micco
Boyd, Daniel, 1:12

Brazos River Reserve, 1:29–30
Brish, Henry C., 1:218, 1:220, letters of, 2:175–179
Britons, 2:145
Broglie, Duc de, 2:57
Brothertons (also spelled Brothertowns), 1:97, 1:136, 1:159, 1:162, 1:182, 1:228, 2:46, 2:156, 2:160, 2:162; removal, 1:26–27
Brown, Jacob, 1:48–49, 1:130, 2:197
Brown, James, 1:42, 2:86
Buck, John, 2:137
Buell, James H., 2:267
Buffalo, New York, 1:156–158, 1:229, 2:113, 2:124, 2:131, 2:132, 2:148, 2:156, 2:161
Buffalo Creek reservation, 1:173, 1:238–239, 1:242, 2:113, 2:124, 2:125, 2:127, 2:137, 2:154, 2:161. See also Treaty of Buffalo Creek
Bushyhead, Jesse, 1:42
Butler, Elizur, 1:89, 1:187, 1:197, 1:270
Butrick, Daniel S., 1:27–28, 1:187, 1:270; journal of, 2:245–261
Buzzard Roost, 1:57, 2:23

Caddos, 1:94–95, 1:149, 1:181, 1:200, 1:205; removal, 1:29–30; treaty, 1:29
Caldwell, Billy, 1:30–31
Caldwell's Band of Potawatomis, 1:31
Calhoun, John C., 1:47
Canby, E. R. S., 1:35, 1:93
Cannon, B. B., 1:41, journal of 1837 Cherokee emigration party, 2:229–238; route, 1:42–143
Cape Girardeau, 1:41, 1:62, 1:188
Carroll, William, 1:25, 1:31–33, 1:39, 1:67, 1:90, 1:205, 1:233, 1:245
Cass, Lewis, 1:21, 1:24, 1:33–34, 1:51, 1:68, 1:72, 1:90, 1:136, 1:177, 1:179, 1:187, 1:191, 1:204, 1:228; letter to, 2:194–196; report from (1831), 2:34–42
Catholics, 1:177, 2:265
Catlin, George, paintings by, 1:53, 1:142, 1:150
Cattaraugus reservation, 1:157, 1:173, 1:238–239, 1:242–243, 2:113
Cavallo, John (Gopher John), 1:2, 1:5, 1:34–35, 1:52–53, 1:58, 1:91, 1:101, 1:114, 1:115, 1:214

census, 2:105, 2:142, 2:156

Cherokee "civilization," 1:24, 1:38; defense of, 2:50–52

Cherokee Nation v. Georgia, 1:36–37, 1:67, 1:89, 1:192, 1:262, 1:270, 1:272, 2:23

Cherokee Phoenix, 1:24–25, 1:38, 1:65, 1:90, 1:187–88, 1:190, 1:192, 1:245, 1:269, 1:270; letter to, 2:47–50. *See also* Boudinot, Elias, editorials

Cherokees, 1:6–10, 1:13–16, 1:24–26, 1:27–28, 1:67, 1:84–91, 1:101, 1:155–116, 1:185–194, 1:198–200, 1:206–208, 1:231–234, 1:240–241, 1:245–246, 1:262–267, 1:271–273, 2:1, 2:17–19, 2:23–25, 2:31–33, 2:47–48, 2:50–55, 2:59–63, 2:65–69, 2:86, 2:168, 2:169, 2:219, 2:229, 2:238–239, 2:241–242, 2:245–261, 2:261–262; Boudinot removal response, 2:97–107; defense of civilization, 2:50–52; journal of 1837 emigration party, 2:229–238; journal of 1838 emigration party, 2:238–245; memorial and protest by, 2:75–86; removal, 1:9, 1:32, 1:37–43, 1:54, 1:60, 1:154, 1:205, 1:225–227, 1:257, 1:262. *See also* Eastern Cherokees; Treaty Party; Western Cherokees

Chicago, 1:31, 1:17, 1:224

Chickasaw Commission, 1:46, 1:109–110, 1:249

Chickasaws, 1:5, 1:6–10, 1:16–19, 1:32, 1:55–56, 1:56–58, 1:66–67, 1:109–110, 1:125–127, 1:130, 1:142–143, 1:231–234, 1:236–238, 1:243, 1:244, 1:246–250, 1:255, 1:264–266, 2:14, 2:17, 2:19, 2:22, 2:29, 2:67, 2:168, 2:172–173, 2:206–207, 2:222; letter of chiefs to Andrew Jackson, 2:71–75; removal, 1:14–15, 1:44–46

childrearing, 1:268

Chippewas, 1:165–168, 1:206. *See also* Saginaw Chippewa removal

Choctaws, 1:5, 1:6–10, 1:13–16, 1:29, 1:30, 1:44, 1:45, 1:55–56, 1:66–67, 1:79–81, 1:110, 1:122, 1:125, 1:127–129, 1:130, 1:134, 1:142–143, 1:149–150, 1:243–245, 1:246–250, 1:264, 1:265, 1:237, 1:240, 2:14–15,

2:17, 2:18–19, 2:22, 2:29, 2:43, 2:67, 2:168–171, 2:179–186; journal of 1832 emigration party, 2:179–186; removal, 1:6, 1:46–50. *See also* Mississippi Band of Choctaw Indians

Choctaw Agency, 1:13, 1:16, 1:45, 1:93, 1:131, 1:145, 1:214, 2:199, 2:202

cholera, 1:12, 1:15, 1:40, 1:45, 1:46, 1:49, 1:80, 1:135, 1:180, 1:224, 1:264, 2:181, 2:191

cholera infantum, 1:71, 1:74

Christian community, appeal to, on condition and prospect of the New-York Indians, 1:230, 2:126–167

church, 1:103, 1:144, 1:150, 1:160, 1:260, 2:146, 2:152. *See also by denomination*; missionaries; religion

Chuwalookee, 1:42

cities: benefits and dangers of, 2:30, 2:144, 2:146, 2:151, 2:161; eastern in which support sought for Indian "civilization," 1:24, 1:187, 1:190, 1:269, 2:270; Indians brought to, 1:21, 1:23, 1:121, 1:158

citizenship: Cherokee Nation, 1:38, 1:87, 2:93, 2:257; for Indians, 1:82; U.S., 1:26, 1:82, 1:229, 1:275, 2:93, 2:95; in *Worcester v. Georgia*, 1:39

"civilization" programs, 1:24, 1:27, 1:38, 1:62, 1:68, 1:103, 1:107, 1:176–177, 1:204, 1:270, 2:5, 2:7, 2:9–14, 2:17, 2:29–30, 2:43, 2:49, 2:65–66, 2:76, 2:100, 2:115–118, 2:122, 2:129, 2:143–146, 2:160–161, 2:164, 2:166–167

Clarendon, 1:13, 1:45, 1:49

Clark, William, 1:21, 1:33, 1:50–51, 1:119–120, 1:128, 1:133–134, 1:202

Clay, Henry, 1:32, 1:105, 1:259, 1:260

Clinch, D. L., 1:76, 1:77, 1:100, 1:208, 1:210, 1:212

Coacoochee, 1:2, 1:34–35, 1:51–53, 1:78, 1:93, 1:101, 1:114, 1:122, 1:209, 1:214

Coe Hadjo, 1:2, 1:34, 1:51, 1:53–54, 1:114, 1:213–214

Coffee, John, 1:32, 1:55–56, 1:57, 1:66, 1:67, 1:113, 1:128, 1:129, 1:233, 1:244, 1:247

Colbert, Levi, 1:56–58, 1:109, 1:236, 1:265, 1:266. *See also* Treaty of Pontotoc

Cole, Robert, 1:79, 1:128
Collins, R. D. C., 1:16–17, 1:130
colonies, American, 1:12, 1:84, 1:251,
    2:22, 2:60–61, 2:66, 2:139, 2:143–145,
    2:154, 2:162
Colston, Daniel, 1:42
Columbus: Georgia, 1:11, 1:70, 1:73,
    1:96, 1:197–199; Mississippi, 1:147,
    1:198; Ohio, 1:83
Columbus Land Company, 1:126
Comanches, 1:30, 1:77
communities, 1:3, 1:26, 1:61, 1:65,
    1:137–140, 1:154, 1:164–166, 1:171,
    1:174–177, 1:195–196, 1:201–203,
    1:228–232, 1:239, 1:262, 1:265–266,
    1:272–273
Confederate Indian forces and
    sympathizers, 1:93, 1:161, 1:219, 1:255
confederations: Cherokee, 1:64, Creek,
    1:11; Iroquois, 1:156, 1:158–159, 1:217,
    1:242, 1:267; Peoria, 1:172; Tecumseh,
    1:122; Three Fires, 1:176, 1:195
Congregationalists, 1:25, 1:27–28, 1:186,
    1:269, 1:271
Continental Congress, 1:24, 1:61; 1:151
contractors, 1:18, 1:59, 1:81, 1:180,
    1:222, 1:252, 2:204–206, 2:209–210,
    2:224
contracts, 1:12, 1:16–18, 1:42, 1:59,
    1:141, 1:147, 1:193, 1:198–199, 1:223,
    1:253, 1:256, 2:63, 2:77, 2:123, 2:126,
    2:243
corn, 1:15, 1:22, 1:80–82, 1:133, 1:168,
    1:263, 1:265, 1:267, 2:17
cotton, 1:3, 1:7, 1:15, 1:47, 1:48, 1:57,
    1:125, 1:127, 1:142, 1:143, 2:17
Cowaya, John. See Cavallo, John
Crawford, Hartley, 1:17, 1:18,
    1:257–258, 2:137
Crawford County, Ohio, 1:273–274
Creeks, 1:3, 1:5, 1:6–10, 1:11, 1:14–17,
    1:32, 1:53, 1:55, 1:68, 1:69–71,
    1:72–74, 1:75–82, 1:84–88, 1:93, 1:96,
    1:112, 1:114, 1:126, 1:160–161, 1:186,
    1:198–199, 1:207, 1:210, 1:212, 1:224,
    1:231, 1:250, 1:254, 2:1; removal,
    1:146–149. See also McIntosh Creeks;
    Muscogees (Creeks); Poarch Band of
    Creek Indians
Creek War: of 1813, 1:111, 1:174: of
    1836, 1:8, 1:70, 1:73, 1:87, 1:96,

1:147, 1:174, 1:199, 1:224, 1:225,
    1:251–252, 1:263–264, 2:81
crimes, 1:70, 1:232, 1:244, 1:257
Cudjo, 1:4, 1:54, 1:214
cultivation, soil, 2:9, 2:12, 2:20, 2:22,
    2:48–49, 2:81, 2:117–119, 2:122,
    2:129, 2:144, 2:156
Currey, Benjamin, 1:39–40, 2:82–83,
    2:91
Cussetas. See Kasihtas

Daniel, Moses, 1:42
Danville, Illinois, 1:177–178, 2:225–227
Davis, William A., 2:84
Deas, Edward, 1:41–42, 1:59–60; journal
    of 1837 Creek emigration party,
    2:219–224; journal of 1838 Cherokee
    emigration party, 2:238–245
debts, tribal, 1:44, 1:57, 1:62, 1:72, 1:85,
    1:107–108, 1:125, 1:139, 1:220,
    1:250–251
Delawares, 1:78, 1:103, 1:107,
    1:117–118, 1:209, 1:273, 1:275;
    removal, 1:60–63. See also Munsee
    Delawares
Democrats, 1:19, 1:33, 1:153, 1:197,
    1:198, 1:256–257, 1:259–261, 1:270
Detroit, 1:33, 1:164, 1:222
diet during removal, 1:73, 1:134–135,
    1:178–179
Drane, G. S., 1:42, 1:226
Drane Contingent of Cherokees,
    2:261–263
Drew, John, 1:43, 1:193
Dutch Reformed church, 1:204
DuVal, William, 1:70

Eastern Band of Cherokees v. The United
    States and the Cherokee Nation, 1:65
Eastern Cherokees, 1:64–65; 1:188,
    1:204, 1:233
Eaton, John Henry, 1:32, 1:33, 1:55,
    1:66–67, 1:72, 1:83, 1:113, 1:128–129,
    1:241, 1:244, 1:247, 1:251, 2:52
Econchatimico, 1:11
Ecore Fabre, 1:13, 1:14, 1:48–49, 1:129
Eel River, 1:139, 2:18, 2:21
Elk River, 2:179, 2:220
Ellsworth, Henry L., 1:1, 1:53, 1:68–69,
    1:106, 1:133, 1:204–205
Emathlachee, 1:11

emigration, 1:7–8, 1:25, 1:49, 1:53, 1:57, 1:72, 1:83–84, 1:111–112, 1:146–147, 1:161, 1:196, 1:199–200, 1:221, 1:225, 1:250, 1:274, 2:15–16, 2:18–19, 2:32, 2:47–48, 2:82–83, 2:127–129, 2:133, 2:164, 2:194–196, 2:219–220, 2:224, 2:238–239, 2:241, 2:263–267, 2:269–273, 2:276. *See also* Alabama Emigrating Company; Sanford Emigrating Company; *individual tribes and their removal*

Eneah Emathla (Neamathla), 1:11, 1:12, 1:69–71, 1:73, 1:96, 1:199, 1:207

Eneah Micco (Neamicco), 1:70, 1:72–74, 1:96, 1:199, 1:251

enforcement, 1:22, 1:34, 1:119, 1:168, 1:272, 2:23, 2:33, 2:54

England, 1:85, 1:164, 1:231, 2:64, 2:118, 2:143, 2:162–163

Episcopal church, 1:175

Erath, George, 1:29

Erie Canal, 1:139, 1:156–158, 1:242

escaped slave advertisements, 2:168–175

Evarts, Jeremiah, 1:27, 1:67, 2:55–70

Everglades, 1:99, 1:215, 1:216, 1:234, 1:235

factionalism, tribal, 1:79, 1:170–171, 1:230, 1:239, 1:242

Fanning, Alexander, 1:51

farmers, 1:7, 1:11, 1:113, 1:143–144, 1:160–161, 1:168, 1:171, 1:198, 1:233, 1:267, 2:89, 2:253

federal government, 1:36–37, 1:62–63, 1:75–76, 1:87–89, 1:97–98, 1:107–108, 1:140–141, 1:146–147, 1:151–153, 1:154, 1:158–160, 1:162–163, 1:195–196, 1:209–211, 1:218–219, 1:231–232, 1:272–274

First Seminole War, 1:1, 1:69, 1:76, 1:208

Five Civilized Tribes, 1:46–47, 1:106, 1:144

flatboats, 1:10, 1:40, 1:41, 1:43, 1:193, 1:212, 1:241, 2:220

Florida and Indian removal, 1:75–79

Folsom, David, 1:79–81

food, 1:81–82

Forsyth, John, 1:104, 2:24

Fox Indians. *See* Sauk and Musquakie (Fox)

Fox River, 1:26, 1:97, 1:135–136, 1:162, 1:182, 1:228

Franklin, J., 2:4

Franklin, State of, 1:232

Franklin, Tennessee, 1:66, 1:128, 1:143, 1:243, 1:247

French and Indian War, 1:61, 1:122

Fuckalusti Harjo, 2:203

Fuller, Andrew, 2:278

Fulsom, David, 2:184

Fulton, John T., 2:178

Gadsden, James, 1:11, 1:76, 1:204, 1:211

Gaines, Edmund P., 1:2, 1:86, 1:186, 1:224

Gallatin, Albert, 1:31, 2:4

gambling, 2:170, 2:250–253, 2:256

Gardiner, James B., 1:83–84, 1:217, 1:219–221, 2:187–190

Garland, John, 1:79–80

Garland, Samuel, 1:127–128

Gasconade River, 2:192, 2:236

Gates, William, 1:52

General Allotment Act, 1:106

Georgia: act of 1828 to appropriate Cherokee territory within state, 2:23–24; and Indian removal, 1:84–91; legislature, 1:28, 1:36–38, 1:89, 1:103–104, 1:190, 1:197, 1:271; penitentiary, 1:88, 1:270–271, 2:31–32, 2:79, 2:250

Georgia Committee Report, 2:24–27

Georgia Compact, 1:31, 1:84, 1:102, 1:124, 1:127, 1:227, 1:262, 2:1–4

Georgia Guard, 1:38, 1:89–90, 1:188, 1:190, 1:197–198, 1:265, 2:31, 2:80, 2:82, 2:255

Gilmer, George R., 1:32, 1:40, 1:90, 1:197–198, 2:34

Glasgow & Harrison, 1:16, 1:17

gold, 1:32, 1:38, 1:88, 1:187, 1:192, 1:197, 2:31, 2:34, 2:79, 2:105–107, 2:256

Gopher John. *See* Cavallo, John

governance, 1:152, 1:169, 1:171, 1:229, 1:239, 1:243, 1:260

Green Bay, 1:97, 1:135–137, 1:159, 1:162, 1:183, 1:228

Halleck Tustenuggee, 1:35, 1:92–94, 1:101, 1:214, 1:235

Harkins, George, 1:129, 1:150, 1:244
Harris, Carey A., 1:113, 1:233, 1:256, 2:224
Harris, Joseph W., 1:40
Harrison, William Henry, 1:19, 1:62, 1:107–108, 1:202, 1:257, 1:260
Haughton, Richard, 2:170
Heckaton, 1:94–95, 1:181, 1:200
Henry (McHenry), Jim, 1:70, 1:71, 1:73, 1:95–97, 1:199, 1:224
Hernandez, Joseph M., 1:34, 1:51–52, 1:54
Hichitis, 1:11, 1:69, 1:70, 1:72, 1:95, 1:96, 1:199
Hicks, Elijah, 1:42, 2:82, 2:86
Hicks, George, 1:42, 2:256
Hilderbrand, Peter, 1:42
Hitchcock, Ethan Allen, 1:6–19, 1:79, 1:207, 1:209, 1:260
Ho-Chunk Indians, 1:22; removal, 1:97–98, 1:159, 1:162–163, 1:203, 1:206. See also Winnebagos
Hogan, John B., 1:73
Hog Creek Shawnees, 1:83, 1:218, 1:222, 1:273, 2:186
Honey Creek, 1:25, 1:189, 1:191
Hopewell Treaty, 1:104, 1:231–232
Horse, John. See Cavallo, John
Hulbutta Micco (Billy Bowlegs), 1:1, 1:3, 1:26, 1:99–100, 1:215–216, 1:234–236
Hulbutta Tustenuggee (Alligator), 1:2, 1:35, 1:52–53, 1:77, 1:100–101, 1:208, 1:213
humanity, 2:8, 2:14, 2:16, 2:26, 2:30, 2:41, 2:50, 2:78–79, 2:81, 2:84, 2:114–115, 2:117–118, 2:122
Humboldt, Baron, 2:57
Humphreys, Gad, 1:70
hunters, 2:20, 2:26, 2:30, 2:40, 2:43, 2:51–52, 2:203; bounty, 1:235; Caddo, 1:29; gold, 1:192; slave, 1:12, 1:101, 1:214

Illinois, 1:20, 1:21–24, 1:31, 1:41, 1:50, 1:97, 1:119, 1:122, 1:133–134, 1:168–169, 1:172, 1:202–203, 1:224, 2:18, 2:186, 2:190, 2:225–226
Indiana and removal, 1:107–109
Indian Removal Act, 1:3, 1:6, 1:9, 1:32, 1:34, 1:38, 1:62, 1:66, 1:68, 1:76, 1:102–106, 1:111–112, 1:153, 1:154, 1:259, 2:27–29
Indian Territory, 1:106–107
Indian Vaccination Act, 1:135, 1:166
Indian women: during removal, 1:262–267; roles and removal, 1:267–269
Iroquois, 1:156, 1:158–159, 1:170–172, 1:217, 1:238–239, 1:241–243, 1:267
Ishtehotopa, 1:46, 1:109–110, 1:238, 1:264, 2:75

Jackson, Andrew, 1:6, 1:8, 1:10, 1:11, 1:16–19, 1:21, 1:23, 1:25, 1:31–32, 1:33, 1:39, 1:41, 1:47, 1:55, 1:66–67, 1:102–105, 1:111–113, 1:143, 1:153–154, 1:187, 1:220, 1:224–225, 1:233, 1:243–244, 1:247, 1:256–258, 1:259–260, 2:113, 2:127; letter from Chickasaw chiefs to, 2:71–75, second annual presidential message, 2:29–31
Jacksonian Era, 1:34, 1:43, 1:56, 1:68–69, 1:106–107, 1:113, 1:129, 1:155, 1:167, 1:197, 1:205, 1:245, 1:258, 1:261
Jacksonville, 1:13, 1:178–179
jail, 1:23, 1:71, 1:96, 1:235, 1:237, 2:32, 2:82, 2:168–175
Jarvis, Nathan, 1:54
Jefferson, Thomas, 1:6, 1:13, 1:102, 1:108, 1:151, 1:153, 1:201; "civilization" program, 1:62
Jefferson Barracks, 1:20, 1:23, 1:121
Jesup, Thomas S., 1:2, 1:5, 1:52, 1:54, 1:70, 1:73, 1:77–78, 1:114, 1:208–209, 1:224–225, 1:252, 1:254–255
Jim Boy. See Tustenuggee Emathla
Johnson, Joseph, 1:26
Jones, Evan, 1:27–28, 1:115–116, 1:269–270
Jones, Sam, 1:99–100, 1:234
journals of emigration parties, 2:179–186, 2:186–194, 2:196–203, 2:203–219, 2:219–224, 2:224–228, 2:229–238, 2:238–245, 2:245–261, 2:263–279
Jumper, John, 1:2, 1:53, 1:77, 1:78, 1:100, 1:208–209, 1:213, 1:215, 1:235–236
jurisdiction, 1:6, 1:32–33, 1:36–39, 1:79, 1:89, 1:103, 1:112, 1:147, 1:187, 1:192,

1:243, 1:245, 1:250, 1:270, 1:272, 2:1,
2:3, 2:26, 2:35–36, 2:43, 2:47, 2:53,
2:68, 2:78, 2:80, 2:92, 2:113, 2:126
justice, 1:26, 1:36–37, 1:39, 1:68, 1:89,
1:109, 1:147, 1:179, 1:251, 1:262,
1:264, 1:272, 2:7–9, 2:13–14, 2:34,
2:36, 2:49–50, 2:54–55, 2:58, 2:63–65,
2:70, 2:82, 2:85, 2:91, 2:96, 2:122,
2:140–141, 2:252

Kansas, 1:23, 1:31, 1:53, 1:62–63,
1:108–109, 1:119–122, 1:137, 1:140,
1:161–162, 1:164–166, 1:172, 1:185,
1:203, 1:274–275, 2:114, 2:127, 2:194
Kansas-Nebraska Act, 1:63, 1:117, 1:275
Kansas territory and Indian removal,
1:117–118
Kasihtas (Cussetas), 1:70, 1:73, 1:96,
1:199, 1:251–252
Kaskaskias. See Peoria-Kaskaskia-
Piankeshaw-Wea removal
keelboats, 1:40–41, 1:146–147, 1:198,
1:212–213, 1:241, 2:197
Kennekuk, 1:119–120, 1:122, 1:133–134,
1:168–169
Keokuk, 1:120–122
Kickapoos, 1:133–134, 1:168–169, 1:172;
removal, 1:122–123
Kingsbury, G. P., 1:17
Kishko, 1:119

land cession treaties, 1:33, 1:51, 1:176,
1:238, 1:242, 1:273
land speculation, 1:6, 1:32, 1:44, 1:70,
1:72, 1:143–144, 1:174, 1:195,
1:197–198, 1:238, 1:242, 1:244, 1:248,
1:253, 1:256, 1:266; and Indian
removal, 1:124–127
Lane, J. F., 1:81, 1:84, 1:221, 2:187,
2:193
languages, Indian, 1:25, 1:27, 1:64–65,
1:72, 1:89, 1:115, 1:139, 1:140, 1:159,
1:230, 1:269–270, 2:131, 2:172, 2:174,
2:262
LeFlore, Greenwood, 1:47–48, 1:66,
1:79–80, 1:127–129, 1:149, 1:244
legislation, removal, 1:6, 1:27, 1:87,
1:102–106, 1:108, 1:112, 1:135, 1:140,
1:187, 1:262, 2:27, 2:36, 2:44, 2:49,
2:58, 2:76–77, 2:79, 2:94, 2:101, 2:165;
Great Society, 1:145

Lewis, Meriwether, 1:50
Lillybridge, Clark, 1:40
Little Rock Office of Removal and
Subsistence, 1:130–131
Little Turtle, 1:15, 1:184
Longhouse religion, 1:113, 1:127
Louisiana, 1:29, 1:48–49, 1:95, 1:106,
1:125, 1:181, 1:225, 2:66
Louisiana Purchase, 1:6, 1:13, 1:50,
1:103, 1:181, 1:201
Lowrey, George, 1:4, 1:190

Makataimeshekiakiak. See Black Hawk
Manypenny, George, 1:117
marriages, 2:74, 2:118; intermarriage,
1:268, 2:195
Marshall, John, 1:36, 1:39, 1:89, 1:173,
1:262, 1:270–273
Martin, John, 1:90, 2:80, 2:86
Mashpees, 1:154–155; Revolt, 1:154
Maumee River, 1:164
McCauley, Clay, 1:79, 1:209–210
McCoy, Isaac, 1:67, 1:106, 1:115, 1:119,
1:132–133, 2:176–177
McHenry, Jim. See Henry, Jim
McIntosh, Roley, 1:71, 1:255
McIntosh, William, 1:7, 1:70, 1:72, 1:76,
1:85, 1:146, 1:160, 1:161, 1:186,
1:210–211, 1:227
McIntosh Creeks, 1:197–198, 1:204
McKenney, Thomas, 1:56; removal
report, 2:14–23
Mecina, 1:122, 1:133–134, 1:168–169
medicine and disease, 1:134–135
Memphis, 1:13–15, 1:42, 1:44–45, 1:49,
1:59–60, 1:110, 1:147–149, 1:198–199,
1:222, 1:233, 1:252–253, 1:255, 1:266
Menominee (chief), 1:109, 1:177
Menominees, 1:26, 1:97, 1:159–160,
1:162–163, 1:182–183, 1:228–229,
2:203–204, 2:209–212, 2:222, 2:240;
removal, 1:135–137; statement
concerning treaties, 2:46–47,
2:128–129, 2:148
merchants, 1:9, 1:19, 1:44, 1:46, 1:80,
1:108, 1:126, 1:185, 1:233, 1:244
Mesquakie (Fox) Indians. See Sauk and
Mesquakie (Fox)
Methodists, 1:96, 1:106, 1:118, 1:119,
1:154, 1:159, 1:273, 1:275
Metoxin, John, 1:137, 1:238

Mexican War, 1:29–30, 1:207
Mexico, 1:35, 1:252–253
Miamis, 1:107–108, 1:152, 1:184–185,
    1:228, 1:235; removal, 1:137–140
Miccosukees, 1:69, 1:92–93, 1:99,
    1:140–141, 1:215–217, 1:234, 1:236
Miccosukee Seminole Nation,
    1:140–141, 1:236
Michigan, 1:33–34, 1:106, 1:124, 1:139,
    1:151, 1:166, 1:176, 1:195–196, 1:205,
    1:222
Michigan Ottawas, 1:164–166
Miconopy, 1:1–3, 1:34, 1:51, 1:54,
    1:77–78, 1:99, 1:100, 1:114,
    1:141–142, 1:208, 2:213–214
migrations, 1:22, 1:47, 1:136–137, 1:140,
    1:172
minko, 1:46, 1:56, 1:109–110, 1:236,
    1:238, 1:264
missionaries, 1:24, 1:27–28, 1:47, 1:50,
    1:61–62, 1:66, 1:106, 1:115–116,
    1:122, 1:129, 1:132, 1:138, 1:150,
    1:187, 1:196–198, 1:269–271, 2:8,
    2:25, 2:51, 2:79, 2:113–114,
    2:126–127, 2:132, 2:146, 2:176, 2:245,
    2:252–253, 2:255. See also by
    denomination; church; religion
Mississippi (state), 1:6, 1:9, 1:32, 1:44,
    1:47–48, 1:56, 1:57, 1:79, 1:84, 1:102,
    1:112, 1:125, 1:127, 1:128–129, 1:237,
    1:243–244, 1:266; and Indian
    removal, 1:142–143
Mississippians, white, 1:47, 1:50,
    1:142–143
Mississippi Band of Choctaw Indians,
    1:7, 1:50, 1:144–146
Mississippi River, 1:22–23, 1:40,
    1:42–43, 1:73, 1:77, 1:94, 1:130,
    1:205, 1:212
Mississippi Swamp, 1:14, 1:42, 1:45,
    1:49, 1:252, 1:255, 1:264
Monmouth, 1:149, 1:254–255, 1:264
Monroe, James, 1:47, 1:102, 1:111,
    1:270; pro-removal presidential
    message, 2:4–6
Montgomery, Alabama, 1:8, 1:71, 1:73,
    1:96, 1:148, 1:199, 1:254
Montgomery, Hugh, 2:83, 2:183
Mooney, James, 1:64
mountains, 1:29, 1:64–65, 1:93, 1:157,
    1:231, 1:233, 2:7, 2:49, 2:69, 2:92,

    2:105–106, 2:121, 2:202, 2:217, 2:220,
    2:222, 2:230
Mouth of Cache, 1:13, 1:45, 1:49
Mulatto King, 1:11
Munsee Delawares, 1:227–228
Munsees, 1:62, 1:136, 1:228–229, 2:44,
    2:128, 2:160, 2:162. See also
    Stockbridge-Munsees
Muscle Shoals, 1:10, 1:43, 1:231, 2:221
Muscogees (Creeks), 1:5, 1:11–12, 1:14,
    1:46, 1:58–60, 1:67–70, 1:72, 1:96,
    1:114, 1:126, 1:130, 1:146–148,
    1:209–211, 1:240, 1:250, 1:252–253;
    journal of 1836 emigration party,
    2:203–219; journal of 1836 emigration
    party, 2:219–224; removal, 1:4, 1:7,
    1:14, 1:59, 1:146–149. See also Creeks
Mushulatubbee, 1:47, 1:79–80,
    1:128–129, 1:149–150, 1:244

Nas-wa-kay, 2:225–226
National Party, 1:39, 1:188, 1:245
Neamathla. See Eneah Emathla
Neamicco. See Eneah Micco
Neapope, 1:20, 1:21, 1:169
negro-Indians, 1:5
Ne-ta-ki-jah, 2:170
New Orleans, 1:4, 1:12, 1:31, 1:52, 1:71,
    1:73, 1:96, 1:99, 1:101, 1:111, 1:130,
    1:148, 1:213–215, 1:254
newspapers, 1:83–84, 1:115, 1:154,
    1:224, 1:240. See also Cherokee Phoenix
Nitakechi, 1:48, 1:80, 1:128–129, 1:144,
    1:149, 1:244
Northwest Ordinance, 1:151–153
nullification, 1:112–113, 1:127, 1:243,
    1:270, 1:272, 2:24, 2:29; and removal,
    1:153–155

Oath Act, 1:28
Occom, Samson, 1:26
Ogden, David A., 1:157
Ogden Land Company, 1:124, 1:136,
    1:137, 1:156–159, 1:169–171,
    1:228–229, 1:238–239, 1:241–243,
    2:113, 2:123, 2:127–128, 2:130, 2:141,
    2:143, 2:165
Ohio (state), 1:24, 1:33, 1:50, 1:61, 1:83,
    1:84, 1:124, 1:152, 1:217–218, 273,
    2:175, 2:186. See also Shawnee
    removal from Ohio

Ohio Indians, 1:25, 1:61, 1:81, 1:83, 1:107, 1:124, 1:132, 1:139, 1:152, 1:222, 1:274, 2:18, 2:21, 2:34, 2:41; journal of 1832 emigration party, 2:186–194
Ohio Ottawas, 1:164–166
Ohio River, 1:40–41, 1:139, 1:146, 1:152, 1:274
Oklahoma Creeks, 1:175
Old Fields, 1:42
Old Settlers, 1:26, 1:189, 1:193
Omnibus Treaty, 1:172, 1:219
Oneidas, 1:26–27, 1:97, 1:136, 1:159–160 1:162, 1:182, 1:217, 1:228, 1:242
Opothleyohola, 1:70, 1:72, 1:86, 1:96, 1:160–162, 1:186, 1:250, 1:253
orphans, 1:19, 1:44, 1:46, 1:126, 1:249, 1:267
Osages, 1:16, 1:94, 1:130, 1:181, 1:200–201
Oscen Tustenuggee, 1:235
Osceola, 1:2, 1:51, 1:54, 1:77–78, 1:100, 1:114, 1:141, 1:208–209, 1:212–214
Oshkosh, 1:136, 1:162–163
Ottawas, 1:24, 1:83, 1:97, 1:132, 1:163–167, 1:169, 1:195, 1:206, 1:218–219, 1:221; removal, 1:163–167. *See also* Michigan Ottawas; Ohio Ottawas
Overton, John, 1:31

Panoahah, 1:122, 1:123, 1:168–169
paper money, 1:115
papers, treaty, 1:53, 1:53, 1:248
Parker, Ely S., 1:169–171, 1:229, 1:239
Parker, Nicholson, 1:171–172, 1:229, 1:239
Pass Christian, Mississippi, 1:8, 1:148–149, 1:254, 1:265
Penn, William, 1:61
Penn, William (pseudonym of Jeremiah Evarts), essays, 2:55–70
Peoria-Kaskaskia-Piankeshaw-Wea removal, 1:172–173
Peorias. *See* Peoria-Kaskaskia-Piankeshaw-Wea removal
Pepper, Abel C., 1:108, 2:24; Potawatomi response to, 2:107–113
Piankeshaws. *See* Peoria-Kaskaskia-Piankeshaw-Wea removal

Pierce, Maris Bryant, 1:173–174, 1:229, 1:230
Poarch Band of Creek Indians, 1:9, 1:149, 1:174–175
Pokagon, Leopold, 1:177, 1:179
Pokagon Band of Potawatomi, 1:176, 1:179–180
politics, 1:31, 1:34, 1:37, 1:90–91, 1:96, 1:104, 1:135, 1:149, 1:154–155, 1:162, 1:172, 1:199, 1:227, 1:231, 1:251, 1:257
Polke, William, 1:178, 2:263
population: African-descended, 1:5; Indian, 1:3, 1:4, 1:8, 1:50, 1:75, 1:121, 1:210, 1:232–233, 2:17, 2:56–57, 2:105–106, 2:120–122, 2:156, 2:158–159; Little Rock, 1:131; unfavorable mixing, 2:106, 2:141, 2:144, 2:151; white American, 1:3, 1:38, 1:102, 1:152, 1:158, 1:202, 1:242, 2:10, 2:29–31, 2:44, 2:48–49, 2:67, 2:69, 2:100, 2:121, 2:147–149, 2:156
postremoval, 1:16, 1:93, 1:207, 1:237, 1:264, 1:269
Potawatomis, 1:24, 1:31, 1:97, 1:107–109, 1:120, 1:132–133, 1:135–136, 1:166, 1:169, 1:175–180, 1:195, 1:223, 1:225–226, 1:266, 2:107–108, 2:224, 2:263, 2:279; journal of 1838 emigration party, 2:263–279; removal, 1:175–180
Potawatomis of Wabash response to Pepper, A. C., 2:107–113
pre-emption claims, 2:78, 2:125, 2:149, 2:155, 2:159, 2:161, 2:163, 2:165
Presbyterians, 1:137, 2:248, 2:256
prison and prisoners, 1:23, 1:28, 1:52, 1:54, 1:71, 1:73, 1:93, 1:100, 1:114, 1:120, 1:141, 1:148, 1:178, 1:214, 1:266, 1:270–271, 2:82, 2:111, 2:246–248, 2:251, 2:260
Proffit, George H., removal journal, 2:224–228
pro-removal sentiment, 1:3, 1:28, 1:80, 1:102, 1:114, 1:128, 1:142, 1:187, 1:204, 1:206, 1:208, 1:229, 1:233, 1:249, 1:260

Quakers, 1:105, 1:173, 1:220, 1:239, 1:242, 2:114, 2:127, 2:132, 2:135, 2:140, 2:142–144

Quapaws, 1:16, 1:94–95, 1:130, 1:172, 1:200–201, 1:205; removal, 1:181–182
Quinney, John W., 1:182–183, 1:228

Raines, Austin J., 1:16–17
Red Jacket, 1:157–158, 1:160, 1:238, 1:242, 2:117, 2:139
Red River, 1:6, 1:14, 1:29–30, 1:80, 1:94–95, 1:150, 1:181, 1:200, 1:205, 1:244–245, 2:170, 2:199
Red Stick War, 1:69, 1:76, 1:189, 1:211, 1:253
refugees, 1:12, 1:65, 1:148
religion, 1:119–120, 1:159, 1:162, 1:177, 1:293, 2:30, 2:38, 2:40, 2:50, 2:51, 2:78, 2:122, 2:143, 2:250, 2:251, 2:258. *See also by denomination*; church; missionaries
Revolutionary War, 1:84, 1:85, 1:113, 1:152, 1:159, 1:217, 2:113, 2:126, 2:148
Reynolds, John, 1:22, 1:169, 1:224
Richardville, Jean Baptiste, 1:137–139, 1:184–185
Ridge, John, 1:4, 1:19, 1:24–25, 1:185–189, 1:246, 2:84, 2:95
Ridge, Major, 1:25, 1:189–191, 1:245–246, 2:95, 2:257
Rock River, 1:20, 1:22, 1:168, 1:202–203, 1:224
Rock Roe, 1:14, 1:49, 1:59, 1:71, 1:73, 1:148, 1:161, 1:253, 2:179, 2:183, 2:211
Rollins v. Cherokees, 1:65
Ross, John, 1:4, 1:10, 1:25, 1:28, 1:38, 1:39, 1:42–43, 1:54, 1:64, 1:85, 1:90, 1:114, 1:116, 1:188, 1:190, 1:191–194, 1:207, 1:213, 1:227, 1:233, 1:245–246, 2:75, 2:80; Boudinot response to "Letter to a Friend," 2:97–107, 2:261–262; letter (1836), 2:86–97
Ross, Lewis, 1:42, 2:86

Sabbath, 2:247–251, 2:272, 2:274
Saginaw Chippewa removal, 1:195–197
Sanderson, James S., 1:52
Sandusky River, 1:83, 1:217, 1:219, 1:221
Sanford, John W. A., 1:12, 1:73, 1:89, 1:197–200

Sanford Emigrating Company, 1:12, 1:59, 1:71, 1:73, 1:147, 1:198–199
Sarasin, 1:95, 1:181, 1:200–201
Sauganash. *See* Caldwell, Billy
Sauk and Mesquakie (Fox) Indians, 1:20–23, 1:82, 1:97, 1:106, 1:120–121, 1:135–136, 1:163, 1:168–169, 1:172, 1:206; removal, 1:201–204
Saukenuk, 1:20, 1:22, 1:168, 1:203
Schermerhorn, John F., 1:1, 1:25, 1:32, 1:39, 1:53, 1:68, 1:90, 1:95, 1:106, 1:133, 1:188, 1:192, 1:200, 1:204–205, 1:242, 1:245; 2:81, 2:85, 2:90–94, 2:96, 2:158–259
Schoolcraft, Henry Rowe, 1:166, 1:205–206
schools, 1:11, 1:24–25, 1:33, 1:82, 1:118, 1:144–145, 1:160, 1:170–171, 1:173, 1:175, 1:181, 1:184–185, 1:187–188, 1:190, 1:258, 2:235
Scott, Winfield, 1:10, 1:17, 1:18, 1:41, 1:65, 1:206–208, 1:226, 2:245, 2:261–262
Second Creek War. *See* Creek War of 1836
Second Seminole War, 1:2, 1:12, 1:35, 1:54, 1:67, 1:68, 1:99, 1:206, 1:208–210, 1:212–214, 1:223–225, 1:234–235
self-governance, Indian, 1:37, 1:57, 1:272, 2:88
self-interest, 1:138, 2:55, 2:102
Seminoles, 1:2–6, 1:11–12, 1:16–17, 1:34–35, 1:51–55, 1:67–71, 1:74–79, 1:92–94, 1:99–101, 1:112–114, 1:140–142, 1:204–217, 1:223–225, 1:234–236, 1:240–241, 1:265–266; journal of 1836 emigration party, 2:196–203; removal, 1:1, 1:11, 1:14, 1:51, 1:67, 1:210–216
Seminole Tribe of Florida, 1:216–217
Seminole Wars, 1:75–76. *See also* First Seminole War; Second Seminole War; Third Seminole War
Senecas, 1:16, 1:81, 1:83, 1:130, 1:156–158, 1:170–171, 1:173–174, 1:205, 1:217–222, 1:229–230, 1:238–239, 1:241–242; removal, 1:217–219; of Sandusky, 1:217, 1:220, 2:175, 2:177, 2:186. *See also* Tonawanda Senecas

Senecas of Ohio; Brish letters about removal, 2:175–179

Shawnee removal from Ohio, 1:219–222; journal of 1832 emigration party, 2:186–194

Shawnees, 1:16, 1:31, 1:61, 1:63–64, 1:78, 1:81–82, 1:107, 1:117–118, 1:124, 1:130, 1:205, 1:209, 1:217–222, 1:231, 1:273–274. *See also* Wapakoneta Shawnees

Sherman, William T., 1:52

Situwakee, 1:42, 1:116

slavery, 1:3, 1:75, 1:77, 2:3, 2:39, 2:57, 2:71, 2:166, 2:168–169, 2:171, 2:174–175, 2:243. *See also* escaped slave advertisements

Smith, Archilla, 2:84

Smith, Benjamin, 1:57

soldiers, 1:23, 1:31, 1:41, 1:47, 1:50–51, 1:78, 1:81, 1:109, 1:139, 1:152, 1:185, 1:207, 1:209, 1:213, 1:241, 1:265, 2:81, 2:88, 2:207, 2:215, 2:245–251, 2:255

Southern and Northern Methodist Episcopal church, 1:118

sovereignty: American, 1:33; Indian, 1:27, 1:37–38, 1:65, 1:89–90, 1:105, 1:141, 1:192, 1:262, 1:270, 1:272–273, 2:34, 2:59, 2:70, 2:78, of states, 1:103–104, 1:153, 2:24–27, 2:154, 2:256

Spencer, John, 1:17–18

Sprague, John T., 1:92, 1:199, 1:222–223, 1:252; journal of 1836 Creek emigration party, 2:203–219

Sprague, Peleg, 1:104

St. Augustine, 1:35, 1:52, 1:54, 1:92, 1:213–214

St. Francis County, Arkansas, 1:171–172

St. Francis River, 1:13–14, 1:45, 2:234

St. Louis, 1:16, 1:20, 1:23, 1:50–51, 1:94, 1:119–121, 1:139, 1:177, 1:201, 1:218, 1:274

state militias and removal, 1:223–227

steamboats, 1:7–8, 1:10, 1:14–15, 1:23, 1:40–43, 1:45, 1:49, 1:59, 1:71, 1:139, 1:146–149, 1:198–199, 1:212–215, 1:218, 1:226–227, 1:265–266, 2:175, 2:179, 2:187, 2:197, 2:203, 2:261

Stephenson, J. R., 1:81, 2:218

Stockbridge-Munsees, 1:26–27, 1:137, 1:159–160, 1:162, 1:182; removal, 1:227–229. *See also* Munsees; Stockbridges

Stockbridges, 1:97, 1:136–137, 1:228–229

Stokes, Montfort, 1:1, 1:53, 1:68, 1:106, 1:133, 1:204–205

Stokes Commission, 1:1, 1:53, 1:95, 1:132–133, 2:186

Strong, Nathaniel Thayer, 1:229–230; "Appeal to Christian Community," 2:126–167

Swan Creek, 1:195–196, 1:205, 1:228

Tampa Bay, 1:2, 1:4, 1:34, 1:51–52, 1:77, 1:100, 1:208, 1:212, 1:214, 1:234

Tapanahoma, 1:79, 1:128

Taylor, Richard, 1:42, 1:90, 2:81

Taylor, Zachary, 1:78, 1:100, 1:209

teachers, 1:115, 1:185, 2:16–17, 2:89, 2:120, 2:146, 2:245, 2:250

Tennessee, 1:10, 1:17, 1:28, 1:31–32, 1:38, 1:41, 1:66, 1:90, 1:103, 1:111, 1:189, 1:225–226, 2:18, 2:80–81, 2:229; and Indian removal, 1:231–234

Tennessee River, 1:9–10, 1:40–41, 1:43, 1:57, 1:146–147, 1:193, 1:226, 2:2, 2:17, 2:219–220

Terrell, John, 1:247–249

territories, 1:13–14, 1:22–24, 1:36, 1:47, 1:50–51, 1:61–63, 1:67, 1:76, 1:105–107, 1:117–118, 1:132–133, 1:151–152, 1:156–157, 1:178, 1:202, 1:271–274

Third Seminole War, 1:75, 1:79, 1:99–100, 1:209–210, 1:215–216, 1:22579, 1:234–236

Thomas, William H., 1:65

Thompson, Wiley, 1:54, 1:100

Three Fires Confederation, 1:176, 1:195

Tishomingo, 1:236–238

Tonawandas, 1:158, 1:169–171, 1:238–239, 1:242–243

Tonawanda Senecas, 1:238–239

townships, 1:11–12, 1:26–27, 1:40, 1:60–62, 1:69–70, 1:72, 1:85–86, 1:96, 1:115, 1:182–183, 1:186–187, 1:190, 1:231–232, 1:250–252, 1:254, 1:274–275

trade, 1:3, 1:5, 1:16, 1:31, 1:56, 1:97, 1:106–109, 1:138–139, 1:162, 1:164–165, 1:184–185, 1:196, 1:199–202, 1:216, 1:221, 1:250–251 traders, 1:69, 1:108, 1:138–139, 1:162

Trail of Tears, 1:43, 1:193, 1:240–241; National Historic Trail legislation, 1:241

Treasury. *See* U. S. Department of the Treasury

treaty commissioners, American, 1:23–24, 1:34, 1:47, 1:203, 1:273

Treaty of Buffalo Creek, 1:158, 1:170, 1:171, 1:173, 1:229, 1:238, 1:241–243

Treaty of Chicago, 1:31

Treaty of Dancing Rabbit Creek, 1:6–7, 1:32, 1:48, 1:55, 1:66, 1:80, 1:125, 1:129, 1:130, 1:143–144, 1:149, 1:243–245

Treaty of Doak's Stand, 1:13, 1:47, 1:127, 1:142–143

Treaty of Doaksville, 1:44, 1:57, 1:249

Treaty of Fort Jackson, 1:9, 1:85, 1:149, 1:174

Treaty of Franklin, 1:44, 1:55, 1:57, 1:66, 1:143, 1:244, 1:247, 1:249, 1:265, 2:29

Treaty of Greenville, 1:61, 1:107, 1:164, 1:176, 1:184

Treaty of Indian Springs, 1:7, 1:72, 1:85, 1:86, 1:146–147, 1:160, 1:198

Treaty of Moultrie Creek, 1:1, 1:11, 1:69–70, 1:76, 1:141, 1:211, 1:266

Treaty of New Echota, 1:4, 1:10, 1:25, 1:32, 1:39, 1:60, 1:65, 1:186, 1:188, 1:191–192, 1:205, 1:225, 1:233, 1:245, 1:245–246, 1:271, 2:75, 2:97

Treaty of Payne's Landing, 1:1, 1:5, 1:11, 1:53–54, 1:68, 1:77, 1:101, 1:204, 1:212, 1:246–250

Treaty of Pontotoc, 1:5, 1:9, 1:32, 1:44, 1:56–57, 1:109, 1:126, 1:143, 1:148, 1:236, 1:238, 1:246–250, 1:265

Treaty of Prairie du Chien, 1:51

Treaty of Washington, 1:8, 1:32, 1:47, 1:87, 1:125, 1:147, 1:174, 1:186, 1:197, 1:250–251, 1:253, 1:266, 2:72, 2:74–75

Treaty Party (Cherokee), 1:4, 1:25–26, 1:28, 1:32, 1:39–42, 1:90, 1:188–189, 1:191–193, 1:245, 1:257, 1:271

Troup, George, 1:85–87

Troy, Missouri, 1:218, 2:175

Tuckabatche Hadjo, 1:251–253

Tukose Emathla (John Hicks), 1:70, 1:141

Turner, Nat, 1:3

Tuski Hajo, 1:11

Tustenuggee Emathla (Jim Boy), 1:70, 1:73, 1:96, 1:161, 1:174, 1:225, 1:253–255

Twin Lakes Indians, 1:109, 1:178–179, 1:225–226, 2:263

Tyler, John, 1:18–19, 1:207, 1:257, 1:260–261

United Brethren, 2:256

United Nation of Senecas and Shawnees, 1:204, 1:218, 1:221, 2:186

Upper Sandusky, 1:273–274

U.S. Army, 1:4–5, 1:23, 1:30, 1:31, 1:35, 1:41, 1:52, 1:54, 1:70, 1:73, 1:96, 1:100, 1:111, 1:122, 1:161, 1:214, 1:223, 1:227, 1:254

U.S. Department of the Treasury, 1:18, 1:170, 1:207, 2:2, 2:140, 2:147, 2:152, 2:157

Van Buren, Martin, 1:19, 1:109, 1:173, 1:226, 1:242, 1:256–258, 1:260, 2:259; first annual presidential message, 2:43–45

Van Horne, J., journal of 1832 Choctaw emigration party, 2:179–186; journal of 1836 Seminole emigration party, 2:196–203

Vann, "Rich" Joe, 1:215

Vesey, Denmark, 1:3

Vicksburg, Mississippi, 1:7, 1:48–49, 1:80; 2:179

villages, 1:7, 1:20, 1:22, 1:62, 1:101, 1:109, 1:114, 1:119, 1:139, 1:165, 1:177, 1:202–203, 1:217, 1:225, 1:273, 2:17, 2:146, 2:151, 2:163, 2:176, 2:189, 2:195–196, 2:206, 2:253, 2:265–266, 2:269, 2:275

violence, 1:12, 1:21–24, 1:41, 1:50, 1:61, 1:63, 1:72, 1:113, 1:126, 1:138, 1:148, 1:166, 1:194, 1:202, 1:232, 1:263–264

Walking Purchase Treaty, 1:61

Wapakoneta Shawnees, 1:83, 1:218, 1:220–221, 2:186

war, 1:2–5, 1:15–24, 1:29–35, 1:53–56, 1:64–73, 1:75–79, 1:83–87, 1:92–94, 1:96–101, 1:113–114, 1:121–122, 1:133–136, 1:198–217, 1:222–225,

1:232–236, 1:251–255, 2:4–7, 2:14, 2:22, 2:25, 2:34, 2:39, 2:41–44, 2:52, 2:59, 2:81–82, 2:91, 2:109–110, 2:135–136, 2:148, 2:160, 2:162–163
Ward, William, 1:48, 1:144
Washington, George, 1:152, 1:232, 2:51
Waterloo, 1:10, 1:40–42, 1:147, 1:226
Wea removal. *See* Peoria-Kaskaskia-Piankeshaw-Wea removal
Webster, Daniel, 1:33
Western Cherokees, 1:9, 1:32, 1:38, 1:39, 1:43, 1:60, 1:68, 1:193, 1:204
Whig Party, 1:18–19, 1:27, 1:84, 1:206, 1:258, 1:259–261, 1:270
Whiteley, R. H. K., 1:41–42
Wichita Agency, 1:30
Wildcat. *See* Coacoochee
Winnebagos, 1:22, 1:26, 1:82, 1:136, 1:159, 1:162, 1:169, 1:203, 1:206, 1:228, 2:47, 2:128–128; removal, *see* Ho-Chunk removal

Wirt, William, 1:36, 1:89, 1:261–262
Wisconsin, 1:20, 1:23, 1:26–27, 1:97–98, 1:106, 1:124, 1:136–137, 1:151, 1:159–160, 1:162–163, 1:169, 1:176, 1:180, 1:182–183, 1:228–229
women: during removal, 1:262–267; roles and removal, 1:267–269
Worcester, Samuel A., 1:24–25, 1:27–28, 1:39, 1:89, 1:115, 1:197, 1:232, 1:269–271
Worcester v. Georgia, 1:25, 1:36, 1:39, 1:89, 1:153–154, 1:191, 1:192, 1:271–273
Worth, William J., 1:52, 1:93, 1:99, 1:223, 1:234
Wyandots, 1:117–118, 1:273–275, 2:18; removal, 1:273–275

Yaha Hadjo, 1:2
Young, John S., 1:40
Yuchis, 1:70–71, 1:73, 1:96, 1:199

ABOUT THE EDITORS
AND CONTRIBUTORS

Editors

Daniel F. Littlefield, Jr. is Director of the Sequoyah National Research Center at the University of Arkansas at Little Rock. He is the author or editor of more than twenty books in Native American studies.

James W. Parins is Professor of English and Associate Director of the Sequoyah National Research Center at the University of Arkansas at Little Rock. He is an internationally known biographer of American Indians and an author and editor of nearly twenty books in Native American studies.

Contributors

John P. Bowes is Assistant Professor of History at Eastern Kentucky University. He is the author of *Exiles and Pioneers: Eastern Indians in the Trans-Mississippi West; The Trail of Tears: Removal in the South;* and *Black Hawk and the War of 1832: Removal in the North.* His current book project is titled *Northern Indian Removal: An Unfamiliar History.*

Randall L. Buchman is Distinguished Professor of History Emeritus at Defiance College. He has published extensively on the tribal peoples of Ohio, served on the editorial board of the *Quarterly of Ohio Historical Society* and the editorial advisory board of Collegiate Press, and presented numerous scholarly papers. His current research includes work on Indian removal from Ohio and on General James Winchester and Fort Winchester. Buchman currently serves as City Historian of Defiance, Ohio.

Jim J. Buss is Assistant Professor of History at Oklahoma City University. He has written and presented on the removal of the Miami and Wyandot tribes of the Great Lakes and is the author of "'They Found Her and Left Her an

Indian': Gender, Race, and the Whitening of Young Bear," *Frontiers: A Journal of Women Studies* 29:2–3 (2008): 1–35.

David J. Carlson is Associate Professor of English at California State University, San Bernardino, where he has taught since 2001. Professor Carlson is the author of *Sovereign Selves: American Indian Autobiography and the Law* (University of Illinois Press, 2005) and has published in a variety of journals, including *Studies in American Indian Literatures* and *American Indian Quarterly*. He is also a contributor to the *Encyclopedia of U.S. Indian Policy and Law* (CQ Press, 2009).

Matthew L. M. Fletcher is Associate Professor at Michigan State University College of Law and Director of the Indigenous Law and Policy Center. He is the Chief Justice of the Poarch Band of Creek Indians Supreme Court and also sits as an appellate judge for the Pokagon Band of Potawatomi Indians and the Hoopa Valley Tribe. Professor Fletcher graduated from the University of Michigan Law School in 1997 and the University of Michigan in 1994. He is a citizen of the Grand Traverse Band of Ottawa and Chippewa Indians.

C. Joseph Genetin-Pilawa is Assistant Professor of History at Illinois College. His article "'All Intent on Seeing the White Woman Married to the Red Man': The Parker/Sackett Affair and the Public Spectacle of Intermarriage" was published in the *Journal of Women's History* in 2008. Another article, "Ely Parker and the Contentious Peace Policy," is forthcoming in the *Western Historical Quarterly*. He is currently revising for publication his book-length manuscript entitled "Confining Indians: Ely S. Parker and State Development in Nineteenth-Century America."

Christopher D. Haveman is Assistant Professor of History at the University of West Alabama. He received his PhD from Auburn University, where he wrote a dissertation on the removal of the Creek Indians to present-day Oklahoma. He holds degrees from Western Washington University and Marquette University.

Carolyn Yancey Kent is an independent scholar from Jacksonville, Arkansas, who has written extensively on Indian removal through Arkansas and elsewhere. She has done considerable work for the Arkansas Trail of Tears Association.

Fred E. Knowles, Jr. is the coordinator of the Graduate Program in Criminal Justice at Valdosta State University, as well as a member of the graduate and undergraduate faculties. His research interests include gender, class, and race issues in criminal justice; institutions of social control and socialization; and Native American issues. Dr. Knowles has been involved in Native American rights and sovereignty for many years. As a sergeant and then lieutenant with the Hillsborough County Sheriff's Office in Tampa, he advocated and ensured constitutionally protected practices for Native American inmates and detainees. Further, he was a frequent speaker regarding the delivery of social services to Native populations at conferences held by the Florida Department of Vocational Rehabilitation. Later, as an academic, he took part in successfully challenging the University of Missouri and compelling the repatriation of the remains of ancestors to the Osage and Wyandot People. He has since associated with several organizations that work toward education and Native American sovereignty. He currently serves on the Board of Directors or Advisors for the Mantle Rock Native American Education and Cultural Center in Marion, Kentucky, and the Withlacoochee Native American Cultural Center near Dade City, Florida, as well as in less formal advisory roles with several other organizations. He has published in matters related to Native American criminal victimization and law.

Lavonna Lovern graduated with a BA in philosophy from Central Methodist University in 1984, an MA in philosophy from the University of Missouri–Columbia in 1986, and a PhD in philosophy from the University of Missouri–Columbia in 1995. She taught at Central Methodist University from 1989 to 2003, where she also developed and implemented an ethics program focusing on global issues and diversity in philosophy and religion. In 2003, Lovern moved to Georgia to work more closely with Native American groups in the region and to continue her work with Dr. Carol Locust and the University of Arizona on Indian child welfare, health and wellness, disability, and rights and education in Native American communities.

In addition to working with the Ultimate Potential Corporation in Tucson and Mantle Rock Native American Educational Center in Kentucky, Lovern is a lecturer at Valdosta State University, where she has assisted in the creation of a Native American studies program, developing courses on Native American women, Native American thought, postcolonization in indigenous cultures, and alternative religions of the world. Her publication work is currently in the areas of Native American disability, Native American wellness and unwellness, and, with Dr. Locust, seers and knowers. Both Lovern and Locust bring their Eastern Cherokee heritage to their works.

Dawn G. Marsh is Assistant Professor at Purdue University. She specializes in indigenous theory, indigenous women's history, and comparative indigenous histories. Her recent publications appear in *Ethnohistory* and *Ohio History* journals, and she is currently revising a book-length manuscript centered on the experience of a Delaware woman in colonial Pennsylvania. Current projects study the forced removals in the Old Northwest Territory and their impact on those who were not removed.

Jill E. Martin is Professor and Chair of Legal Studies at Quinnipiac University in Hamden, Connecticut. Her research interests are federal Indian law and policy.

Amada L. Paige, historian and researcher, holds a BA in history and an MA in public history, both from the University of Arkansas at Little Rock. She is the coauthor of a book on Chickasaw removal and has written extensively on Indian removal in Arkansas.

Melissa A. Rinehart is Assistant Professor of Anthropology at Valdosta State University. She has worked with Miami Indian communities for several years covering subjects such as the removal era and language shift. She has interests in Native American ethnohistory, anthropological praxis, language shift and revitalization, and the boarding school era. She is currently working on a book project about a former Indian boarding school, St. Joseph's Indian Normal School, in Rensselaer, Indiana. This project examines boarding school culture from multiple perspectives as well as St. Joseph's participation at the World's Columbian Exposition in Chicago in 1893.

Tony R. Rose is Special Projects Coordinator for the Sequoyah National Research Center and holds mathematics and history degrees from the University of Arkansas at Little Rock. His Indian removal research includes creating an index for thousands of National Archives Cherokee and Creek removal records from Record Group 217 and work on the cholera epidemic of 1832 and how it relates to Choctaw removal. His current research is on Native Americans in Arkansas and images of Native Americans in comic books.

Wendy St. Jean graduated with a BA in history from Yale University in 1993 and earned an MA in history from the University of Connecticut in 2004. She now teaches at Purdue Calumet University in Indiana. Since 1994, she has been researching the Chickasaw Indian nation, which has resulted in eight peer-reviewed articles and a PhD dissertation. Her book, *Chickasaws in Indian Territory, 1830s–1907*, will be published by the University of Alabama Press.